THE EMERGENCE OF MODERN AESTHETIC THEORY

Broad in its geographic scope and grounded in original archival research, this book situates the inception of modern aesthetic theory – the philosophical analysis of art and beauty – in theological contexts that are crucial to explaining why it arose. Simon Grote presents seminal aesthetic theories of the German and Scottish Enlightenments as outgrowths of a quintessentially Enlightenment project: the search for a natural "foundation of morality" and a means of helping naturally self-interested human beings to transcend their own self-interest. This conclusion represents an important alternative to the standard history of aesthetics as a series of preludes to the achievements of Immanuel Kant, as well as a reinterpretation of several canonical figures in the German and Scottish Enlightenments. It also offers a foundation for a transnational history of the Enlightenment without the French *philosophes* at its center, while solidly endorsing historians' growing reluctance to call the Enlightenment a secularizing movement.

SIMON GROTE is currently the Wellesley Faculty Assistant Professor of History at Wellesley College, where he has taught since 2013. He previously spent three years at Princeton University's Society of Fellows in the Liberal Arts after graduating with a Ph.D. in History from the University of California, Berkeley (2010), an M.Phil. in Political Thought and Intellectual History from the University of Cambridge (2006), and an A.B. from Harvard College (2001).

IDEAS IN CONTEXT

Edited by David Armitage, Richard Bourke, Jennifer Pitts, and John Robertson

The books in this series will discuss the emergence of intellectual traditions and of related new disciplines. The procedures, aims, and vocabularies that were generated will be set in the context of the alternatives available within the contemporary frameworks of ideas and institutions. Through detailed studies of the evolution of such traditions, and their modification by different audiences, it is hoped that a new picture will form of the development of ideas in their concrete contexts. By this means, artificial distinctions between the history of philosophy, of the various sciences, of society and politics, and of literature may be seen to dissolve.

The series is published with the support of the Exxon Foundation.

A list of books in the series can be found at the end of the volume.

THE EMERGENCE OF MODERN AESTHETIC THEORY

Religion and Morality in Enlightenment Germany and Scotland

SIMON GROTE

Wellesley College

CAMBRIDGE
UNIVERSITY PRESS

CAMBRIDGE
UNIVERSITY PRESS

University Printing House, Cambridge CB2 8BS, United Kingdom

One Liberty Plaza, 20th Floor, New York, NY 10006, USA

477 Williamstown Road, Port Melbourne, VIC 3207, Australia

314–321, 3rd Floor, Plot 3, Splendor Forum, Jasola District Centre, New Delhi – 110025, India

79 Anson Road, #06-04/06, Singapore 079906

Cambridge University Press is part of the University of Cambridge.

It furthers the University's mission by disseminating knowledge in the pursuit of education, learning and research at the highest international levels of excellence.

www.cambridge.org
Information on this title: www.cambridge.org/9781107110922
DOI: 10.1017/9781316275559

First published 2017

Printed in the United Kingdom by Clays, St Ives plc

A catalogue record for this publication is available from the British Library

Library of Congress Cataloging-in-Publication data
Names: Grote, Simon, 1979– author.
Title: The emergence of modern aesthetic theory : religion and morality in Enlightenment Germany and Scotland / Simon Grote.
Description: New York : Cambridge University Press, 2017. | Includes bibliographical references and index.
Identifiers: LCCN 2017020178 | ISBN 9781107110922 (alk. paper)
Subjects: LCSH: Aesthetics, Modern – History. | Enlightenment – Germany. | Enlightenment – Scotland. | Germany – Religion. | Ethics – Germany. | Scotland – Religion. | Ethics – Scotland.
Classification: LCC BH151.G76 2017 | DDC 111/.850943 – dc23
LC record available at https://lccn.loc.gov/2017020178

ISBN 978-1-107-11092-2 Hardback

To my father and in memory of my mother

Contents

Acknowledgments

This book, like the dissertation on which it is based, bears witness to an education, both intellectual and sentimental, whose effects on me have been so deep and so welcome that I would happily fill page after page with names and reminiscences, showering gratitude on everyone who has had even the remotest connection with it. What restrains me is a sense of the impropriety of self-indulgence, the inadequacy of words to convey my true feelings, and a fear that my faulty memory would turn any pretense of all-inclusiveness into a source of disappointment for everyone whose name I had unfairly and unwittingly omitted. So I confine myself to mentioning, with regrettable but unavoidable brevity and blandness, and with apologies to everyone I have overlooked, some of the people and institutions who have contributed to this book in particularly direct ways.

The initial phase of my research began seventeen years ago, when I spent a summer in Scotland laying the foundation for an undergraduate thesis in history at Harvard College. Of all the people on whose help I relied, and whom I thanked in the pages of that thesis and thank again now, the one who has left the clearest fingerprints on this book is the late Istvan Hont. Together with Clare Jackson, he supervised a year of research at Cambridge University, generously funded by the Gates–Cambridge Trust in 2004–5, essential to this book's fourth and fifth chapters. His advice and support continued during my time in the history PhD program at the University of California, Berkeley and in the years between my graduation from that program in 2010 and his death in 2013. He has my gratitude for those thirteen years of challenging criticism, flattering encouragement, and effective advocacy.

I have based the greater part of this book on research I conducted in Germany over the course of several extended visits to Halle (Saale), beginning in 2007, at the generous invitation of the Francke Foundations and the Interdisciplinary Center for European Enlightenment Research, and more particularly the members of the fellowship selection committee, which included Thomas Müller-Bahlke, Britta Klosterberg, Udo Sträter, and Daniel Fulda. The funding for these visits, for which I am very grateful, came from the Fritz Thyssen Foundation, the German Academic Exchange Service, and the Max Kade Foundation. With help from my hosts in Halle and from many new acquaintances and friends, I became aware of an academic culture and a set of scholarly conversations about Pietism and Enlightenment that have substantially shaped how I understand the significance of my work. These new friends' and colleagues' enthusiasm about me and my project buoyed my confidence and made every departure from Halle bittersweet. The archivists, librarians, and other members of the staff of the Study Center of the Francke Foundations, ably led by Britta Klosterberg, taught me paleography and, together with their colleagues at the Halle-Wittenberg University archive and the university library, helped me find almost all the materials I needed. For useful consultations about the substance of my research during those visits, I thank in particular Alexander Aichele, Ulrich Barth, Frank Grunert, Hans-Joachim Kertscher, Reimar Lindauer-Huber, Christian Soboth, and Udo Sträter. Among my colleagues in Halle, I am especially grateful to Alexander Aichele for giving me the means of publishing some results of my research in 2008 and to Rainer Godel (together with Anita Traninger) for inviting me to develop part of it into a conference presentation in 2013. For important advice on drafts of chapters and other written work, and for countless hours of invigorating conversation in Halle, I also owe special thanks to Dirk Effertz and to two dear friends: Ulrich Diehl and Kelly Whitmer.

In Berkeley, where I produced the dissertation that eventually became this book, many friends gave me both a welcome sense of intellectual community and concrete assistance. These include fellow members of the History Department's intellectual history reading group; Jim Spohrer, who bought reproductions of rare sources for the university library to support my research when time in Germany had run out; and, above all, Johan van der Zande, whose expert critique and openhanded praise of my work, throughout fourteen years of intellectual camaraderie and friendship, have given me a sense of my worth as a scholar. I am likewise grateful to my dissertation committee – Tom Brady, David Lieberman, Niklaus Largier, and Martin Jay – for reading my work attentively, for guiding it with a light but judicious touch, for opening my eyes to aspects of it that I might otherwise never have noticed, and for making a strong case – not only to me but also to others – for its value. For the unflagging care with which Tom and Kathy Brady looked after me *in loco parentium*, I offer fond appreciation.

The other institution that has left a significant mark on this book is the Society of Fellows in the Liberal Arts at Princeton University, whose members taught me – among many other lessons – to aspire to speak to, and seek criticism from, audiences outside my discipline. In addition to thanking all those in whose judgment I deserved an invitation to join that extraordinarily stimulating and harmonious community, I thank in particular several colleagues in Princeton (at Princeton University and at the Institute for Advanced Study) for reading my manuscript with care and offering a wide range of productive critiques: Thomas Ahnert, Christopher Close, Caryl Emerson, James Harris, Daniel Heller-Roazen, Daniel Garber, and Susan Stewart. To them, to my friends Mary Harper, Kerim Yasar, and the late Jim Clark, and to so many others in Princeton, I owe the wonderfulness of those three years.

The last institution that deserves my gratitude is Wellesley College, which has offered me everything I needed to finish this project – including the funding to procure expert assistance with several Latin translations from TextFormations and to hire the research assistants whose careful work has saved me from a myriad of small errors: Felicity Loughlin and Timothy Wright. I thank especially my colleagues in the Department of History for their unwavering confidence in the importance of my work within the broader field of early modern European history.

The many others whom I thank for reading parts of my manuscript and offering valuable advice and other forms of support include Susanna Elm, Christian Flow, Anthony Grafton, Eleanor Johnson, Martin Otero Knott, Joel Lande, Anthony LaVopa, Hartmut Lehmann, Anthony Long, Rebecca Lyman, Boris Maslov, Marcus Meier, Yair Mintzker, James Moore, Martin Mulsow, Alessandro Nannini, Christopher Ocker, Thomas Pfau, David Pugh, Clemens Schwaiger, Olga Katherina Schwartz, Jonathan Sheehan, Walter Sparn, the two anonymous reviewers for Cambridge University Press, David Armitage and his fellow editors of the Ideas in Context series, and all those who organized or attended my presentations of parts of this project outside Halle, Berkeley, Princeton, and Wellesley. The venues included the Transatlantic Doctoral Seminar on early modern Germany (2008), organized by Roger Chickering and Richard Wetzell for the German Historical Institute in Washington, D. C.; the Seminar in Political Thought and Intellectual History at Cambridge University (2009); the Department of Political Science and the Scholars' Circle at Concordia University in Montreal (2012); the Istituto Italiano per gli Studi Filosofici in Heidelberg (2012); and the Departments of History at Boston College and York University (2013). For the invitations I thank, among others, Ulrich Diehl, Ed King, James Moore, Isaac Nakhimovsky, and Martin Sattler.

Words do no justice to my gratitude toward my parents. I wish my mother could see the fruits her indefatigable aspirations for my education have borne. To her and to my father, I dedicate this book with overflowing love.

Abbreviations

AFSt   Archive of the Francke Foundations. Halle (Saale), Germany.

BL   British Library. London, England.

DBA   *Deutsches Biographisches Archiv*. New York: K. G. Saur, 1982–85.

DNB   *The Dictionary of National Biography*. 61 vols. Edited by H. C. G. Matthew and Brian Harrison. Oxford: Oxford University Press, 2004.

EUL   Edinburgh University Library. Edinburgh, Scotland.

HL   *The Letters of David Hume*. Edited by J. Y. T. Grieg. Vol. 1 of 2, *1727–1765*. Oxford: Oxford University Press, 1932.

NLS   National Library of Scotland. Edinburgh, Scotland.

StAndUL   St. Andrews University Library. St. Andrews, Scotland.

TCM   City of Edinburgh. Minutes of the Town Council. Edinburgh City Chambers. Edinburgh, Scotland.

Transcription and Citation

1. Most isolated Greek words and phrases have been transliterated.
2. All abbreviations using superscript letters (e.g., "y^e" for "the") have been written out in full. Most ampersands have been replaced with "and."
3. In the case of William Cleghorn's lecture dictates, all abbreviations have been written out in full, and punctuation has occasionally been changed to increase readability (e.g., commas inserted between elements of a list). The original orthography has been altered in the case of obvious errors that impair the readability of the text, and the frequent capitalization of individual words has been altered (i.e., usually eliminated) to conform more closely to now-current norms. All changes with an obvious, significant bearing on the interpretation of the text have been enclosed in square brackets.
4. William Dalgleish's four-volume set of dictates of William Cleghorn's lectures (EUL MS Dc.3.3–6) is cited according to the pagination of the volumes. The first three volumes (Dc 3.3–5), which are continuously paginated (i.e., 1 to 707, with Dc 3.3 containing pages 1–199, Dc 3.4 pages 201–423, and Dc 3.5 pages 425–707), are accordingly cited as Book I; and the fourth volume (Dc 3.6), which is independently paginated (i.e., 1 to 367), is cited as Book II. For example, the citation "W. Cleghorn, Lectures, EUL, I.413–5" refers to EUL MS Dc.3.4, fols. 413–15.
5. Corrections in original manuscripts have been reproduced as precisely as possible. Struck-through printed text (like ~~this~~) indicates text that is crossed out in the original manuscript. Underlined printed text following a caret (like ~~that~~ ^this) reproduces the text of a handwritten correction or addition.

Introduction

Most histories of aesthetic theory in the Western world begin in earnest with the first decades of the eighteenth century. Conventional wisdom takes this to be the moment when medieval speculative philosophizing about beauty finally began to give way in much of Europe to a recognizably modern enterprise: the systematic and empirically oriented analysis of the perception of beauty as a mental phenomenon.[1] The list of theorists whose work marks this transition is almost as conventional as the transition's date. Many historians of aesthetics mention Joseph Addison (1672–1719) in England; David Hume (1711–76), Alexander Gerard (1728–95), and Archibald Alison (1757–1839) in Scotland; Jean-Pierre de Crousaz (1663–1750) in Lausanne; and Nicolas Boileau-Despréaux (1636–1711), Jean-Baptiste Du Bos (1670–1742), and Charles Batteux (1713–80) in France. Some add Johann Jakob Bodmer (1698–1783) and Johann Jakob Breitinger (1701–1776) in Zurich, or Giambattista Vico (1668–1744) in Naples. But almost all give pride of place to Anthony Ashley Cooper, third Earl of Shaftesbury (1671–1713) in England, Francis Hutcheson (1694–1746) in Ireland and Scotland, and Alexander Gottlieb Baumgarten (1714–62) in Brandenburg-Prussia. Each of them has been influentially credited with breaking important new ground. Shaftesbury has been called the "inventor" of aesthetics and the author of "the first . . . comprehensive and independent philosophy of the beautiful."[2] Hutcheson, a "father" of the Scottish Enlightenment and

---

[1] The many examples of this general view include W. Tatarkiewicz, *History of Aesthetics*, v. 3 of 3 (Paris: Mouton, 1974), xix; W. Tatarkiewicz, *A History of Six Ideas: An Essay in Aesthetics* (London: Nijhoff, 1980), 310–11, 319–20; *Aesthetics*, prod. C. O'Donnell, dir. P. Garcia, 51 min., Films for the Humanities and Sciences, 2004, digital video disc; D. Kliche, "Die Institutionalisierung der Ästhetik," in *Ästhetische Grundbegriffe*, ed. K. Barck et al., v. 1 (Stuttgart: Metzler, 2000), s.v. "Ästhetik/ästhetisch," 318; and G. Dickie, *Introduction to Aesthetics: An Analytic Approach* (Oxford: Oxford University Press, 1997), 9–10.

[2] J. Chytry, *The Aesthetic State: A Quest in Modern German Thought* (Berkeley: University of California Press, 1989), lv; E. Cassirer, *The Philosophy of the Enlightenment*, trans. F. C. A. Koelln and J. P. Pettegrove (Princeton, NJ: Princeton University Press, 1951; repr., Boston: Beacon Press, 1965), 312;

first major exponent of the "moral sense," has been described as the first philosopher "to write a clearly recognizable, extended, and self-contained work on what we would now call aesthetics or the philosophy of art."[3] Baumgarten, professor of philosophy in the cities of Halle and Frankfurt (Oder), coined the very term *aesthetica* in 1735 as the name of a new philosophy and, in Ernst Cassirer's words, allowed philosophical aesthetics to "constitute itself as a philosophical discipline in its own right."[4]

What precisely was modern about early-eighteenth-century aesthetic theories?

Historians of aesthetics usually regard as modern those theories that offer coherent, self-contained, and empirically informed discussion of the constellation of topics comprehended within the philosophical subdiscipline we now call *aesthetics*. They include the metaphysics of beauty; the psychology of human beings' experience of beauty; the nature of art or the arts as such; and various other elements of art-making and criticism, such as taste, imagination, and genius. None of these topics, of course, emerged *ex nihilo* in the eighteenth century. Individual aspects of each of them can be found in treatises and practical manuals on rhetoric, architecture, and painting and the other visual arts, not to mention a plethora of academic textbooks, extending back from the seventeenth century into the Middle Ages and antiquity.[5] But insofar as the eighteenth century saw self-contained analysis of all these topics coalesce into a single genre or philosophical discipline,[6] it witnessed the emergence of aesthetic theories worthy of the designation *modern* in the loose sense of that term.

Historians of aesthetics also tend to measure the modernity of an aesthetic theory by a different, narrower criterion – the degree to which it approximates what many of them have considered the supreme or first important model of modern aesthetic theory: Immanuel Kant's

---

cf. P. Guyer, *A History of Modern Aesthetics*, v. 1 of 3 (Cambridge: Cambridge University Press, 2014), 30.

[3] P. Kivy, "The 'Sense' of Beauty and the Sense of 'Art': Hutcheson's Place in the History and Practice of Aesthetics," *Journal of Aesthetics and Art Criticism* 53 (1995): 355; cf. Guyer, *A History of Modern Aesthetics*, I.98; and *Aesthetics*, prod. Camila O'Donnell.

[4] Cassirer, *Philosophy of the Enlightenment*, 342. Cf. T. Kinnaman, "Aesthetics before Kant," in *A Companion to Early Modern Philosophy*, ed. S. Nadler (Malden, MA: Blackwell, 2002), 578–79; and K. Hammermeister, *The German Aesthetic Tradition* (Cambridge: Cambridge University Press, 2002), 13.

[5] As described in, e.g., Tatarkiewicz, *History of Aesthetics*, v. 1 and 2 of 3; and U. Eco, *Art and Beauty in the Middle Ages*, trans. H. Bredin (New Haven, CT: Yale University Press, 1986).

[6] Guyer, *A History of Modern Aesthetics*, I.21; Hammermeister, *German Aesthetic Tradition*, ix; and, on the difficulty of defining the subject of the discipline: K. Barck, "Einleitung: Zur Aktualität des Ästhetischen," in *Ästhetische Grundbegriffe*, v. 1, s.v. "Ästhetik/ästhetisch," 308–9.

Critique of Judgment, first published in 1790. This narrower criterion is the chief principle by which a mere parade of stars – such as Shaftesbury, Hutcheson, and Baumgarten – has long been presented as a coherent narrative.

Some authors of such narratives present early-eighteenth-century aesthetic theories as valiant but inadequate attempts to pose and solve a problem ultimately and more convincingly addressed by Kant. The central problem is sometimes described as a conflict over whether human judgment of a thing's beauty – or, more generally, whether knowledge itself – is ultimately a matter of sensation or reason. Bernard Bosanquet calls the problem a conflict between "individual" and "universal" philosophical tendencies;[7] Ernst Cassirer describes the problem as "the schematic conflict" between experience and reason;[8] Howard Caygill describes the problem as the paradox, addressed in different ways by two competing traditions, one British and the other German, of how to judge the rules according to which we use our own judgment to achieve a "union of sensible and intelligible";[9] and Ted Kinnaman describes the problem as a paradox arising from the question, bequeathed to the modern world by René Descartes (1596–1650), whether beauty is a "subjective" or an "objective" quality.[10] Kant – so the stories go – resolved these problems.[11]

Other histories of early-eighteenth-century aesthetic theory present pre-Kantian theories as having anticipated concepts that came to fruition with Kant and thereby set the stage for later discussion.[12] The most heavily

---

[7] B. Bosanquet, *A History of Aesthetic*, 2nd ed. (New York: Macmillan, 1904; repr., 1934), 170–76.

[8] Cassirer, *Philosophy of the Enlightenment*, 322. Cf. M. Beardsley, *Aesthetics from Classical Greece to the Present: A Short History* (New York: Macmillan, 1966; repr., Tuscaloosa: University of Alabama Press, 1975), whose seventh and eighth chapters ("Cartesian Rationalism" and "Empiricism") immediately precede the chapter on Kant; A. Riemann, *Die Aesthetik Alexander Gottlieb Baumgartens unter besonderer Berücksichtigung der Meditationes philosophicae de nonnullis ad poema pertinentibus nebst einer Übersetzung dieser Schrift* (Halle: Niemeyer, 1928; repr., Tübingen: Niemeyer, 1973), 76; U. Franke, *Kunst als Erkenntnis: Die Rolle der Sinnlichkeit in der Aesthetik des Alexander Gottlieb Baumgartens*, Studia Leibnitiana, suppl. vol. 9 (Wiesbaden, 1972), 7.

[9] H. Caygill, *Art of Judgment* (Oxford: Basil Blackwell, 1989), 4–7, 37.

[10] Kinnaman, "Aesthetics before Kant," 572.

[11] A similar story, though with the important difference that Kant is presented as having resolved such problems far *less* convincingly than his German predecessors, can be found in F. Beiser, *Diotima's Children* (Oxford: Oxford University Press, 2009).

[12] The explicit purpose of such histories is sometimes, but not always, a deeper understanding of Kant himself, as in studies of Baumgarten by Bernard Poppe, Karl Raabe, and Alfred Bäumler. Franke, *Kunst als Erkenntnis*, 6. Cf. K. Raabe, *A. G. Baumgarten aestheticae in disciplinae formam redactae parens et auctor*, PhD diss. (University of Rostock, 1873); B. Poppe, *Alexander Gottlieb Baumgarten: Seine Bedeutung und Stellung in der Leibniz-Wolffischen Philosophie und seine Beziehungen zu Kant* (Borna-Leipzig, 1907); and A. Bäumler, *Das Irrationalitätsproblem in der Ästhetik und Logik des 18. Jahrhunderts bis zur Kritik der Urteilskraft*, 2nd ed. (Tübingen: Niemeyer, 1967; repr., Darmstadt: Wissenschaftliche Buchgesellschaft, 1975).

cited of these is the concept of the "aesthetic attitude," a particular type of contemplative experience characterized by "disinterestedness" and "autonomy," in the sense that the judgment it involves is subject to its own rules and is not directed toward any goal outside itself. What precisely the aesthetic attitude entails, and whether it is distinguishable from other kinds of experience, has long been a subject of controversy, and the lack of consensus about it among twentieth-century aesthetic theorists is reflected in the variety of stories about how it emerged as an object of investigation among eighteenth-century predecessors of Kant. Benedetto Croce, for example, writing at the turn of the twentieth century, traced his own concept of aesthetic experience as a type of nonconceptual cognition, or *intuition*, back through Kant to Vico, and, in an imperfect form, to Baumgarten.[13] Jerome Stolnitz, in a series of articles beginning in 1961, developed the influential argument that a concept of "disinterested aesthetic experience" – much like his own – first appeared in the work of Shaftesbury and Hutcheson before Kant gave it more elaborate exposition.[14] Paul Guyer, in a more recent argument untarnished by the heavy criticism endured by Stolnitz,[15] has looked to Shaftesbury, Hutcheson, Du Bos, Addison, and, above all, Baumgarten for anticipations of Kant's concept of aesthetic experience as necessarily involving the free play of the imagination.[16]

---

[13] B. Croce, "The 'Aesthetica' of Baumgarten," in *Philosophy, Poetry, History: An Anthology of Essays*, trans. C. Sprigge (Oxford: Oxford University Press, 1966); cf. P. Romanell, introduction to *Guide to Aesthetics*, by B. Croce (Indianapolis, IN: Bobbs-Merrill, 1965; repr., Indianapolis, IN: Hackett, 1995), ix. Umberto Eco evidently has Croce's aesthetic theory in mind as he measures the modernity of medieval aesthetics in *Art and Beauty in the Middle Ages*, 1.

[14] J. Stolnitz, "On the Origins of 'Aesthetic Disinterestedness,'" *Journal of Aesthetics and Art Criticism* 20.2 (1961), 133; M. Rind, "The Concept of Disinterestedness in Eighteenth-Century British Aesthetics," *Journal of the History of Philosophy* 40.1 (2002), 67–68; and summarizing Stolnitz, G. Dickie, "Stolnitz's Attitude: Taste and Perception," *Journal of Aesthetics and Art Criticism* 43.2 (1984), 195–98.

[15] E.g., by Rind, "The Concept of Disinterestedness," 70–74 (most convincingly, 73); Dickie, "Stolnitz's Attitude," 201; and P. Guyer, *Kant and the Experience of Freedom* (Cambridge: Cambridge University Press, 1993), 48–130, cited in Guyer, *A History of Modern Aesthetics*, I.37. Evidence that Stolnitz's discovery of the aesthetic attitude in the works of Shaftesbury can no longer be accepted uncritically is provided by P. Ayres, introduction to *Characteristicks*, by Shaftesbury (Oxford: Oxford University Press, 1999), xxviii. Ayres notes scholarly agreement that Shaftesbury moved *toward* aesthetic disinterestedness, thereby implicitly acknowledging that Stolnitz's discovery of aesthetic disinterestedness itself in Shaftesbury has been rejected.

[16] P. Guyer, "The Origins of Modern Aesthetics, 1711–1735," in *Values of Beauty: Historical Essays in Aesthetics*, by P. Guyer (Cambridge: Cambridge University Press, 2005), 5, 28–36; cf. Guyer, *A History of Modern Aesthetics*, I.9 (and I.339–40) on the pleasure of the "free exercise of our human capacities of mind and . . . body," one of three ideas around which Guyer organizes his narrative of the history of modern aesthetic theory in the eighteenth, nineteenth, and twentieth centuries. Other histories of aesthetic theory that measure pre-Kantian theorists by the degree to which they anticipated a paradigm established by Kant include Hammermeister, *German Aesthetic Tradition*.

Kantian concepts are equally central to another category of histories of aesthetic theory: those oriented not toward unearthing the origins of Kant's ideas, the origins of problems Kant tried to solve, or the origins of later aesthetic theories, but rather toward answering questions addressed famously by Walter Benjamin and Theodor Adorno, among others, about the connections between aesthetic theory and fascist or capitalist ideologies. Like their counterparts among historians of aesthetics who avoid all trace of Marxist vocabulary, authors of these histories tend to take the concept of "autonomous" aesthetic experience, articulated influentially by Kant, as the essential element of modern aesthetic theory and to discuss Kant's predecessors with a view to establishing the ways in which they anticipated later uses of the concept.[17] Their histories, too, in other words, present Shaftesbury, Hutcheson, and Baumgarten as milestones on the road to Kant and beyond.

Nor does the road adorned by these milestones lead only to modern aesthetic theory. According to a significant body of recent scholarship, it also leads to recognizably modern artistic institutions and cultural norms. Eighteenth-century Europe, on one influential account, witnessed the emergence of concepts of the "fine arts" as distinct from crafts and of the artist as distinct from the craftsman – distinctions unknown in the Middle Ages and antiquity.[18] By contrast with the craftsman, the artist was a person of genius: inspired, spontaneous, and original. These new artists, as imagined in the eighteenth century, produced their work not primarily for a

---

[17] Examples of this kind of approach include works by Terry Eagleton, Jonathan Hess, and Christoph Menke. Eagleton traces the concept of the autonomous aesthetic artifact – which he takes to be the essential subject of aesthetic theory – through the canon of aesthetic theorists, warning contemporary representatives of "Left moralism" not to forget that in the eighteenth century and at every later stage in its history, the concept not only reinforced bourgeois ideology, as is often assumed, but also served as a bulwark against "instrumentalist" thinking and provided the foundation for Marx's critique. Hess uses an analysis of works by Karl Philipp Moritz and Kant to argue that the concept of aesthetic autonomy did not emerge as a defense of high culture under pressure from burgeoning consumerism (contra Martha Woodmansee), and should be considered neither "protofascist" (contra Walter Benjamin) nor a progenitor of the public sphere (contra Jürgen Habermas), but was developed specifically as a means of ascribing freedom to intellectuals under an absolute monarchy. Menke reconstructs and elaborates on Theodor Adorno's use of Kant's concept of "antinomy" to resolve the tension between apparently mutually contradictory conceptions of aesthetic experience as "autonomous" and as "sovereign." T. Eagleton, *Ideology of the Aesthetic* (Oxford: Basil Blackwell, 1990), esp. 3, 8–9; J. Hess, *Reconstructing the Body Politic* (Detroit, MI: Wayne State University Press, 1999), esp. 16–23, 31–32, 59–80; C. Menke, *The Sovereignty of Art*, trans. N. Solomon (Cambridge, MA: MIT Press, 1998), vii–xi.

[18] L. Shiner, *The Invention of Art* (Chicago: University of Chicago Press, 2001), elaborating on P. O. Kristeller, "The Modern System of the Arts," *Journal of the History of Ideas* 12 (1951): 496–527 and 13 (1952): 17–46; and P. O. Kristeller, "Origins of Aesthetics: Overview," in *Encyclopedia of Aesthetics*, ed. M. Kelly (Oxford: Oxford University Press, 1998).

commissioning patron but for the emerging art market, driven in large part by growing middle-class demand in societies reaping the economic benefits of commercial expansion and the growth of manufacturing. Their works were to be enjoyed not for crass utilitarian reasons but primarily for the refined pleasure that a person of good taste could derive from contemplating them in a "disinterested" way. These new ideals were reflected in, and reinforced by, a slew of art-related institutions that developed simultaneously with them, including art museums, concert halls, and theaters.[19] Why exactly the concept of disinterested aesthetic experience began to emerge amid these other cultural and institutional developments is a matter of debate,[20] but its centrality to those developments is seldom disputed.[21]

Among all these histories of aesthetic theory that look to Shaftesbury, Hutcheson, and Baumgarten as Kant's forerunners, many contain a great deal of truth. But almost every one of them unites the protagonists of its story with an ahistorical bond: to a greater or lesser extent, they all produced approximations of a theory – or participated in the construction of a discipline – that none of them knew would emerge. The story is coherent, but from the perspective of a historian interested primarily in the early eighteenth century, its coherence must seem disappointingly teleological. Insofar as the theories resembled each other, the causes of that resemblance still demand explanation. The occasional suggestion that the theorists themselves had common aims usually bears no weight, signaling instead a momentary lapse in the conscientiousness with which historians need to distinguish what foreshadows a later innovation from what their history's protagonists intended to achieve. George Dickie illustrates the problem well in his own introduction to aesthetic theory, when he purports, in a historical prelude, to "trace the central, organizing strains of the field and thereby set the stage for discussion of present-day problems in aesthetics."[22] Even putting aside the question of whether a single field of aesthetics has in fact persisted from the eighteenth century to

---

[19] Shiner, *Invention of Art*, 3–7, 79–146.

[20] Various proposals can be found in, e.g., Shiner, *Invention of Art*, 130–51; M. Woodmansee, *The Author, Art, and the Market: Rereading the History of Aesthetics* (New York: Columbia University Press, 1994), 11–33; and Hess, *Reconstructing the Body Politic*. Cf. Guyer, *A History of Modern Aesthetics*, I.9–10, I.21.

[21] Important exceptions include J. Porter, "Is Art Modern? Kristeller's 'Modern System of the Arts' Reconsidered," *British Journal of Aesthetics* 49.1 (2009): 1–24; J. Porter, "Reply to Shiner," *British Journal of Aesthetics* 49 (2009): 171–78; J. Porter, "Why Art Has Never Been Autonomous," *Arethusa* 43.2 (2010): 165–80; and J. O. Young, "The Ancient and Modern System of the Arts," *British Journal of Aesthetics* 55.1 (2015): 1–17. Cf. Guyer, *A History of Modern Aesthetics*, I.28.

[22] Dickie, *Introduction to Aesthetics*, ix.

the present, Dickie's silence about whether early aesthetic theorists perceived the "central, organizing strains" of the field as we now perceive them opens the door to the questionable inference that in addressing questions and problems occupying aesthetic theorists today, eighteenth-century theorists were intentionally organizing their concepts and theories exclusively around those questions and problems.[23]

My purpose is to forestall this inference by offering an alternative to the conventional history of modern aesthetic theory before Kant, an alternative history whose coherence is not teleological. This history accepts the widespread designation of early-eighteenth-century theories as *modern* in the minimal sense that they contained coherent discussions of still-familiar aesthetic topics, and in that respect it accepts the classification of Shaftesbury, Hutcheson, and Baumgarten as modern aesthetic theory's pioneers. At the same time, it leaves aside the question of how closely their theories resembled Kant's, and by extension, it excludes any assessment of the validity of their theories relative to his. Instead, it excavates another, broader intellectual context in which these authors were working, in order to bring to light a different set of questions and problems they consciously designed their own theories to address. The result is a causal explanation for the creation of those theories and, thereby, a substantial basis – more substantial than the mere fact of their modernity – for including them in the same historiographical narrative. This narrative turns out to be considerably different from the histories of aesthetics in which early-eighteenth-century theories have hitherto featured so prominently.

According to this new narrative, aesthetic theories were part of a larger pattern of responses in the late seventeenth and early eighteenth centuries, in much of Europe, to what could be called aspects of the Augustinian legacy of early modern Christianity.[24] For all its shortcomings, probably the most lucid portrait of this larger pattern remains Hugh Trevor-Roper's "Religious Origins of the Enlightenment," a forty-page comparative study, now more than fifty years old, of proto-Enlightenment repudiations of seventeenth-century Calvinism in Holland, England, Scotland, France,

---

[23] Alexander Broadie's summary of aesthetics in the Scottish Enlightenment, a brief tour of eighteenth-century Scottish philosophical treatments of several problems important to modern aesthetic theory, exemplifies the consequences of this inference: the problems have been highlighted primarily because of their later importance. A. Broadie, "Art and Aesthetic Theory," in *Cambridge Companion to the Scottish Enlightenment*, ed. A. Broadie (Cambridge: Cambridge University Press, 2003).

[24] A condensed version of the following several paragraphs can be found in *Encyclopedia of Aesthetics*, 2nd ed., ed. M. Kelly (Oxford: Oxford University Press, 2014), s.v. "Origins of Aesthetics: Theological Origins of Aesthetics," by Simon Grote. Reused here by permission of Oxford University Press.

and Switzerland.[25] Trevor-Roper portrays the birth of the Enlightenment in all these places as, in essence, a restaging of the famous 1524–25 pamphlet exchange between Martin Luther (1483–1546) and Desiderius Erasmus (c. 1467–1536) on the freedom of the human will. One of the chief points of conflict in that exchange had been the extent to which sinful human beings are naturally capable of improving their own prospects for salvation. Against Luther, who insisted that salvation be regarded as an utterly unmerited gift bestowed on sinful human beings by an inscrutable but merciful God, Erasmus protested that God is also supremely just, and as such he must have given human beings a capacity to perform the virtuous actions he explicitly commands. By the late seventeenth century, following the lead of such theologians as Jacob Arminius (1560–1609) and Hugo Grotius (1583–1645) in the Netherlands, resurgent partisans of Erasmus within Europe's established churches and among a variety of dissenting groups had placed the heirs of John Calvin (1509–64), Theodor Beza (1519–1605), George Buchanan (1506–82), and John Knox (1505–72) ("What a gallery of intolerant bigots, narrow-minded martinets, timid conservative defenders of repellant dogmas, instant assailants of every new or liberal idea, inquisitors and witch-burners!"[26]) on the defensive. What united these "Erasmian" and "Arminian" bearers of Enlightenment's torch was not only their endurance of a wide range of slurs – including *Arminianism, Socinianism, deism, Pelagianism,* and *atheism* – but also their general antipathy toward the hitherto mainstream Protestant teaching that as a consequence of original sin, human beings are by nature radically depraved, which is to say, naturally incapable of doing good in this life without the supernatural assistance of divine grace.[27]

---

[25] H. Trevor-Roper, "The Religious Origins of the Enlightenment," in *Religion, the Reformation and Social Change*, 3rd ed. (London: Secker and Warburg, 1984). The usefulness of Trevor-Roper's study can be appreciated especially if his descriptions of the evidence are salvaged from the polemical frame (that the Enlightenment should be regarded as the legacy of the political Right rather than the Left) in which he presents them.

[26] Trevor-Roper, "Religious Origins," 206.

[27] Attention to the rise of "Arminianism" as a largely pan-European phenomenon has not become standard in scholarly overviews of Enlightenment Christianity, where the greatest emphasis has long fallen on the development of "rationalism." Classic examples of the latter emphasis include G. R. Cragg, *The Church and the Age of Reason, 1648–1789* (New York: Penguin, 1960, repr. 1990); and, still definitive for the study of Christianity in eighteenth-century Germany, K. Aner, *Die Theologie der Lessingzeit* (Halle: Niemeyer, 1929). Cragg's emphasis more or less persists in M. Heimann, "Christianity in Western Europe from the Enlightenment," in *A World History of Christianity*, ed. A. Hastings (Grand Rapids, MI: Eerdmans, 1999). Trevor-Roper corrects not only this emphasis but also Paul Hazard's somewhat exaggerated association of the rise of theories of natural morality with the abandonment of "the Christian system," in *European Thought in the Eighteenth Century* (Cleveland, OH: Meridian Books, 1963), 160. Essentially in line with Trevor-Roper are Cassirer, *Philosophy of the Enlightenment*, 137–60; and, more recently, J. McManners, "Enlightenment: Secular and Christian (1600–1800)," in *The Oxford Illustrated History of Christianity*, ed. J. McManners

The dynamics of this controversy, sketched so vividly by Trevor-Roper and elucidated with greater precision by others after him,[28] can be observed in the churches and universities of all the places in which historians and philosophers have recently observed aesthetic theory's emergence – and not only in the context of theological debate. They were also evident in the university-taught subjects of moral philosophy and natural jurisprudence, where the subject of the controversy had by the early eighteenth century acquired a common name: "the foundation of morality" or, in the German-speaking world, *Grundlage der Moral*.[29] At issue, in schematic terms, was the extent to which human beings can become genuinely virtuous by exercising faculties they naturally possess. Crucial subquestions included (1) the identity of the natural faculties that needed to be exercised and (2) the extent to which the exercise of these faculties must involve discovering God's existence and understanding divine law.[30] In the Scottish Presbyterian and German Lutheran versions of this debate, two of the versions now best reconstructed by modern scholarship – and, happily, best suited to illuminate the goals of Baumgarten, Hutcheson, and the closest disciples of Shaftesbury, if not Shaftesbury himself – two basic positions were represented.

One position held that human beings in their natural state are simply incapable of acting in accordance with moral principles, including divine law, with any motivation other than the crass self-interest represented by a fear of divine punishments and a desire for divine rewards. Genuine virtue,

(Oxford: Oxford University Press, 1990), 289–92; and J. G. A. Pocock, *Barbarism and Religion: The Enlightenments of Edward Gibbon, 1737–1764*, v. 1 of 4 (Cambridge: Cambridge University Press, 1999), 50–71.

[28] Exemplary recent accounts of the controversy's many aspects and regional inflections can be found in I. Rivers, *Reason, Grace, and Sentiment*, 2 v. (Cambridge: Cambridge University Press, 1991–2000); T. Ahnert, *The Moral Culture of the Scottish Enlightenment, 1690–1805* (New Haven, CT: Yale University Press, 2014); A. Schubert, *Das Ende der Sünde: Anthropologie und Erbsünde zwischen Reformation und Aufklärung* (Göttingen: Vandenhoeck und Ruprecht, 2002); T. O'Connor, *An Irish Theologian in Enlightenment France: Luke Joseph Hooke 1714–96* (Dublin: Four Courts Press, 1995); and T. O'Connor, *Irish Jansenists: Religion and Politics in Flanders, France, Ireland and Rome* (Dublin: Four Courts Press, 2008).

[29] In English, one variation was the "foundation of morals." On the prominence of the term in England and Scotland: D. F. Norton and M. Kuehn, "The Foundations of Morality," in *The Cambridge History of Eighteenth-century Philosophy*, ed. K. Haakonssen, v. 2 of 2 (Cambridge: Cambridge University Press, 2006), 941–44.

[30] This account of the central questions harmonizes with Rivers, *Reason, Grace, and Sentiment*, II.199–237; G. Hartung, *Die Naturrechtsdebatte: Geschichte der Obligatio vom 17. bis 20. Jahrhundert* (Freiburg: K. Alber, 1998); and K. Haakonssen, "German Natural Law," in *The Cambridge History of Eighteenth-Century Political Thought*, ed. M. Goldie and R. Wokler (Cambridge: Cambridge University Press, 2006). Alternative accounts include Norton and Kuehn, "The Foundations of Morality," which tends to elide the question of human beings' capacity for virtue with the question of moral distinctions' existence, and which implausibly denies the importance of these questions in the early-eighteenth-century German-speaking world.

on this view, requires a fundamental change or "regeneration" of the human soul by God in the course of a person's life, such that the motivation to act in accordance with moral principles ceases to be a desire for reward and fear of punishment and becomes instead a disinterested love of God and neighbor. In early-eighteenth-century Scotland, this view was represented by so-called orthodox Presbyterians. Key aspects of it – above all the assumption that human beings are naturally motivated only by crass self-interest – were understood by its critics, albeit sometimes unfairly, to reside also in the works of other authors familiar to Scottish university students, including Thomas Hobbes (1588–1679), Samuel Pufendorf (1632–94), and Bernard Mandeville (1670–1733).[31] In Halle, the Brandenburg-Prussian university city where Baumgarten began developing his aesthetic theory, a similar view was represented by a number of theologians and jurists who defy easy placement under a single heading but who included canonical representatives of German Pietism and putative adherents to a tradition of natural jurisprudence with roots in the works of Pufendorf.[32]

Another position in the debate, represented by many of Trevor-Roper's "Erasmians," held that without paying attention to the rewards and punishments attached to divine law, human beings are indeed capable of reaching a substantial degree of virtue, simply by cultivating and exercising a naturally inborn, more or less instinctive human desire for virtue itself. Elements of this view have been traced by modern scholars not only to Erasmus but also to ancient and medieval accounts of *synderesis* as a spark of divinity within the human soul, such as that of Thomas Aquinas (ca. 1225–74); to the well-known argument by Grotius that natural law would remain obligatory even if it were conceded that God does not exist; and to the "federal theology" of Reformed theologian Johannes Cocceius (1603–63), which introduced late-seventeenth-century Calvinism and Lutheranism to the possibility of human beings' progressive moral improvement, thereby undermining long-standing notions of original sin.[33] Between 1720 and 1750, the best-known and most committed Scottish representative of this view was Francis Hutcheson, who devoted his career as a moral theorist and university professor to demonstrating that human beings possessed an

---

[31] I thank Katerina Mihaylova for impressing upon me the respects in which this characterization of Pufendorf by his critics was unfair.

[32] E.g., Johann Franz Buddeus (1667–1729), Nicolaus Hieronymus Gundling (1671–1729), and Christian Thomasius (1655–1728) – on all of whom, see Chapter 1.

[33] E.g., R. A. Greene, "Instinct of Nature: Natural Law, Synderesis, and the Moral Sense," *Journal of the History of Ideas* 58.2 (1997): 175–98; Schubert, *Das Ende der Sünde*; S. Borchers, *Die Erzeugung des ganzen Menschen* (Berlin: de Gruyter, 2011), esp. 136–62.

instinctive benevolence, that virtue could by definition only be motivated by this benevolence, and that his students and other fellow countrymen should cultivate benevolence in themselves. In the German lands, including Baumgarten's Brandenburg-Prussia, the most important representative of a similar view was another professor: Christian Wolff (1679–1754), who attributed virtue to the exercise of the so-called rational appetite, a natural impulse that would invariably prompt human beings unencumbered by their passions to choose a course of action that their own rational faculties and experience had led them to conclude would contribute to the perfection of themselves and others.

Learned controversy among representatives of these two positions on the foundation of morality received thorough attention in the lecture halls of eighteenth-century Scottish and German universities as well as in the pages of philosophy textbooks, treatises, dissertations, sermons, and periodicals. This attention was by no means purely theoretical. At stake was the education of university students and, more broadly, the beliefs of those whose ranks many students were about to join: the lawyers, officials, physicians, clergymen, and others in a position to wield state, church, and other institutional powers and thereby to inculcate political preferences, moral conduct, and religious teachings in the population at large. What these people believed about the foundation of morality mattered a great deal, a fact nowhere more obvious than in the heatedness with which Scottish and German professors struggled among themselves to control how the issue would be taught in universities. In Scotland, Hutcheson supported a campaign in the mid 1740s to prevent the appointment of David Hume (1711–76) to the vacant professorship of moral philosophy at the University of Edinburgh, apparently fearing that Hume would undermine the moral-educational project to which Hutcheson himself had devoted his career. Like many of his colleagues, Hutcheson regarded this project as essential to upholding the legitimacy of the Whig establishment and the new monarchy brought to power by the Glorious Revolution of 1688; essential to ensuring the successful reform of the Church of Scotland; and essential to producing a Scottish population capable of enjoying the economic boons of the 1707 union with England while escaping the accompanying dangers of moral corruption and political apathy. In Brandenburg-Prussia, the stakes were similarly high. Controversy over the foundation of morality in early 1720s Halle between Wolff and his Pietist colleagues on the Theology Faculty led to Wolff's dismissal from the university and forceable expulsion from the land. The conflict turned on how to legitimate the Calvinist Hohenzollern regime in a land with a Lutheran church and nobility; how to reform the established Lutheran church; and how to produce a pious and industrious population capable of sustaining the economic and military projects central to Hohenzollern state-building.[34] Each of these notorious incidents in the history of academic politics registers how important the participants perceived correct education about the foundation of morality to be, and why they devoted so much energy to debating it.

These incidents also suggest why aesthetic questions began to receive similarly intense scrutiny. As Hutcheson's presence among the more Erasmian participants in the foundation-of-morality debate indicates, aesthetic theories were first developed largely as a means of bolstering the Erasmian position. Most authors of such theories in both Germany and Scotland, drawing on long traditions of reflection upon the nature of beauty and moral obligation, proposed that contemplating beauty in works of art and in the natural world, independent of any revealed knowledge of God or of divine law, could lead the contemplator to virtue. In doing so, they afforded themselves and their audiences – including their critics – ample occasion for psychologically well-informed, theoretical consideration of the questions involved: what beauty is, how we human beings perceive it, how it affects us, and how to produce its effects by artistic means. Theories of art and beauty, in other words, functioned as arenas for implicit or explicit debate about the foundation of morality, even as they were coalescing into a self-contained philosophical genre distinct from moral philosophy.

This is not to say that German and Scottish theorists understood themselves to be engaging in a single conversation with one another across the transnational republic of letters. English and French aesthetic writings certainly attracted attention in early-eighteenth-century Scotland; Addison and Shaftesbury were widely read, and Hutcheson himself, for example, claimed to have read Crousaz's 1715 *Treatise on Beauty* before writing

---

[34] These very general formulations borrow from aspects of overviews such as J. Moore, "Natural Rights in the Scottish Enlightenment," in *Cambridge History of Eighteenth-Century Political Thought*, 291–304; K. Haakonssen, "Natural Jurisprudence and the Identity of the Scottish Enlightenment," in *Philosophy and Religion in Enlightenment Britain: New Case Studies*, ed. R. Savage (Oxford: Oxford University Press, 2012); N. Phillipson, "The Scottish Enlightenment," in *Enlightenment in National Context*, ed. R. Porter and M. Teich (Cambridge: Cambridge University Press, 1981); and, with reference to Brandenburg-Prussia, e.g., essays by P. G. Dwyer, R. Gothelf, C. Clark, and J. van der Zande in *The Rise of Prussia, 1700–1830*, ed. P. G. Dwyer (Harlow: Pearson, 2000); I. Hunter, "Multiple Enlightenments: Rival *Aufklärer* at the University of Halle, 1690–1730," in *The Enlightenment World*, ed. M. Fitzpatrick et al. (New York: Routledge, 2004); W. Neugebauer, "Brandenburg-Preußen in der Frühen Neuzeit. Politik und Staatsbildung im 17. und 18. Jahrhundert," in *Handbuch der Preussischen Geschichte*, ed. W. Neugebauer, v. 1 (Berlin: De Gruyter, 2009); and Haakonssen, "German Natural Law," esp. 253.

his own.[35] But German aesthetic writings such as Baumgarten's appear to have gotten no public mention there, if they were read at all. Likewise, while Baumgarten and his early-eighteenth-century German contemporaries were familiar with texts by English-language authors such as Shaftesbury, Addison, and, to a lesser extent, Hutcheson – either directly or indirectly through translations, reviews, and references in other texts;[36] before the 1740s and 1750s, they appear to have directed most of their attention to their fellow countrymen and toward the French and the Swiss.[37] But if Scots and Germans did not write primarily for each other, they nonetheless did share a vocabulary, drawing key terms such as *perfection*, *beauty*, and *obligation* not only from the ostensibly "aesthetic" French and English texts they were reading in common but also from a different and more expansive repertoire of ancient and modern texts on metaphysics; natural law; theology; moral philosophy; the history of philosophy; and the practice and criticism of art, architecture, and literature. These texts were available throughout much of Europe and routinely featured – again, directly or indirectly through descriptions and excerpts in other texts – in the curricula of German and Scottish universities.[38] The terms employed in these texts provided their readers with the building blocks from which

[35] D. Raynor, "Hutcheson's Defence against a Charge of Plagiarism," *Eighteenth-Century Ireland* 2 (1987), 178–79; and on the reception of Du Bos by Hume, P. Jones, *Hume's Sentiments: Their Ciceronian and French Context* (Edinburgh: Edinburgh University Press, 1982), esp. 106–13. Cf. J. Friday, introduction to *Art and Enlightenment: Scottish Aesthetics in the Eighteenth Century* (Charlottesville, VA: Imprint Academic, 2004), 1.

[36] As described in B. Fabian, "English Books and Their Eighteenth-Century German Readers," in *Selecta Anglicana*, by B. Fabian (Wiesbaden: Harrassowitz, 1994), 11–94.

[37] Cf. S. Buchenau, *The Founding of Aesthetics in the German Enlightenment* (Cambridge: Cambridge University Press, 2013), 10–11. On the German reception of Shaftesbury's and Addison's writings before the 1740s: M.-G. Dehrmann, *Das "Orakel der Deisten": Shaftesbury und die deutsche Aufklärung* (Göttingen: Wallstein, 2008); R. Horlacher, *Bildungstheorie vor der Bildungstheorie: die Shaftesbury-Rezeption in Deutschland und der Schweiz im 18. Jahrhundert* (Würzburg: Königshausen und Neumann, 2004); and on the reception of Addison, e.g., M. Bragg, *Bodmer and Breitinger's Main Sources, Leibniz and Addison* (New York: Ballhorn Press, 1978); and M. Fritz, *Vom Erhabenen* (Tübingen: Mohr Siebeck, 2011), 208–14, 220–22. Accounts of early-eighteenth-century German engagement with French aesthetic texts include Riemann, *Die Ästhetik Alexander Gottlieb Baumgartens*, 5–14; and *Ästhetische Grundbegriffe*, v. 1, s.v. "Ästhetik/ästhetisch, I. Der europäische Kontext einer deutschen Gründung" and "Ästhetik/ästhetisch, V. Der europäische Begriffstransfer."

[38] Concise histories of the diffusion of these terms and of the concepts to which they refer abound. On *beauty*: e.g., *Encyclopedia of Aesthetics*, 2nd ed., s.v. "Beauty"; J. Haubrich, *Die Begriffe "Schönheit" und "Vollkommenheit" in der Ästhetik des 18. Jahrhunderts*, PhD diss. (Mainz, 1998), esp. 39–133; and Tatarkiewicz, *A History of Six Ideas*, Chapters 4 and 5. On *perfection*: e.g., Haubrich, *Die Begriffe "Schönheit" und "Vollkommenheit"*; *Ästhetische Grundbegriffe*, v. 6, s.v. "Vollkommen/Vollkommenheit"; *Historisches Wörterbuch der Philosophie*, ed. J. Ritter, v. 3 (Darmstadt: Wissenschaftliche Buchgesellschaft, 1974), s.v. "Ganzes/Teil"; and, focusing on Christian Wolff's sources, C. Schwaiger, *Das Problem des Glücks im Denken Christian Wolffs: Eine quellen-, begriffs-, und entwicklungs-geschichtliche Studie zu Schlüsselbegriffen seiner Ethik* (Stuttgart-Bad

they could construct theories that we now regard as aesthetic but that, from their own early-eighteenth-century perspectives, bore directly upon the moral-philosophical and natural-jurisprudential questions central to the discourses in which many of the terms featured prominently.

This, in brief, is a general history of the emergence of modern aesthetic theory in the early eighteenth century. The credibility of the thesis embedded within this history, that the emergence of aesthetic theories in early-eighteenth-century Scotland and Germany can be explained as an outgrowth of simultaneous and similar debates about the foundation of morality, depends upon the soundness of an argument with essentially two steps: (1) there were similar debates about the foundation of morality in Scotland and in Germany in the first half of the eighteenth century and (2) traditionally important aesthetic theories in both places should be construed as similar contributions to those debates. These two steps cross ground already traveled by other scholars. Although the foundation-of-morality controversy in eighteenth-century Scotland has received only a modicum of sustained, explicit scholarly attention as a phenomenon in its own right,[39] it has long received attention – and is now well understood – as a subject of disagreement between Francis Hutcheson and David Hume.[40] That Hutcheson developed his ethical theory as a contribution to the foundation-of-morality debate, and that he used his aesthetic theory to reinforce his ethical theory, is also well known.[41] This last observation accords well with the more general view that Shaftesbury and many of his Scottish readers ascribed beauty to the souls of virtuous human beings, saw art as an important tool of moral education, and thereby took for granted the interrelations between ethics, aesthetics, and politics.[42] On the German

---

Cannstatt: Frommann-Holzboog, 1995). On *obligation*: e.g., Hartung, *Die Naturrechtsdebatte*, 11–166; Haakonssen, "German Natural Law"; Haakonssen, "Natural Jurisprudence and the Identity of the Scottish Enlightenment"; and *Historisches Wörterbuch der Philosophie*, v. 7, s.v. "Pflicht."

[39] The most important examples known to me are Rivers, *Reason, Grace, and Sentiment*, I.199–237; and Norton and Kuehn, "The Foundations of Morality."

[40] See Chapter 5. A rehearsal of Hume and Hutcheson's disagreement about the foundation of morality constitutes L. Turco, "Moral Sense and the Foundations of Morals," in *The Cambridge Companion to the Scottish Enlightenment*, 136–56; with a fuller picture of the controversy's other participants provided by J. A. Harris, "The Early Reception of Hume's Theory of Justice," in *Philosophy and Religion in Enlightenment Britain*.

[41] In addition to Turco (note 40, above), see Chapter 5, note 13, for the scholarship on which Turco's article is based. Cf. R. Norton, *The Beautiful Soul: Aesthetic Morality in the Eighteenth Century* (Ithaca, NY: Cornell University Press, 1995), Chapter 1.

[42] As described with reference to England and Scotland in J. Barrell, *The Political Theory of Painting from Reynolds to Hazlitt* (New Haven, CT: Yale University Press, 1986), esp. 1–68; to Scotland and Germany in Norton, *The Beautiful Soul*; and Caygill, *Art of Judgment*; and with reference to Scotland in Friday, *Art and Enlightenment*, 11; and L. Brown, *Artful Virtue: The Interplay of the Beautiful and*

side, although the term *Grundlage der Moral* is seldom applied, a substantial outline of the controversy to which it refers is available in the case of Christian Wolff and some of his critics among professors of law at the University of Halle in the 1710s, 1720s, and 1730s.[43] And as research on Baumgarten has progressed in the past several decades, conducted in many cases by scholars either uninterested in his resemblance to Kant or interested in illuminating the value of his achievements by contrast with Kant's,[44] implications of his aesthetic theory not only for moral education but also more specifically for the foundation of morality and its theological implications have come into view.[45]

Terra incognita nonetheless remains, and establishing the relevant similarities between Scottish and German aesthetic theories requires that several parts of it be mapped precisely. On the Scottish side, although the persistent importance of Shaftesbury's moral and aesthetic ideas in the eighteenth century is widely accepted, the details of its reception remain hazy. In particular, the deviation of Hutcheson from Shaftesbury and the relative marginality of Hutcheson's aesthetic theory by the middle of the century, by comparison with Shaftesbury's, warrants careful attention.[46] Contrary to many histories of pre-Kantian aesthetics, from an historical perspective, the best Scottish point of comparison with German theorists such as Baumgarten is not Hutcheson but rather several contemporaries of his who, while more obscure today, better represent the mainstream in their wholehearted adoption of Shaftesbury's ideas of aesthetic and moral education. The little-known William Cleghorn (1718–54) is probably an ideal representative.[47]

---

the *Good in the Scottish Enlightenment* (Burlington, VT: Ashgate, 2015). My thanks to Leslie Brown for the opportunity to read a draft of her manuscript before its publication.

[43] Most notably, in G. Hartung's large-scale survey, *Die Naturrechtsdebatte*.

[44] The latter purpose frames F. Beiser, *Diotima's Children* (Oxford: Oxford University Press, 2009), and Buchenau, *The Founding of Aesthetics*, a contextualization of Baumgarten's aesthetics within the history of logic and theories of invention; whereas the former perspective characterizes Borchers, *Die Erzeugung des ganzen Menschen*, a contextualization of Baumgarten's aesthetics within the reception of federal theology in late-seventeenth-century and early-eighteenth-century German Lutheranism.

[45] E.g., Caygill, *Art of Judgment*, esp. 104–71; Norton, *The Beautiful Soul*, esp. 55–99; J. Jacob, *Heilige Poesie* (Tübingen: Niemeyer, 1997), 17–54; C. Schwaiger, "Ein 'missing link' auf dem Weg der Ethik von Wolff zu Kant," *Jahrbuch für Recht und Ethik* 8 (2000): 247–61; E. Müller, *Ästhetische Religiosität und Kunstreligion* (Berlin: Akademie, 2004), 45–53; P. Bahr, *Darstellung des Undarstellbaren* (Tübingen: Mohr Siebeck, 2004), 11–170; S. Grote, "Pietistische *Aisthesis* und moralische Erziehung bei Alexander Gottlieb Baumgarten," *Aufklärung* 20 (2008): 175–98; C. Schwaiger, "Baumgartens Ansatz einer philosophischen Ethikbegründung," *Aufklärung* 20 (2008): 219–38; E. Stöckmann, *Anthropologische Ästhetik* (Tübingen: Niemeyer, 2009), 25, 104–10; C. Schwaiger, *Alexander Gottlieb Baumgarten: ein Intellektuelles Porträt* (Stuttgart-Bad Cannstatt: Frommann-Holzboog, 2011); Borchers, *Die Erzeugung des ganzen Menschen*, 136–62; Fritz, *Vom Erhabenen*, esp. 230–83; and Buchenau, *The Founding of Aesthetics*, 10, 178–92, 235–36.

[46] See Chapter 4.   [47] See Chapter 5.

On the German side, substantially more needs uncovering. First, the extent
of the importance of the foundation-of-morality debate in the early German Enlightenment needs clearer demonstration. Although information
about Christian Wolff's disagreement with contemporary natural jurists
about the issue can be found in recent scholarship, the connection between
this disagreement and Wolff's better-known quarrel with the Pietist theologians in Halle, who engineered his 1723 expulsion from Brandenburg-
Prussia, requires further illumination. Disagreement over the foundation
of morality was in fact the axis on which both these controversies turned.[48]
Second, Alexander Baumgarten's intellectual debts to many of those Pietist
theologians in Halle continue to require careful scrutiny, as does the relationship between his aesthetic theory and those theologians' quarrel with
Wolff.[49]

The chapters that follow dispel the mists around these features of the
two historical landscapes, German and Scottish, in which several canonical pre-Kantian aesthetic theories took form. As the mists disperse, the
landscapes reveal themselves to be, for all their differences, astonishingly
alike. In fact, far more than simply allowing anyone who cares about the
history of aesthetics to make an imaginative leap from one historiographical
framework to another – that is, from pre-Kantianism to a more variegated
history of debate about natural law, theology, and morality – the newly
apparent similarities of the two historical settings suggest how a new history of early-eighteenth-century aesthetic theory could be told. Aesthetic
theories in Scotland and Germany did not resemble each other only by
virtue of the simple fact that they developed in connection with debates
over the foundation of morality; rather, they also shared crucial concepts
and deployed those concepts in similar ways, to similar ends, and at similar times in a pair of debates that not only shared a name and a subject
but also unfolded similarly in multiple stages parallel to one another. The
history of early-eighteenth-century aesthetic theory can be told in terms
of the unfolding of these debates. Admittedly, this history may end up

---

[48] See Chapter 1.
[49] Most older treatments of Baumgarten that do not examine him primarily in relation to Kant (see
above, note 12) nonetheless do not give very much attention to his immediate, German intellectual
milieu, often preferring to discuss his predecessors and contemporaries among French aesthetic
theorists – e.g., Riemann, *Die Aesthetik Alexander Gottlieb Baumgartens* – and almost always treating
his aesthetic theory as a contribution to epistemology rather than as a contribution to then-current
debates about ethics. See, e.g., Franke, *Kunst als Erkenntnis*; and Steffen Gross, *Felix Aestheticus. Die
Aesthetik als Lehre vom Menschen* (Würzburg: Königshausen und Neumann, 2001). Indicators that
this tide has turned include the works mentioned above in notes 44 and 45 as well as Kliche, "Die
Institutionalisierung der Ästhetik," in *Ästhetische Grundbegriffe*, s.v. "Ästhetik/ästhetisch."

looking surprisingly unlike its old self. There is little mention of autonomy and the aesthetic attitude in the following pages. Francis Hutcheson,
a familiar protagonist of the pre-Kantian story, has had to make room for
William Cleghorn. But by comparison with that pre-Kantian story, the
result is at least as coherent, situated in a more elaborate historical context,
less teleological, and more faithful both to the purposes of the theorists it
examines and to the character of the theories themselves.

CHAPTER I

Christian Wolff's Critics and the Foundation of Morality

In 1723, Pietist theologians at the University of Halle engineered the dismissal and forceable expulsion of their colleague in the Philosophy Faculty Christian Wolff (1679–1754). In doing so, they inadvertently produced what has long been regarded as one of the great set pieces of eighteenth-century intellectual history and a seminal moment in the history of ideas. Pitting the most influential eighteenth-century German academic philosopher before Kant against the most institutionally powerful exponents of German Pietism, the story of Wolff's expulsion has been described in the last hundred years as the outgrowth of deep conflict between distinct intellectual currents of the early Enlightenment: between a yearning for intellectual freedom and a protectiveness of the clergy's prerogative to defend orthodoxy; between quasi-Spinozistic determinism and a Christian commitment to the idea of human freedom; between approval and suspicion of the very enjoyment of life; between two university faculties, philosophy and theology, fighting to institute mutually exclusive programs of educational reform; and, most pervasively of all, between neo-Scholastic confidence in human beings' rational cognitive faculties and Pietist anxiety about conversion.[1] As for the consequences of the controversy, Wolff's critics

---

[1] Accounts like these, brutally schematized here for the sake of concision, can be found in, for example, W. Schrader, *Geschichte der Friedrichs-Universität zu Halle*, 2 v. (Berlin, 1894), I.168–81, I.204–26; F. J. Schneider, "Das geistige Leben von Halle im Zeichen des Endkampfes zwischen Pietismus und Rationalismus," *Sachsen und Anhalt* 14 (1938): 137–66; M. Wundt, *Die deutsche Schulphilosophie im Zeitalter der Aufklärung* (Tübingen: Mohr, 1945; repr., Hildesheim: Olms, 1992), 230–44; C. Hinrichs, *Preussentum und Pietismus* (Göttingen: Vandenhoeck & Ruprecht, 1971), 388–441; B. Bianco, "Freiheit gegen Fatalismus: Zu Joachim Lange's Kritik an Wolff," in *Zentren der Aufklärung I: Halle*, ed. N. Hinske, Wolffenbütteler Studien zur Aufklärung 15 (Heidelberg: Lambert Schneider, 1989); H. Poser, "Pietismus und Aufklärung – Glaubensgewißheit und Vernunfterkenntnis im Widerstreit," in *Aufklärung und Erneuerung*, ed. G. Jerouschek et al. (Halle: Werner Dausien, 1994), 170–81; J. Holloran, "Professors of Enlightenment at the University of Halle, 1690–1730" (PhD diss., University of Virginia, 2000), esp. 309; J. Israel, *Radical Enlightenment* (Oxford: Oxford University Press, 2001), 541–58; J. J. Fehr, *"Ein wunderlicher nexus rerum": Aufklärung und Pietismus in Königsberg unter Franz Albert Schultz* (Hildesheim: Olms, 2005), 115–52; and A. Beutel, "Causa Wolffiana: Die Vertreibung Christian Wolffs aus Preußen in 1723 als Kulminationspunkt des theologisch-politischen

have been credited with exposing the fundamental inability of the so-called Leibniz–Wolffian philosophical system – the reigning orthodoxy among academic philosophers in early-eighteenth-century Germany for well over a generation – to give a credible account of human freedom, thereby laying the groundwork for its demise at the hands of Immanuel Kant.[2]

This controversy also deserves careful study for one of its lesser-known consequences: the impetus it gave Alexander Baumgarten, studying theology and philosophy in Halle in the 1730s, to develop what ultimately became the first aesthetic theory to bear the name. In 1721, six years before Baumgarten arrived in Halle, as the story is conventionally told, Christian Wolff, *ordinarius* professor of mathematics and philosophy at Halle since 1706,[3] had delivered a public lecture on the practical philosophy of the Chinese and had thereby given his long-standing critics on the university's Theology Faculty an opportunity to attack him openly.[4] The result was a denunciation of the lecture from the pulpit by a member of the Theology Faculty, Joachim Justus Breithaupt (1658–1732); an investigation of Wolff's philosophical writings by the Theology Faculty as a whole; and sustained though initially unsuccessful maneuvering by three of the faculty's biggest stars – Breithaupt, August Hermann Francke (1663–1727), and their colleague Joachim Lange (1670–1744) – to secure a denunciation of Wolff's lecture from the Brandenburg-Prussian court.[5]

Konflikts zwischen Halleschem Pietismus und Aufklärungsphilosophie," in *Reflektierte Religion*, by A. Beutel (Tübingen: Mohr Siebeck, 2007). My thanks to Erik Midelfort for alerting me to Jonathan Holloran's work.

[2] Bianco, "Freiheit gegen Fatalismus," 112–13, 116–17, 122–26.

[3] Schrader, *Geschichte der Friedrichs-Universität zu Halle*, I.169, II.550.

[4] G. V. Hartmann, *Anleitung zur Historie der Leibnitzisch-Wolffischen Philosophie* (Leipzig, 1737; repr., Hildesheim: Olms, 1973), 665. The conventional account of the story, as repeated in various retellings in the past century, is derived largely from sources friendly to Wolff, above all Carl Günther Ludovici and Georg Volckmar Hartmann. For the sake of presenting a concise chronology, I have extracted only the outlines of the conventional story, omitting as much as possible the tendentious causal explanations and commentary provided by Hartmann and Ludovici. It should be noted, though, that even the conventional chronology, beginning with Wolff's lecture on Chinese practical philosophy, is somewhat misleading. August Hermann Francke noted his concern about Wolff years before the provocative lecture, and he began to keep a dossier on allegedly suspicious teachings by Wolff in 1717 at the latest. Lange's warnings to students about Wolff can be traced as far back as 1712. See Hinrichs, *Preussentum und Pietismus*, 397–401; Beutel, "Causa Wolffiana," 132–33, drawing primarily on Francke's *Journal* and Hartmann's *Anleitung*; and, taking issue with aspects of Hinrichs's and Beutel's chronologies, S. Grote, "Religion and Enlightenment Revisited: Lucas Geiger (1682–1750) and the Allure of Wolffian Philosophy in a Pietist Orphanage," *Pietismus und Neuzeit* 41 (2015): 32–56.

[5] Holloran, *Professors of Enlightenment*, 293–302; cf. C. G. Ludovici, *Ausführlicher Entwurf einer vollständigen Historie der Wolffischen Philosophie*, v. 1, 3rd ed. (Leipzig, 1738; repr., Hildesheim: Olms, 2003), 8.

The conflict between Wolff and his critics reached a fever pitch two years later, in 1723, with the publication – encouraged by Joachim Lange – of a critique and denunciation of Wolff's metaphysics by a former student of his, Daniel Strähler. In the midst of the ensuing fight over whether Strähler should be punished for violating the university statute against issuing such denunciations in public, and amid attempts on both sides to win university and royal support, the verbal abuse escalated. Lange began a long series of thinly veiled printed attacks against Wolff's metaphysics and ethics, prompting a series of indignant and derogatory responses by Wolff. The same year, a direct appeal by Francke to King Friedrich Wilhelm I (1688–1740), circumventing Wolff's supporters at court, had an effect more momentous even than the denunciation Wolff's critics had ostensibly sought: the king issued orders that Wolff leave his territories immediately, which Wolff obeyed, taking up a professorship in Marburg that had been offered to him the year before.[6]

Over the next several years the polemical exchanges continued. Critiques of Wolff from the University of Jena at the hands of *ordinarius* professor of theology Johann Franz Buddeus (1667–1729) and his son-in-law, *ordinarius* professor of rhetoric, later also of poetry and theology, Johann Georg Walch (1693–1775) appeared in print shortly after Wolff's banishment. By 1726, critiques like those raised by Strähler, Lange, Buddeus, and Walch were being debated in universities throughout the German lands.[7] In 1727, citing concern that Wolff was finding an alarming number of supporters, Francke and Lange succeeded in convincing the king to ban the sale and teaching of Wolff's metaphysics and ethics, under threat of fine.[8] Five months after the ban was imposed, Alexander Baumgarten arrived in Halle. Only nine years later, one year after Baumgarten's first public call for the creation of aesthetics as a philosophical discipline, was the ban lifted.[9]

Whether Baumgarten's development of an aesthetic theory represented in any way a response to the controversy over Wolff is not immediately obvious. The obscurity stems in part from the fact that the controversy was not entirely about ideas. At the time, Wolff and several of his supporters repeatedly alleged that the real source of the animus against him was bitterness over his attempt in 1723 to secure a recently vacated professorship of philosophy at Halle for a student of his, Ludwig Thümmig (1697–1728), thereby causing candidates preferred by Lange, Francke, and most of the rest of the Theology Faculty to be passed over. This allegation, however

---

[6] Holloran, *Professors of Enlightenment*, 327–65.   [7] Holloran, *Professors of Enlightenment*, 413.
[8] Holloran, *Professors of Enlightenment*, 419.   [9] Schneider, "Das geistige Leben," 145.

partial to Wolff's cause, does find some support in surviving contemporary documents.[10] Among the other plausible motivations for the attacks against Wolff are Lange's jealousy over Wolff's popularity among students, who seem to have been flocking from Lange to Wolff throughout the 1720s, and irritation among honor-conscious members of the Theology Faculty over Wolff's unpleasant habit of aggrandizing himself and belittling his theological colleagues.[11] And yet objections were also raised against Wolff's philosophical works throughout the 1720s and 1730s by critics who lived and worked far from Halle and had no personal investment in the internal maneuverings of Halle's professors. Personally motivated or not, in other words, the critiques of Wolff took on a life of their own shortly after they appeared in print.[12]

The charges themselves followed a pattern largely set by Joachim Lange at the outset, confirmed by Buddeus and Walch in 1723, and then repeated by others with little substantial variation for the next thirteen years and in most summaries of the debate long afterward. Wolff's teachings were frequently alleged to endanger piety and foster immorality among university students.[13] Wolff himself faced a variety of slurs: he was denounced as an advocate of Spinozism, Stoicism, fatalism, and atheism.[14] Other attacks were more elaborate. Wolff's critics argued, among other things, (1) that by endorsing Leibniz's description of the relationship between mind and body as a "preestablished harmony," and by adopting Leibniz's theory of monads, he had effectively denied that the human soul ruled over the body, thereby denying human freedom and "mechanizing" the soul; (2) that he rejected the soundest and most convincing proofs of God's existence; (3) that he portrayed God as a source of evil as well as good; and (4) that he described natural law as if it could exist even in God's absence, thereby undermining the foundations of religion and morality.[15] This last type of critique is one with which Alexander Baumgarten appears to have grappled

---

[10]　Hinrichs, *Preussentum und Pietismus*, 405–9; Holloran, *Professors of Enlightenment*, 310–21, 338.

[11]　Holloran, *Professors of Enlightenment*, 376; J. C. von Dreyhaupt, *Pagus neletici et nudzici, oder diplomatisch-historische Beschreibung des Saal-Kreÿses*, rev. and expanded by J. F. Stiebritz (Halle, 1773), II.168–9; Hinrichs, *Preussentum und Pietismus*, 398–400; and, quoted by Holloran, Nicolas Veridicus Impartialis Bohemus [=Nicolaus Hieronymus Gundling], *Unpartheyisches Sendschreiben* (Wittenberg [=Halle?], 1724), 13, 31, 33 – on which, see pp. 57–58.

[12]　Holloran, *Professors of Enlightenment*, 412.

[13]　Poppe, *Alexander Gottlieb Baumgarten*, 6; Holloran, *Professors of Enlightenment*, 360, 400.

[14]　Poppe, *Alexander Gottlieb Baumgarten*, 7–9.

[15]　As described by Poppe, *Alexander Gottlieb Baumgarten*, 6; Schneider, "Das geistige Leben," 140; Wundt, *Die deutsche Schulphilosophie*, 235–37; T. J. Hochstrasser, *Natural Law Theories in the Early Enlightenment* (Cambridge: Cambridge University Press, 2000), 158–59.

throughout his career, from his days as a student in Halle in the early 1730s onward, and he developed his aesthetic theory partly in order to address it.

The meaning of this critique and the reasons for its importance to Baumgarten and his contemporaries can be extracted from synopses of the conflict by two modern investigators. According to Albrecht Beutel, the more recent of the two,

> the substantive reason for the conflict that Wolff had to fight out with the Halle Pietists lay in the controversial question of cognitive method: whether, to put it biblically, fear of God, or, in Wolff's terms, the power of the human intellect is the beginning of wisdom.[16]

An earlier suggestion, anticipating Beutel's in some ways, comes from Ferdinand Josef Schneider. Recalling a remark by Joachim Lange that "nowhere else is the conversion of the audience the chief aim, the way it is in Halle,"[17] Schneider explains why Lange and his colleagues perceived Wolff to be so dangerous:

> Pietism's very zeal for conversion seemed in Halle to be called into question. Once anyone had taken the poison of Wolffianism, it was difficult to lead him back to the humble sensibility of a sinful creature wearing itself out in penitential struggle.[18]

Schneider does not refer explicitly to "the controversial question of cognitive method" mentioned by Beutel, but he implicitly places it, or something very much like it, at the center of the conflict between Wolff and his critics. The question of whether fear of God is the beginning of wisdom, or whether wisdom begins instead with the exercise of the human intellect independent of such fear, corresponds directly to the question of whether regarding oneself as a sinful creature and undertaking

---

[16] Beutel, "Causa Wolffiana," 128:

> Der sachliche Grund des Konflikts, den Wolff mit den halleschen Pietisten auszufechten hatte, lag in der strittigen Frage der Erkenntnismethode: ob, biblisch gesprochen, die Furcht Gottes oder aber, mit Wolff zu reden, die Kraft der menschlichen Verstandes der Weisheit Anfang sei.

[17] Schneider, "Das geistige Leben," 140:

> Zu seiner und seiner Amtsgenossen Verteidigung machte später Lange einem einstigen Schüler des Philosophen gegenüber vor allem den Grund geltend, daß man an keinem anderen Ort "die Bekehrung der Zuhörer zum Hauptzweck habe, so wie in Halle."

[18] Schneider, "Das geistige Leben," 141:

> Der ganze Bekehrungseifer des Pietismus schien in Halle tatsächlich in Frage gestellt zu sein. Wer da das Gift des Wolffianismus einmal in sich aufgenommen hatte, war schwer noch zur demütigen Gesinnung einer im Bußkampf sich aufreibenden sündlichen Kreatur zurückzuführen.

a penitential struggle is the necessary condition of moral improvement. Put another way, the question at issue for Wolff and his critics was whether fear of God and the kind of knowledge that produces such fear – namely, knowledge of God's will and of the dangers of disobeying his will – are the only adequate foundation of morality. Wolff's apparently negative answer to this question seemed to his critics to be false and therefore dangerous.

Wolff's Defense of Natural Obligation

At the heart of the controversy stood Christian Wolff's defense of what he called "natural obligation" (*obligatio naturalis* or *natürliche Verbindlichkeit*).[19] Wolff had explained the meaning of this term in his *German Ethics*, a textbook first published in Halle in 1720, one year before his provocative lecture on Chinese practical philosophy, and then again in 1722 and 1728 with additions reflecting his awareness of the controversy that had ensued. In the preface to the 1722 edition, Wolff credits himself with having described natural obligation in a newly illuminating way, and he makes its significance obvious. "When one wants to direct a human being," he explains, "one can go about it in one of two ways. Either one directs him by force like cattle, or with the help of reason, like a rational creature." Natural obligation refers to the latter: it is a means of directing human actions that uses human reason to produce "internal obedience" – which is to say, genuine virtue – while preserving the freedom of those who act in accordance with it. All other kinds of obligation refer explicitly to the "will of a superior" and involve the use of force, violence, and fear to produce merely "external discipline." To be sure, compulsion and fear are indispensable for restraining certain people from doing what they want, but only in the case of those people who, like cattle, lack a well-functioning intellect and the capacity to reason. Those whose rational faculties function well need only natural obligation.[20] The chief implication of this account, which Wolff repeatedly stresses, is that by virtue of natural obligation, people whose rational faculties are intact and who are

[19] Dieter Hüning has described Wolff's development and explanation of this concept in an essay generously adorned with pertinent quotations and comparative textual references, which I have taken as my point of departure: "Christian Wolffs Begriff der natürlichen Verbindlichkeit als Bindeglied zwischen Psychologie und Moralphilosophie," in *Die Psychologie Christian Wolffs*, ed. O.-P. Rudolph and J.-F. Goubet, Hallesche Beiträge zur Europäischen Aufklärung 22 (Tübingen: Niemeyer, 2004): 143–67.

[20] C. Wolff, *Vernünfftige Gedancken von der Menschen Thun und Lassen, zu Beförderung ihrer Glückseeligkeit* [= *Deutsche Ethik*], 4th ed. (Frankfurt (Main), 1733), preface to 2nd ed. [xx–xxii] (cf. preface to 3rd ed., §10).

either unaware of the will of God or do not acknowledge his existence – which is to say, atheists – are nonetheless obliged to act virtuously.[21]

Wolff's account of natural obligation depends explicitly on a substantial number of psychological, metaphysical, and ontological presuppositions. The word *obligation* itself Wolff defines simply as motivation, which he understands to be, in his words, "a reason to want or to not want something."[22] The source of natural obligation in particular, according to Wolff, is the human conscience, passing judgment on whether an action is good or bad, understood by Wolff to mean whether an action conduces to the perfection (*Vollkommenheit*) of the actor or not.[23] Underlying Wolff's account of natural obligation, therefore, is an explanation of what perfection is; how the human mind passes judgment on whether any given action conduces to it or not; and how this judgment moves the will, such that the will is directed toward good actions and away from bad actions without the use of fear and coercion.

In general, perfection or *Vollkommenheit*, the idea of which Wolff called "the source of my practical philosophy," refers to the relationship among the parts of a larger whole. The greater the extent to which those parts function together in such a way as to promote the purpose for which the whole exists, the greater the perfection of the whole. In Wolff's words, perfection is "unity amid variety" (*consensus in varietate* or *Zusammenstimmung des mannigfaltigen*), where "unity" (*consensus*) refers specifically to a thing's tendency to achieve some purpose (*tendentia ad idem aliquod obtinendum*).[24] A mechanical watch is Wolff's paradigmatic example: it is perfect insofar as its many component parts function together, such that its hands show the correct time. In the case of a human being, all the individual actions over the course of an entire life are the "parts" that constitute the "whole" of that life. A particular person's life is perfect to the extent that the individual actions "harmonize" with each other to promote his life's ultimate

---

[21] Wolff, *Deutsche Ethik*, preface to 3rd ed., §§4, 10; cf. Hüning, "Christian Wolffs Begriff der natürlichen Verbindlichkeit," 147.

[22] Wolff, *Deutsche Ethik*, §8: "To obligate someone to do something or to stop doing something," in Wolff's words, "is nothing other than to attach to it a motivation (*Bewegungsgrund*) to want or to not want [to do it]." Cf. Hüning, "Christian Wolffs Begriff der natürlichen Verbindlichkeit," 145–46.

[23] Wolff, *Deutsche Ethik*, §§41, 75.

[24] C. Wolff, *Vernünfftige Gedancken von Gott, der Welt und der Seele des Menschen, auch allen Dingen überhaupt* [= *Deutsche Metaphysik*], 11th ed. (Halle, 1751), §§152–54; cf. C. Wolff, *Philosophia prima, seu Ontologia* (Leipzig, 1736), §503ff. (See also below, Chapter 3, notes 23 and 24.) On Wolff's derivation of the concept of perfection from Leibniz, and on his assimilation of it to the concept of *Endzweck* or "ultimate purpose" in his *German Ethics*: Schwaiger, *Das Problem des Glücks*, 91–110. My thanks to Dirk Effertz for several illuminating conversations about these terms.

purpose, which Wolff takes to mean the extent to which the person lives in accordance with the essence and nature of a human being in general.[25] "Conformity to the essence and nature of a human being" in turn means achieving the best possible condition of the essential parts of the human being, namely, the greatest possible health of the body and the best possible functioning of the perceptive powers of the soul.[26] The result of achieving complete perfection, by engaging only in actions that harmonize with each other in promoting the health of the body and the perceptiveness of the soul, is in turn happiness, which consists of joy.[27]

The task of perceiving which actions contribute to one's own perfection Wolff assigns to the conscience (*Gewissen*). By virtue of what Wolff calls the interconnection or "nexus" of things (*nexus rerum* or *Zusammenhang der Dinge*), the fact that all things are connected with one another by an invariable relationship of cause and effect – which is to say, with Wolff, that each thing has a *Grund* or reason for its existence and that this reason is to be found in another thing – the question of whether a particular thing actually promotes one's perfection is a matter of fact.[28] This fact is discoverable through the application of a maxim established by the memory and the imagination on the basis of repeated experience, stating whether things of that type in general promote one's perfection. The human conscience, in turn, is responsible for applying the maxim, which it does by constructing syllogisms. The perception of the thing in question as a thing of a particular type is the major premise, the maxim (i.e., that things of this type do or do not promote one's perfection) is the minor premise, and the conclusion is that the thing in question does or does not promote one's perfection – in other words, the thing is either good or bad.[29]

This conclusion by the conscience, on Wolff's account, necessarily moves the will, which Wolff explicitly calls the "rational appetite" (*appetitus rationalis*).[30] The mechanism by which the complete subservence of the will to the conscience can be explained is that obeying the conscience produces tranquillity, whereas disobeying produces restlessness and therefore unhappiness, and the will invariably prefers tranquility.[31] The capacity

---

[25] Wolff, *Deutsche Ethik*, §14; Wolff, *Deutsche Metaphysik*, §§168, 144, 146.

[26] Wolff, *Deutsche Ethik*, §§19, 225.

[27] Wolff, *Deutsche Ethik*, §§45, 51–53; and, explicating this issue and much of the content of the following two paragraphs in greater detail, Schwaiger, *Das Problem des Glücks*, 120–88.

[28] Wolff, *Deutsche Ethik*, §§5, 90; Wolff, *Deutsche Metaphysik*, §§30, 912–13.

[29] Wolff, *Deutsche Ethik*, §192; Wolff, *Deutsche Metaphysik*, §§238, 266, 337–38.

[30] Wolff, *Deutsche Metaphysik*, pt. II: *Ausführliche Anmerckungen*, §155; cf. Hüning, "Christian Wolffs Begriff der natürlichen Verbindlichkeit," 157.

[31] Wolff, *Deutsche Ethik*, §§90, 128.

of the will to effect action, in turn, corresponds to the strength of the desire or motivation produced by the conscience, which depends on the degree to which the conclusion of the conscience is certain (*gewiss*), and therefore the degree to which the terms of the syllogism employed by the conscience are distinct (*deutlich*). The conscience leads most reliably to action when the perception of the thing in question (the major premise) and the perceptions from which the memory and imagination construct the maxim (the minor premise) are as distinct as possible.[32] Admittedly, clear but indistinct perceptions, produced by the senses and the imagination, also produce motivation and thereby lead to action, but the conclusions based on such perceptions are less certain and are more likely to confuse real perfection with merely apparent perfection.[33] Moreover, clear and indistinct perceptions, which on Wolff's account cause action by arousing affections[34] rather than by stimulating the rational appetite, thereby detract from the freedom of the actions to which they lead. "By means of the affections," Wolff writes,

> a human being is drawn to do and to avoid this and that, and they [the affections] make sensate desire and sensate aversion stronger than they would otherwise be. . . . But because a human being in a state of affection doesn't consider what he is doing, and accordingly no longer has control over his actions, he is forced both to do and to avoid what he otherwise would not do or avoid if he distinctly grasped what it was. Therefore, because the affections arise from the senses and the imagination, the rule of the senses, the imagination, and the affections constitutes the slavery of the human being. And one therefore calls *slaves* those who let their affections rule and who stay simply with the indistinct perception of the senses and the imagination.[35]

The motivation produced by the affections therefore cannot be described as the natural obligation whose existence Wolff wishes to prove, since

---

[32] Wolff, *Deutsche Metaphysik*, §§206–9, 238, 266, 326, 333, 337–38.
[33] Wolff, *Deutsche Metaphysik*, §§414–16, 502; Wolff, *Deutsche Ethik*, §§94, 180–81.
[34] Here and elsewhere, I follow eighteenth-century English usage, referring to *affects* as *affections*.
[35] Wolff, *Deutsche Metaphysik*, §§490–91:

> Durch die Affecten wird der Mensch hingerissen dieses und jenes zu thun oder zu lassen, und machen sie die sinnliche Begierde und den sinnlichen Abscheu stärcker, als er sonst seyn würde. . . . Da nun aber bey den Affecten der Mensch nicht bedencket, was er thut, und er demnach seine Handlungen nicht mehr in seiner Gewalt hat; so wird er gleichsam gezwungen zu thun und zu lassen, was er sonst nicht thun, noch lassen würde, wenn er deutlich begriffe, was es wäre. Derowegen weil die Affecten von den Sinnen und der Einbildungs-Kraft herrühren; so macht die Herrschaft der Sinnen, der Einbildungs-Kraft und Affecten die Sclaverey des Menschen aus. Und nennet man dannenhero auch Sclaven diejenigen, welche sich ihre Affecten regieren lassen, und bloß bey der undeutlichen Erkäntniß der Sinnen und Einbildungs-Kraft verbleiben.
>   Cf. Wolff, *Deutsche Ethik*, §§87, 180–83, 186.

the obligation to act virtuously can by no means involve force, let alone slavery. Rather, the effectiveness of natural obligation must correspond to the degree of distinctness and therefore the degree of certainty in the syllogism on which the conscience bases its conclusion.

Moral education, accordingly, depends primarily on training the conscience to draw conclusions as distinctly as possible, and on accustoming oneself to use the conscience's conclusions as the exclusive basis of one's actions. This is mostly a matter of habituation. Among the exercises Wolff recommends are taking time before bed to reflect upon whether the actions one performed during the day in fact conduced to one's own perfection, and taking time upon waking up to consider which actions tomorrow will best further one's own perfection. This process of reflection, he explains, involves rehearsing the syllogisms employed by the conscience. Continual repetition of the process leads to greater ease and facility in deduction.[36] The ultimate aim, which Wolff calls the highest degree of wisdom, is to be able to order all one's intentions and actions, such that they are all subservient to the single ultimate purpose of furthering one's own perfection.[37]

What moral education does not necessarily involve, by contrast, is learning to perceive the will of God as such. On the one hand, Wolff does argue that human beings are naturally obliged to recognize God's perfections and, as a consequence of that recognition, to discover what he wills.[38] The obligation to recognize God's perfections, Wolff explains, follows from the obligation to promote one's own perfection, because we can infer from God's perfections that he wishes us to be perfect, which invariably strengthens our motivation to become as perfect as possible.[39] Atheists, moreover, who lack this strengthened motivation, are for that reason incapable of as high a degree of virtue as those who perceive the existence and perfections of God.[40] On the other hand, Wolff also repeatedly emphasizes that even atheists, the relative weakness of their motivation notwithstanding, are naturally obliged to act virtuously; and the natural law that prescribes the pursuit of perfection and that obliges human beings by means of their own consciences would persist even in God's absence.[41] Wolff does admit

---

[36] Wolff, *Deutsche Ethik*, §§173–75, 188.

[37] Wolff, *Deutsche Metaphysik*, §§908–9, 914–20. Cf. Wolff, *Deutsche Ethik*, §§140, 146.

[38] Wolff, *Deutsche Ethik*, §§650–51. Here Wolff's argument is admittedly somewhat unclear: a human being cannot in fact promote the perfection of God, since God is unchangeable, and so "nothing is left but that he recognize the perfections of God and use them as motivations of his actions [*Derowegen bleibt nichts übrig, als daß er die Vollkommenheiten GOttes erkennet und sie zu Bewegungs-Gründen seiner Handlungen brauchet*]."

[39] Wolff, *Deutsche Ethik*, §§654–60.   [40] Wolff, *Deutsche Ethik*, §§47, 71, 675.

[41] Wolff, *Deutsche Ethik*, §§20–21.

that among those who have neither a "taste" (*Geschmack*) for virtue nor a habitual aversion to vice, a servile fear (*knechtliche Furcht*) of God can be a useful corrective tool, but it is by no means universally necessary.[42]

Wolff's defense of natural obligation as an effective basis for a program of moral education was precisely what disturbed some of his most prominent critics. According to Gottlieb Stolle (1673–1744), professor of politics at Jena and one of Wolff's contemporary supporters, those opponents of Wolff who find fault with his metaphysics "don't want to be satisfied with his moral philosophy either, because the one is based on the other." What those opponents object to, Stolle explains, are three things: (1) that human actions are good or bad in themselves, independent of God having willed them or not, (2) that human actions would remain good or bad even if there were no God, and (3) that God does not direct human beings by means of lordship (*Herrschaft*), so that the natural laws by means of which he guides them are accordingly not "laws in the strict sense of the word."[43] Stolle makes no effort to hide his partisanship for Wolff, but his description of the crucial points at issue is faithful to the critics' own words. The proof is supplied by representatives of variations on the central critique, Johann Liborius Zimmermann (1702–34) and Nicolaus Hieronymus Gundling (1671–1729), and by colleagues and teachers of theirs – Johann Franz Buddeus, Johann Georg Walch, and above all Christian Thomasius (1655–1728) – with whose ideas they were engaging and in whose shadows they stood.

Johann Liborius Zimmermann

According to his most recent biographer, writing more than a century ago, Johann Liborius Zimmermann was a gifted preacher, spiritual counselor, and theologian who deserves some credit for the Pietist "awakening" in his home town of Wernigerode in Saxony, and who commanded respect among members of the Halle Theology Faculty and their students during Alexander Baumgarten's time there.[44] Before joining that faculty as a colleague in the last years of his short life, he had not always been its most enthusiastic supporter. As an adolescent attending school in the city of Halberstadt, Zimmermann had been swayed by a friend's unrelenting hostility toward Halle Pietism, and for his university education he therefore

---

[42] Wolff, *Deutsche Ethik*, §706.

[43] G. Stolle, *Anleitung zur Historie der Gelahrheit* (Jena, 1727), III.i, §64.

[44] E. Jacobs, "Johann Liborius Zimmermann und die pietistische Bewegung in Wernigerode," *Zeitschrift des Harz-Vereins für Geschichte und Altertumskunde* 31 (1898): 121–226, here 121, 181, 188.

chose Jena over Halle. But upon beginning his studies there in 1721, at age nineteen, he fell in with a circle of professors and students sympathetic toward Halle Pietism and outspoken in their opposition to Wolff. This circle included most importantly Johann Franz Buddeus, its chief sponsor, and Johann Georg Walch.[45] Zimmermann is attested to have attended philosophical lectures by Walch and the first part of Buddeus's lectures on moral theology.[46]

On the basis of letters between Zimmermann and several friends at Jena, it seems that Zimmermann soon became much more sympathetic toward Pietism than he had been as a student in Halberstadt. Encouraged by fellow students from Wernigerode, he took part in voluntary devotional gatherings (*collegia pietatis*) organized by Buddeus. Soon he appeared to his friends to be engaged in a penitential struggle, and to be reading such standard texts of the Pietist canon as Johann Arndt's (1555–1621) *True Christianity*.[47] Zimmermann eventually moved into Buddeus's house as a boarder, and it is clear from the dedication of his first dissertation, among other sources, that Buddeus directed and encouraged his theological studies.[48] He became an instructor in philosophy at Jena in 1725, and with Buddeus's support he began delivering lectures on philosophy in conjunction with holding devotional gatherings of his own. He endorsed and adopted, in other words, what Joachim Lange alluded to in his claim that in Halle "the conversion of the audience is the chief aim": the characteristically Pietistic association of two roles, philosophical instructor and moral and spiritual guide, in the person of the professor, whose joint task was accordingly to develop the student's knowledge (*Wissenschaft*) and, at least as importantly, to help reform the student's character.[49]

What Zimmermann conceived this reform to entail becomes particularly clear in his best-known work, and the only one to reach an international audience: *The Excellency of the Knowledge of Jesus Christ*, a sermon he delivered as court preacher to Count Christian Ernst of Stolberg-Wernigerode (1691–1771), after poor health had forced him in 1728 reluctantly to abandon his teaching duties in Jena. The count's wife, Sophie Charlotte (1695–1762), had been so impressed by Zimmermann's preaching during his visit to Wernigerode the previous year that she had

[45] Jacobs, "Johann Liborius Zimmermann," 135.   [46] Jacobs, "Johann Liborius Zimmermann," 132.

[47] Jacobs, "Johann Liborius Zimmermann," 136–37; S. Lau, "Erbauungs- und Gedächtniß-Rede," in *Wernigerodisches Denckmal* (Wernigerode, 1734), 10–11.

[48] Jacobs, "Johann Liborius Zimmermann," 135–38; J. H. Zedler, *Universal-Lexicon*, s.v. "Zimmermann, Johann Liborius."

[49] Jacobs, "Johann Liborius Zimmermann," 145.

decided to enlist him as her spiritual counselor, and the sermon repeats many of the themes discernible in letters Zimmermann had already written to her in this capacity.[50] In conformity with Lutheran tradition, Zimmermann draws explicitly on Paul's Letter to the Romans to portray the reform of a person's character as having three aspects, which Zimmermann presents as chronologically sequential phases. In the first phase, the *Welt-Mensch* or "worldly man" lives under the control of his own sinful desires, with no awareness of God and no concern for the state of his soul. Becoming aware of the existence of God and of divine law, he then enters the second phase, life "according to the law" (*Gesetz*). His conscience prompts him to fear that God will punish his transgressions of divine law, and he therefore begins the penitential struggle or *Bußkampf,* attempting to reform his character and thereby become worthy of God's approval. Only after repeatedly failing in these attempts, and suffering under the torments of his conscience, can he become convinced of his own "paltriness" (*Nichtigkeit*). He accepts that his lack of faith in God's mercy is the source of the corruption of his character, and that genuine faith is not in his power.[51] This experience enables him, with God's help, to pass into the third phase, life "according to the gospel" (*Evangelium*). Now he thinks of God as a loving and forgiving parent, rather than a vengeful tyrant; his troubled conscience throws away its cares; his fear is replaced by a love of God and a desire that God direct his will; his trust in God begins to exert influence over how he lives (it develops a "living power" or *lebendige Kraft*); and his soul reaches a state of tranquillity.[52] Quoting Paul's Letter to the Philippians, Zimmermann describes this third phase as the "excellence of the knowledge of Jesus Christ" (*überschwengliche Erkenntnis Jesu Christi*), a phrase he obviously cherished.[53]

Zimmermann repeatedly emphasizes that the passage into this third phase, though ultimately the result of a miraculous act of grace by God, is facilitated by a process with pronounced sensory and experiential aspects. One the one hand, there is the experience of one's own corruption, described by Zimmermann in visual terms, and consequently a willing submission to God's justice under the law:

[50] Jacobs, "Johann Liborius Zimmermann," 146–48, 157–59.
[51] J. L. Zimmermann, *Die Überschwengliche Erkenntnis Jesu Christi* (Halle, 1731), 28–45.
[52] Zimmermann, *Überschwengliche Erkenntnis*, e.g., 45, 53, 96.
[53] Lau, "Erbauungs- und Gedächtniß-Rede," 4; Jacobs, "Johann Liborius Zimmermann," 205–6; Phil 3:8. This English translation follows the first published English translation of Zimmermann's sermon: *The Excellency of the Knowledge of Jesus Christ* (London, 1772).

A person has to *experience* the law, to the point that he *sees vividly before his eyes* his deep corruption and complete powerlessness, recognizes God's severe treatment of sin, and thereby infers the absolute necessity of the justice of Jesus Christ together with a sanctified and pure heart.[54]

The indispensibility of experience (*Erfahrung*) in the transition from law to gospel – that is, from a life under the law to a life of faith – runs throughout Zimmermann's writings and biography. In devotional gatherings he conducted in Jena, Zimmermann is reported to have focused his energies on producing in students the experience of the presence of the Holy Spirit.[55] "Penance, faith, and rebirth," he declared in one session, "must be experienced, sensed, and felt."[56] Then there is the traditional visual exercise to which Zimmermann returns again and again in his best-known sermon, which he prescribed in letters to Sophie Charlotte: contemplation of the wounds and blood of Christ, from which should follow the recognition that Christ has "obliterated" our sins, and that they will therefore be forgiven.[57] Hymn-singing was another of the exercises Zimmermann valued; a friend from Jena, Samuel Lau (1703–46), reported often hearing him singing in his own room, alone, from the *Halle Hymnal* published by August Hermann Francke and colleagues of his in Halle.[58] (In light of the emphasis he laid on these visual and musical exercises, Zimmermann's own pronounced talents as a painter and singer come as no surprise.[59]) The task of the preacher, moreover, Zimmermann described as the encouragement of all these exercises, as well as the presentation of a "blameless example" to his congregation, assisted by the Holy Spirit.[60] If his own reputation as a moving speaker is any indication, the auditory effect of a preacher's words, too, appears to have played for Zimmermann an important role in facilitating the transition from law to gospel in his audience. As in Wernigerode, where his

---

[54] Zimmermann, *Überschwengliche Erkenntnis*, 109:

> [E]in Mensch [muß] das Gesetz in so fern erfahren, daß er sein tiefes Verderben und gäntzliche Ohnmacht lebendig vor Augen sehe, GOttes Ernst über die Sünde daher erkenne, und die höchste Nothwendigkeit der Gerechtigkeit JEsu CHristi, nebst eines geheiligten und reinen Herzens daraus ersehe.
>
> Emphasis added. Cf. J. L. Zimmermann, *Das evangelische Predigt-Amt, wie es denen Menschen zur Seligkeit gereichen soll* (Wernigerode, 1728), 19, 44.

[55] Samuel Lau, qtd. in Jacobs, "Johann Liborius Zimmermann," 145.

[56] J. L. Zimmermann, *collegium* taken down by S. Lau (ULB Sachsen-Anhalt, Handschriften-Abteilung, Wernigerode Bestand, Sig. Zd 104), qtd. in Jacobs, "Johann Liborius Zimmermann," 224: "Buße, Glaube, und Wiedergeburt muß erfahren werden, empfunden und gefühlt sein."

[57] Zimmermann, *Überschwengliche Erkenntnis*, 93, 110; Jacobs, "Johann Liborius Zimmermann," 159.

[58] Lau, "Erbauungs- und Gedächtniß-Rede," 12.

[59] Jacobs, "Johann Liborius Zimmermann," 123–25.

[60] Zimmermann, *Das evangelische Predigt-Amt*, 31.

preaching had made such a strong impression on Sophie Charlotte, Zimmermann is attested to have impressed audiences in Halle, where in 1731 he was called to take up the *ordinarius* professorship of theology recently vacated by Johann Jakob Rambach (1693–1735). Zimmermann accepted the position, and upon hearing him preach, Johann Peter von Ludewig (1668–1743), professor of law, is reported to have remarked, "The boys must be asses if they didn't hear the man!"[61]

But what Zimmermann brought to Halle was not only a powerful preaching style and a conception of moral education as a three-stage process whose second major transition was facilitated by sensory experience and sensory exercises. He also brought with him a forceful critique of Wolff, which he had developed during his studies at Jena and incorporated into his philosophical teaching, and which reflected his view of the first major transition, from life as a "worldly man" to life according to the law. The substance of the critique can be found in an explicitly anti-Wolffian dissertation entitled *De actionum humanarum moralitate* (On the morality of human actions), delivered and defended by Zimmermann in Jena in 1728. The circumstances under which Zimmermann delivered the dissertation soon became widely known. According to a published report by Joachim Lange, students of Wolff's allies in Jena learned that Zimmermann was to deliver a critique of Wolff and spent the night before it in an uproar. The streets of Jena were filled with shouts of "Vivat Wolff!" and "Pereat Zimmermann!" During the defense itself, the students accompanied Zimmermann's comments with "tumultuous laughter, foot-stamping, hand-clapping, and whistling through their fists." Afterwards, the still-tumultuous students harassed Zimmermann and prevented him from returning to his lodgings at Buddeus's house. One observer, Lange claims, later passed a judgment to the effect that before witnessing the whole affair, "he had not had a good impression of the Wolffian philosophy, but now he has seen with astonishment that it makes human beings absolutely inhuman."[62] This quotation, which Lange admits is not exact,

---

[61] Qtd. in Jacobs, "Johann Liborius Zimmermann," 169.

[62] J. Lange, *Hundert und Dreyßig Fragen aus der neuen Mechanischen Philosophie* (Halle, 1734; repr., Hildesheim: Olms, 1999), 140–42:

> [D]er ältere Herr Graf Reuß, wie von Ihm damals referiret worden, . . . wo nicht gäntzlich den Worten, doch dem Sinne nach, also geurtheilet: Sie hätten zwar von der Wolfianischen Philosophie bereits vorher keine gute Idee gehabt, nunmehro hätten sie mit Erstaunen gesehen, daß sie aus Menschen rechte Unmenschen mache[.]

Lange's report appears to have served as the principal source for the many other accounts that appeared in the following decades, which include Ludovici, *Ausführlicher Entwurf*, I.§385; Zedler, *Universal-Lexicon*, s.v. "Zimmermann, Johann Liborius"; and Dreyhaupt, *Pagus neletici et nudzici*.

conveniently summarizes the lesson that Lange hoped the story of Zimmermann's dissertation would convey: Wolff's philosophy undermines the foundation of morality. In Lange's words, the story is one of many examples of "the fruits" of Wolff's philosophy, showing that it "scraps natural and revealed religion together with the entirety of moral philosophy."[63] This assessment by Lange also captures the thrust of the dissertation itself.

The fundamental problem with Wolff's moral philosophy, as Zimmermann diagnoses it, is the norm Wolff proposes for judging human actions to be morally good or bad. Instead of taking the criterion of a morally good action to be the human actor's freely chosen obedience to the will of God, a just lawgiver, Wolff takes the criterion to be the success of the action, measured by its consequences, in promoting the perfection of the actor.[64] In place of divine law, in other words, Wolff substitutes the precept, "Do what makes you and your condition more perfect."[65] Wolff does offer a defense of his precept, arguing that actions have divinely ordained, necessary consequences: they subsist in a stable nexus of cause and effect, which God created and which therefore represents the will of God, or if you like, the "law" of God that good consequences will follow some actions, and bad consequences others. All this, Zimmermann concedes.[66] But he finds Wolff's self-defense deceptive and inadequate and insists that although Wolff's precept can be accepted as a norm for judging human actions to be *naturally* good or bad,[67] by definition it is not a norm for judging human actions to be *morally* good or bad, because for various reasons it cannot be regarded as a divine law in the strict sense of that term. First: Wolff's nexus of cause and effect can be discerned without reference to God at all and would persist, according to Wolff, even in God's absence. So Wolff may call the causal nexus a divine law, but he describes this "law" as if it existed independently of God's will – that is, as if it were a law without a lawgiver, which is a manifest contradiction.[68] Wolff's own assertions that the causal nexus is nonetheless willed by God, moreover, suggest that Wolff is willing to attribute to God the evil actions performed by human beings.[69] Then there is the problem of Wolff's use of the word *law* (*lex*). On Wolff's account, Zimmermann explains, a law is simply a precept to which rewards

[63] Lange, *Hundert und Dreyßig Fragen*, 123–24.
[64] J. L. Zimmermann, *De actionum humanarum moralitate nec non de obligatione iuris, legibusque stricte dictis* (Jena, 1728), 1, 3.
[65] Zimmermann, *De actionum humanarum moralitate*, 3.
[66] Zimmermann, *De actionum humanarum moralitate*, 3, 8–9.
[67] Zimmermann, *De actionum humanarum moralitate*, 4.
[68] Zimmermann, *De actionum humanarum moralitate*, 9.
[69] Zimmermann, *De actionum humanarum moralitate*, 9.

and punishments are attached. This conception of law excludes all consideration of whether the lawgiver has any right to govern (*ius imperandi*), and for Zimmermann the lawgiver's right to govern is precisely what qualifies his decree as a law rather than a "counsel" or "recommendation" (*consilium*). Wolff calls his moral precept a law, but by Zimmermann's definition it is merely a recommendation.[70]

This difference in definitions was no inconsequential quibble over terminology. It went right to the heart of Zimmermann's conviction – apparent in his famous sermon, *The Excellency of the Knowledge of Jesus Christ* – that moral education requires, in its early stages, a penitential struggle, a period of striving to conform to God's law. For Zimmermann, genuine law could be an effective instrument of moral education in a way that a mere command or recommendation could not. Law was more than simply a norm of action. It could obligate a lawgiver's subjects to obey; it could exert a "force" (*vis*) that recommendations could not muster.[71] The reason, on Zimmermann's account, is that only law can enlist the support of the conscience:

> *Conscience* is a judgment or reasoning about whether our actions are good or bad. We feel its force when, in accordance with the various reasons for our actions, it excites various affections and sensations in us, i.e. hope or fear, mental unease or tranquillity. The greatest use of conscience is that by means of it we are called away from committing crimes and sins, and we are pushed by a strong instinct toward whatever things are eminent and prescribed by law.[72]

For Zimmermann, as for Wolff, conscience arouses sensations of desire or aversion in response to actions that it judges to be good or bad, respectively. But unlike Wolff, Zimmermann holds that conscience deliberates not about whether our actions are *naturally* good or bad (*commodum* or *incommodum*), but rather about whether they are *morally* good or bad, which is to say, whether they conform to a moral norm defined by a lawgiver with the right to command. The power of conscience to excite our affections and sensations such that we instinctively shun bad deeds and are impelled to commit good deeds therefore depends entirely on a prior

---

[70] Zimmermann, *De actionum humanarum moralitate*, 9.

[71] Zimmermann, *De actionum humanarum moralitate*, 21–22.

[72] Zimmermann, *De actionum humanarum moralitate*, 25:

> Conscientia iudicium vel ratiocinatio est de actionibus nostris, utrum bonae sint, an malae: vim autem illius sentimus, quando varios in nobis pro actionum diversa ratione adfectus sensionesque excitat, spem videlicet aut metum, inquietem animi vel tranquillitatem. Maximus conscientiae usus est, quod beneficio illius a sceleribus peccatisque committendis revocemur, ad praeclara autem quaevis legeque prae<c>epta valido instinctu permoveamur.

judgment that the lawgiver indeed has the right to command.[73] When a lawgiver is presumed either not to exist or to exist but without the right to command, then conscience withholds its endorsement of obedience. In Zimmermann's words, conscience loses all its efficacy (*efficacia*), and obligation therefore "goes up in smoke."[74]

As far as Zimmermann was concerned, this meant that Wolff's equation of moral good and evil with natural good and evil effectively robbed moral education of its most effective tool. His so-called moral precept that human beings should strive for perfection, which made no reference to God's right to command and therefore no appeal to conscience as Zimmermann understood it, did not have the necessary force to induce human beings to make fundamental changes to their own desires. Like the law laid down by a tyrant, whose rewards and punishments are essentially no different from any other natural goods and natural evils, Wolff's precept could perhaps in some cases change a person's "outer life," but power (*potentia*) alone could lead no one either to the pursuit of virtue nor "to the true emendation and cultivation of the soul," which is to say, to the cultivation of a genuine love of God.[75] On the one hand, the natural evils described by Wolff as the "punishments" of imperfection were ineffective; they hardly had the corrective power of punishments inflicted by a discernibly just ruler, presumably for the good of his subjects.[76] On the other hand, Wolff's precept seemed to make the natural goods, or "rewards," ends in themselves, with zeal for the glory of God and obedience to God's will merely instruments for promoting one's own perfection, rather than an outgrowth of love of God for his own sake. In practice, Zimmermann feared, this would have the effect of diminishing the zeal with which human beings strove for the glory of God, since such zeal would appear to be only a means to a further – private – end. Here Zimmermann saw in Wolff the specter of Pufendorf, who had derived human duties to God from the "necessity of social life" (*socialitas*) – which is to say, from the necessity of social life as a mere means to the

---

[73] Zimmermann, *De actionum humanarum moralitate*, 22.
[74] Zimmermann, *De actionum humanarum moralitate*, 25.
[75] Zimmermann, *De actionum humanarum moralitate*, 28.
[76] Zimmermann, *De actionum humanarum moralitate*, 25–27. Here, Zimmermann was articulating a view evident in August Hermann Francke's instructions to the instructors in his schools: punishment needed to be inflicted with obvious reluctance and a clear display of fatherly concern, and without any trace of anger, lest the punished child be inflamed with hatred of the instructor and the punishment therefore have the opposite of the intended, correctional effect. See A. H. Francke, *Instruction für die Praeceptores, was sie bei der Disciplin wohl zu beachten haben,* in *Pädagogische Schriften,* by A. H. Francke, ed. H. Lorenzen (Paderborn: Schöningh, 1957); P. Menck, *Die Erziehung der Jugend zur Ehre Gottes und zum Nutzen des Nächsten: Die Pädagogik August Hermann Franckes* (Tübingen: Niemeyer, 2001), 48–55. See also below, Chapter 2, pp. 78–79.

attainment of indispensable natural goods for oneself – and had therefore robbed those duties of their force.[77]

In his capacity as professor of philosophy at Jena, Zimmermann therefore proposed a course of moral education whose aim was systematically to develop what he thought Wolff's metaphysics could not provide: "living cognition of God" (*lebendige Erkenntnis Gottes*), which is to say, a perception of God that can consistently and effectively move the will to perform good actions, actions that promote the honor of God and the happiness of human beings, motivated by an "orderly" love of God. This course of moral education certainly did not involve neglecting the intellect: Zimmermann agreed with Wolff that the intellect's distinct perception of something as perfect produces an "internal motivation" to engage in an action whose aim is union with the thing in question, and that the intellect should be trained to develop concepts that are as true, as certain, as distinct, and as "living" (*wahr, gewiß, deutlich*, and *lebendig*) as possible.[78] But unlike Wolff, he identified the perfection of the human being directly and unequivocally with union with God and accordingly identified "living cognition" of good and bad with the judgment not that an action conduces or does not conduce to the perfection of the actor, but rather that it conforms or does not conform to God's will.[79] God's will, in turn, Zimmermann says must be gathered in part from God's positive law as recorded in the Bible, and in part from the "ultimate ends of things" (*Endzwecke der Dinge*), which are themselves to be deduced from the necessary, and necessarily eternal, existence of a cause of the world, namely, God, and from his relationship to the world as its creator.[80] Here, Zimmermann has recourse to the so-called *notitia Dei* or "inborn recognition of God," a proof of the existence and attributes of God characteristic of seventeenth-century Lutheran dogmatic theology: the absolute dependence of all things on God, and the status of God as therefore the supreme and ultimately sole benefactor of mankind, is the basis of God's right to command,[81] and it implies that God has made all things for the purpose of his own glorification.[82] Moral education therefore

---

77 Zimmermann, *De actionum humanarum moralitate*, 17–19.
78 J. L. Zimmermann, *Natürliche Erkenntnis Gottes, der Welt und des Menschen* (Jena, 1730), §§50, 52, 125. On the importance of training the intellect, see also §§533, 535, 617, 618, 622, 633, 635, as well as J. L. Zimmermann, *Gründliche Anweisung zum eigenen Nachsinnen*, in *Kurzer Abriß einer Vollständigen Vernunft-Lehre* (Jena, 1730), §47.
79 Zimmermann, *Natürliche Erkenntnis*, §622; Zimmermann, *Gründliche Anweisung*, §§39, 47.
80 Zimmermann, *De actionum humanarum moralitate*, §3; Zimmermann, *Natürliche Erkenntnis*, §§809, 525; Zimmermann, *Gründliche Anweisung*, §68.
81 Zimmermann, *Natürliche Erkenntnis*, §§60, 796; Zimmermann, *Gründliche Anweisung*, §§6, 11, 15.
82 Zimmermann, *Natürliche Erkenntnis*, §68; Zimmermann, *Gründliche Anweisung*, §§19, 39.

must begin, in Zimmermann's view, with a training in metaphysics whose aim is to convey to students as distinctly as possible, by the application of the rules of logic to allegedly incontestable and immediately graspable truths about the world, that there is a God who created the world for the purpose of his own glorification and the happiness of rational creatures, who therefore wills that this purpose be furthered by those creatures, and on whom human beings are absolutely dependent.[83]

But while moral education should begin with a training in metaphysics and logic, according to Zimmermann, it cannot end there. We may conclude intellectually that our own perfection comes from union with God, Zimmermann warns, but because of Adam and Eve's original sin our wills are so inescapably corrupt, so "horribly weighed-down by disorderly love," that the attainment of genuinely "living cognition" of those perfections, producing a love of God and a desire for union with him, is impossible. Zimmermann tends to account for this impossibility in two ways. On the one hand, as a result of the will's corruption, the intellect is consigned to "ignorance, error, and foolishness" and is hardly capable of attaining the degree of truth, certainty, and distinctness necessary to produce living cognition of God's perfections.[84] For, as Zimmermann repeatedly emphasizes, the will is not simply the slave of the intellect; the very act of cultivating the intellect to pass certain and distinct judgments at all, let alone about God's perfections, must itself be motivated, and a corrupt will is unlikely to supply the requisite motivation. On the other hand, even those few who have managed to achieve certain and true perception of God's perfections, presumably motivated by love of the honor, money, or other pleasures it may bring them, do not thereby develop a love of God:

> What use is knowledge, even true knowledge, ultimately, to most people, given that it remains in their intellect, completely dead and devoid of force? Some philosophers talk and prove a lot about the greatest good in its length and width, but in reality nothing is less esteemed in their eyes. The slightest honor, worldly comfort, and monetary sum is capable of inciting most people's will to undertake the most difficult task; knowledge of God, however, doesn't motivate them enough to lift a single foot from its place.[85]

---

[83] Zimmermann, *Natürliche Erkenntnis*, §§809, 811, 825.
[84] Zimmermann, *Gründliche Anweisung*, §47.
[85] Zimmermann, *Natürliche Erkenntnis*, §405:

> [W]as hilfft endlich alle, auch wohl wahre Erkenntniß den allermeisten, da sie bloß in ihrem Verstande gantz todt und unkräfftig verbleibet. Mancher Welt-Weiser redet und demonstriert viel von dem höchsten Gute in die Länge und in die Breite, nach der Wahrheit aber ist wol nichts weniger geachtet in seinen Augen. Die geringste Ehre, Comodität dieses

The will cannot be reformed, nor disorderly love eradicated, by the exercise of the intellect alone.

This is why distinct knowledge that human perfection consists of union with God and obedience to God's will must be accompanied by two other discoveries: the threat that those who do not conform to his will will be punished justly, and the reality of one's own inability to conform. The result is necessarily fear of God, the only reliable means of developing an aversion to sin and an outward obedience to God's will. Hence the necessity that God be understood not only as a merciful father but also as a lord or *Herr*, capable of anger and of punishment. In Zimmermann's words,

> If human beings in the course of their vices only kept a merciful God in mind, and had no punishments to await, they would hardly consider themselves miserable in putting their disgraceful lusts into practice; experience teaches that most people in such a condition don't even once desire union with God or a better happiness.[86]

Only by encountering the threat of just punishment at the hands of God can human beings be made to realize that the happiness they seek in vice is in fact misery, and convinced to seek a superior happiness by laying the foundation for a transition, assisted by God's grace, into "life according to the gospel": a genuine love of God, accompanied by genuine tranquillity of mind.

Zimmermann died young, at age thirty-two, and never acquired renown or exerted influence as extensive as that of his older colleagues in the Halle Theology Faculty. But he nonetheless merits attention from historians of aesthetic theory by virtue of having presented theology students in 1730s Halle, such as Alexander Baumgarten, with a lucid position in the widespread controversy about the foundation of morality, one that carried the authority and amplified the influence of Zimmermann's teachers at Jena, Johann Georg Walch and Johann Franz Buddeus. Both in his specific criticisms of Wolff and in many of the basic elements of the

---

Lebens und Geldes werth ist vermögend den Willen der mehresten zur beschwerlichsten Arbeit anzutreiben: die Erkenntnis Gottes aber vermag bey ihnen nicht so viel, daß sie einen Fuß aus der Stelle setzen solten.

[86] Zimmermann, *Natürliche Erkenntnis*, §740:

> Denn wenn nur die Menschen bey ihren Untugenden einen gnädigen GOtt behielten, und keine Straffen desfalls zu erwarten hätten, würden sie sich in Ausübung ihrer schändlichen Lüste nicht eben gar elend schätzen; wie denn die Erfahrung lehret, daß die meisten in solchem Zustande die Vereinigung mit GOtt, und eine bessere Glückseligkeit nicht einmal begehren.

> Cf. Zimmermann, *Natürliche Erkenntnis*, §§647, 741–45, 807; Zimmermann, *De actionum humanarum moralitate*, §10.

system of moral education that he proposed as an alternative, he was aligning himself with them. Each of them had attacked Wolff in print, Zimmermann quoted each of them approvingly, and each of them likely had a hand in the construction of the arguments in Zimmermann's 1728 *De actionum humanarum moralitate*, over which Buddeus himself presided.

On the level of polemic, the similarities between Zimmermann and Buddeus are clear. In his opening salvo in 1724, Buddeus had charged Wolff with, among other things, dismantling "morality and all religion" by disabling the human conscience and leaving no effective replacement. Foreshadowing Zimmermann's dissertation, Buddeus attacked Wolff for asserting that natural law could obligate atheists, since the very idea of a law, strictly speaking, required the idea of a legislator.[87] Nor was Wolff's proof of the existence of God adequate to give natural law obligatory force. Wolff had cast doubt on "the usual and most solid proofs of the existence of God," including above all the *notitia Dei*, and had replaced them with the idea of a "substance that represents the entire universe distinctly to itself," which is to say, a God who is essentially passive.[88] Wolff had explained God's governance of the world by recourse to Leibniz's theory of preestablished harmony, thereby accepting an idea that he himself admitted had been the foundation of denials of divine providence by Aristotle and by the Epicureans, and making it into the foundation – and therefore the fundamental weakness – of his own philosophical system.[89] As in Zimmermann's dissertation, the problem for Buddeus was that Wolff had proposed a conception of God, and by extension a conception of God's relationship to the universe, that was powerless to effect moral change in the person contemplating it, while at the same time he had appealed to the stringent requirements of mathematical demonstrations as a reason to reject conceptions of God with far more moral-educational force. Atheists, those who had not even taken the first step away from the self-oriented desires that dominated them, could not be moved by Wolff, and in fact their numbers were likely to grow: "If people are brought to the point of considering the most powerful convictions of the conscience to be groundless opinion, isn't it certain that ultimately atheism will be the result?"[90] The essentially passive

---

[87] J. F. Buddeus, *Bedencken über die Wolffianische Philosophie mit Anmerckungen erläutert von Christian Wolffen* (Frankfurt (Main), 1724; repr., Hildesheim: Olms, 1980), 33–34, 37.
[88] Buddeus, *Bedencken*, 8–15, 38–39, 84–85.   [89] Buddeus, *Bedencken*, 42–43, 96.
[90] Buddeus, *Bedencken*, 30: "Wenn nun die Menschen dahin gebracht werden, daß sie die kräfftigsten Überzeugungen des Gewissens *pro vana persuasione* halten, muß denn nicht endlich der Atheismus daraus entstehen?"

God that Wolff proposed as a replacement for the just, lawgiving, prov-
idential God whose decrees engage the conscience could not have the
same effect: "Why should I pray to and serve a God who knows nothing of me, and who neither punishes evil nor rewards good?"[91] Loosely
speaking, this was the position that Zimmermann would defend and
expand in 1728.

Zimmermann's position bears more precise resemblance to that of
Walch, who, more clearly and elaborately than Buddeus, portrayed the
critical weakness in Wolff's philosophical system as the inadequacy of
"natural obligation" as a foundation of morality. The clearest and most
concise of Walch's various such portrayals appears in the entry "Morality"
(*Moralität*) in the 1726 edition of his famous *Philosophical Lexicon*.[92] With
the initial exchanges in 1724 between Buddeus, Wolff, and himself in the
background, Walch summarizes their discussion of moral obligation so
as to defend Buddeus's critique of Wolff and refute Wolff's rebuttals. In
his response to Buddeus's initial objections, Wolff had denied that the
disagreement between them pertained to the question of whether there
can be moral obligation independent of divine law. Although Wolff agreed
that in his *German Ethics* he had claimed that what binds human beings to
the natural law is "nature" and "reason," he had also asserted that natural
law was legislated by God, and that God in fact obliges human beings to
obey it.[93] On the question of the origin of moral obligation, therefore, and
whether natural law is strictly speaking a law, Wolff claimed that Buddeus
was wrong to assert any disagreement. Rather, the question at issue was
whether God has reasons for what he wills. By denying Wolff's assertion
that actions are *per se* morally good or bad, antecedent to God's commanding them or prohibiting them, Buddeus had – so Wolff claimed – effectively
denied that God had reasons for commanding some things and prohibiting
others. Buddeus was thereby defending the view that divine justice is arbitrary: the principle of *justitia arbitraria* asserted by Pufendorf in the late
seventeenth century to the consternation of many Lutheran theologians,
and defended by Christian Thomasius while Buddeus himself was studying
in Halle.[94]

In his article on morality, Walch takes issue with this portrayal of the
substance of the dispute. On Walch's account, the question is not whether

[91] Buddeus, *Bedencken*, 39–44, 45: "[W]arum solte [*sic*] ich einen solchen Gott anbeten, und ihm
dienen, der nichts von mir weiß, der auch weder das Böse bestrafft, noch das Gute belohnet?"
[92] J. G. Walch, *Philosophisches Lexikon* (Leipzig, 1726), s.v. "Moralität."
[93] Buddeus, *Bedencken*, 31(t).
[94] Buddeus, *Bedencken*, 32(u), 33–34(x). On Thomasius and Buddeus, see below.

God has reasons for what he wills. Walch readily grants that God does have reasons: "the quality of the thing is the reason why he has commanded one thing and forbidden another," since God only wills what conforms to his own sanctity (*Heiligkeit*), and God therefore could not have enacted any natural law other than the one he in fact enacted.[95] Rather, the question is whether moral obligation only arises from an act of legislation by God – whose actual result is divine law, as revealed in the form of natural law – or whether humans would be obliged even if God had not acted.[96] According to Walch, Buddeus can hold the first of these positions (and in fact does hold it), while at the same time holding, like Wolff, that there are discernible reasons for the divine law that God in fact issued. These reasons, Walch explains, can be discerned in the world that God created – as Wolff would agree. In issuing divine law, God's will should therefore be understood to have been informed by his intellect, examining that created world, even if creation itself must be understood as an act of divine will whose reasons are inscrutable to the human intellect.[97] This answer to Wolff may of course seem to be a mere quibble over how to define the term *moral obligation*, as Wolff claimed it was, but Walch's citation of Paul's Letter to the Romans in support of his own position tells a different story. According to Walch, Paul correctly understood that the recognition of one's sins can only come from recognition of divine law, and the very ideas of good and bad must therefore derive from the law.[98] For Walch, just as for Zimmermann two years later, the dispute over the origin of moral obligation amounted to a dispute over whether moral reform required knowledge of God's law as such.

Naturally, Zimmermann's debt to his teachers extended beyond the repetition and expansion of the arguments they had used in their engagement with Wolff. Zimmermann had clearly absorbed the underlying moral-educational system on which those arguments were based. It was a system that Buddeus had been developing for decades and had expounded in a series of textbooks that by 1728 had found widespread use in universities throughout the German-speaking world.[99] Though Buddeus's

---

95 Walch, "Moralität," 1829, 1830.   96 Walch, "Moralität," 1828–29.
97 Walch, *Bescheidene Antwort*, 30–35; Walch, "Moralität."   98 Walch, "Moralität."
99 These included primarily Buddeus' textbooks on moral philosophy and moral theology, the *Elementa philosophiae practicae* (1697) and the *Institutiones theologiae moralis* (1711). *Geschichte der Universität Jena*, I.199. The sometimes-overlooked fact that Buddeus had developed his philosophical system before his public engagement with Wolff's is pointed out by Wundt, *Die deutsche Schulphilosophie*, 63. On the propagation of Buddeus' textbooks: A. F. Stolzenburg, *Die Theologie des Jo. Franc. Buddeus und des Chr. Matth. Pfaff* (Berlin: Trowitzsch, 1927; repr., Aalen: Scientia, 1979), 396–97; Zedler, *Universal-Lexicon*, s.v. "Buddaeus, Joann Francisc."

psychological vocabulary in those books bears less resemblance to Wolff's than Zimmermann's does, substantial continuities with Zimmermann's ideas are clear. Buddeus repeatedly emphasizes that the intellect and the will are distinct faculties of the soul, that the cultivation of the intellect alone is incapable of effecting moral improvement in its possessor, and that moral education must therefore aim primarily to improve the will, by techniques that Buddeus purports to adopt from the practice of medicine. The attraction of the unregenerated soul to pleasure, honor, and wealth is to be treated as a sickness, and the model of health at which the cure aims, the *sanitas mentis*, is the overriding love of God characteristic of the regenerated soul.[100] The cure is ultimately the result of divine grace,[101] but it is necessarily preceded by a process whose three phases are familiar from Zimmermann's sermon, *The Excellency of the Knowledge of Jesus Christ*: a false sense of tranquillity is followed by the discovery of divine law and a period of fearful servitude to God, followed ideally, with the help of God's grace, by faith in God, genuine tranquillity, and obedience to God's law, motivated only by love and gratitude.[102] In Buddeus's account, therefore, as in Zimmermann's, the improvement of the will requires attaining knowledge of God's law, a knowledge which is revealed in the text of the Bible but which is also available in a less complete but more universally accessible form through the exercise of the human intellect, scrutinizing itself and the world.

Like Zimmermann, Buddeus refers to this universal means of acquiring knowledge of God as the *notitia Dei* or "inborn recognition of God," accepting the conventional classification of this *notitia* as *insita* (that is, acquired by reflection on one's own intellect) or *acquisita* (acquired by reflection on the wider world) and explicitly including the former among the "usual and most solid proofs of the existence of God" whose denial by Wolff he identified as dangerous to the foundation of morality.[103] It is through the *notitia Dei* that every human being, by exercise of his intellect, can discover that God is his creator and preserver, as well as the creator and preserver of everything in the universe, and that as a mere creature, he absolutely depends on God for everything that he is. From here it is for Buddeus a very small step to the firm belief that one "has not been

---

[100] J. F. Buddeus, *Einleitung in die Moral-Theologie* (Leipzig, 1719), Vorrede [v–vi]; J. F. Buddeus, *Elementa philosophiae practicae*, 3rd ed. (Halle, 1707; repr., Hildesheim: Olms, 2004), I.vi. §§1–3.

[101] E.g. J. F. Buddeus, *Institutiones theologiae moralis* (Leipzig, 1727; repr., Hildesheim: Olms, 2007), I.1. §36.

[102] Buddeus, Einleitung in die Moral-Theologie, II.Vorbericht. §8.

[103] C. Ratschow, *Lutherische Dogmatik zwischen Reformation und Aufklärung*, v. 2 of 2 (Gütersloh: Mohn, 1966), 29–32; Buddeus, *Institutiones theologiae dogmaticae*, e.g., III.ii.§4; and on Wolff's denial of the *notitia Dei insita*, see above.

created and furnished with such immense favors by [God] so that he may present God with hatred, but rather so that he may love him,"[104] and to the conviction that God has both the power and the just cause to oblige human beings to obey his law, which is revealed both to those who examine human nature with a healthy intellect and, more clearly, to those who read the Bible.[105] The result of this conviction is fear of God. It arises from the discovery by the conscience that the powers of one's soul, corrupted by original sin, are unable to obey divine law, and from an awareness that God is supremely just and will condemn the disobedient to eternal punishment after death. Revealing human sin and producing fear, for Buddeus as for Luther, is in fact the very purpose of divine law.[106]

The fear it produces is moreover an indispensable stimulus to the attempt to reform one's corrupted will by a means that Buddeus calls "philosophical" and describes as a regimen of sensory exercises in affection-control. The God-fearing person subjects his will to intense scrutiny; deliberately refrains from activities that he knows excite his base desires; tries to observe and imitate examples of genuine virtue, including in books; disciplines his imagination by contemplating exclusively "serious, pious, and upright things"; and tries above all to cultivate the two virtues most important for the suppression of vices, namely, constancy (*constantia*) and patience (*patientia*).[107] Buddeus describes these exercises as having a twofold result. On the one hand, little by little they reform the will, like a medicine whose effectiveness depends on repeated doses: as the base affections slowly wane, love of God slowly waxes.[108] On the other hand, their effect on the will is ultimately minimal. This ineffectiveness – and therefore the depth of one's own depravity – becomes increasingly clear, and the result is desperation.[109]

The awareness of God's goodness, however, prompts one to believe that there must be another means of satisfying him, and if it cannot be discovered by reason alone, then it must have been revealed by God himself, and moreover in the text of the Bible.[110] At this point a new regimen of

---

[104] Buddeus, *Elementa philosophiae practicae*, I.vi.§29.
[105] Buddeus, *Einleitung in die Moral-Theologie*, II.ii.§§8, 6.
[106] Buddeus, *Einleitung in die Moral-Theologie*, I.i.§§7, 11, II.Vorbericht.§8; cf. also the summary of Buddeus's teachings, allegedly drawn from his textbooks and lectures, by J. D. König: *Kürzester und leichtester Weg, die Grundsätze und Beschaffenheit einer grundlichen Moral und Politic zu erlernen* (Leipzig, 1723), 71, 78, 101.
[107] Buddeus, *Elementa philosophiae practicae*, I.vi.§§30–46.
[108] Buddeus, *Elementa philosophiae practicae*, I.vi.§§32, 34.
[109] Buddeus, *Elementa philosophiae practicae*, I.vi.§§48–58.
[110] Buddeus, *Elementa philosophiae practicae*, I.vi.§§58–64.

spiritual exercises is added to the old regimen. These new exercises, which recall those advocated by Zimmermann, include meditation on scripture and tireless prayer, all in the hope that by the grace of God one's will can be healed.[111] Like Zimmermann, Buddeus describes the ideal result as a new perception of God, one that incites love rather than fear: it is "living cognition" (*lebendige Erkenntnis*), cognition that is not only true (*vera*) and certain (*certa*) but also, most importantly, living (*viva*) and effective (*efficax*), and it necessarily involves a sense (*sensum*) and experience (*experientia*) of divine things.[112] What necessarily flows from this living cognition is what the medical treatment of the will aims at: an overriding love of God.

Buddeus lacked confidence that Wolff's program of moral education could have the same result. This lack of confidence becomes abundantly clear, more clear in many respects even than in his relatively brief published criticism of Wolff, in his conceptual outline of the history of philosophy, continual references to which are one of the most obvious hallmarks of Buddeus's writings. In proposing a system of theology whose ultimate aim was to reform the human will, Buddeus consistently represented himself as engaged in a struggle against the "Scholastics" and their far less edifying theological systems. As for the actual errors encompassed by this historical label, Buddeus of course presented their intellectual origins as distant, primarily in the philosophy of Aristotle and his medieval admirers, but his primary concern was with his contemporaries. Buddeus admired the early Protestant reformers, above all Luther and Philipp Melanchthon (1497–1560), and found much to admire even in some Lutheran theologians of the seventeenth century, including Johann Wilhelm Baier (1647–95). The influence of the Wittenberg theologians who effectively founded and dominated Lutheran dogmatic theology in the seventeenth century, however, above all Johann Friedrich König (1619–64) and Johann Andreas Quenstedt (1617–88), Buddeus associated with a "Scholastic" period, in which the influence of Catholic theology, he thought, had become excessive.[113]

---

[111] Buddeus, *Elementa philosophiae practicae*, I.vi.§65; Buddeus, *Einleitung in die Moral-Theologie*, I.i.§§13, 15; c.f. König, *Kürzester und leichtester Weg*, 20–21, 106.

[112] Buddeus, *Institutiones theologiae moralis*, I.prolegomena.§§8–9. Note that according to J. D. König, Buddeus considered *Gewissheit* to be a consequence of "historical" *Erkenntnis* of a thing, engendered by meditation. König, *Kürzester und leichtester Weg*, 47. On historical cognition, cf. below, Chapter 2, p. 97, n. 131.

[113] F. Nüssel, introduction to *Institutiones theologiae dogmaticae*, by Buddeus (Hildesheim: Olms, 1999), vi; K. Heussi, *Geschichte der theologischen Fakultät zu Jena* (Weimar: Böhlau, 1954), 155–56; A. F. Stolzenburg, *Die Theologie des Jo. Franc. Buddeus*, 240–42; M. Wundt, *Die Philosophie an der Universität Jena* (Jena: Fischer, 1932), 66.

The problems with these new "Scholastics" were allegedly manifold. They lay too much emphasis on Aristotle's distinction among the four causes and produced theological systems full of "vain, otiose, and inept" principles rather than trying to draw attention to the beauty of God and of theology; they followed the lead of their own curiosity without paying attention to the utility of their investigations; they assumed that perception by the intellect alone, which they considered the source of the highest perfection for man as well as for God, was an adequate means to virtue, and that virtue itself was a means to genuine happiness rather than a consequence of love of God; they falsely denied that God's will could be understood with the same exactness as his being; and they falsely asserted that God's commands were in fact commands of reason (*recta ratio*), and that there could be a divine law in the absence of a divine lawgiver.[114] These and Buddeus's other specific criticisms are of course not all identical to one another, but at least one common thread is obvious: the so-called Scholastics' theological systems engaged the intellect but for various reasons did not have the requisite medicinal effect on the will. Buddeus saw himself as part of a modern response to this Scholastic error, led by Descartes, Pufendorf, and, by virtue of their attention to the improvement of character, Philipp Jakob Spener (1635–1705) and Johann Arndt.[115] Wolff, on the other hand, who had erred in insisting that human actions could be recognized as morally good or bad without reference to divine law, Buddeus readily classified among the Scholastics. The Scholastics' error, he explained, had been defended unconvincingly by Grotius and then revived by Leibniz, Wolff, and their adherents. Unsurprisingly, Walch and Zimmermann repeated Buddeus's genealogy.[116]

The critical posture toward Wolff adopted by Buddeus, Walch, and most pointedly by Zimmermann could not have escaped Alexander Baumgarten during his theological and philosophical studies in Halle in the early 1730s. The works of Buddeus and Walch had already been well known in Halle for years, and they found frequent use in theological and philosophical lectures.[117] Buddeus himself was obviously well liked by several

---

[114] Nüssel, introduction to *Institutiones theologiae dogmaticae*, vii–ix; J. F. Buddeus, *De eo, quod in theologia pulchrum est* (Jena, 1715), 18–19, 23; J. D. König, *Kürzester und leichtester Weg*, 85–87, 97–98; Buddeus, *Einleitung in die Moral-Theologie*, II.Vorbericht.§§3–4.

[115] Heussi, *Geschichte der theologischen Fakultät zu Jena*, 155–56; Stolzenburg, *Die Theologie des Jo. Franc. Buddeus*, 242–43; Buddeus, *Institutiones theologiae moralis*, I.i.§§21, 26.

[116] Buddeus, *Bedencken*, 36–37; Zimmermann, *De actionum humanarum moralitate*, §1; Walch, "Moralität," 1829–30.

[117] Examples can be found in virtually every semester between 1730 and 1735: *Catalogi lectionum . . . publicati in Academia Fridericiana* (Halle, 1730–35).

members of the theology and philosophy faculties. His friendships with Joachim Lange and August Hermann Francke were demonstrably close, and he had at various points taken in their student and later colleague, Zimmermann's predecessor at Halle, Johann Jakob Rambach,[118] as well as Francke's son, Gotthilf August (1696–1769), as boarders in Jena while they were still students.[119] Upon joining the Halle Theology Faculty in 1731, invited principally by Gotthilf August Francke to help replenish the faculty's ranks after the departure of Rambach and the death of Francke's father, Zimmermann began to represent Buddeus's views in person. In his lectures, which Alexander Baumgarten attended, Zimmermann read from Buddeus's textbooks on dogmatic and moral theology.[120] Upon Zimmermann's death after a mere four semesters, Baumgarten's brother Siegmund Jacob (1706–57) – who succeeded Zimmermann as *ordinarius* professor of theology – observed in his memorial sermon that Zimmermann had "venerated" Buddeus and had adopted substantial elements of Buddeus's theological teachings and arguments.[121]

As for Alexander Baumgarten's attitude toward Zimmermann, the evidence is regrettably thin. Even the best evidence that can be mustered from his brother's memorial sermon, itself at best an indirect source of Alexander's views, is difficult to evaluate. On the one hand, his praise is effusive. "In writing and arguing," Siegmund Jacob comments, Zimmermann "had few equals and no superiors,"[122] and he "produced more men schooled in solid erudition, integrity of religion, and zeal for promoting virtue and knowledge of Christ than many other learned men have listeners over the course of their entire lives."[123] Zimmermann's life, though not long, was "extremely fruitful" (*fructuosissima*), and he could not have spent his final years more gloriously or more usefully.[124] And yet it is difficult not to imagine that in his evaluation of Zimmermann's "extremely worthy" (*dignissima*) textbook on metaphysics, Siegmund Jacob Baumgarten meant to convey some disaffection behind the veneer of praise demanded by the occasion. That Zimmermann "could have become one of the best in this discipline," as Baumgarten puts it, "if he hadn't devoted himself fully

[118] On whom, see below, Chapter 2.
[119] Stolzenburg, *Die Theologie des Jo. Franc. Buddeus*, 249–52.
[120] G. F. Meier, *Alexander Gottlieb Baumgartens Leben* (Halle, 1763), 10; *Catalogi lectionum . . . publicati in Academia Fridericiana* (Halle, Winter 1731–Spring 1733).
[121] S. J. Baumgarten, *In funus summe rever. Jo. Liborii Zimmermanni,* in *Opuscula,* by S. J. Baumgarten, ed. G. C. Bake (Halle, 1746), 60–63, 73.
[122] S. J. Baumgarten, *In funus summe rever. Jo. Liborii Zimmermanni,* 58.
[123] S. J. Baumgarten, *In funus summe rever. Jo. Liborii Zimmermanni,* 63.
[124] S. J. Baumgarten, *In funus summe rever. Jo. Liborii Zimmermanni,* 64, 67.

to theology," has the ambiguity of a back-handed compliment.[125] It is perhaps telling, that whereas Siegmund Jacob Baumgarten, as Zimmermann's successor, was obliged to deliver a memorial sermon, the task of delivering the oration at Zimmermann's funeral fell to Zimmermann's friend, Gotthilf August Francke.[126] Whatever the case may be, it is at least clear that what Zimmermann had taught, including his publicly critical attitude toward Wolff, was well known both to Siegmund Jacob Baumgarten and to his brother Alexander.

Nicolaus Hieronymus Gundling

The same can be said, if perhaps less conclusively, about another of Wolff's public critics among the Halle professoriate, Nicolaus Hieronymus Gundling. By 1727, the year Alexander Baumgarten arrived in Halle and enrolled in Francke's Latin School, Gundling's life was nearly over. As he took up the pro-rectorship of the university for the last time in 1729, his doctor and predecessor as pro-rector, Friedrich Hoffmann, doubted that he would live to pass the academic scepter to a successor.[127] Gundling's death the same year, the first time a pro-rector of the university had died in office, proved Hoffmann right. But when Baumgarten entered the university one year later, in 1730, Gundling's legacy was still potent. Even if we assume that Baumgarten never heard him speak, it is difficult to imagine how he could have escaped an encounter with the memory of Gundling and the ideas Gundling had recorded in his voluminous writings.[128] Gundling had arrived in Halle thirty years earlier, in 1698. He had already studied theology for several years at the universities of Altdorf and Jena, gathered a year of preaching experience in Nürnberg, near his home town, and seemed to be headed toward a pastoral and theological career like his father's. But in Halle he fell under the spell of Christian Thomasius, who inspired

---

[125] S. J. Baumgarten, *In funus summe rever. Jo. Liborii Zimmermanni*, 73.

[126] Jacobs, "Johann Liborius Zimmermann," 181.

[127] C. F. Hempel, *Nicolai Hieronymi Gundlings Umständliches Leben und Schriften* (Leipzig, 1736), 7054.

[128] Although the presence of a book in the auction catalog of Alexander Baumgarten's library, published shortly after his death in 1762, by no means proves conclusively that Baumgarten read or even knew of the book, it does make Baumgarten's acquaintance with the book seem more likely. It is therefore worth mentioning that a significant number of Gundling's works were sold as a part of Baumgarten's library after his death. These included Gundling's *Otia* (Frankfurt (Main), 1706), volumes from *Gundlingiana* (Halle, 1715–32), *Via ad veritatem* (1713), *Historia philosophiae moralis* (Halle, 1706), and *Ius naturae* (1728). *Catalogus librorum a viro excellentissimo amplissimo Alexandro Gottlieb Baumgarten* (Frankfurt (Oder), 1762).

him to redirect his professional ambitions and devote himself to the academic study of law. After receiving his doctoral title in 1703, Gundling soon acquired a long string of professorships in unusually quick succession: he became *extraordinarius* professor of philosophy (*professor philosophiae universae*) in 1705 and *ordinarius* professor of philosophy in 1707, succeeded the late renowned Christoph Cellarius (1638–1707) as professor of antiquities and rhetoric (*antiquitatum et eloquentiae*) in 1707, and took up the professorship of the law of nature and of nations (*iuris naturae et gentium*) in the Law Faculty in 1712.[129] The variety of the subjects on which Gundling lectured, and the volume of writing he produced, were enormous, and one hardly needs to accept uncritically the high praise of his most thorough biographer, Christian Friedrich Hempel, to appreciate the breadth of his learning. He published dozens of volumes of essays and book reviews, as well as numerous textbooks, and more than ten thousand pages of his lectures were published in the decade after his death.[130] Beginning in 1731, Gundling's admiring student and first biographer, Professor Friedrich Wideburg (1708–58), used textbooks by Gundling as the basis for several of his own lectures, and, like Gundling before him, he based his seminar on politics on the third part of Buddeus's *Institutiones theologiae moralis* (Institutes of moral theology).[131] As for Gundling's friends among the professors who survived him, they included not only Wideburg but also the supervisor of Alexander Baumgarten's first dissertation,[132] Christian Benedict Michaelis (1680–1764), whom Gundling had asked to share the task of looking after his children's education after his death, and who supervised the auction of Gundling's vast library.[133] Johann Jakob Rambach delivered the memorial sermon at Gundling's funeral.[134]

That Gundling's legacy in the controversy over Christian Wolff and the foundation of morality was his outspoken and unrelenting defense of a position very much like Zimmermann's and Buddeus's should come as a surprise, given what is currently known about the relationship between

[129] Zedler, *Universal-Lexicon*, s.v. "Gundling, Nicolaus Hieronymus"; *DBA*, s.v. "Gundling, Nicolaus Hieronymus"; Hempel, *Nicolai Hieronymi Gundlings Umständliches Leben und Schriften*, 7018–48.

[130] Hempel's catalog of Gundling's writings takes up more than four hundred pages: Hempel, *Nicolai Hieronymi Gundlings Umständliches Leben und Schriften*, 7084–536 (Chapter 7).

[131] H. Schröder, *Lexikon der hamburgischen Schriftsteller*, v. 8 (Hamburg, 1883; repr., *DBA*), s.v. "Wiedeburg, Friedrich"; Hempel, *Nicolai Hieronymi Gundlings Umständliches Leben und Schriften*, 7544, 7548; *Catalogi lectionum . . . publicati in Academia Fridericiana* (Halle, 1732–35).

[132] On which, see below, Chapter 2, pp. 90–91.

[133] Hempel, *Nicolai Hieronymi Gundlings Umständliches Leben und Schriften*, 7082; C. B. Michaelis, ed., *Catologus bibliothecae Gundlingianae* (Halle, 1731).

[134] J. J. Rambach, *Gedächtniß-Rede von dem Geheimniß der Evangelischen Weisheit*, 1st ed. (Halle, 1730), 2nd ed. (Halle, 1732).

Gundling and Buddeus. The trend of the last fifty years of research on early-eighteenth-century German natural law theory has been to place them on opposite sides of a controversy over the legacy of the teacher and colleague they had in common during their years in Halle: Christian Thomasius. In 1688, as lecturer at the University of Leipzig, two years before he arrived in Halle as a teacher of philosophy and jurisprudence at the city's *Ritterakademie* and six years before the *Ritterakademie* was granted the privileges that transformed it into a university, Thomasius had produced his *magnum opus*, the *Institutes of Divine Jurisprudence*. It was a textbook on natural and divine law in which he purported to prove and strengthen the principles laid out in Samuel Pufendorf's 1673 *On the Duty of Man and Citizen according to Natural Law*, which he quoted at great length.[135] But in the late 1690s and early 1700s, as his contemporaries soon perceived, Thomasius changed his mind about several substantial elements in the natural law theory he had articulated in his *Institutes*. This change of mind, which has been described repeatedly as an intellectual "crisis," appears to have followed from changes in Thomasius's fundamental conception of the human will and how it can be regenerated.[136] The consequences of these changes for Thomasius's natural law theory became evident in a set of "improvements" to his *Institutes*, published in 1705 under the title *Foundations of the Law of Nature and of Nations*.[137] In his preface to the *Foundations*, while claiming that he neither regrets having defended Pufendorf in the *Institutes* nor wants to weaken or overturn anything he argued there, Thomasius nonetheless expressly purports to set his natural law theory on a new foundation and to present the entire "edifice of morality" (*Gebäude der Moral*) in a new way.

The principal error of Pufendorf, and by extension the 1688 *Institutes*, according to Thomasius, was the presumption that "universal divine positive law," the law issued expressly by God to all human beings, has the same obligatory force as human law, and that like human law, it

---

[135] On Thomasius's arrival in Halle: Schrader, *Geschichte der Friedrichs-Universität zu Halle*, 15–16; Holloran, *Professors of Enlightenment*, 93–121. On Thomasius's *Institutes*: F. Grunert, introduction to *Grundlehren des Natur- und Völkerrechts*, by C. Thomasius (Hildesheim: Olms, 2003), v.

[136] E.g., W. Schneiders, *Naturrecht und Liebesethik* (Hildesheim: Olms, 1971), 241, 246–47; H. D. Kittsteiner, *Die Entstehung des modernen Gewissens* (Frankfurt (Main): Suhrkamp, 1995), 254; Hochstrasser, *Natural Law Theories in the Early Enlightenment*, 129; and the most differentiated account of the changes in Thomasius's thinking, Thomas Ahnert's *Religion and the Origins of the German Enlightenment* (Rochester, NY: University of Rochester Press, 2006), 27–42.

[137] C. Thomasius, *Fundamenta iuris naturae et gentium* (Halle, 1705). I have drawn primarily on the German translation, *Grundlehren des Natur- und Völkerrechts*, translated Johann Gottfried Zeidler (1655–1711) in cooperation with Thomasius, which appeared in Halle in 1709. On the circumstances of the translation: Grunert, introduction to *Grundlehren*, xv–xvi.

obliges human beings by means of the threat of punishment attached to it by a lawgiver.[138] What Pufendorf overlooked was that divine punishment, unlike human punishment, has a "natural connection" with human transgressions of divine law.[139] From Thomasius's point of view, the consequences of this overlooked fact are enormous. Briefly put, it means that knowledge of God's will, which Pufendorf proposed as the source of moral obligation, is not in fact a reliable inducement to virtue. The reason for this, Thomasius explains with reference to a conceptual structure that he elaborated repeatedly and at great length in his *Foundations*. At its center is the distinction Thomasius draws between internal and external obligation. Both types of obligation induce action by arousing hope and fear in the obligated person, but their sources differ: whereas *internal* obligation (*innerliche Verpflichtung*) arises when the conscience perceives an unavoidable natural connection between an action and its good or bad consequences for the actor, *external* obligation (*äusserliche Verpflichtung*) arises when the conscience perceives a potentially avoidable connection, established by an arbitrary decision on the part of a human being. Thomasius further defines the source of internal obligation as a "recommendation" (*Rath* or *consilium*), and the source of external obligation as "lordship" (*Herrschaft* or *imperium*).[140] The former, he adds, makes use primarily of logical deductions (*Vernunft-Schlüsse*), while the latter makes more use of force (*Gewalt*).[141] Thomasius diverges from Pufendorf in categorizing divine law as a recommendation (*Rathschlag*), and therefore a source of internal, not external, obligation:

> [G]uard yourself . . . against the thought that the natural and positive, divine and human types of law have the same nature. Natural and divine law belong more to recommendations than to lordship; human law in the genuine sense indicates only the rule of lordship.[142]

As a result, a large category of human beings, namely, those who cannot be induced to action by internal obligation as easily as by external obligation, cannot be made more virtuous by any consciousness of divine law – which

---

[138] Thomasius, *Grundlehren*, Vorrede.§§8–10.   [139] Thomasius, *Grundlehren*, Vorrede.§10.
[140] Thomasius, *Grundlehren*, I.iv.§§61–2.   [141] Thomasius, *Grundlehren*, I.iv.§§55–56.
[142] Thomasius, *Grundlehren*, I.v.§34:

> Hüte dich demnach, daß du nicht meinest, als wenn das natürliche und gegebene, das göttliche und menschliche Gesetze Arten von einerley Natur wären: Das natürliche und göttliche Gesetze gehöret mehr zu den Rathschlägen, als zu denen Herrschafften; das menschliche Gesetze in dem eigentlichen Verstande genommen wird nur von der Norm der Herrschaft gesaget.

Thomasius denies is a law in the strict sense.[143] These are the so-called fools (*Narren*). By contrast with the "wise," whom Thomasius describes as being primarily internally obligated to virtue by their consciousness of its natural advantages and by their perception of the will of God, whom they fear in a childlike (*kindlich*) rather than a servile (*knechtisch*) way,[144] fools do not perceive virtue's natural advantages and can only be induced to become wise by means of external obligation – more precisely, by the application of force on the part of the wise, in the form of the threat of punishment attached to human law. In contrast to divine punishments and rewards, Thomasius explains,

> the punishments of promulgated law are more graspable and visible, and are therefore also more suitable for instilling fear in fools, just as the rewards of promulgated law, too, are more apparent.[145]

Of course this is not to say that the moral education of fools by the wise is a matter simply of coercion by means of the brute force of the law.[146] Thomasius emphasized the necessity that the teacher exert force in a "friendly" way and present himself as an example of the virtues he is trying to inculcate, so as not to disturb the student's trust and contented obedience to the teacher's will. There is nonetheless no mistaking Thomasius's abandonment of the perception of God's will as a sufficiently forceful impetus to the reform of the human will in the earliest stages of moral education.

This change in Thomasius's thinking had significant consequences for his intellectual legacy, and it has become standard to describe those consequences in terms of the formation of two "schools," defined by their members' attitudes toward Thomasius's *Foundations*. Those admirers of Thomasius's *Institutes* who continued to voice approval of Pufendorf's natural law theory after 1705 and did not agree with the innovations of the *Foundations*

---

[143] Thomasius, *Grundlehren*, I.vi.§6.   [144] Thomasius, *Grundlehren*, I.iv.§64, I.v.§§41–42.

[145] Thomasius, *Grundlehren*, I.v.§57:

> Aber die Straffen des publicirten Rechts sind handgreiflicher und sichtbarer, daher sind sie auch geschickter denen Narren eine Furcht einzujagen. Wie denn auch die Belohnungen des publicirten rechts gleichfals mehr in die Augen fallen.

[146] Contra Werner Schneiders, who presents Thomasius's description of obligation in the *Foundations* similarly to the discussion above, but lays unmitigated emphasis on the role of force in Thomasius' conception of the moral education of fools, in *Naturrecht und Liebesethik*, 259–60. Cf. H. Holzhey, "Christian Thomasius und der Beginn der deutschen Aufklärung," in *Grundriß der Geschichte der Philosophie: die Philosophie des 17. Jahrhunderts*, v. 4, Das heilige Römische Reich, ed. H. Holzhey and W. Schmidt-Biggemann (Basel: Schwabe, 2001), 1195–97.

constitute the "first" school, whereas those who found the *Foundations* convincing constitute the "second" school.[147] Nor was this short-hand classification unknown in the eighteenth century. As Hinrich Rüping, its most visible recent exponent, has pointed out, description of the controversy over Thomasius's *Foundations* can be found in the 1729 edition of Gottlieb Stolle's *Anleitung zur Historie der Gelahrheit* (Introduction to the history of learning), and a list of the two schools' members appears in Christian Friedrich Georg Meister's *Biblioteca iuris naturae et gentium* (Library of the law of nature and of nations) (1749–57).[148] Rüping, like Meister, numbers Buddeus among the members of the first school and Gundling among the members of the second school.[149]

In light of the lack of extensive and detailed research on the vast bodies of work produced by the members of these schools, the accuracy of the "two-school" classification is difficult to judge, but in the case of Buddeus, it certainly contains some truth. Buddeus was called to Halle in 1693, three years after Thomasius, to take up a professorship of moral philosophy. Over the next twelve years he produced his own first major works – several textbooks that quickly became standard reading in many universities outside Halle[150] – in the shadow of Thomasius's 1688 *Institutes*. His relationship with Thomasius was in many respects close during this period. Buddeus's documented contributions to the learned journal founded by Thomasius illustrate their intellectual cooperation,[151] and this cooperation was clearly fruitful. Essential elements of Thomasius's thinking are obvious, for example, throughout Buddeus's textbook, *Elementa philosophiae practicae* (Elements of practical philosophy), first published in 1697.[152] Among the many positions of Thomasius that Buddeus apparently found sympathetic were his derivation of natural law from the will of God and his rejection of *moralitas objectiva*, the idea that actions are morally good or bad *per se*, which Wolff would later make central to his *German Ethics*.[153]

But with the publication of Thomasius's *Foundations*, their intellectual relationship apparently cooled. Thomasius, evidently perceiving Buddeus's

---

[147] H. Rüping, "Budde und die Naturrechtslehre der Thomasius-Schule," in *Grundriß der Geschichte der Philosophie: die Philosophie des 17. Jahrhunderts*, v. 4, 1203; H. Rüping, "Christian Thomasius und seine Schule im Geistesleben des 18. Jahrhunderts," in *Recht und Rechtswissenschaft im mitteldeutschen Raum*, ed. H. Lück (Köln: Böhlau, 1998), 129–31.

[148] Rüping, "Budde und die Naturrechtslehre," 1203.

[149] Rüping, "Christian Thomasius und seine Schule," 130, 132.   [150] See above, note 99.

[151] *Observationes selectae ad rem litterarium spectantes* (Halle, 1700–37). Heussi, *Geschichte der theologischen Fakultät zu Jena*, 157; Stolzenburg, *Die Theologie des Jo. Franc. Buddeus*, 304.

[152] W. Sparn, introduction to *Elementa philosophiae practicae*, by J. F. Buddeus (Hildesheim: Olms, 2004), 26–27.

[153] Stolzenburg, *Die Theologie des Jo. Franc. Buddeus*, 304.

unenthusiastic reception of the book's deviation from Pufendorf, criticized him for "half-heartedness."[154] For his part, Buddeus, who had once expressed equal admiration of Thomasius and Pufendorf,[155] began to reserve his praise of Thomasius explicitly for the *Institutes*. In naming the most noteworthy contributors to the history of natural jurisprudence, Buddeus mentions Pufendorf, Johann Nikolaus Hertius (1651–1710), Jean Barbeyrac (1674–1744), Gottlieb Gerhard Titius (1661–1714), Andreas Adam Hochstetter (1668–1717), and Thomasius's *Institutes of Divine Jurisprudence*. About Thomasius's later work, he proceeds with a vagueness that suggests thinly veiled disapproval: Thomasius published the *Foundations* "because some principles in [the *Institutes*] didn't suit the author himself, who had changed his mind about some points of divine law."[156]

Buddeus's admiration of Pufendorf, on the other hand, was obvious long after the publication of Thomasius's *Foundations*. In his own 1719 *Einleitung in die Moral-Theologie* (Introduction to moral theology), moreover, Buddeus repeatedly singled out for praise one essential element of Pufendorf's natural law theory that Thomasius had decided to discard. Pufendorf's chief success, Buddeus explained, was in showing that positive divine law created universally binding moral obligations that could be deduced with precision and certainty by means of human reason, examining human nature in its corrupt state.[157] Admittedly, the single principle from which Pufendorf had deduced all those obligations, namely, the necessity of maintaining social life, was for the purposes of Buddeus's lectures on moral theology too limited. Buddeus himself wanted to expound on the obligations of Christians, and he therefore proposed to discover the first principle of human obligations by examining human nature in its *regenerated* state, drawing not only from the evidence of God's will supplied by human reason but also on the evidence revealed – far more precisely and vividly – in the text of the Bible. Unlike Pufendorf, Buddeus's first principle was the necessity that faithful Christians unite with God (*Vereinigung der Wiedergeborenen mit Gott*).[158]

---

[154] Stolzenburg, *Die Theologie des Jo. Franc. Buddeus*, 305.

[155] Stolzenburg, *Die Theologie des Jo. Franc. Buddeus*, 304.

[156] Buddeus, *Einleitung in die Moral-Theologie*, II.Vorbericht.§20n:

> Weil aber in derselben [jurisprudentia divina] dem Herrn verfasser selbst einige sätze mißfielen, als welcher seine meynung in etlichen puncten des göttlichen rechts geändert hatte, als hat er aufs neue *fundamenta juris naturae & gentium* . . . , zu Halle 1705. in 4. heraus gegeben.

[157] Buddeus, *Einleitung in die Moral-Theologie*, Vorrede [ix].

[158] Buddeus, *Einleitung in die Moral-Theologie*, Vorrede [ix–x].

His method of deducing obligations from a first principle had nonetheless come, he asserted, from Pufendorf, and he readily agreed with Pufendorf that divine law, as discoverable by human reason in the way Pufendorf had proposed, was "the supreme and strongest bond of human society" (*das höchste und feste Band der menschlichen Gesellschaft*). It served both the "political" aim of restraining the sinful from vice by engendering fear of divine punishment, as well as the "theological" aim of motivating them to try to overcome their sinfulness.[159]

Given the substance of Buddeus, Walch, and Zimmermann's criticism of Christian Wolff for having undermined the foundation of morality, it is therefore not difficult to imagine where in the *Foundations* the danger of Thomasius's innovations on Pufendorf must have appeared particularly clearly. Pufendorf's specification of the necessity of sociability as the principle from which all moral obligations could be derived may not have met with unadulterated praise from Buddeus and Zimmermann, but Thomasius's *Foundations* must have seemed far more objectionable. Whereas Pufendorf had shown that natural law was in fact divine with respect to its source, was universally recognizable as such, and was therefore obligatory, Thomasius had described divine law as a mere recommendation, effectively obligatory only on the "wise," who had the task of inculcating virtue in the "fools" largely by means of fear induced by the threat of punishment attached to human law. This of course undermined the idea that moral education must begin with knowledge of God's will, as a stimulus to the re-examination of one's own corrupt character and the initiation of the penitential struggle, and it stood in direct contradiction to the psychological foundation on which Zimmermann, drawing from the published writings and personal advice of Buddeus and Walch, had built his critique of Wolff's ethics. Like Thomasius, Zimmermann considered law, issued by a superior, in most cases a far more effective instrument of moral education than a mere recommendation. Wolff's maxim, "Do what makes you and your condition more perfect," could not engage the conscience, because it was not clearly the dictate of a lawgiver. But for Zimmermann, unlike Thomasius, the effectiveness of law as an instrument of moral education derived primarily from the lawgiver's recognizable possession of the *ius imperandi* or right to command. Divine law was therefore the ultimate source of moral obligation – and not only for the "wise" – because all human beings endowed with reason could recognize that God had created the world, was human beings' greatest benefactor,

---

[159] Buddeus, *Einleitung in die Moral-Theologie*, II.Vorbericht.§8.

and therefore had the right to command. In fact, human law, too, derived its effectiveness as an instrument of moral education from having been pronounced by a human lawgiver with the right to command. In no case could force alone, represented by the mere threat of punishments or promise of rewards, suffice. Thomasius's description of divine law as a type of recommendation rather than a mode of lordship (*Herrschaft*), therefore, and less effective than human law in the moral education of "fools" because its punishments were "natural" rather than artificially instituted by human beings, must have been deeply unpersuasive to Zimmermann, Walch, and Buddeus.[160]

By contrast, Nicolaus Hieronymus Gundling's alleged membership in the "second Thomasian school" – that is, those admirers of Thomasius who, unlike Buddeus, largely approved of Thomasius's *Foundations* – would seem to imply that he must have found Thomasius's new view of divine law persuasive. Among the many respects in which Gundling has been identified as having followed the lead of Thomasius's *Foundations* are his "Hobbesian" view that human beings can only be made sociable by means of force exerted by a sovereign,[161] and his distinction, allegedly more "decisive" than even Thomasius's, between internally and externally enforceable obligations.[162] Gundling is also known to have differed from Buddeus, with whom he undoubtedly had substantial contact during their seven years together in Halle, on several questions relevant to their respective attitudes toward Thomasius. Martin Mulsow, taking Gundling and Buddeus as representatives of two kinds of Enlightenment, one "liberal" and "skeptical" (Gundling), the other "conservative" and "theological" (Buddeus), and referring to them as representatives of "two wings of the Thomasian school that were drifting apart,"[163] has drawn attention to several other distinct but probably interrelated issues on which Gundling and Buddeus differed. These included Gundling's highly controversial assertion that Plato, among many other ancient philosophers whose conceptions of God Buddeus had defended in print, was an atheist like Benedict

---

[160] This conclusion resonates with Gottlieb Stolle's remark in his 1727 *Anleitung zur Historie der Gelahrheit*, quoted above (p. 28), that Wolff, too, had denied that God promotes human happiness by means of *Herrschaft* – a position, Stolle notes, "which the Herr Privy-counselor Thomasius, in accordance with his insight into this kind of truth, pointed out long ago [*welches der Herr Geheimde Rath Thomasius nach seiner Einsicht in diese Art der Wahrheiten längst erinnert*]."

[161] M. Mulsow, *Moderne aus dem Untergrund* (Hamburg: Meiner, 2002), 346–47.

[162] Rüping, "Budde und die Naturrechtslehre," 1203–4, 1213; Rüping, "Christian Thomasius und seine Schule," 130–31, 132n19.

[163] Mulsow, *Moderne aus dem Untergrund*, 35, 309, 311, 348.

Spinoza (1632–77);[164] and Gundling's insistence, contra Buddeus, (1) that the human intellect in its original, prelapsarian form was not substantially different from its present form and had not been radically darkened by the Fall, and (2) that the lost perfection for which human beings ought to strive must therefore reside solely in the will rather than partly in the intellect.[165] That these two controversies between Gundling and Buddeus were publicly known is demonstrated by apologetic mention of them in Hempel's biography of Gundling, as well as the attention drawn to them in a fictional dialog between Buddeus and Gundling "in the realm of the dead," published in 1731, two years after their deaths.[166]

On the other hand, even in the absence of a comparative systematic reconstruction of Gundling's and Buddeus's moral and political philosophies, there is good reason to believe that what has come to pass for conventional wisdom about the two men's adversarial relationship overschematizes a more complicated reality. Signs that Gundling and Buddeus had much in common, as well as great respect for each other, abound. Hempel, for example, includes Buddeus among seven named people whom Gundling considered his close friends (*seine besondere Freunde*), and he remarks that upon arriving in Halle, Gundling "seemed to hear his [Buddeus's] philosophical and historical lectures with contentment."[167] Given Hempel's obvious desire to paint as positive as possible a picture of the two men's relationship, unsubstantiated assertions such as these cannot be accepted at face value, but other assertions by Hempel to the same effect can be substantiated. Hempel correctly points out, for example, that Gundling used the third book of Buddeus's *Institutiones theologiae moralis* as the basis for his own lectures on politics, calling it the best book he could find and finding much to praise in it, even if he did not agree with Buddeus on every particular issue.[168] Hempel moreover reports that Gundling's respect for Thomasius did not prevent him from voicing disagreement with him, and

---

[164] Mulsow, *Moderne aus dem Untergrund*, 289–97; cf. Hempel, *Nicolai Hieronymi Gundlings Umständliches Leben und Schriften*, 7597–99.

[165] Mulsow, *Moderne aus dem Untergrund*, 315–24; M. Mulsow, "Gundling vs. Buddeus," in *History and the Disciplines*, ed. D. Kelley (Rochester, NY: University of Rochester Press, 1997), 105–15. This quarrel is explained similarly by Hempel, in *Nicolai Hieronymi Gundlings Umständliches Leben und Schriften*, 7563.

[166] [Anonymous], *Besonders Gespräch in dem Reich derer Todten zwischen N. H. Gundling und J. F. Buddeus* (Frankfurt (Main), 1731).

[167] Hempel, *Nicolai Hieronymi Gundlings ... umständliches Leben und Schriften*, 7029, 7650–51.

[168] Hempel, *Nicolai Hieronymi Gundlings ümstandliches Leben und Schriften*, 7029; cf. N. H. Gundling, *Discours über Buddei ... Philosophiae Practicae Pt. III. die Politic* (Leipzig, 1733), prolegomena.§1; J. A. Franckenstein, *Vorrede, Discours über Buddei ... Philosophiae Practicae Pt. III. die Politic*, by N. H. Gundling, 13–14.

the issue Hempel selects as an example of their disagreement is telling. Gundling voiced disagreement with Thomasius, Hempel reports, over the "well-known controversy, that the law of nature is not, strictly speaking, a law."[169] This is also an issue in which Gundling and Buddeus had much in common.

Not surprisingly, Gundling's closer proximity to Buddeus on this issue than his alleged membership in the "second Thomasian school" would seem to imply can be discerned in Gundling's long-standing antagonism toward Christian Wolff. In 1713, ten years before Wolff's heated quarrel with members of Halle's Theology Faculty ended with his departure for Marburg, Gundling had attacked Wolff in print, on the suspicion that either Wolff himself or a student of Wolff's must be the author of an anonymous pamphlet attacking Gundling's recently published textbook of logic.[170] Gundling's suspicion was false, but his animosity toward Wolff did not diminish. Eleven years later, shortly after Wolff's expulsion from Halle, Gundling issued a pseudonymous account of the whole quarrel between Wolff and his critics on the Theology Faculty, entitled *Unpartheyisches Sendschreiben* (Nonpartisan missive), by "Nicolas Veridicus Impartialis Bohemus." Gundling's "nonpartisan" account was hardly flattering to Wolff. Although Wolff's avowed defender, Carl Günther Ludovici (1707–78), without identifying Gundling, claimed that "the author takes neither Wolff's side nor the side of the Halle theologians, but rather shows himself to be a friend of the now departed Christian Thomasius," in fact Gundling dealt Wolff by far the heavier blows.[171] While admitting that the theologians – represented primarily by Joachim Lange – displayed an exaggerated contempt for philosophy and could not expect to make theologians out of students who lacked intellectual ability or received no training in logic, Gundling at the same time defends Daniel Strähler's arguments against Wolff and insinuates his own charges.[172] For all their vagueness, these charges clearly indicate a view of Wolff's intellectual

---

[169] Hempel, *Nicolai Hieronymi Gundlings ümstandliches Leben und Schriften*, 7029. Hempel correctly refers the reader to Gundling's *Via ad veritatem iurisprudentiae naturalis* (Halle, 1714), Chapter I.

[170] Ludovici, *Ausführlicher Entwurf*, III.§17; [N. H. Gundling], *Aufrichtiges Sendschreiben eines Gundlingischen Zuhörers an Herrn Christoph August Heumann . . . darinnen er den ungezogenen* Auctorem Salebrarum *nach Verdiensten züchtiget . . .* (Alt-Rannstadt, 1713). The anonymous pamphlet attack to which Gundling reacted was *Salebrae in via ad veritatem* (n.d., n.p.), in fact by Wolff's colleague in the Philosophy Faculty, Johann Friedemann Schneider.

[171] Ludovici, *Ausführlicher Entwurf*, I.§266: "Der Verfasser hält es weder mit Wolffen noch mit den Hällischen Gottesgelehrten, sondern zeiget sich als einen Freund des nunmehr seel. Hrn. Christian Thomasius." Ludovici does not explain his comment further.

[172] [Gundling], *Unpartheyisches Sendschreiben*, 16, 19, 21, 23–24.

heritage that corresponds to Buddeus's, Walch's, and Zimmermann's. According to Gundling, Wolff should be considered a faithful reviver of "Scholasticism," above all the teachings of Thomas Aquinas, and he was understandably lauded to no end by the Jesuits.[173] Again and again, Gundling hints at the theme emphasized by Buddeus in his own critical references to Scholasticism: it aims at the cultivation of the intellect to the exclusion of the will. He strategically recalls, as an example, the comment of a "certain distinguished man of learning" that "Mr. Wolff's philosophy is so abstract and subtle as to be almost useless."[174]

In addition to the anti-Scholastic, anti-Wolffian innuendo of the *Unpartheyisches Sendschreiben*, Gundling advanced in other published works a more substantial criticism of Wolff's theory of natural obligation, and in doing so he clearly adopted essential parts of the position defended by Buddeus, Walch, and Zimmermann. A hint of Gundling's criticism is to be found in the memorial sermon for Gundling, delivered by Johann Jakob Rambach in 1730. At Gundling's request, Rambach devoted the sermon to an exposition of Luke 10:21–22 and an explanation of how, as the two verses indicate, "the mystery of the wisdom of the gospel . . . remains hidden to the wise and the prudent of this world," and "how it will be revealed to the children."[175] Among the themes that Rambach emphasizes are the insufficiency of knowledge or *Wissenschaft*, however systematic and thoroughly grounded, as a means of pleasing God. Learning and knowledge are a gift of God and have many important uses, he explains,

> But at the same time one has to keep in mind that human sciences [*Wissenschaften*] make no one better and more pleasing to God; a simple farmer, who fears him and goes about with humility, pleases him much more than a proud and inflated man of learning.[176]

It is no accident that Rambach mentions fear, the motivation behind the penitential struggle, as one of the two identifying characteristics of the man

---

[173] [Gundling], *Unpartheyisches Sendschreiben*, 10, 20–23.

[174] [Gundling], *Unpartheyisches Sendschreiben*, 21: "Des Herrn Wolffens *Philosophie* wäre schon so *abstract* und *subtil*, daß sie fast nicht zu brauchen."

[175] J. J. Rambach, *Gedächtniß-Rede von dem Geheimniß der Evangelischen Weisheit*, 2nd ed. (Halle, 1732), 12, 54. Rambach proposes to consider "Das Geheimniß der Evangelischen Weisheit. I. Wie solches den Weisen und Klugen dieser Welt verborgen bleibe. II. Wie es den Unmündigen offenbaret werde" (12).

[176] Rambach, *Gedächtniß-Rede von dem Geheimniß der Evangelischen Weisheit*, 20–21:

> Allein man muß dabey gleichwol bedencken, daß die menschlichen Wissenschaften vor GOtt niemand besser und angenehmer machen; dem vielmehr ein einfältiger Bauer, den ihn fürchtet, und in der Demuth wandelt, besser gefällt, als ein stoltzer und aufgeblasener Gelehrter. Rambach cites here Thomas à Kempis' *De imitatione Christi*, I.ii.

pleasing to God. As he explains later in the sermon, there is only a single correct order of stages through which one must pass in preparation for escaping the corruption of the will by means of God's grace, and the painful recognition of one's own sinfulness cannot be circumvented:

> There is simply no other way to heaven than this one: that one humbly recognize and painfully feel one's own sinful misery, one's inborn blindness and foolishness, and one's deep incapacity for everything good, that one come to Jesus Christ like a small child, seek from him forgiveness of one's sins, clothe oneself in his justice, and let oneself be illuminated, transformed, and sanctified by his spirit.[177]

This is one of the central lessons Rambach draws from Gundling's verses, and if it does not necessarily reflect Gundling's own understanding of the verses, it certainly resonates with Gundling's public reasons for finding fault with Wolff's moral philosophy.

Gundling made those reasons clear in the pages of *Gundlingiana*, a learned journal he founded in 1715 as an organ for the publication of his own essays.[178] In 1724, one year after Wolff's departure from Halle, Gundling decided to add his own voice to the controversy over the foundation of morality in the form of an essay on the question, "Whether natural laws arise from the essence of human nature or from the will of God."[179] His answer is very much like Walch's response to Wolff in the same year:[180] the key issue is not whether divine law originates ultimately from God's will or God's intellect and wisdom, since God's will cannot be separated from his intellect and wisdom.[181] Like Walch, Gundling dismisses as obviously untenable the position that Wolff attributes to Buddeus, and he instead adopts the position attributed to Buddeus by Walch: moral obligation derives from the will of God, but God exercises his will in conformity with

---

[177] Rambach, *Gedächtniß-Rede von dem Geheimniß der Evangelischen Weisheit*, 69:

> Es ist einmal . . . kein andrer Weg zum Himmel als dieser, daß man sein sündlich Elend, seine angebohrne Blindheit und Thorheit, und sein tiefes Unvermögen zu allem guten demüthig erkenne, schmertzlich fühle, als ein kleines Kind zu JESU Christo komme, bey ihm Vergebung der Sünden suche, sich in seine Gerechtigkeit einkleiden, und durch seinen Geist erleuchten, verändern und heiligen lasse.

[178] N. H. Gundling, *Gundlingiana, darinnen allerhand zur Jurisprudentz, Philosophie, Historie, Critic, Litteratur und übrigen Gelehrsamkeit gehörige Sachen abgehandelt werden* (Halle, 1715–32); Hempel, *Nicolai Hieronymi Gundlings Umständliches Leben und Schriften*, 7047.

[179] N. H. Gundling, "Ob die natürliche Gesetze von dem Wesen der menschlichen Natur, oder von dem göttlichen Willen entstanden," *Gundlingiana* 33 (1724): 275–92.

[180] See above, pp. 40–41.

[181] Gundling, "Ob die natürliche Gesetze von dem Wesen der menschlichen Natur, oder von dem göttlichen Willen entstanden," §§1–10.

the nature of human beings and the world, which he himself created.[182] The real debate, Gundling continues, is therefore not about the source of moral obligation, but rather about how human beings can learn God's will by examining human nature, and equally importantly, how human beings can be reliably induced to act on what they learn. On the first of these questions, Gundling grants that Grotius and Pufendorf, in specifying the necessity of sociability as the essential part of human nature from which God's will can be learned, gave a plausible answer to the first question. But he adds that "Grotius and the Scholastics" – which can be taken to include Wolff, given Gundling's association of Wolff with the "Scholastics" in his *Unpartheyisches Sendschreiben* – were wrong to suggest that human beings would be obliged to obey natural law even if there were no God. As Jakob Thomasius (1622–84), Christian's father, correctly pointed out, "If there were no God, there would be nothing, and nothing would endure, not even the essences of all things." Gundling continues: "It would therefore be more tolerable if they had said that even if God were ignored, the natural laws would nonetheless produce obligation."[183]

But even here, Gundling finds fault with "Grotius and the Scholastics" for failing to perceive that the very knowledge that God is the author of natural laws is necessary to induce human beings to obey those laws. It is perhaps "more tolerable" to say that natural law obliges even those who have no knowledge of God than it is to say – obviously falsely – that human nature and the causal nexus would persist even if there were in fact no God, but it is still hardly satisfactory. As in the case of an atheist who learns mathematical principles without having knowledge of the creator of those principles, Gundling explains,

> To the same extent it is undoubtedly possible that [an atheist] could also grasp moral truths that have a connection with human nature. But here it is important to observe that the truths under consideration in moral philosophy and natural jurisprudence are practical. Theory is not enough, here;

---

[182] Gundling, "Ob die natürliche Gesetze von dem Wesen der menschlichen Natur, oder von dem göttlichen Willen entstanden," §10.

[183] Gundling, "Ob die natürliche Gesetze von dem Wesen der menschlichen Natur, oder von dem göttlichen Willen entstanden," §16:

> Nur sind die Scholastici samt Grotio zu weit gegangen, wann sie gemeinet, etiam sublato Deo leges naturae humanae congruentes futuras. Jacobus Thomasius aber antwortet hierauf in seinen dilucidationibus Stahlianis nicht unrecht: Sublato DEO nihil esse nihilque substiturum, eoque nec rerum omnium essentias mansuras. Darum wäre es leidentlicher gewesen, wann sie gesaget, ignorato licet DEO leges naturales nihilominus obligationem producturas.

practice, too, must be successfully carried out. Carrying it out is opposed to our concupiscence and affections, and therefore there has to be a means available, by which a person is more certainly and powerfully constrained to live according to these truths, so that the most dangerous acts are not undertaken without paying attention to all knowledge and recognition of the truth. In the opposing position, there is nothing left to keep me from stealing, murdering, or insulting someone except *utilitas*, or usefulness.[184]

The problem with insisting that those who have no knowledge of God are obliged to obey natural law, Gundling claims, is that human beings are naturally prone to desire what natural law forbids. Dominated by concupiscence and self-oriented affections, the human will naturally chooses actions that seem to promote one's own "utility" (*utilitas*), and there are all kinds of situations in which *utilitas* seems to oppose what the natural law commands. Gundling takes the example of an atheist who encounters Paul, his sworn enemy, on a deserted road. If you are an atheist, Gundling asks, what is to keep you from murdering Paul if you are certain that the crime will not be discovered? Nothing. "To the contrary," Gundling explains, "it is a great advantage for you, if your enemy lies on the ground. You have no fear of God, since God is unknown to you. You are an atheist. What is supposed to hold you back?"[185] The same thought can be applied to kings whose subjects are atheists: only a lack of force prevents their subjects from overthrowing them. "I therefore conclude," Gundling continues, "that if a moral philosophy is to hold up in practice, it is impossible to leave God out of the system. Fear of God is

---

[184] Gundling, "Ob die natürliche Gesetze von dem Wesen der menschlichen Natur, oder von dem göttlichen Willen entstanden," §§17–18:

> Und in so weit ist es wol möglich, daß er auch moralische Wahrheiten, welche mit der menschlichen Natur eine Connexion haben, begreiffe. Aber es ist allhier wol zubeobachten. daß es practische Wahrheiten seyn, welche in der Moral und natürlichen Rechts-Gelahrheit fürkommen. Allhier ist die Theorie nicht genug, sondern es muß auch die Ausübung erfolgen. Die Ausübung ist unserer Concupiscenz, und Affecten zuwieder; und darum muß auch ein Mittel fürhanden seyn, wodurch man gewisser und kräfftiger constringiret werde, nach solchen Wahrheiten zuleben, daferne nicht, aller Wissenschaft und Erkäntnüß der Wahrheit ungeachtet, die allergefährlichsten Thaten sollen fürgenommen werden. In der gegenseitigen Meinung bleibet nichts, als utilitas, oder die Nutzbarkeit übrig; welche mich abhalten soll, daß ich nicht stehle, nicht morde, oder jemand beleidige.

[185] Gundling, "Ob die natürliche Gesetze von dem Wesen der menschlichen Natur, oder von dem göttlichen Willen entstanden," §17:

> Hingegen ist es eine grosse Avantage für dich, wann dein Feind zu Boden lieget. Vor GOtt fürchtest du dich nicht. Dann dieser ist dir unbekandt. Du bist ein Atheiste. Was soll dich nun abhalten?

the beginning of wisdom. Without God, all moral philosophy is an empty nothing."[186]

This criticism of Grotius and the "Scholastics" in the pages of *Gundlingiana*, which later appeared as a criticism of "Grotius and Wolff" in the published text of Gundling's lectures on moral philosophy in Halle,[187] reveals how far Gundling diverged from Thomasius's *Foundations*, and how closely he approached Buddeus, Walch, and Zimmermann, on the closely related questions of whether divine law is a law in the strict sense of the word, and whether knowledge of God's will is a necessary precondition for successful moral education. Whereas Thomasius had decided in his *Foundations* to present human law and the punishments associated with it as the only reliable means of inculcating virtue in "fools," with divine law by contrast a recommendation with obligatory force only on the wise, Zimmermann and his teachers in Jena insisted that divine law was in fact a law in the strict sense, that it was universally perceptible as such, and that the perception of it was moreover the only reliable means of convincing human beings to attempt to reform their own desires and thereby begin the process of preparing themselves for the gift of divine grace that could genuinely transform their naturally corrupt wills. They worried that making divine law a mere recommendation, as Wolff had done, implied that the only motivation to behave virtuously was *utilitas*. But because the human will was naturally corrupt, the search for *utilitas* could only lead one to indulge one's vicious desires. For this reason, Wolff's program for a moral education that relied in its early stages primarily on inculcating an awareness of "natural obligation" could not work. Rather, as Zimmermann insisted, the conscience needed to be engaged by an awareness of divine law. Gundling shared this worry, and he saw it as a reason to take issue with Thomasius's *Foundations*. At first, as Gundling remarked in a lecture on moral philosophy, Thomasius had followed his father Jakob's lead by refuting Grotius's claim that moral obligation would persist in the absence of God. "Then," Gundling added, "he defended [Grotius] again in the *Foundations*, for which reason Wolff praised him."[188] But

---

[186] Gundling, "Ob die natürliche Gesetze von dem Wesen der menschlichen Natur, oder von dem göttlichen Willen entstanden," §18:

> Darum schliese ich, daß es nicht möglich sey, bey einer Morale, welche die Probe halten soll, GOtt aus dem Systemate heraus zulassen. Die Furcht GOttes ist der Weisheit Anfang. . . . Ohne Gott ist die gantze Morale ein eitles nichts.

[187] N. H. Gundling, *Philosophischer Discourse . . . oder Academische Vorlesungen uber seine* Viam ad veritatem moralem *und* Kulpisii Collegium Grotianum (Frankfurt (Main), 1740), 289–94, here 289.

[188] Gundling, *Academische Vorlesungen uber seine* Viam ad veritatem moralem, 289–90.

Gundling thought that in doing so, Thomasius had in fact made moral obligation less "firm." In Gundling's view, "if a rational moral philosophy is not to become contemptible, one has to believe in an immortal soul and in a God who punishes transgressors." Moral education had to begin not with an appeal to *utilitas*, but rather with the "constraint" provided by awareness of God's will and of God's intention to punish those who violate it.[189]

Admittedly, it would be an exaggeration to say that Gundling's position resembled Zimmermann's, Walch's, and Buddeus's in all important respects. Although Gundling does insist that moral education requires an awareness of God's justice, he does not explicitly assert that moral education must begin specifically with an awareness of God's right to command; his emphasis is clearly on the importance of constraint. The purpose of this constraint, however, is ultimately the inculcation of genuine virtue, not simply the coercion of external obedience – and in explaining this position, Gundling resembles Zimmermann and Buddeus on a number of important points. Gundling agrees, for example, that the aim of moral philosophy is to help a person achieve genuine happiness by attaining 'living cognition" of the highest good, namely, God.[190] The moral truths one learns by means of one's own intellect (*ex ratione*) lead one to inquire into the truths revealed by God in the Bible, which serve as a supplement to what one has learned independently of revelation.[191] Ultimately, attaining living cognition of God requires that one perfect one's nature rather than allowing one's nature to remain in its current, corrupt state; and perfecting one's nature means reforming one's will.[192] This reform must begin with an attempt to control one's antisocial desires, such that one lives in conformity with the norms of justice, motivated by a fear of punishment. Gundling is careful to point out that since the virtue that moral education ultimately aims to inculcate is love of God, and since love by its very nature cannot be forced, "force makes no one virtuous [*Zwang macht niemanden tugendhaft*]."[193] Force does, however, serve as an indispensable preparation for becoming virtuous. Perfect virtue is difficult for human beings, Gundling explains, and

---

[189] Gundling, "Ob die natürliche Gesetze von dem Wesen der menschlichen Natur, oder von dem göttlichen Willen entstanden," §19; cf. Gundling, *Philosophischer Discourse . . . oder Academische Vorlesungen*, 293.

[190] Gundling, *Academische Vorlesungen uber seine* Viam ad veritatem moralem, 8–11.

[191] Gundling, *Academische Vorlesungen uber seine* Viam ad veritatem moralem, 9, 18.

[192] Gundling, *Academische Vorlesungen uber seine* Viam ad veritatem moralem, 18, 280.

[193] Gundling, *Academische Vorlesungen uber seine* Viam ad veritatem moralem, 32.

one must therefore try at the very least to establish merely external peace, which happens in natural jurisprudence or natural law, which recommends and inculcates just actions in human beings on account of external fear.[194]

Only once this "external peace" is achieved can those who enjoy it attempt to attain "internal tranquillity."[195] The precise relationship between external peace enforced by the threat of punishment and internal tranquillity maintained without any such threat, Gundling does not discuss at length, but he does suggest that the attainment of internal tranquillity must be indirectly produced by the same "constraint" that he considers indispensable to the external discipline of atheists in situations where human punishment poses no threat: namely, the threat of divine punishment.

As far as the means by which this threat ultimately produces internal tranquillity, although Gundling does not invoke the penitential struggle explicitly, he does allude to it. In repudiating pastors who make excessive use of punishment, misguidedly claiming God himself to be their model, Gundling points out that

> God does not intend to make anyone immediately virtuous by means of his punishments; rather, he intends to give those who have been punished an opportunity to beat themselves on the inside, and, by means of this kind of humiliation, to recognize their own misery of their own free will.[196]

It would seem that Johann Jakob Rambach's interpretation of the verses chosen by Gundling for the sermon at his funeral was not unfaithful to Gundling's own perception of the indispensibility of the penitential struggle in moral education. Here too, Gundling resembled Buddeus, Walch, and Zimmermann.

Conclusion

It is therefore fair to say, together with Albrecht Beutel and Ferdinand Josef Schneider, that Wolff and several of his most outspoken critics clashed

---

[194] Gundling, *Academische Vorlesungen uber seine* Viam ad veritatem moralem, 26:

> Alle Menschen werden jedoch schwerlich vollkommen tugendhafft werden. Und darum muß man wenigstens doch nur externam pacem zu etabliren suchen, als welches in jurisprudentia naturali, oder dem jure naturae geschiehet, so den Menschen die actiones justas ob timorem externum recommendiret und inculciret.

[195] Gundling, *Academische Vorlesungen uber seine* Viam ad veritatem moralem, 23–24.

[196] Gundling, *Academische Vorlesungen uber seine* Viam ad veritatem moralem, XI.394:

> ... Gott will durch seine Strafen niemand unmittelbar tugendhaft machen, wohl aber den gestraften Gelegenheit geben, daß sie in sich schlagen, und durch dergleichen Demüthigung ihr Elend selbsten freywillig erkennen.

over the question of whether fear of God is the beginning of wisdom, and whether moral education must entail a penitential struggle. What the comparison between Gundling, Zimmermann, Buddeus, and Walch illuminates is the argumentative contours of that clash. It reveals their fundamental disagreement with Wolff about the natural capacities of the human will and, therefore, about the best means of reforming it. Wolff had proposed that moral obligation, the motivation to become virtuous, was ultimately a function of the human perceptive faculties. Exercises in making perception as distinct as possible, at the expense of affection-arousing indistinct perception, were the best means of increasing the effectiveness of the conscience, such that even a person with no knowledge of God could attain a considerable degree of virtue by correctly judging whether any given action conduced to his own perfection or not. Force, whether in the form of the threat of divine punishment or the domination of the intellect by affections, was both unnecessary and in most cases undesirable. Wolff's critics, on the other hand – even Johann Liborius Zimmermann, the critic of his who had obviously learned the most from him – perceived him to have made the same basic mistake that they placed at the center of their polemic against "Scholasticism": he had failed to see that the cultivation of the intellect does not necessarily lead to the reform of the will. The intellect could perhaps be trained to perceive as distinctly as humanly possible, but even the most exact knowledge of how to live in conformity with one's own nature and thereby "perfect" oneself could not on its own persuade the corrupt will to produce genuinely virtuous actions. Instead, what the reform of the will required was a long process of affection-control, and ultimately a deeply felt recognition of the will's intractability, in preparation for the divine grace by which the will could in fact be reformed.

But the corruption of the will made even the beginning of this process unlikely. In the absence of an external constraint, the preexisting, natural desire for one's own *utilitas* would never come into question. The question for Wolff's critics was what this constraint should be. As of 1705, Christian Thomasius had identified human law as the constraint necessary to initiate the process of reforming the human will, given the relative ineffectiveness of the "natural" punishments attached to divine law. His colleagues Buddeus and Gundling, on the other hand, disagreed. They considered Thomasius's abandonment of the view he had once held, that perception of divine law was an effective and even indispensable instrument of moral education, unwarranted. From their perspective, only the perception of divine law and the fear of divine punishment – as well as, in Buddeus's view, the perception of God's justice as conveyed by the *notitia Dei* – could effectively engage the conscience to constrain the corrupt will and set in motion the process of re-examining and trying to reform one's own desires. In opposition first to Thomasius and later to Wolff, they therefore insisted that for moral education to succeed, divine law must first be perceived as a law in the strict sense of the word. This perception of divine law was, in their view, the "foundation of morality" that Wolff's program of moral education threated to undermine. For Alexander Baumgarten, it would be the task of aesthetic theory to indicate how the threat could be avoided.

CHAPTER 2

Pietist Aisthēsis, *Moral Education, and the Beginnings of Aesthetic Theory*

If Alexander Baumgarten developed what he famously called an "aesthetic philosophy" in response to the debate between Christian Wolff and his critics about the foundation of morality, is not immediately obvious from Baumgarten's few statements about his own motives. The most explicit of these statements can be found in Baumgarten's well-known *Meditationes philosophicae de nonnullis ad poema pertinentibus* (Philosophical considerations of some things pertaining to poetry).[1] This was the dissertation in which, at age nineteen, he first issued his famous call for the creation of aesthetics as a philosophical discipline. Baumgarten opens with some introductory reminiscences about Martin Christgau (1697–1776), the teacher who he claims instilled in him a lifelong love of poetry, and then proceeds to explain the occasion that prompted him to write. In his first stint as a teacher of poetry and logic in August Hermann Francke's Latin School, he thought it reasonable to "put the principles of philosophizing into practice," and, rather than simply repeat what his own teachers had taught him, to demonstrate the characteristics of a perfect poem.[2]

The concise self-portrait contained in these lines – a young lover of poetry, driven by a thirst for philosophical certainty to formulate what would come to be known as aesthetic theory – has hardly faded with time. It was readily taken up and elaborated upon by Baumgarten's friends and colleagues, whose accounts of Baumgarten's aims and motivations remain the unavoidable starting point for all modern investigations. Those eighteenth-century accounts tell us that the young lover of poetry acquired his thirst for philosophical certainty as a university student in Halle from an encounter with the philosophy of Christian Wolff.[3] Arriving in Halle

---

[1] A. G. Baumgarten, *Meditationes philosophicae de nonnullis ad poema pertinentibus* (Halle, 1735).
[2] A. G. Baumgarten, *Meditationes*, 4.
[3] E.g., T. Abbt, *Alexander Gottlieb Baumgartens Leben und Character* (Halle, 1765), 8–13.

four years after Wolff's expulsion, Baumgarten could not attend lectures by Wolff himself, but he encountered Wolff's ideas in print and in conversation, and like many other Halle students of the 1720s and 1730s he made the trip to the University of Jena, where teaching Wolff's ethics and metaphysics had not been banned, to hear lectures on what could not be taught openly in Halle. In time, Baumgarten's biographers tell us, he found himself inflamed by an insatiable craving for unassailable knowledge, the kind that he had come to believe only philosophy could supply. He saw that philosophers – even Wolff – had given little serious attention to some of the things he himself most cared about, such as the rules for evaluating poems and for cultivating the parts of the mind primarily responsible for the creation of good poetry. He therefore decided to fill that gap himself.

To put this traditional story still more precisely, what motivated Baumgarten to develop an aesthetic theory was a deep appreciation for the value of *Wissenschaft* or "science": knowledge whose incontestable certainty derived from its being openly deduced from indubitable first principles, such that every proposition could be defended with reference to an earlier proposition (the "principle of sufficient reason"), and such that no proposition contradicted any other (the "principle of noncontradiction").[4] Christian Wolff had been attempting to create in all fields of knowledge this same kind of certainty – the kind that could be found in mathematics – by applying the "mathematical method" of geometric proof,[5] but he had not yet sufficiently addressed either the fine arts and literature (the so-called *schöne Künste*) or the cognitive faculties associated with the practice of them. As a lover of poetry, we are told, Baumgarten therefore decided to apply Wolff's "mathematical method" to the arts, particularly the art of poetry, and to the cognitive faculties employed by writers and readers of poetry, and thereby to provide a philosophically sound account of how to improve them.[6]

---

[4] Baumgarten's definition of *Wissenschaft* or *scientia* can be found in his *Philosophia generalis* (Halle, 1770), §31: "Science is certain cognition derived from things that are certain [*Scientia est certa cognitio ex certis*]." This corresponds to the strictest definition of *Wissenschaft* given by J. G. Walch in his *Philosophisches Lexikon*, second index ("of things"), s.v. "Wissenschaft."

[5] T. Frängsmyr, "Christian Wolff's Mathematical Method and its Impact on the Eighteenth Century," *Journal of the History of Ideas* 36.4 (October 1975): 655–57.

[6] W. Strube, "Die Entstehung der Ästhetik als einer wissenschaftlichen Disziplin," *Scientia Poetica* 8 (2004), 15; C. Wolff, *Discursus preliminaris de philosophia in genere* (Frankfurt (Main), 1732), §§30, 72. Cf. F. Copleston, *A History of Philosophy*, v. 4, Wolff to Kant (Westminster, MD: Newman Press, 1960), 116; C. Zelle and G. Schwering, "Vorbemerkung," in *Ästhetische Positionen nach Adorno*, ed. Zelle and Schwering (Munich: Fink, 2002), 7; Beiser, *Diotima's Children*, 50, 123–24; Buchenau, *The Founding of Aesthetics*, 115.

This story is difficult to resist. Its proponents include a formidable array of eyewitnesses and second-hand observers – Carl Günther Ludovici,[7] Georg Friedrich Meier (1718–77),[8] Moses Mendelssohn (1729–86),[9] Thomas Abbt (1738–66),[10] and Johann Gottfried Herder (1744–1803),[11] for example – some of whom can claim a philosophical stature and historical impact comparable to Baumgarten's own. And yet there is good reason not to leave these early commentators with the last word. Their tendency to present Baumgarten as essentially a committed follower of Wolff – and thereby to suggest that although Baumgarten was well-acquainted with the conflict between Wolff and his critics, the critics' arguments must have left barely a mark on him – probably reflects the polarization of the intellectual landscape in which they found themselves. From the perspective of Ludovici, writing in the 1720s and 1730s, that landscape was inhabited by two communities locked in conflict, Wolffians and anti-Wolffians, and Baumgarten belonged unequivocally among the Wolffians. Meier and Abbt, writing in the 1750s and 1760s, essentially endorsed Ludovici's judgment. In Meier's view, Baumgarten spent the 1730s in Halle loosening himself from the grip of anti-Wolffian polemic. "He had read and heard many charges against Wolff," Meier writes, but as a thoughtful young man who had himself attended lectures on Wolff in Jena, he refused to "jump to

---

7   In 1737, Ludovici quoted a reader of Baumgarten's *Meditationes* as having been convinced by it "that the mathematical method is applicable even in things that appeared most foreign to it, like poetry." Ludovici, *Ausführlicher Entwurf*, II.§509.

8   Meier (*Alexander Gottlieb Baumgartens Leben*, 14) claims that while studying poetry at Francke's orphanage school, Baumgarten began "to wonder whether the so-called 'fine sciences' [*schöne Wissenschaften*] could not after all become that which they had long been called [i.e., sciences], and whether one could not deduce general, certain basic principles for them."

9   In 1757, after Baumgarten had published part of his *Aesthetics*, Moses Mendelssohn claimed that through Baumgarten's and Meier's forays into aesthetics, "philosophy is making a new conquest and is taking possession of an entire part of human cognition that one hitherto could not have called a 'science' without abusing the word." M. Mendelssohn, Review of *Auszug aus den Anfangsgründen aller schönen Künste und Wissenschaften*, by G. F. Meier, in *Ästhetische Schriften*, by M. Mendelssohn, ed. A. Pollok (Hamburg: Meiner, 2006), 107.

10   Abbt portrays Baumgarten as driven to delineate a new science of poetics – and more generally, a new science of aesthetics – by a desire to endow the rules of artistic production with a certainty that they had hitherto lacked, by applying the method of demonstration that he had learned from Wolff. T. Abbt, *Leben und Charakter Alexander Gottlieb Baumgartens* (Berlin, 1780), repr. in *Vermischte Werke*, by T. Abbt, v. 4 of 6 (Hildesheim: Olms, 1978), 222–23.

11   Herder's description of Baumgarten's *Meditationes* clearly borrows from Abbt's. J. G. Herder, "Entwurf zu einer Denkschrift auf Alexander Gottlieb Baumgarten, Johann David Heilmann, und Thomas Abbt" and "Von Baumgartens Denkart in seinen Schriften," in *Sämmtliche Werke*, by J. G. Herder, v. 32, ed. B. Suphan (Berlin, 1899), 175–77 and 178–92. On connections between Herder and Baumgarten: F. Solms, *Disciplina aesthetica: Zur Frühgeschichte der ästhetischen Theorie bei Baumgarten und Herder* (Stuttgart: Klett, 1990); and H. Adler, *Die Prägnanz des Dunklen: Gnoseologie, Ästhetik, Geschichtsphilosophie bei Johann Gottfried Herder* (Hamburg: Meiner, 1990).

conclusions and condemn what he himself had not yet sufficiently investigated and confirmed."[12] Abbt presented Baumgarten's affinity for Wolff as still more clear-cut. Wolff's enemies scorned philosophy, he explains, and Baumgarten embraced it:

> Even after Wolff had left Halle, the rage of his enemies there continued. The pulpits resounded not only with continual refutations but also with continual malicious accusations against his philosophy. Above all, the mathematical method of demonstration, which Wolff employed, was condemned, and therewith almost all rational demonstrations. Young people were scared away from that which is most excellently peculiar to genuine philosophy, namely, the precise delineation and correct specification of concepts; and they became accustomed to prove with biblical sayings principles that are perceived by reason, and to condemn whatever cannot be proven that way as unnecessary, useless, or even harmful. . . . Baumgarten, as he himself once affirmed to me, never looked back at those days without a special sentiment. For perhaps he simply had to thank this peculiar confluence of circumstances for the fact that his genius broke through all the more powerfully for having encountered resistance.[13]

The anti-Wolffian polemics, as described by Abbt, had no hold on Baumgarten whatsoever. They were merely the "resistance" encountered by Baumgarten's genius before it "broke through."

Abbt's vivid, bitter, and influential account of Baumgarten's encounter with Wolff's critics in post-1723 Halle, which he added to a second edition of his biography of Baumgarten after the danger of censorship in Halle had passed, illustrates precisely why the story of Baumgarten's straightforward extension of Wolffian philosophy into the aesthetic realm cannot be accepted at face value. It has all the signs of unfair caricature.

---

[12] Meier, *Alexander Gottlieb Baumgartens Leben*, 11–12.

[13] Abbt, *Leben und Charakter*, 219–20:

> [A]uch nachdem Wolf Halle verlassen hatte, währte das Wüten seiner Feinde daselbst fort. Die Katheder erschallten, nicht allein von beständigen Widerlegungen, sondern auch von beständigen gehässigen Beschuldigungen wider seine Philosophie. Besonders ward die mathematische Methode im Demonstriren, der sich Wolf bediente, und mit derselben beynahe alle vernünftige Demonstrazion verworfen. Die jungen Leute wurden von dem, was der ächten Philosophie vorzüglich eigen ist, von der genauen Zergliederung und richtigen Bestimmung der Begriffe abgeschreckt; und gewöhnt, Sätze welche die Vernunft erkennt, durch biblische Sprüche zu beweisen, und was daraus nicht bewiesen werden kann, als unnöthig, oder unnütz, oder gar als schädlich zu verwerfen. . . . Baumgarten sah niemals, ohne eine besondere Empfindung, wie er mich ehemals selbst versichert hat, auf diese Zeiten zurück. Denn vielleicht hatte er es bloß diesem seltsamen Zusammenlaufe von Umständen zu danken, daß sein Genie, welches nunmehro Widerstand fand, desto mächtiger durchbrach.

Abbt's characterization of the Halle Pietists as antiphilosophical fundamentalists, though affirmed by a tradition of scholarship that stretches from the present day back into the 1730s,[14] flies in the face of hard evidence, not least of all the fact that August Hermann Francke made mathematics and logic, taught in part from textbooks by Wolff, staples of his schools' curricula.[15]

Abbt's characterization of Baumgarten himself similarly strains credibility. Obviously he did not know how to handle Baumgarten's sentimentality about his Halle years.[16] Baumgarten's own account of those years, albeit presented in the persona of "Aletheophilus," anonymous author of "philosophical letters" published by Baumgarten in 1741 for an interested lay public, conveys far less bitterness. Having begun to study Wolff's writings, Aletheophilus recalls, "I developed a desire to write down and, as usual, defend some things that I had become convinced of." More recently, he continues, "I discovered this pamphlet, not without laughter, in a catalog of Wolffian texts." Amusingly, it seemed to have been placed in the catalog simply because "I had divided my text into §'s and referred in each [section] to the previous one"[17] – hardly a sign that the author subscribed to everything Wolff taught. To those who ask him whether he is a "Wolffian," Aletheophilus explains, he therefore prefers "not to answer until I know what you understand a 'Wolffian' to be." He professes to be one, however, insofar as he is at least largely convinced by Wolff's philosophical system.[18] Aletheophilus presents himself, in other words, as a man amused by the pervasive fear of an ill-defined "Wolffianism," stimulated by its critics to learn more about it, and ultimately convinced by much of it. The story is at least partly fictionalized, insofar as it deviates from facts about Baumgarten's life as preserved in more authoritative sources. But whether or not it conveys Baumgarten's own response to Ludovici's classification of his 1735 *Meditationes* as a Wolffian text, or his own attitude toward Wolff's philosophical system, at the very least it does not exude the vitriol toward Halle Pietism that Abbt took for granted. Baumgarten's relationship

---

[14] E.g., Steffen Gross's characterization of Pietism as "hostil[e] towards logical thinking and abstractions in general," in S. Gross, "The Neglected Programme of Aesthetics," *British Journal of Aesthetics* 42.4 (October 2002): 407; corrected in S. Gross, *Cognitio Sensitiva: ein Versuch über die Ästhetik als Lehre von der Erkenntnis des Menschen* (Würzburg: Königshausen und Neumann, 2011), 47–108. Cf. Grote, "Religion and Enlightenment Revisited."

[15] As brought to light in K. Whitmer, *The Halle Orphanage as Scientific Community: Observation, Eclecticism and Pietism in the Early Enlightenment* (Chicago: University of Chicago Press, 2015).

[16] Abbt, *Alexander Gottlieb Baumgartens Leben und Character*, 9.

[17] [A. G. Baumgarten], *Philosophische Briefe von Aletheophilus* (Leipzig, 1741), 3.

[18] [A. G. Baumgarten], *Philosophische Brieffe*, 4.

with the Halle theologians, among Wolff's other critics, was clearly more complex and more sympathetic than Abbt, recalling it in the 1760s, understood or wished to acknowledge.

After all, Baumgarten had already spent eight formative years among those theologians before issuing his influential call for an aesthetic philosophy in 1735. In 1727, at age thirteen, he had been sent from Berlin to Halle to attend Francke's Latin School on the instructions of his late father, Jacob Baumgarten (1668–1722), who had himself been a student of Joachim Justus Breithaupt in the 1690s and inspector of Francke's other school, the *Pädagogium Regium*, in the 1710s. Alexander spent three years at Francke's Latin School before enrolling as a theology student at the university in 1730. There he attended lectures by Halle Pietism's leading lights: Joachim Lange, Christian Benedict Michaelis, Gotthilf August Francke, and particularly notably, Buddeus's and Walch's disciple Johann Liborius Zimmermann.[19] His constant educational guide was his older brother, Siegmund Jacob, who had himself attended August Hermann Francke's schools and studied theology under Pietist professors in Halle. Close to the elder and younger Franckes since arriving in Halle in 1722, Siegmund Jacob served as inspector of the Latin School during Alexander's time there as a student; became adjunct on the Halle Theology Faculty in 1732; succeeded Zimmermann as *ordinarius* professor in 1734; and encouraged Alexander to teach in Francke's Latin School while studying at the university.[20] It is therefore easy to imagine that Baumgarten's aesthetic theory, in contrast to Abbt's caricature of Baumgarten as merely an anti-Pietist enthusiast for Wolff's mathematical method, must reflect the impact of his Pietist teachers and their critiques of Wolff. But how?

These teachers' impact appears particularly suggestively in the very text in which Baumgarten called for the development of an aesthetic theory: his 1735 *Meditationes*.[21] Ostensibly, Baumgarten set out in this treatise

> to demonstrate that many things that have been said a hundred times, but scarcely ever proven, can be proven from the single concept of a poem that has been firmly in my mind for a long time.[22]

[19] Meier, *Alexander Gottlieb Baumgartens Leben*, 10–11.
[20] Abbt, *Leben und Charakter*, 218–23; Meier, *Alexander Gottlieb Baumgartens Leben*, 5–19; Zedler, *Universal-Lexicon*, s.v. "Baumgarten, Siegmund Jacob."
[21] What follows is an expanded and revised version of S. Grote, "Pietistische *Aisthesis* und moralische Erziehung bei Alexander Gottlieb Baumgarten," *Aufklärung* 20 (2008): 175–98. Reused with permission from Felix Meiner Verlag. Further elaborations on this article's subject can now be found in Fritz, *Vom Erhabenen*, esp. 230–83, 324–56; and Gross, *Cognitio Sensitiva*, esp. 47–158.
[22] A. G. Baumgarten, *Meditationes*, 4: "ut enim ex una, quae dudum mente haeserat, poematis notione probari plurima dicta iam centies, vix semel probata posse demonstrarem."

The fulfillment of this intention occupies most of the rest of the text. Baumgarten begins his proof with a definition of a poem as "perfect sensate discourse" (*oratio sensitiva perfecta*).[23] From this definition, Baumgarten deduces the general characteristics of a perfect poem. The principal characteristic of such a poem, according to Baumgarten, is that it is written such that it tends, to the greatest extent possible, to produce "sensate ideas" (*representationes sensitivae*) in the mind of its reader.[24] Applying terms influentially described by Leibniz in 1684, employed by Wolff with some modifications in the 1720s, and in general use by the 1730s, Baumgarten calls those ideas *clear* and *confused* (*clarae* and *confusae*).[25] An idea is clear, in that it allows us to recognize what thing is being represented, because it contains representations of those characteristics of the thing that allow us to distinguish it from other things.[26] An idea is confused, as opposed to *distinct*, in that those distinguishing characteristics are not made explicit, so that the thing represented cannot immediately be classified according to a definition.[27] Unlike a logical proof, in other words, a poem does not contain words and phrases that denote general concepts and correspond obviously to definitions. Rather, it contains words and phrases that represent particular objects of the senses.[28] But Baumgarten adds that these words should not simply convey "dead mental images" (*phantasmata mortua*).[29] From the principle that the perfect poem produces as many sensate ideas in the mind of its reader as possible, Baumgarten concludes that the most perfect poems produce not only imagined sense impressions of particular objects but also another kind of sensate idea, namely, ideas of "momentary changes" (*mutationes praesentes*) in the human mind.[30] Baumgarten's term is "sensual ideas" (*repraesentationes sensuales*), and he includes among them ideas of "affections" (*affectus*),[31] which he calls "noticeable degrees of pain and pleasure" (*notabiliores taedii et voluptatis gradus*) in a person indistinctly representing something to himself as bad or good.[32] The most perfect poems, therefore, arouse in their readers as many and as strong affections as possible.

---

[23] A. G. Baumgarten, *Meditationes*, §9.   [24] A. G. Baumgarten, *Meditationes*, §8.
[25] A. G. Baumgarten, *Meditationes*, §§12–15. On Leibniz's and Wolff's use of these terms: Schwaiger, *Das Problem des Glücks*, 137–53.
[26] A. G. Baumgarten, *Meditationes*, §13. Cf. G. W. Leibniz, "Meditations on Knowledge, Truth, and Ideas," in *Philosophical Essays*, by G. W. Leibniz, trans. R. Ariew and D. Garber (Indianapolis, IN: Hackett, 1989), 24; C. I. Gerhardt, *G. W. Leibniz: Die philosophischen Schriften*, 7 v. (Berlin, 1875–90), IV.422–26.
[27] A. G. Baumgarten, *Meditationes*, §14; Leibniz, "Meditations," 24.
[28] A. G. Baumgarten, *Meditationes*, §25.   [29] A. G. Baumgarten, *Meditationes*, §29.
[30] A. G. Baumgarten, *Meditationes*, §24.   [31] See above, Chapter 1, note 34.
[32] A. G. Baumgarten, *Meditationes*, §25–27.

After explaining the various rules for choosing and arranging the contents of a poem so as to produce as many sensate ideas as possible, Baumgarten calls for the philosophical treatment of a new type of knowledge – which is to say, he calls for the creation of a new branch of philosophy, one that teaches the perception of truth not through the "higher" cognitive faculties of the soul, such as reason, the improvement of which has traditionally been considered the ambit of logic, but through the "lower" faculties, such as the imagination and the memory, which play a more direct role in the generation of sensate ideas and therefore a more direct role in the creation of and response to poetry as Baumgarten defines it. As a name for this new branch of philosophy, Baumgarten suggests *aesthetica*.[33]

This word is one end of a thread that can be followed from Baumgarten's first aesthetic foray through some of his Pietist teachers' many intellectual projects – their hermeneutic theories and biblical criticism, their assessments of poetry's value, their theories of moral education. It leads ultimately to the conclusion that Baumgarten called for a new branch of philosophy in sympathy with many of those projects, as well as with his teachers' critique of Wolff. Like many of his teachers, and in contrast with the "Scholastics" among whom they numbered Wolff, Baumgarten held that moral education and the "living cognition" at which it aimed required training the human affections through the exercise of the lower cognitive faculties of the soul.

Pietist *Aisthēsis* and Moral Education

Baumgarten has occasionally been honored as the coiner of the term *aesthetic*,[34] but Baumgarten himself declined this honor, explicitly tracing the source of its ancient Greek cognate *aisthētikē* to the word *aisthēta*, used by "the Greek philosophers and the Church Fathers" to refer to sensible things perceived by means other than reason.[35] What Baumgarten apparently never mentioned in print, but certainly knew, is that by 1735 the Greek word *aisthēsis*, another cognate of *aisthēta* and *aisthētikē*, had already been in prominent use among theologians in Halle for several decades, in connection with a debate over the means by which God communicates with human beings, and over the involvement of human affections in that process of communication. One of these theologians was August Hermann Francke himself, who had given *aisthēsis* a significant place in his

---

[33] A. G. Baumgarten, *Meditationes*, §§115–16.
[34] E.g. K. Aschenbrenner and W. B. Holther, introduction to *Reflections on Poetry*, by A. G. Baumgarten (Berkeley: University of California Press, 1954), v.
[35] A. G. Baumgarten, *Meditationes*, §116.

Delineatio doctrinae de affectibus (Outline of doctrine concerning the affections), an addendum to his Latin introduction to reading the Bible, *Manuductio ad lectionem scripturae sacrae* (Guide to the reading of holy scripture), first published in 1693.[36]

Francke mentions *aisthēsis* in connection with what he calls "expository" reading of the Bible, one of the seven types of biblical reading that altogether constitute a "complete study of divinity," and one of four types that aim at understanding the "spirit" of the text, as opposed to the "letter."[37] In Francke's words, an expository reading of a biblical text expounds "the literal sense as intended by the Holy Spirit," and the meaning it seeks is communicated without need of "labored interpretations," just as the will of God was communicated to the earliest Christians by the Apostles. The hermeneutic techniques by which one arrives at this meaning are many. One must consider, among other things, the *scopus* or purpose of the passage in question; the context of the passage; parallelisms with other biblical texts that may shed light on the meanings of particular words or ideas (otherwise known as the "analogy of faith"); the order in which the biblical authors typically expound their subjects; the circumstances referred to in the passage in question; and the affections or emotional state of the author of the passage.[38] In the course of explaining this last consideration in his *Manuductio* Francke directs his readers to the much more extensive discussion of it in his *Delineatio*, where he invokes *aisthēsis* by name.

In mentioning *aisthēsis*, Francke, like Baumgarten, very likely had several "Greek philosophers and church fathers" in mind, but his most obvious source, one that he quotes, was Paul, who prays in his Letter to the Philippians "that your love may overflow more and more with knowledge and full insight [*pasēi aisthēsei*] to help you determine what is best."[39] Paul's reference to *aisthēsis* had of course been interpreted and elaborated upon

---

[36] E. Peschke, introduction to *Manuductio ad lectionem scripturae sacrae*, in *Schriften zur biblischen Hermeneutik* I, by A. H. Francke, ed. E. Peschke (Berlin: Walter de Gruyter, 2003), 28–30. Francke himself appears to have given lectures in Halle on the *Manuductio* from 1698 through 1702. Later editions appeared in 1700 (Halle), 1706 (London), and 1709 (Halle). A full précis of these texts can be found in E. Peschke, *Studien zur Theologie August Hermann Franckes*, v. 2 of 2 (Berlin: Evangelische Verlagsanstalt, 1966), 15–31, 97–110.

[37] A. H. Francke, *Manuductio*, 36–37, 61.   [38] A. H. Francke, *Manuductio*, 61–71.

[39] 1 Phil 1:9–10 (New Revised Standard Version); Paul, Letter to the Philippians, in *The Greek New Testament*, ed. K. Aland et al. (Stuttgart: Württemberg Bible Society, 1966), 1:9–10: "ἵνα ἡ ἀγάπη ὑμῶν ἔτι μᾶλλον καὶ μᾶλλον περισσεύῃ ἐν ἐπιγνώσει καὶ πάσῃ αἰσθήσει, εἰς τὸ δοκιμάζειν ὑμᾶς τὰ διαφέροντα" Francke reproduces Paul's pairing as "σολιδα ... ἐπιγνώσει, αἰσθήσει" in his *Manuductio*, 92. Martin Luther's translation, as published by Francke in 1714, reads: "daß eure liebe je mehr und mehr reich werde in allerley erkäntniß und erfahrung, Daß ihr prüfen möget, was das beste sey."

for many centuries before Francke's birth, and descriptions of the word's meaning in this context were easily available to him. Francke found in the *Philologia Sacra* (Sacred philology) of the seventeenth-century Lutheran theologian Salomon Glassius (1593–1656), for example, an explication of *aisthēsis* as "the internal experience of the soul, or the internal testimony of the Holy Spirit in the heart, about God's grace and election to salvation [*experientia interior animae seu interius Spiritus sancti in corde testimonium, de gratia Dei, & adoptione ad salutem*]."[40] Both elements of this description – the "internal experience" and the "testimony of the Holy Spirit" – were central to Francke's understanding of the word.

On Francke's account, *aisthēsis* is what allows someone to perceive the affections of a sanctified soul, and therefore the affections of the sanctified people whose words are recorded in the Bible. It is not available to everyone. The only people who seriously strive to attain *aisthēsis* and are capable of it, according to Francke, are those people who have themselves been "reborn" (*rennatus* or, more familiarly in German, *wiedergeboren*), and who have therefore had personal experience of the "*habitus* of a soul that has been sanctified and endowed with divine wisdom."[41] This *habitus*, in fact, is the essential distinguishing mark of rebirth. It is the predominance of "spiritual" (*spiritualis*) over "natural" (*naturalis*) affections. Humility, serenity, love of God, and a desire to seek God's glory and the edification of mankind, for example, outweigh the perversely self-interested, turbulent desire for one's own private pleasure.[42] This experience of moral reform among the reborn is the precondition of *aisthēsis*.

According to Francke, *aisthēsis* and what it makes possible – i.e., the perception of the affections of a sanctified soul – are important because they allow a reader of the Bible to understand not only the literal meaning of the text, the so-called shell (*cortex* or *Schale*), but also the spiritual truths contained in the text, the so-called kernel (*nucleus* or *Kern*).[43] That the literal meaning cannot be understood reliably without *aisthēsis* follows in part from two key premises. The first of these premises is drawn from the very nature of all verbal discourse: affections are what cause people

---

[40] S. Glassius, *Philologia Sacra* (Leipzig, 1705), 1809. The description of *aisthēsis* and its cognates is to be found in the context of a discussion of "metaphors that are derived from and refer to the human being," under the heading *Rhetorica Sacra*. Cf. G. Pasor, *Lexicon Graeco-Latinum In Novum Domini Nostri Jesu Christi Testamentum* (Leipzig, 1686), s.v. "*aisthēsis*." On Glassius's importance for Francke: C.-W. Kang, *Frömmigkeit und Gelehrsamkeit* (Basel: Brunnen, 2001), 335.

[41] A. H. Francke, *Manuductio*, 91–92: "illum animae sanctificatae & sapientia divina donatae habitum."

[42] A. H. Francke, *Manuductio*, 93–94.   [43] A. H. Francke, *Manuductio*, 88.

to make statements in the first place, and they are inseparable from language and its meaning.[44] "Everyday experience in familiar discourse," Francke writes, "testifies... how the same words, uttered differently on account of a different affection, differ in meaning."[45] One must therefore perceive the affections of a writer or speaker in order to say with confidence what the writer or speaker intended his or her words to mean.[46] The second premise is that the human authors of the words recorded in the Bible indeed had affections like those of the reborn, such that the reborn can apply an understanding of the authors' affections, derived from their own experience, to the interpretation of the authors' words.

That a biblical passage's spiritual meaning, too, can only be grasped by means of *aisthēsis* follows not only from these two premises but also from Francke's view of what it means to grasp the spiritual truth of a text. In the important case of interpreting the divine commandments, grasping the spiritual truth means not only identifying a precept issued by God and being able to apply it to oneself but also being able to understand and strive more fully to attain the spiritual *habitus* to which the precept ultimately refers. Francke's final exhortation in the *Delineatio* summarizes this thought as it applies to biblical interpretation in general:

> Rule XI: *And so, in examining affections, we profit most of all by an imitation and pious emulation of those affections that we have perceived in the holy authors.*
>
> For the more we adopt the same affection, the more skillfully and deeply we will be able to seek it, assess it, and show it in the holy texts. And so whenever an affection of the holy authors presents itself to us, let us diligently try under the same circumstances to obtain the same affection in ourselves, and indeed the same degree of the affection, if possible; and let us try, with the help of God's grace, to correct every faulty [affection] we have discovered. The meaning of scripture, grasped in this way by the heart rather than the head, will penetrate to the very marrow of our bones, and will transform our souls "from glory to glory,"[47] and we will experience truly that the word of God is effective [*efficacem*], and sharper than any two-edged sword, piercing all the way to the division of mind and spirit, of

---

[44] A. H. Francke, *Manuductio*, 88.

[45] A. H. Francke, *Manuductio*, 66:

> Testis etiam est quotidiana in familiari sermone experientia, quantum pondus addat, ad recte comprehendum sensum dicentis, affectus, & quam varium eadem verba, diversimode ob diversum affectum pronunciata, sortiantur sensum.

[46] C.f. A. H. Francke, *Einleitung zur Lesung Heiliger Schrift*, in *Schriften zur biblischen Hermeneutik* I, ed. E. Peschke, 141.

[47] II Cor 3:18.

joints and marrow, and that it discerns the thoughts and intentions of the heart.[48]

On Francke's account, grasping the spiritual truth of a biblical text means being morally transformed by the text, not only on the superficial level of behavior, but on the deeper level of one's own affections. To be sure, experience of spiritual affections on the part of the reader is a precondition of grasping the spiritual meaning of the text, but it is also the result. Recognizing the spiritual affections of the holy authors is the indispensable means of further strengthening those affections in oneself by a process of imitation, at the expense of the "faulty" natural affections that they outweigh. Implicit in Francke's hermeneutic discussion of *aisthēsis*, therefore, is a theory of moral education.

References to this theory can be found throughout Francke's published discussions of pedagogy, which themselves indicate how deeply it informed the design of the educational institutions he developed and administered. In his *Kurzer und einfältiger Unterricht wie die Kinder zur wahren Gottseligkeit und Christlichen Klugheit anzuführen sind* (Short and simple instruction in how to lead children to true godliness and Christian prudence), a pedagogical manual used by teachers in Francke's schools, Francke describes the purpose of education as *cultura animi* or *Gemüths-Pflege*: the cultivation of the child's soul, such that the child comes to love God and therefore makes honoring God its highest, overriding aim.[49] This process necessarily involves training both the will and the intellect,[50] and Francke's account of how the will should be trained recalls unmistakably his biblical hermeneutic theory. More important than any other means of

---

[48] A. H. Francke, *Manuductio*, 98:

> Reg. XI. *Tandem in scrutinio affectuum potissimum proficimus imitatione, piaque aemulatione eorum, quos in Scriptoribus S. semel perspexerimus affectuum.* Quo enim magis eundem induerimus affectuum, eo solertius, ac profundius eum in Textibus sacris rimari, perpendere, ac demonstrare poterimus. Quoties itaque affectus se nobis sistet Scriptorum S. toties posito vel ficto eodem casu, eundem in nobis ipsis affectum, imo eundem affectus gradum, quoad ejus fieri potest studiose quaeramus, deprehensumque defectum per gratiam DEi auxiliatricem corrigere studeamus. Sic Scripturae sensus, corde potius quam cerebro comprehensus, ad medullas usque ossium penetrabit, nostramque animam transformabit ἀπὸ δόξης εἰς δόξαν, & revera experiemur, sermonem DEi esse efficacem, & penetrantiorem quovis gladio, utrinque incidente, ac pertingente usque ad divisionem animae simul ac Spiritus; compagumque ac medullarum, & discretorem cogitationum & intentionum cordis.

[49] A. H. Francke, *Kurzer und einfältiger Unterricht wie die Kinder zur wahren Gottseligkeit und Christlichen Klugheit anzuführen sind* (Halle, 1733), 5; Menck, *Die Erziehung der Jugend*, 99–102.

[50] A. H. Francke, *Kurzer und einfältiger Unterricht*, 5.

producing love of God in children of a tender age, Francke repeatedly stresses, is the power of a good example.[51] By presenting himself as virtuous, and as possessed of a genuine love of God as a result of having already experienced the conversion (*Bekehrung*) that he aims to induce in his pupils, the teacher will awaken in them a similar love and an attraction to virtue. The reason for this, Francke explains, lies primarily in the psychology of young children: they remember and imitate virtually everything they see and hear.[52] Moreover, even though what they imitate is merely behavior, and therefore "external," when the behavior is genuinely good the children "will thereby be inculcated, unconsciously, with a *love* of virtuous behavior."[53] Francke does add that teachers should accompany their presentation of examples with clear and distinct explanations of what exactly is meant to be exemplary, but the means by which the imitation of virtuous behavior produces love of virtuous behavior is below the level of the child's consciousness and does not itself involve the intellect.

Although Francke does not describe this psychological mechanism with great precision, his repeated stress on the importance of sensory impressions, "external" *habitus*-formation, and imitation as a means of awakening love of virtue and love of God helps to fill in some of the details. He recommends, for example, that teachers "paint the virtues and vices with lifelike [*lebendig*] colors," adding that the "heathens" considered this "a good way to awaken virtue and to pull people away from vices."[54] In the supremely important case of presenting children with the perfect model of virtue, Jesus Christ, this means presenting him frequently (*öfters*), movingly (*beweglich*), and with love and gentleness (*Liebe und Sanftmuth*), so that the children "acquire a longing to always carry in their memory and their heart the perfect picture of the lord Jesus – how he was made for their wisdom, justice, sanctification, and salvation."[55] The origin of the love of God that this longing represents is ultimately, it would seem, the child's experience of God's love, evoked by the teacher's portrayal of it in a lifelike way.[56]

---

[51] A. H. Francke, *Kurzer und einfältiger Unterricht*, 6–7. Cf. Fritz Osterwalder's suggestively similar summary of the pedagogical writings of Fénelon: F. Osterwalder, "Theologische Konzepte von Erziehung. Das Verhältnis von Fénelon und Francke," in *Das Kind im Pietismus und Aufklärung*, ed. J. N. Neumann and U. Sträter (Tübingen: Niemeyer, 2000), 84.

[52] A. H. Francke, *Kurzer und einfältiger Unterricht*, 55.

[53] A. H. Francke, *Kurzer und einfältiger Unterricht*, 8 [emphasis added].

[54] A. H. Francke, *Kurzer und einfältiger Unterricht*, 25 (cf. 4).

[55] A. H. Francke, *Kurzer und einfältiger Unterricht*, 19–20.

[56] This is Peter Menck's conclusion about the psychological mechanism on which Francke's based his educational theory. Menck, *Die Erziehung der Jugend*, 101–2.

Francke did not accord experience this kind of power only in the case of young children. In one of his "exhortatory lectures" (*lectiones paraeneticae*), a long series of presentations to Halle's theology students during the weekly seminars that Francke and his colleague Breithaupt developed for the purpose of fostering the students' own conversion and thereby aiding their theological training, Francke makes the importance of experience as a pedagogical instrument particularly clear.[57] Having just read aloud from one theology student's written account of his own struggle against temptation and his quest to increase his love of God, Francke explains why, in order to comfort and instruct those in the room who have had similar experiences, he has quoted the student instead of retelling the story in his own words:

> It is the case, as the moralists are careful to remind us, that when one describes the signs of virtues and vices as they express themselves, one can present the thing much more vividly, than when one gives mere definitions. In the same way, when a temptation like this, a struggle like this that happens within one's heart, is described by means of the experience of the person who feels it, it imprints itself better and is also more instructive than when one says a lot of abstract things about it and describes it this way or that.[58]

Conveying the felt experiences of a particular person rather than describing those experiences in the abstract, in Francke's view, has the same benefit as describing the characteristics of people with particular virtues and vices rather than describing those virtues and vices in the abstract. Because the thing to be conveyed is presented vividly, in the form of a lifelike example to which the listener's own similar experiences allow him to relate, it imprints itself more deeply into the listener's character and can thereby have a more salutary effect on his affections. In other words, Francke conceives of the good teacher as making use of a psychological mechanism much like the one by means of which the inspired authors of the Bible communicate spiritual truths to reborn readers capable of *aisthēsis*.

---

[57] A. H. Francke, *Lectiones paraeneticae*, v. 1, 2nd ed. (Halle, 1730), Vorrede.
[58] A. H. Francke, *Lectiones paraeneticae*, I.271–72:

> Es ist damit so beschaffen, wie die Moralisten gar wohl zu erinnern pflegen, daß wenn man die characteres virtutum & vitiorum beschriebe, wie sie sich äusserten, man die Sache viel lebhafter vorstellen könne, als wenn man blosse definitiones davon gebe. So ist es darinnen auch, wenn eine solche Anfechtung, ein solcher Kampf, der im Gemüthe vorgehet, mit der eigenen Ehrfahrung dessen, der sie empfindet, beschrieben wird, so dringets besser ein, und ist auch lehrreicher, als wenn man sonst gleich vieles in abstracto davon redet, und es so oder so beschreibet.

Unsurprisingly, Francke's conception of a moral education that engages the lower cognitive faculties in a character-transforming quest for *aisthēsis* looks more like Johann Liborius Zimmermann's and Johann Franz Buddeus's moral-educational theories than like Christian Wolff's. It fits seamlessly into the tripartite schema articulated by Buddeus and later adopted by Zimmermann, occupying that middle phase in which the Christian who has come to recognize his own inability to obey divine law with the help of philosophy alone therefore turns to meditation on the Bible and a new regimen of sensory exercises in the hope of healing his diseased soul with the help of the Holy Spirit. Like Francke, and following Salomon Glassius explicitly, Buddeus called the culmination of this process, the experience of the Holy Spirit, *aisthēsis*.[59] *Aisthēsis* was, in other words, precisely the "living cognition" that Zimmermann and Buddeus considered the aim of moral education.

Nor were Buddeus and Zimmermann Francke's only sympathizers on this point. A conception of moral education like Francke's appears to have been common currency among a large group of theologians befriended with Francke, sympathetic to Halle Pietism, and sensitive to the marked quality of the term *aisthēsis*. Joachim Lange, who had been Francke's student in Leipzig in the 1670s and 1680s before joining him on the Halle Theology Faculty, emphasized the importance of *aisthēsis* – which he called "spiritual taste" (*gustus spiritualis*) – in his own *Medicina mentis* (Medicine for the mind), a pedagogical manual that found use in Francke's schools.[60] Francke also found an ally in another former student and colleague on the Theology Faculty, Johann Jakob Rambach, who essentially endorsed Francke's views in two well-known textbooks on hermeneutics.[61] For Rambach, as for Francke, "perception of affections is necessary for an accurate

---

[59] Buddeus, *Institutiones theologiae moralis*, I.prolegomena.§§8–9; Buddeus, *Einleitung in die Moral-Theologie*, I.Vorbericht.§§8–9. On Buddeus's moral-educational theory, see above, Chapter 1, pp. 41–44.

[60] J. Lange, *Medicina mentis* (Berlin, 1704), II.3.§37.

[61] J. J. Rambach, *Institutiones hermeneuticae sacrae* (Jena, 1723); and J. J. Rambach, *Erläuterung über seine eigene Institutiones hermeneuticae sacrae*, ed. E. F. Neubauer (Giessen, 1738). Rambach's relationship with Francke was close. Born in Halle in 1693, he attended Francke's orphanage schools from 1708 to 1712 and then enrolled as a theology student at the University of Halle until 1715, where he is attested to have studied hermeneutics with Francke. After working on a new edition of the Hebrew Bible with Francke's colleague in the Halle Theology Faculty, Johann Heinrich Michaelis, he spent two years studying in Jena and then returned to Halle in 1723 to take up an adjunct position in the Halle Theology Faculty and an inspectorship at Francke's schools. Upon Francke's death in 1727, Rambach became *ordinarius* professor of theology, leaving Halle again in 1731 to take up a professorship in Giessen. Zedler, *Universal-Lexicon*, s.v. "Rambach, (Joh. Jac.)"; F. W. Strieder, *Grundlage zu einer hessischen Gelehrten-und-Schriftsteller-Geschichte*, v. 2 (Hessen, 1797; repr., *DBA*), s.v. "Rambach, Johann Jacob."

interpretation," and "no sane person can think that affection is absent from the style of sacred [authors]."[62] Affections, Rambach explains, are "the soul of discourse" (*anima sermonis*), the transmission of which allows readers to benefit fully from the words of biblical authors, such that the words "fill[] our own hearts with good and holy affections."[63] Like Francke, Rambach calls the capacity to perceive these affections *aisthēsis*, which he translates as "spiritual sensation" (*geistliche Empfindung*) and ascribes exclusively to the reborn.[64]

Divine Inspiration and Sacred Poetry

Francke's conception of divine communication and moral education through the arousal of human affections, stressing the indispensability of *aisthēsis*, was clearly controversial, and not only insofar as it became a central component in the Pietist critiques of Wolff in the 1720s and 1730s. Already in the 1690s, when Francke's *Manuductio* and *Delineatio* first appeared, it underlay Francke and his sympathizers' self-definition as "Pietist" reformers of a church mired in the "sterility" and "Scholasticism" of what has come to be known as Lutheran late orthodoxy.[65] By the 1720s, after nearly three decades of quarreling between Pietists and their Lutheran critics, the fundamental doctrinal disagreements had come into sharp focus. One of these disagreements, and the source of many others, concerned the nature, origins, and effects of faith or *Glaube*. The Pietists' insistence that faith be understood as an inner renewal of the human soul, produced by the effect of the Holy Spirit inhabiting the individual reader of God's word and experienced by that individual as rebirth, stood in stark contrast to late orthodoxy's teaching that faith constitutes publicly confessed assent to sound doctrine and is prompted simply by hearing God's word and receiving the sacraments.[66] An extended quarrel in the 1710s

---

[62] Rambach, *Institutiones*, 123; Rambach, *Erläuterung*, 381.
[63] Rambach, *Erläuterung*, 377–78. Cf. A. Bühler and L. Cataldi Madonna, "Von Thomasius bis Semler. Entwicklungslinien der Hermeneutik in Halle," in *Hermeneutik der Aufklärung*, ed. A. Bühler and L. Cataldi Madonna (Hamburg: Meiner, 1993), 58–59.
[64] Rambach, *Erläuterung*, 388–89.
[65] On the meaning of this concept: J. Wallmann, "Pietismus und Orthodoxie. Überlegungen und Fragen zur Pietismusforschung," in *Pietismus-Studien: Gesammelte Aufsätze*, v. 2, by J. Wallmann (Tübingen: Mohr Siebeck, 2008).
[66] How much weight to ascribe to particular teachings in distinguishing Pietism from late orthodoxy has long been a matter of scholarly dispute – on which, see Wallmann, "Pietismus und Orthodoxie." My formulation leans on S. Lodewigs, *Der Pietismus im Spiegel seiner theologischen Kritiker*, PhD diss. (Göttingen, 1972), esp. 172–73. My thanks to Christian Soboth for recommending Lodewigs' work.

between Joachim Lange and the Wittenberg theologian and defender of late orthodoxy *par excellence*, Valentin Ernst Löscher (1674–1749), revealed that the central question, simply put, was how to understand Luther's well-known teaching that God's word alone is the means of salvation. The point of conflict was what both parties referred to as the doctrine of "illumination" and recognized as the "center" of Halle Pietist theology."[67] Whereas Löscher insisted that God's word illuminates the minds of all human readers, even impious ones, Lange defended Francke's *aisthēsis*-oriented hermeneutic and moral-educational ideas, arguing that illumination comes only to reborn readers who can see the spiritual meaning beneath the letter of the text.[68] This debate and the various subsidiary questions it raised – especially about the nature of divine inspiration, about how best to defend the Bible's status as a divinely inspired text, and about the educational value of poetic language – persisted for decades, even after Francke's death in 1727 left Lange and Rambach the most prominent defenders of his positions.[69]

One point at issue was the nature of divine inspiration or *theopneustia*, and more specifically whether God's direct communication with prophets through inspiration by the Holy Spirit involved a dampening of the prophets' human affections. The centrality of this question becomes clear when one considers two objections to Francke's position, dealt with explicitly and at length both by Francke in 1693 and by Rambach decades later.[70] The first objection, as Francke puts it, is that "one who attributed affections to the divinely inspired authors . . . would be doing an injustice to the Holy Spirit, since the holy scripture must be credited not to the holy authors, but to the Holy Spirit, speaking through their mouth[s]."[71] The alleged danger, Rambach explains, is that attributing affections to human authors of

---

[67] J. G. Walch, *Historische und Theologische Einleitung in die Religionsstreitigkeiten der Evangelisch-Lutherischen Kirche*, v. 2 (Jena, 1730), §§53, 253.

[68] Greschat, *Zwischen Tradition und neuem Anfang*, 262–78.

[69] Contemporary dissertations taking a position on the controversy included Johann Georg Pritius, *De renatorum experientia spirituali* (Jena, 1723), as described by E. Koch in "*De Theologia experimentali*. Akademische Diskurse um 1700 in Leipzig, Halle und Wittenberg," in *"Aus Gottes Wort und eigener Erfahrung gezeigt": Erfahrung – Glauben, Erkennen und Handeln im Pietismus. Beiträge zum III. Internationalen Kongress für Pietismusforschung*, ed. Christian Soboth and Udo Sträter (Halle: Franckesche Stiftungen, 2012).

[70] Cf. Peschke, *Studien zur Theologie August Hermann Franckes*, II.97–100; J. Dyck, *Athen und Jerusalem* (Munich: Beck, 1977), esp. 114–22.

[71] A. H. Francke, *Manuductio*, 90:

> Existimare aliquis posset, illum fore in ipsum Spiritum S. injurium, qui Scriptoribus θεοπνεύστοις sive ex afflatu divino scribentibus affectus tribuerit; neque enim Scripturam S. esse Scriptoribus S. sed Spiritui S. per ipsorum os loquenti acceptam ferendam.

scripture excludes the possibility that those authors were inspired, because inspiration necessarily involves the suppression of human affections by the Holy Spirit. To this objection, Francke and Rambach give similar answers: the inspired authors clearly did not write the biblical texts "like blocks, without sense or *aisthēsis*."[72] To the contrary, the Holy Spirit should be seen not only as having illuminated the intellects of the holy authors but also as having stirred up their wills "with pious, holy, and ardent emotions [*motibus*]";[73] having been at work in their "phantasy, intellect, and will";[74] and having "accommodated" itself to their human mental characteristics – including their individual temperaments and their characteristically human inability to grasp any representation of God as a pure essence.[75]

A second objection, according to Francke and Rambach, was that looking to the affections of scriptural authors as the key to the meaning of their words renders those words ambiguous and their meaning uncertain, such that a reader can derive from them whatever meaning he or she may want.[76] The alleged danger again appears to be that assuming the language of biblical authors to be laden with affections excludes the possibility that it is inspired, since inspired words must by their nature be unambiguous, and affection-laden words are not. To this objection, Francke and Rambach offer a simple rebuttal: it is simply a fact, verifiable by our experience with everyday language, that the meaning of an utterance depends on the affections of the utterer. Paying attention to those affections is therefore the only way to eliminate ambiguity and uncertainty.[77]

Francke's and Rambach's controversial insistence on the importance of perceiving and imitating the affections of divinely inspired biblical authors as a means of moral improvement implied a similarly controversial defense of poetry as a verbal means of communicating divine truths and improving the affections of a reader or listener. The character of this defense is hinted at in a slim booklet of poems and poetic fragments by Martin Luther, published in Magdeburg in 1729 by Johann Justus von Einem (b. 1685), who had studied biblical hermeneutics and rhetoric under Francke between 1706 and 1708.[78] In defense of reading and writing poetry as activities

---

[72] A. H. Francke, *Manuductio*, 90. Rambach writes, "completely without *Empfindung*." Rambach, *Erläuterung*, 378.

[73] A. H. Francke, *Manuductio*, 90.   [74] Rambach, *Erläuterung*, 377.

[75] Rambach, *Erläuterung*, 377, 389, 411.

[76] A. H. Francke, *Manuductio*, 90; Rambach, *Erläuterung*, 378.

[77] A. H. Francke, *Manuductio*, 90; Rambach, *Erläuterung*, 374–9.

[78] Einem dedicates the book to Francke's and Rambach's colleague on the Halle Theology Faculty, Joachim Justus Breithaupt ("easily the prince, father, patron, and instructor of the poets of this age"), whose lectures on dogmatics and morals (*Grundsätze der Glaubens- und Sittenlehre*) Einem

worthy of a holy person, Einem asserts that Luther himself took delight in reading ancient poets, whose style he compared to the style of holy scripture. Luther moreover claimed to have found the poetic passages of scripture – in the Psalms, above all – much more moving than the prosaic ones. In withdrawing to the monastery in Erfurt, Einem claims, Luther left behind all his books, even his books on law, with a single exception: the poetry of Vergil. Vergil's affections, Luther thought, had come "not from nature or the vulgar tribe of the Muses, but rather as a gift of the spirit, imbued by Jesus Christ."[79] Einem's characterization of Luther as an admirable poet and great lover of poetry of course implied that poetry should not be condemned outright as the product of inspiration by the Muses, or as the product of no inspiration at all, but rather ought to be admired as – at least in some cases – a gift of the Holy Spirit, capable of moving human beings in a salutary way.

This view found more elaborate and explicit articulation in Rambach's preface to *Poetische Fest-Gedancken von den höchsten Wohlthaten Gottes* (Poetic thoughts in celebration of God's supreme benefactions), a collection of his own spiritual poetry published in 1727, two years before Einem's booklet. In discussing the "abuse and correct use of poetry," Rambach condemns at great length and in no uncertain terms all poetry that is used as an instrument of "carnal desire, love of honor, and love of money" (*Wohllust, Ehrgeiz, und Geldgeiz*), singling out for special attention the poems of Anacreon, Ovid, Catullus, Tibullus, and Propertius, for undermining their readers' chastity, modesty, and fear of God.[80] The danger of such poems arises, according to Rambach, by virtue of the mechanism by which words exert power over the character of their readers: they awaken feelings by causing the reader to imagine the things to which the words refer, and the more frequently one imagines things that arouse a particular desire, the deeper such desire impresses itself into the reader's heart.[81] Dangerous poems describe "things that violate the purity of one's character" by arousing a "fleshly desire for pleasure."[82]

But poetry itself was not to be simply condemned. An avid poet himself and admiring student of the master of erotic spiritual and secular poetry in

---

is said to have heard during his years in Halle, and whom Alexander Baumgarten is also attested to have heard. J. A. Trinius, *Beytrag zu einer Geschichte berühmter und verdienter Gottesgelehrten auf dem Lande*, v. 1 (Mansfeld, 1751; repr., *DBA*), s.v. "Einem, Johann Justus von"; J. J. von Einem, *Martini Lutheri poemata* (Magdeburg, 1729), Vorrede; Meier, *Alexander Baumgartens Leben*, 10.

[79] Einem, *Martini Lutheri poemata*, Vorrede.
[80] J. J. Rambach, *Poetische Fest-Gedancken* (Jena, 1727), Vorrede, §§1–3.
[81] Rambach, *Poetische Fest-Gedancken*, Vorrede, §6.
[82] Rambach, *Poetische Fest-Gedancken*, Vorrede, §6.

early-eighteenth-century Halle, Christian Hunold (1681–1721),[83] Rambach happily called poetry a "noble gift of the Highest One" (*eine edle Gabe des Höchsten*), capable of being used as an instrument for improving the reader's character as well. It must be written

> to honor God; to celebrate his boundless perfections, his most lovable qualities, his venerable majesty, which the prophets describe in a style so sublime that the reader cannot but be overcome by spiritual trembling.[84]

The effect on readers of poems that fulfill these conditions, is that

> their hearts can be awakened to reverence for God, to love of Jesus Christ, to understanding of the creator, to perception of their own insignificance, to longing for His holy community, and to holy conduct and godly life.[85]

Poetry, for Rambach, was an instrument of moral education, usable at all stages of a Christian's progress from worldliness to faith, whose effectiveness derived from its power to awaken spiritual affections in its readers by means of a sublime style, much like the power of the affection-laden words uttered by the divinely inspired human authors of the Bible.[86]

Baumgarten's Defense of Divine Inspiration

Alexander Baumgarten's enlistment in Francke's and Rambach's constellation of controversial arguments marked by the polarizing term *aisthēsis* – above all, their arguments that the Holy Spirit elevated rather than suppressed the affections of the Bible's human authors, that this regenerated moral *habitus* constituted the spiritual truth communicated by those authors' words, and that poetry should therefore be regarded as a suitable means of divine communication – is suggested by a plethora of evidence.

---

[83] W. Miersemann, "Ein 'Liebes-Poet' als geistlicher Dichter: Zu dem Menantes-Gedicht 'Bey Betrachtung der Liebe Gottes,'" in *Menantes: Ein Dichterleben zwischen Barock und Aufklärung*, ed. C. Hobohn (Jena: Quartus, 2006).

[84] Rambach, *Poetische Fest-Gedancken*, Vorrede, §11:

> zur Ehre GOttes, zur Besingung seiner unendlichen Vollkommenheiten, seiner liebenswürdigsten Eigenschaften, seiner anzubetenden Majestät (deren Beschreibung die Propheten mit einer so erhabenen Schreibart verrichten, daß dem Leser dabey ein heiliger Schauer überfallen muß).

[85] Rambach, *Poetische Fest-Gedancken*, Vorrede, §11:

> daß ihre Herzen dadurch zur Ehrfurcht vor GOtt, zur Liebe JEsu Christi, zum Lobe des Schöpfers, zur Erkäntniß ihrer Nichtigkeit, zum Verlangen nach seiner seligen Gemeinschaft, zum heiligen Wandel und gottseligen Leben erwecket werden können.

[86] For elaboration on this point, see Fritz, *Vom Erhabenen*, esp. 240–43.

By the time he wrote his *Meditationes*, Baumgarten was certainly acquainted with the issues, since he had encountered the key texts by Francke, Rambach, and others during his years as a student in Halle. All students in Francke's Latin School – attended by Baumgarten from 1727 to 1730 – were required to read Francke's German introduction to reading the Bible, in which the *Manuductio* is explicitly mentioned.[87] Baumgarten probably acquired detailed knowledge of Rambach from lectures by Christian Benedict Michaelis, *ordinarius* professor in the Faculties of Theology and Philosophy at Halle, friend of Francke's, and a respected philologist who taught biblical languages and biblical interpretation to two generations of theology students.[88] Between 1731 and 1732, Michaelis taught hermeneutics from Rambach's textbook.[89] Baumgarten's other source, of course, was his older brother, Siegmund Jacob, who had himself studied theology with Rambach and Michaelis, and who lectured on Rambach's textbook in 1735.[90] In his own hermeneutics textbook of 1745, he recommends reading Francke's *Manuductio* and parts of Rambach's textbook.[91]

Baumgarten's enlistment in these projects, above and beyond mere acquaintance with them, can be inferred from his involvement in another, larger polemical effort, well under way in Halle by the 1730s, of which Francke's and Rambach's controversial hermeneutic and moral-educational theories were one support among many. Neither merely indicative of an intra-Lutheran quarrel nor primarily an instrument of Pietist self-definition, this larger polemical effort aimed at proving that the authors of biblical texts were divinely inspired at all. Its connection with the controversy over affection-laden divine communication finds a particularly vivid illustration in hermeneutical writings by Baumgarten's brother, Siegmund Jacob. According to Siegmund Jacob Baumgarten, many passages in the Bible appeared to make no sense to any reader who did not keep in mind that divine inspiration had put the human authors of those passages in a

---

[87] *Album scholae latinae* (1712–29), AFSt /S L2, fols. 331–32; Freylinghausen and G. A. Francke, *Ausführlicher Bericht von der Lateinischen Schule des Wäysenhauses yu Glaucha vor Halle zum Dienst derer die Nachfrage zu tun pflegen* (Halle, 1736), 97–99; A. H. Francke, *Einleitung zur Lesung Heiliger Schrift*, 133.

[88] Baumgarten is attested to have attended his lectures between 1730 and 1735. Meier, *Alexander Gottlieb Baumgartens Leben*, 10. On Michaelis's relationship to Nicolaus Hieronymus Gundling, see above, p. 48.

[89] *Catalogus lectionum aestivalium* (Halle, April 1732).

[90] Meier, *Alexander Gottlieb Baumgartens Leben*, 11; *Index acroasium ex omni scientiarum et disciplinarum bonarum genere* (Halle, September 1735).

[91] S. J. Baumgarten, *Unterricht von Auslegung der heiligen Schrift* (Halle, 1742), 3.

state of "strong, sensate emotion" (*starke sinnliche Gemüthsbewegung*). This included passages where

> general truths are uttered in a very concrete [*sinnlich*] way; . . . fully equivalent or at least very similar and interchangeable expressions are repeated; . . . absent people and even unthinking and lifeless objects are spoken to; . . . short, broken-off sentences and comments appear; . . . dedicatory words appear, which the context and the completeness of the meaning didn't call for; . . . the discussion is interrupted by interpolated ideas that are not relevant to the comprehensibility of the things being discussed . . .

and so on.[92] The danger, it seems, was that the divine inspiration of biblical authors could be called into question if apparently senseless or internally contradictory passages could not be proven to be suitable products of divinely inspired authorship. The occasional presence of unsuitably affection-laden language was evidently one reason for this danger.

The immediate sources of the danger were of course those biblical critics, well known to modern students of Enlightenment religion, who had called the divine inspiration of the biblical authors into question along precisely these lines.[93] One of the most prominent, and the most relevant to an investigation of Alexander Baumgarten's role in the controversy, was the Genevan theologian and man of letters, Jean Le Clerc (1657–1736). In 1685, Le Clerc had published, in French, a critique of Richard Simon's (1638–1712) *Critical History of the Old Testament* in epistolary form.[94] In the eleventh and twelfth letters of the critique, published five years later in English as the first two chapters of Le Clerc's *Five Letters Concerning the Inspiration of the Holy Scriptures*, Le Clerc insists that the "sense" of biblical authors' words was perhaps in some cases inspired, in that God imparted to some prophets, for example, a "clear and distinct idea" about the future, but that the words themselves in most cases cannot have been God's. Even disregarding several biblical authors' explicit denials that the Holy Spirit dictated their texts word-for-word, Le Clerc explains, it is clear from the various contradictions in the historical books, the apparently haphazard

---

[92] S. J. Baumgarten, *Unterricht von Auslegung*, 47–48:

> von algemeinen Wahrheiten sehr sinlich geredet wird; . . . gantz einerley Ausdrucke oder doch sehr änliche und gleichgültige wiederholt werden; . . . sonderlich abwesende Personen auch wol unvernünftige und leblose Dinge angeredet werden; . . . kurtz abgebrochene Sätze und Reden vorkommen; . . . Zueignungsworte vorkommen, die der Zusammenhang und die Volständigkeit des Verstandes eben nicht erforderte; . . . die Rede durch eingeschaltete Vorstellungen unterbrochen wird, die zur Verständlichkeit der vorgetragenen Sachen nicht gehören. . . .

[93] As described in, e.g., J. Sheehan, *The Enlightenment Bible* (Princeton, NJ: Princeton University Press, 2005), 1–53.

[94] S. L. Golden, *Jean LeClerc* (New York: Twayne, 1972), 31.

variations of vocabulary, and the vagueness about dates and numbers in general, that biblical authors' words were in most cases not the result of divine inspiration at all.[95]

Corresponding to Le Clerc's incredulity about the divine origins of most biblical words, it seems, was a presupposition that divinely inspired discourse must by its nature meet the standards to which Le Clerc thought human beings should aspire in their own use of language. One of the most important standards was "perspicuity of style."[96] In an essay on "True and False Eloquence," Le Clerc devotes ten pages to the discussion of the three canonical styles, but he virtually omits discussion of the "pleasing" and "sublime" styles, devoting far more space to describing and praising the "simple and proper style," which he appears to take as a model of perspicuity:

> The principal rock, which we ought to avoid in this simple and natural language is obscurity, and 'tis for that reason that we carefully shun everything that may produce it, as equivocal terms, too great plenty of figures, and an ill disposition of words and thoughts.[97]

Among the several dangers of deviating from a perspicuous style, according to Le Clerc, is the perpetuation of an ethical "disorder" that false eloquence tends to produce in the world. "[I]f the end of the discourse be to correct the faults of the readers and auditors," Le Clerc writes,

> the multitude of impertinent words, the weakness of the reasonings, and the [in?]judicious choice of the thoughts, produce but very sorry effects. As we are persuaded without knowing why or wherefore, and have no clear and continued principles to preserve ourselves from errour, and to regulate our conduct aright, our manners will infallibly derive an unhappy tincture from the disorder of our minds; we do good and evil without discerning them so distinctly as we ought to do, and our lives become a perpetual mixture of a little virtue and a great deal of vice. We know the general rules of good and evil confusedly, and we apply them almost by mere accident to the particular actions of life.[98]

Ethically effective eloquence, Le Clerc implies, ought to use a perspicuous style to convey "general rules of good and evil" such that they can be understood clearly and distinctly.

---

[95] [J. Le Clerc], *Five Letters Concerning the Inspiration of the Holy Scriptures* (London, 1690), 20–41.

[96] [J. Le Clerc], *Parrhasiana* (London, 1700), 79. In quotations from this anonymous translation, capitalization and most spelling without bearing on the meaning of the text have been silently modernized.

[97] [Le Clerc], *Parrhasiana*, 82.   [98] [Le Clerc], *Parrhasiana*, 65–66.

Le Clerc's reservations about poetry as an instrument of moral education therefore come as no surprise. While claiming to deny "that poets are altogether unuseful,"[99] Le Clerc nonetheless expresses caution at every turn: everything about a poem that creates "sensible pleasure" in its audience – its beautiful style, its power to arouse the passions, or the agreeable sounds of its words and cadence – blind the audience to all the "false thoughts" the poem contains.[100] Le Clerc moreover asserts that the intent of a poet to communicate a particular moral lesson by means of a poem cannot be reliably discerned from the poem itself. In his view,

> there never was any narration in the world from which some sort of a moral might not be deduced, altho' the author of it never dreamt of any such thing. . . . Therefore to be assured that any poet had a design to give us certain lessons, 'tis necessary that he should tell us so himself, or at least set it down in his writings after such a manner that no body cou'd doubt it.[101]

The effect of a poem on its reader's or listener's affections, in other words, is not a sufficient indicator of the moral truth that the poet wished to convey. Le Clerc's view is a far cry from the position of Francke and Rambach, who took the affections aroused by divinely inspired words as themselves an important "spiritual truth" and one of the indispensable indicators of the meaning of those words. Le Clerc's lack of interest in the sublime style and lack of confidence that poetry can be used for educational purposes, moreover, stands in contrast to Rambach's defense of poetry in his *Poetische Fest-Gedancken*.

Le Clerc's challenge to the divine inspiration of the bible's human authors was answered by none other than Alexander Baumgarten, under the direction of Christian Benedict Michaelis, an open critic of Le Clerc. In 1733, Michaelis had assigned an older classmate of Alexander's, Johann Christian Meisner, the task of writing a dissertation defending the authorship of Exodus 36 by Moses, whose authorship had been called into question by Spinoza, Richard Simon, and Le Clerc. The danger of allowing that some author later than Moses had inserted the chapter, Michaelis explained in a published review of Meisner's dissertation, was twofold. First, it made the exegesis of all the other chapters uncertain, by unsettling the conviction that Moses wrote the passages that had traditionally been ascribed to him. Moreover, it seemed to argue against the divine inspiration of the author of the chapter in question. In Michaelis's words, "How could a

99 [Le Clerc], *Parrhasiana*, 41.
100 [Le Clerc], *Parrhasiana*, 6–7, 9–10, 20–21.   101 [Le Clerc], *Parrhasiana*, 42–43.

God-driven man have inserted a new part into the laws of Moses without indicating its distinctness from Moses's own laws?"[102] Michaelis's defense of the divine inspiration of the biblical authors continued in 1735, when he assigned Alexander Baumgarten the task of "saving" a number of verbal expressions whose usage in Genesis had been criticized – by Le Clerc, among others – as chaotic, imprecise, and unbefitting an author inspired by a perfect God.[103] The result was Baumgarten's *Dissertatio chorographica* (Chorographic dissertation), a defense of biblical authors' use of the words *superus* and *inferus* ("above" and "below") as internally consistent rather than haphazard. The usage may appear haphazard to those interpreters who "scarcely blush at imputing the mark of invalidity [*akurologia*] to the style of the sacred book," Baumgarten explains, but this appearance of haphazardness is simply the result of the words' having been used in a variety of senses, corresponding to the various aspects of the things to which the words are attached; sometimes they refer to physical locations, sometimes to moral qualities, and sometimes the physical and the moral aspects are connected with each other.[104] Baumgarten presented this dissertation, apparently to great acclaim, six months before completing his *Meditationes*.[105]

In light of this context, it is difficult not to read between the lines of Baumgarten's *Meditationes* and find in it a purposeful defense of the Bible as a divinely inspired text.[106] Having already offered an explicit defense of the precision of the Bible's diction in his *Dissertatio chorographica*, Baumgarten now presents in the *Meditationes* implicit but direct reinforcement for the positions articulated by Francke and Rambach and challenged by Le Clerc: divine inspiration can and should produce affection-laden discourse, and poetry is a divinely sanctioned means of moral improvement. The strength of this reinforcement comes primarily from Baumgarten's argument that

---

[102] C. B. Michaelis, [Review of Meisner], *Wöchentliche Hallesche Anzeigen* XXXV (24 August 1733), 553–56.

[103] C. B. Michaelis, Review of *Dissertatio chorographica*, by A. G. Baumgarten, *Wöchentliche Hallesche Anzeigen* XI (14 March 1735), 166–71; XII (21 March 1735), 181–85.

[104] A. G. Baumgarten, *Dissertatio chorographica notiones* superi *et* inferi, *indeque adscensus et descensus in chorographiis sacris evolvens*, praes. C. B. Michaelis (Halle, 1735), in *Commentationes theologicae*, ed. J. C. Velthusen, C. T. Kuinoel, and G. A. Rupert (Leipzig, 1798), 401, 404–5.

[105] According to the records of the Philosophy Faculty at Halle, the text of Baumgarten's *Meditationes* was submitted to the faculty censor, Johann Heinrich Schulze, on 9 August 1735. Halle Universitätsarchiv, Rep. 21, III.261, fol. 74.

[106] Such a reading may also be justified by setting Baumgarten's *Meditationes* in the context of the contemporary controversy over the *Wertheim Bible*, as suggested in U. Goldenbaum, "Mendelssohn's Spinozistic Alternative to Baumgarten's Pietist Project of Aesthetics," in *Moses Mendelssohn's Metaphysics and Aesthetics*, ed. R. Munk (New York: Springer, 2011), 300. But see also below, Chapter 3, pp. 120–28.

a poem is capable of perfection, and that a poem is moreover perfect in proportion to its tendency to arouse affections in the mind of the reader through the presentation of indistinct ideas. The implicit conclusion is clear: using indistinct ideas to arouse affections also befits a perfect God, who would only use a perfect means of communication.[107]

Baumgarten himself suggests this conclusion at several points in the *Meditationes* where it becomes clear that his subject is not only poetry in general but also biblical poetry in particular. He describes miracles, for example, as well as prophetic predictions whose accuracy is verifiable (because the events they describe have already come to pass), as subjects that tend to contribute to the perfection of a poem.[108] Baumgarten's allusions to biblical stories and prophecies can hardly be accidental.[109] That God himself can be conceived as a poet is another of Baumgarten's implicit arguments for regarding poetry as divinely sanctioned. He describes the development of a poem's theme as similar to the creation of a world: the ideal ordering principle of representations in a poem corresponds to the order "in which things in the world follow one another, such that the glory of the Creator is revealed – the highest and ultimate theme of an immense poem, so to speak."[110] As if to endorse all these inferences by an attentive reader, Baumgarten offers near the end of his *Meditationes* a particularly explicit marker of his sympathy for Francke's and Rambach's positions: a reference to a 1710 dissertation written under the supervision of the Helmstedt theologian (and one-time teacher of Johann Justus von Einem) Johann Andreas Schmidt (1652–1726), entitled *De modo propagandi religionem per carmina* (On the method of propagating religion by means of poems).[111] The dissertation itself describes "poetic theology" as having flourished in various ancient communities, where poems were the standard vehicle of transmitting divine law and true religion before Moses.[112] Baumgarten invokes it as an authority for the claim that

---

[107] Cf. W.-L. Federlin, *Kirchliche Volksbildung und bürgerliche Gesellschaft* (New York: Lang, 1993), 89–91, although Federlin interprets these aspects of Baumgarten's text as implicitly critical of Pietist biblical hermeneutics. For an explicit corrective to parts of Federlin's position, see Grote, "Pietistische *Aisthesis*," esp. 176–77, 197.

[108] A. G. Baumgarten, *Meditationes*, §64.

[109] At any rate, Baumgarten's reason for including them cannot have been simply that they follow from his criteria of perfection in a poem, for he does not test every possible subject of a poem against those criteria – contra Strube, "Die Entstehung der Ästhetik als einer wissenschaftlichen Disziplin," 15.

[110] A. G. Baumgarten, *Meditationes*, §71, cf. §68.

[111] J. A. Schmidt, praes., *Dissertatio historico-theologica de modo propagandi religionem per carmina*, def. L. G. Gelhud (Helmstadt, 1710). A second edition of the dissertation appeared in 1728. Einem is attested to have studied under Schmidt in 1705. See Trinius, *Beytrag*, s.v. "Einem, Johann Justus von."

[112] Schmidt, *Dissertatio*, e.g., §§3, 5, 6, 9.

virtue and religion have been promoted for a very long time by means of fictional stories fashioned into poems.[113]

Probably the most persuasive confirmation that a defense of divine inspiration indeed lay just beneath the surface of Baumgarten's *Meditationes*, available to readers willing and able to draw theological inferences from an explicitly philosophical dissertation, can be found in the most extensive known record of Baumgarten's own theology: a series of lectures he began giving approximately a decade after the publication of his *Meditationes*, within the first eight years of his tenure as professor of philosophy in Frankfurt (Oder).[114] Originally presented by Baumgarten as a philosophical introduction to "thetic" (i.e., dogmatic) theology,[115] the lectures leave no doubt that in Baumgarten's view, aesthetic theory provided a powerful philosophical argument for considering the Bible divinely inspired. Subjecting scripture to aesthetic critique, he explained, reveals a degree of perfection so far beyond what contemporary ancient authors produced, that it cannot have been the effect of merely natural human ability and is very likely attributable to divine inspiration.[116] If this argument can be read back into the 1735 *Meditationes*, then in calling for the creation of an aesthetic philosophy whose purpose was to aid the lower cognitive faculties in attaining knowledge and perceiving truth,[117] Baumgarten must also have envisioned the discovery of rationally demonstrable criteria by which the affection-laden verbal expressions of the Bible's human authors – and the affection-laden mental state or "spiritual truth" communicated by those expressions – could be judged to be divinely inspired.

Anti-Stoic Resistance to Wolff

Baumgarten's call for an aesthetic theory that could buttress the Bible's status as a divinely inspired text reflected not only his enlistment in the

---

[113] A. G. Baumgarten, *Meditationes*, §58.

[114] A. G. Baumgarten, "Isagoge philosophica in theologiam theticam," taken down by J. G. Beneke, 3 v. [1748], Berliner Staatsbibliothek Ms theol. lat. Oct. 48; and A. G. Baumgarten, *Praelectiones theologiae dogmaticae*, ed. J. S. Semler (Halle, 1773). Beneke's text, ostensibly written in 1748, appears to be a fair copy of a set of student notes. A plethora of small but substantive discrepancies makes it difficult to know for certain whether Semler – who claimed to have made tacit editorial corrections to the single set of student notes on which he based his edition – was using Beneke's text or not. On the assumption that Beneke's 1748 text reflects Baumgarten's own words more closely than Semler's posthumously emended edition, I have relied primarily on Beneke.

[115] A. G. Baumgarten, "Isagoge philosophica," §§92–94.

[116] A. G. Baumgarten, "Isagoge philosophica," §41 and §§42–69. The criteria Baumgarten applies correspond directly to the criteria of aesthetic perfection in his *Aesthetics* – on which, see below, Chapter 3, p. 107.

[117] A. G. Baumgarten, *Meditationes*, §115.

multigenerational campaign by his Pietist teachers to repudiate biblical critics such as Jean Le Clerc but also his sympathy for their continuing concern that Christian Wolff's "Scholastic" program of moral education posed a threat to the foundation of morality. Here again, looking below the surface of the *Meditationes* offers a glimpse of Baumgarten's implicit position. In presenting affection-arousing poetry as a suitable means of divine communication, Baumgarten clearly presupposed, like Francke and Rambach, that moral education could and should engage the lower cognitive faculties and enlist rather than suppress the human affections. This presupposition in turn implied a deviation from Christian Wolff's view that moral education required suppressing the affections in favor of the rational appetite. That Baumgarten consciously deviated from Wolff in this way – and moreover that he envisioned aesthetic theory as a tool of moral education that could succeed where Wolff had failed – is of course hard to conclude from the text of the *Meditationes* alone. But it becomes more apparent in light of other texts produced in the 1730s and 1740s by fellow students and instructors in Halle, closely acquainted with Baumgarten, who voiced similar doubts about Wolff's program of moral education even as, like Baumgarten himself, they adopted Wolff's "mathematical method" as a model for philosophical argument and happily employed Wolff's technical vocabulary.

The closest to Baumgarten, of course, was his older brother. Siegmund Jacob Baumgarten, Alexander's mentor in Halle, was understood by many of his contemporaries to hold Wolff's philosophy in high regard, and this judgment has hardly been challenged since.[118] But behind Siegmund Jacob Baumgarten's obviously Wolffian terminology lay a view of moral education in many respects like Francke's. Moral education, Baumgarten explained in his textbook of moral theology, requires conversion (*Sinnesänderung* or *Bekehrung*), a process of transformation that Francke describes in his *Delineatio* as a replacement of carnal by spiritual desires. For Baumgarten, as for Francke, the man under the law is supernaturally transformed into the man under grace. By acquiring "living cognition" (*lebendige Erkenntnis*) of his own sinfulness, the man whose *habitus* of "observing the law as well as possible"[119] is merely pseudo-virtue (*Scheintugend*), motivated by an overbearing and disorderly self-love (*Eigenliebe*), is converted by

[118] Meier, *Alexander Gottlieb Baumgartens Leben*, 11; cf. M. Schloemann, *Siegmund Jacob Baumgarten* (Göttingen: Vandenhoeck und Ruprecht, 1974), esp. 66–79.

[119] S. J. Baumgarten, *Unterricht vom recht-mäßigen Verhalten eines Christen oder Theologische Moral* (Halle, 1744), 594.

divine grace into the man of genuine virtue (*Tugend*). The virtuous man's observance of divine law is motivated by "living cognition" of God: an "inclination of his character toward God, such that [he] takes God to be his God and his highest good, and expects his well-being to come from Him."[120]

In describing this process of transformation, Siegmund Jacob Baumgarten most obviously deviates from Wolff not only in the importance he places on recognizing one's own sinfulness but also in his repeated emphasis on the importance of indistinct ideas and the affections they produce. In Baumgarten's view, Paul indicated in his letter to the Philippians that increasing one's love of God requires *aisthēsis*, understood by Baumgarten literally as sensation (*Empfindung*) but metonymically as "all knowledge and experience gained from feeling and observation of one's sensations," be those sensations internal or external.[121] Clear and distinct knowledge that God is our highest good is useful and should certainly be striven for, Baumgarten grants, but the ultimate goal is to move the will, and for this purpose indistinct ideas need to be enlisted. In Baumgarten's words,

> the inner effect of God extends not only to distinct ideas, and therefore the higher powers of the soul, but also to indistinct and dark ones, which not only make the necessary impression of distinct perception onto the heart in the case of adults, but are also indispensable in the special case of children before they can use their reason.[122]

Here, Baumgarten uses terms recognizable from his brother's *Meditationes* to advance a position like Francke's and Rambach's. Whereas Francke and Rambach assert that God works on the will and arouses the emotions of the authors and prophets he inspires, and that spiritual truths must be grasped through sensation (*Empfindung*), Siegmund Jacob Baumgarten insists that God's "inner effect" on one's character ultimately works through indistinct and obscure ideas, graspable by the lower rather than the higher

---

[120] S. J. Baumgarten, *Unterricht vom recht-mäßigen Verhalten eines Christen*, 115–16: "Neigung des Gemüths gegen Gott, daß ein Mensch Gott für seinen Gott und höchstes Gut annimmt, und seine Wohlfahrt von demselben erwartet."

[121] S. J. Baumgarten, *Auslegung der Briefe Pauli an die Galater, Epheser, Philipper, Colosser, Philemon und Thessalonicher*, ed. J. S. Semler (Halle, 1767), 381–82.

[122] S. J. Baumgarten, *Unterricht vom recht-mäßigen Verhalten eines Christen*, 680 (cf. 118–19):

> Die innere Wirckung Gottes . . . [erstreckt] sich nicht nur auf deutliche Vorstellungen, und folglich obere Kräfte der Seele, sondern auch auf undeutliche und dunckele [Vorstellungen] . . . , die sowol bey erwachsenen Personen den nötigen Eindrück der deutlichen Erkentnis ins Gemüt verursachen, als sonderlich bey Kindern vor dem Gebrauch des Verstandes unentbehrlich sind.

cognitive faculties of the soul.[123] These lower faculties, therefore, need to be cultivated effectively.[124] In this sentiment, articulated by Siegmund Jacob Baumgarten in 1738 at the latest,[125] the echo of Alexander Baumgarten's call for an aesthetic philosophy to aid in the cultivation of those faculties is unmistakable.

A similar and still more striking resistance to Wolff's program of moral education can be observed in another acquaintance of Alexander Baumgarten's in Halle, Gottfried Profe (1712–70). One of many academically inclined classmates of Baumgarten's whose careers and writings have enjoyed – and perhaps deserved – far less attention from posterity than Baumgarten's own, the nearly forgotten Profe nonetheless warrants attention for the unusually direct glimpse he offers us into Baumgarten's immediate intellectual environment in the 1730s. The similarities between his and Baumgarten's biographies are uncanny. By turns simultaneously and in close succession, they spent several years in Francke's schools; enrolled as students of theology and philosophy at the University of Halle; attended lectures by the luminaries of Halle Pietism; grew interested in Christian Wolff; ventured to Jena to hear lectures by Wolff's supporters and opponents there, including Johann Georg Walch; returned to Halle and began teaching in Francke's schools; finished their university degrees; and taught at the university until departing to take up philosophy professorships elsewhere. Their careers were of course hardly identical. Profe counted mathematics among his primary interests, accepted a three-year teaching position outside Halle during his career as a university student, and ultimately ended up in Denmark. But in other respects, their educational and career paths could hardly have been more similar, and they clearly spent their formative years between ages thirteen and twenty-seven in close proximity. Profe is attested to have been supervised by Siegmund Jacob Baumgarten both as a pupil in Francke's schools and as a university student; he was in Halle when Alexander's *Meditationes* appeared; and he and Alexander taught simultaneously both in Francke's schools and at the university.[126]

---

[123] In general, the use of a philosophical vocabulary to describe what earlier Pietists tended to describe in other terms is characteristic of Siegmund Jacob Baumgarten, according to A. Bühler and L. Cataldi Madonna, "Von Thomasius bis Semler. Entwicklungslinien der Hermeneutik in Halle," 61–62.

[124] S. J. Baumgarten, *Unterricht vom recht-mäßigen Verhalten eines Christen*, 602.

[125] I.e., the date of the earliest edition of Baumgarten's *Unterricht vom recht-mäßigen Verhalten eines Christen* that I have found.

[126] F. C. G. Hirsching, *Historisch-litterarisches Handbuch berühmter und denkwürdiger Personen* (Leipzig, 1810; repr., *DBA*), s.v. "Profe, Gottfried."

That they knew of each other is hard to doubt; that they knew each other well is easy to imagine.

Like the Baumgarten brothers, Profe appears to have harbored reservations about Wolff's moral-educational program, and he expressed them in a way that reveals how obvious the implicit deviation from Wolff in Baumgarten's *Meditationes* must have been to a philosophically educated reader. Profe built his own critique of Wolff into a dissertation he supervised in 1739, shortly before his and Baumgarten's departure from Halle. Titled *De affectibus demonstratio philosophica* (Philosophical demonstration on the affections), this dissertation makes no mention of Wolff, but to any reader with even the most elementary knowledge of Wolff's philosophy it must have looked on the surface like an admiring treatment of the *German Ethics*. It restates Wolff's well-known definition of the law of nature as the imperative to seek one's own perfection, repeats Wolff's warning that the affections generated by confused ideas are likely to lead one astray, and insists that the only way to avoid moral slavery is to conquer one's affections and act only according to distinct judgments about good and evil.[127] But about half way through, Profe changes course. Affections, he explains, are appetites that differ from the rational appetite only by their greater "vehemence" (*vehementia*), and the degree of vehemence in an appetite corresponds to the extent to which the ideas that produce that appetite are confused.[128] Since all ideas possess at least a small amount of confusion, he continues, all appetites have a certain degree of vehemence, and they can all be described as affections.[129] Moreover, it is better to have a more vehement appetite for perfection than a less vehement one.[130] Therefore, affections should not be expunged, and the confused ideas that generate them should not necessarily be rendered as distinct as possible, lest all action and cognition become impossible.[131]

Ignoring this warning, Profe points out, means repeating the error of the ancient Stoics, who falsely asserted that virtue must be recognized by

---

[127] G. Profe, praes., *De affectibus demonstratio philosophica* (Halle, 1739), §§14, 46–47.
[128] Profe, *De affectibus*, §§32–35.   [129] Profe, *De affectibus*, §§38, 40, 51.
[130] Profe, *De affectibus*, §§57, 61–62.
[131] Profe, *De affectibus*, §§50–52, 55; cf. Profe's argument that "historical" (i.e., sensate) cognition is the foundation of philosophical knowledge, in G. Profe, *Mathesis philosophiae filia, non mater* (Halle, 1738). Profe draws explicitly on the threefold classification of cognition as either historical, philosophical, or mathematical articulated in G. B. Bilfinger, *De triplici rerum cognitione, historica, philosophica, et mathematica* (Jena, 1722), and G. B. Bilfinger, *Dilucidationes philosophicae de deo, anima humana, mundo, et generalibus rerum affectionibus* (Tübingen, 1725), §279. Cf. below, Chapter 3, p. 105. On Wolff's similar notion that symbolic cognition must terminate in intuitive cognition, albeit unaccompanied by a corresponding valorization of the affections: Schwaiger, *Das Problem des Glücks*, 131.

reason alone and that affections, which arise only from false opinions about good and evil, are entirely absent from the soul of the wise man.[132] In other words, the same position that had prompted Buddeus, Walch, and others to attack Wolff as a Scholastic – namely, Wolff's insistence on the rational appetite's reliability and sufficiency as a virtuous motivation independent of the affections – also opened Wolff to the charge of Stoicism.[133]

Profe's divergence from Wolff's proscription of affections, together with his tacit assimilation of Wolff's position to a Stoic error, not only anticipates a central line of argument explicit in Baumgarten's later metaphysical, ethical, and aesthetic writings[134] but also amplifies an otherwise muffled resonance between Baumgarten's 1735 *Meditationes* and a tradition of anti-Stoic rhetoric characteristic of German academic dissertations on the affections stretching back into the seventeenth century. Often known as *pathologia* or "pathology" (literally, the study of the passions), the subject of these dissertations traditionally invited an author to rehearse the ancient quarrel between the Stoics and Aristotelians, as described in antiquity by Cicero, among other authors, and either simply to find the Stoic position wanting, or to find the usual representation of it so implausible as to warrant denying that the Stoics' disagreement with the Aristotelians could have been more than merely verbal.[135] Like many of his predecessors in this tradition, who openly or implicitly brought the categories of the ancient Stoic-Peripatetic debate to bear on the psychological and ethical theories of their contemporaries – notably those of Descartes or Christian Thomasius – Profe saw Wolff through this same lens. In arguing against the suppression of the affections, he was clearly following an anti-Stoic argumentative trail that had been tread upon for centuries, and that any student of philosophy would have recognized immediately.

The same can be said of others around him who advanced arguments to similar effect, even without explicit reference to the Stoics but with an obvious anti-Stoic resonance. Those included not only Rambach and Francke,

---

[132] Profe, *De affectibus*, §§52, 54.
[133] Cf. similar twenty-first-century assessments in Buchenau, *The Founding of Aesthetics*, 229; and Beiser, *Diotima's Children*, 264.
[134] See below, Chapter 3.
[135] Examples of such disputations, far too numerous to list comprehensively here, include L. Weger, *Pathologia generalis sive de affectibus in genere dissertatio* (Königsberg, 1627); L. Pollio, *Pathologia sive de affectibus* (Leipzig, 1678); J. B. Niemeier, praes., *Disputatio ethica ... de stoicorum ἀπάθεια* (Helmstadt, 1679); and J. Reichius, praes., *Disputatio moralis de nature et indole adfectuum* (Halle, 1700). One recent guide to this discourse is R. Campe, *Affekt und Ausdruck: zur Umwandlung der literarischen Rede im 17. und 18. Jahrhundert* (Tübingen: Niemeyer, 1990). My thanks to Joel Lande for referring me to Campe's work.

whose *Delineatio doctrinae de affectibus* bore a title much like dissertations on pathology, but also Alexander Baumgarten. Only two years after the publication of Profe's dissertation, and seven years after the publication of his own implicitly anti-Stoic *Meditationes*, Baumgarten published an explicit refutation of the position conventionally attributed to the Stoics, denying that even the Stoics can truly have rejected what Aristotle and "all reasonable [*vernünftig*] people" have recognized, namely, that "strong desire [*heftige Begierde*]" or "sensate, very strong emotions [*sinnliche stärkere Bewegungen*]" can lead us to "the most noble virtues [*den edelsten Tugenden*]" and therefore should not necessarily be suppressed.[136]

Conclusion

The fact that Baumgarten's *Meditationes* reflects a sympathy with several of his Pietist teachers' intellectual projects does not preclude the possibility that Baumgarten also consciously departed from those projects in various respects. Baumgarten's invocation of *aisthēta*, for example, cannot be assumed to imply his agreement with Francke's and Rambach's view that *aisthēsis*, a perceptive ability available only to the reborn and the chief means of moral improvement for a reader of the Bible, was absolutely indispensable for understanding the spiritual meaning of a biblical text. Direct, unambiguous signs of disagreement are not obvious, but Alexander's brother, Siegmund Jacob Baumgarten, did deviate from Francke and Rambach's position. While allowing that "experience of the things described by the words" makes the perceptions of an aspiring biblical exegete more distinct and more reliable, Baumgarten stops short of describing it as indispensable, asserting in fact that "the unconverted as well as the converted can discern the correct sense of holy scripture."[137] Whether Alexander Baumgarten agreed with his brother or with Francke and Rambach on this issue is difficult to discern.[138]

A deviation from Rambach is easier to discern in Baumgarten's frequent endorsement of mythological figures as images appropriate to a perfect

---

[136] [A. G. Baumgarten], *Philosophische Brieffe*, 88.

[137] S. J. Baumgarten, *Öffentliche Anzeige seiner diesmaligen Akademischen Arbeit* (Halle, 1734), §10; S. J. Baumgarten, *Unterricht von Auslegung der Heiligen Schrift*, 18. Cf. M. Schröter, *Aufklärung durch Historisierung: Johann Salamo Semlers Hermeneutik des Christentums* (Berlin: De Gruyter, 2012), 40, 49.

[138] The most likely sources of information are A. G. Baumgarten's "Isagoge philosophica in theologiam theticam" (§§55, 73) and *Praelectiones theologiae dogmaticae*, where Baumgarten nonetheless does not address the issue directly. Cf. Aletheophilus's account of how belief that illumination and rebirth require supernatural grace can produce "enthusiasm" in those insufficiently versed in empirical psychology, in [A. G. Baumgarten], *Philosophische Brieffe*, 81–84.

poem.[139] By contrast, Rambach worries in his *Poetische Fest-Gedancken* that the "heathen religion" nourishes the fleshly desire for pleasure.[140] To be fair, as one contemporary reviewer noted, Rambach himself did not always avoid mythological subjects in his own poems: in one of them he "forgets himself," making reference to Apollo and the Muses.[141] In general, though, his wariness of mythological subjects stands in clear contrast with Baumgarten's enthusiasm for them.[142] While the conventional wisdom that Halle's Pietist theologians regarded beauty and the arts *per se* with hostility flies in the face of hard evidence and no longer commands a scholarly consensus, it is nonetheless probably fair to characterize Baumgarten's generation as open to poetic forms and subjects that their teachers regarded as morally treacherous.[143]

But even if Baumgarten did not simply endorse Francke's and Rambach's ideas about poetry and moral education in every detail, what he does seem to have endorsed suggests how much he learned from their writings while studying in Halle. Francke and Rambach had taken what they themselves portrayed as a controversial position in a debate about biblical hermeneutics: the spiritual meaning of a biblical text consists of its power to reform the affections of a reader who has had the experience of conversion. This position, marked by Francke's and Rambach's reference to *aisthēsis*, presupposed another controversial view, namely, that divine inspiration reformed rather than suppressed the human affections of the people subject to it. Furthermore, Francke and Rambach conceived of moral education in

---

139 This endorsement is echoed by the indirect praise of Homer as an effective moral teacher and the direct praise of the "scandalous poets" in a 1741 dissertation by one of Baumgarten's students in Frankfurt (Oder): S. W. Spalding, resp., *De vi et efficacia ethices philosophiae*, praes. A. G. Baumgarten (Frankfurt (Oder), 1741), §24, on which see also below, Chapter 3, pp. 139–40.

140 Rambach, *Poetische Fest-Gedancken*, Vorrede, §3.

141 Review of *Johann Jacob Rambachs geistliche Poesien*, in *Unschuldige Nachrichten von Alten und Neuen Theologischen Sachen*, ed. V. E. Löscher (Wittenberg, 1736), 785–87.

142 A. G. Baumgarten, *Meditationes*, e.g., §36. Other signs of the disagreement between Baumgarten and Rambach on the appropriate subject of a good poem can be found in Baumgarten's *Kollegium*, in Poppe, *Alexander Gottlieb Baumgarten*, e.g., §183, where Baumgarten expressly denies that a beautiful poem must necessarily express praise of God (*Lob der Gottheit*). On this text, see below, Chapter 3, p. 106. I have not yet seen compelling evidence for the apparently standard view that this represents a repudiation of the Pietist attitude toward *adiaphora* – on which, see W. Martens, *Literatur und Frömmigkeit in der Zeit der frühen Aufklärung* (Tübingen: Niemeyer, 1989), esp. 129–72.

143 Fritz, *Vom Erhabenen*, 247. The older tendency to characterize Pietists as enemies of beauty and the arts can be found in, e.g., W. Schmitt, *Die pietistische Kritik der 'Künste,'* PhD diss. (Univerität Köln, 1958), and Martens, *Literatur und Frömmigkeit*. Resistance to this tendency can be found in not only Fritz's *Vom Erhabenen* but also, e.g., T. Müller-Bahlke, "Der Hallesche Pietismus und die Kunst: Bemerkungen zu einem alten Vorurteil," in *Das Echo Halles: Kulturelle Wirkungen des Pietismus*, ed. R. Lächele (Tübingen: Niemeyer, 2001).

general as a process of reforming one's own affections, and they considered imitation of other people's spiritual affections to be one of this educational process's important methods. Poetry, moreover, was among its most important tools. In the idiom of Leibniz and Wolff, as employed by Alexander and Siegmund Jacob Baumgarten, Gottfried Profe, and countless others, they were describing divine inspiration, biblical interpretation, and moral education as processes that make use of "confused" or indistinct ideas.

Alexander Baumgarten absorbed all of this. By the time he called for philosophers to study the method of perfecting the lower cognitive faculties of the soul, he had been exposed to Francke's and Rambach's ideas of hermeneutics and moral education from several directions as a student in Francke's Latin School and the University of Halle; he had written a dissertation in defense of the divine inspiration of the Bible under Christian Benedict Michaelis; and he was aware of the controversy over poetry's suitability as a means of divine communication. His 1735 *Meditationes* reflects what he had learned, not only by its use of the word *aesthetica* but also by its implicit defense of the divine inspiration of biblical poetry and by its implicitly anti-Stoic and anti-Wolffian lines of argument. Baumgarten's first foray into aesthetic theory, in other words, represented much more than an enthusiastic application of Wolff's "mathematical method" to the poetry-writing he had learned to love early in life. It represented Baumgarten's sympathy for ideas about moral education upon which his teachers had founded their critiques of Wolff.

CHAPTER 3

Alexander Baumgarten's Intervention

In the later 1730s, 1740s, and 1750s, while teaching at Halle and then Frankfurt (Oder), Alexander Baumgarten continued to produce a published record of his own philosophical system, text by text, the last piece of which contained much of the aesthetic philosophy that he had first declared a desideratum in 1735. As these pieces fell into place, the relationship between aesthetic theory and the rest of Baumgarten's system – including especially his natural jurisprudence and moral philosophy – became clearer, and the Pietist sympathies and resistance to Wolff already evident in 1735 likewise resolved into a better defined and more clearly self-conscious position in the controversy over the foundation of morality.

For all this clarity, however, Baumgarten's intervention in the controversy is hard to characterize. His texts certainly reflect the impact of participants on both sides, but the extent to which Baumgarten should be placed on one side or the other is harder to determine. One possibility, that Baumgarten meant to strike a middle position between the two sides, or more generally to "reconcile the traditionally irreconcilable oppositions between Pietism and Wolffianism,"[1] has found several proponents among modern scholars.[2] Whether this reconciliation can be characterized more specifically as an attempt to shield Wolff from Pietist critiques[3] raises the difficult question, of course, whether Baumgarten's divergences from Wolff's position should be regarded as superficial or deep.

It is clear, in any case, that Baumgarten did diverge from Wolff in a way that reflected his alertness, already evident in his 1735 *Meditationes*, to

---

[1] Schwaiger, "Ein 'missing link,'" 259.
[2] The most probing and original recent articulations and justifications of this view, especially with regard to Baumgarten's moral philosophy, can be found in Schwaiger, "Ein 'missing link'"; Schwaiger, "Baumgartens Ansatz," esp. 229–30; and the revised versions of these and several other essays that compose Schwaiger, *Alexander Gottlieb Baumgarten*, e.g., §§3, 5, 10, 24–28, 46, 54. Cf. Poppe, *Alexander Gottlieb Baumgarten*, 32; and Gross, *Cognitio Sensitiva*, 104–6.
[3] As in Schwaiger, "Ein 'missing link,'" 259; and Schwaiger, "Baumgartens Ansatz," 229, 230.

the dangers of "Scholasticism" that his teachers had long warned against. On the one hand, he granted, with Wolff, that a degree of genuine virtue was possible for atheists and others who had not arrived at faith. On the other hand, he maintained, contra Wolff, that clear and confused ideas, not only clear and distinct ideas, were a source of moral obligation, and by extension that the cultivation of the lower cognitive faculties was essential to moral education.[4] This divergence from Wolff, integral to Baumgarten's own metaphysics and moral philosophy, constituted an obvious justification for Baumgarten's project to produce a science of perfecting the lower cognitive faculties. That science, Baumgarten's aesthetic theory, should therefore be construed as part of a systematic response to Wolff's critics. It grew out of Baumgarten's acceptance of criticisms such as Zimmermann's, Walch's, and Buddeus's that Wolff had undermined the foundation of morality.

The Aesthetic Cultivation of Living Cognition

The most substantial of Baumgarten's divergences from Wolff, which appears most explicitly in his *Metaphysics* (first published in 1739) but also resonates throughout his aesthetic and ethical writings, is in the concept of living cognition, or *lebendige Erkenntnis* – the very thing that Zimmermann claimed Wolff's program of moral education could not produce. In his *German Ethics*, Wolff had openly granted that indistinct cognition (*undeutliche Erkenntnis*) of God's perfections on the part of a "simple person" could be more certain, more living, and productive of a greater love of God than the distinct knowledge of God possessed by an "astute philosopher." But this was a special case. Wolff was comparing a simple Christian, helped by the power of the Holy Spirit, to a philosopher bereft of supernatural assistance. Under natural conditions, living cognition was produced by certainty (*Gewissheit*), and certainty was produced by distinct cognition. Even in the case of the simple Christian helped by the Holy Spirit, distinct cognition was not to be scoffed at; all other things being equal, greater distinctness of cognition produced even greater certainty than the help of the Holy Spirit alone.[5] On this point, Baumgarten went his own way. While he agreed that the simple, genuine Christian had a "truer" cognition than the unreborn but doctrinally correct philosopher,[6] he discarded

---

[4] Cf. Schwaiger, "Ein 'missing link,'" 257; Schwaiger, *Alexander Gottlieb Baumgarten*, e.g., 83, 88, 120–21, 132–39.

[5] Wolff, *Deutsche Ethik*, §681.

[6] A. G. Baumgarten, *Kollegium über die Ästhetik*, in Poppe, *Alexander Gottlieb Baumgarten*, §556.

Wolff's presupposition that under natural conditions, certain and therefore living cognition must be distinct. Rather, he proposed that what in fact makes cognition living is its "magnitude" (*magnitudo absoluta, quantitas continua, stetige Größe*).[7] The definition of this term and its central function in Baumgarten's metaphysics is the key to understanding Baumgarten's position in the quarrel between Wolff and his critics.[8]

For Baumgarten, "magnitude" refers to the number of "internal characteristics" that allow one thing to be distinguished from another.[9] As in his 1735 *Meditationes*, where he distinguishes distinct ideas from clear but confused ideas according to whether the ideas represent things whose distinguishing characteristics allow them to be classified according to a definition (in the case of distinct ideas) or merely to be perceived as different from one another (in the case of clear but confused ideas), Baumgarten in his 1739 *Metaphysics* classifies the internal distinguishing characteristics of a thing according to whether they are perceived clearly and distinctly or are perceived clearly but confusedly.[10] Characteristics perceived distinctly, Baumgarten calls "qualities" (*qualitates*), whereas characteristics perceived clearly but confusedly he calls "quantities" (*quantitates*).[11] Crucially, the "magnitude" of the idea itself does not depend on whether the distinguishing characteristics of the thing it represents are quantities or qualities – that is, whether the distinguishing characteristics are perceived confusedly or distinctly. Rather, they must simply be perceived clearly, and the more of them there are, the greater the magnitude of the idea. The distinctly perceived characteristics of a thing, in other words, add no more to the magnitude of the idea of that thing than do the clearly but confusedly perceived characteristics.

The greater the magnitude of the idea, in turn, the greater the idea's "force" (*vis*) or "strength" (*robur*),[12] understood as an idea's power to change

---

[7] A. G. Baumgarten, *Metaphysica*, ed. and trans. G. Gawlick and L. Kreimendahl (Stuttgart-Bad Cannstatt: Frommann-Holzboog, 2011), §159; A. G. Baumgarten, *Metaphysik*, trans. G. F. Meier (Halle, 1783), §122. Meier translates *continua* here as "stetig," on which cf. Wolff, *Deutsche Metaphysik*, §§20, 58. In the notes that follow, *Metaphysik* refers to Meier's 1783 translation, whereas *Metaphysica* refers to the Latin of the fourth (1757) edition, as edited by Gawlick and Kreimendahl.

[8] Cf. Schwaiger, *Alexander Gottlieb Baumgarten*, 77, 120–21, 133, 141.

[9] A. G. Baumgarten, *Metaphysica*, §§159, 517; *Metaphysik*, §§122, 381.

[10] A. G. Baumgarten, *Metaphysica*, §§36, 67; *Metaphysik*, §§31, 52. Baumgarten's words for what I am calling "characteristics" are *determinationes*, *notae*, and *praedicata*. These characteristics are, without exception, the "distinguishing characteristics" of the things in which they inhere. Baumgarten accordingly refers to them as *discrimina*, *differentiae*, *characteres*, *notae*, and *notae characteristicae* – the same words he uses for them in his *Meditationes*.

[11] A. G. Baumgarten, *Metaphysica*, §§68–69; *Metaphysik*, §53.

[12] *Robur*, Baumgarten's word for a high degree of *vis* in an idea, does not yet appear in the first (1739) edition of Baumgarten's *Metaphysica*. A. G. Baumgarten, *Metaphysica*, §§197, 515; *Metaphysik*, §379.

the state of mind of the person in whose mind the idea arises. There are many types of force, not all of which are directly related to the "living" power of an idea to cause action,[13] but the same principle applies to each kind: all other things being equal, ideas of greater magnitude have greater force. Ideas specifically capable of "living force" are produced for the most part by the faculty of judgment, which evaluates the degree to which a given thing is perfect or imperfect. Things judged to be perfect cause pleasure (*voluptas*) and therefore desire (*appetitio*) in the person judging. "Living perception" (*cognitio viva*) refers specifically to those perceptions of perfection that have living force. Whether they are primarily sensate or primarily distinct, such perceptions have enough magnitude to produce a desire great enough to cause the perceiving person to try to bring about the desired thing.[14] It is therefore possible for an idea of perfection perceived clearly but confusedly to have a greater magnitude and a greater degree of living force than the idea of perfection perceived distinctly.

This simple conclusion, so similar to the conclusion advanced by Gottfried Profe that same year,[15] justified Baumgarten's project to develop an aesthetic theory. Because the generation of confused or "sensate" ideas is the task of the so-called lower faculties of the mind, according to Baumgarten, the exercise of the lower faculties is essential for the generation of ideas with as great a magnitude and as high a degree of living force as possible. And explaining how the lower faculties could best be cultivated was in fact, according to Baumgarten, the express purpose of "aesthetic science" (*scientia aesthetica*)[16] and of Baumgarten's own textbook on the subject. In the preface to that textbook, Baumgarten claims to have been asked, in 1742, to "present, in a new set of lectures, some suggestions about how to direct the lower faculties in apprehending the truth."[17] To this request — already issued by Georg Bernhard Bilfinger (1693–1750) to readers of his own metaphysics textbook, such as Baumgarten and Profe, in 1725[18] — Baumgarten responded dutifully by giving such lectures for several years at

---

[13] A. G. Baumgarten, *Metaphysica*, §531; *Metaphysik*, §393.
[14] A. G. Baumgarten, *Metaphysica*, §§663–71; *Metaphysik*, §§489–95.
[15] See above, Chapter 2, pp. 97–98.   [16] A. G. Baumgarten, *Metaphysica*, §533.
[17] A. G. Baumgarten, *Aesthetica*, ed. and trans. D. Mirbach (Hamburg: Meiner, 2007), praefatio: "quaedam consilia dirigendarum facultatum inferiorum in cognoscendo vero, novam per acroasin, exponere." Unless noted otherwise, quotations from the Latin text of Baumgarten's *Aesthetica* follow Mirbach's edition, including her minor typographical emendations to the 1750–58 edition.
[18] On Bilfinger's 1725 call for a science of directing the lower faculties, and its importance for Baumgarten: Franke, *Kunst als Erkenntnis*, 17. Cf. Bilfinger, *Dilucidationes*, §268; A. G. Baumgarten, *Aesthetica*, §11. Cf. Gawlick and Kreimendahl, introduction to *Metaphysica*, by A. G. Baumgarten, XVI.

Frankfurt (Oder). Eight years later, he published the first installment of a heavily revised version of the lectures in the form of a textbook that he then began to use in the classroom.[19] This first volume of Baumgarten's *Aesthetics* appeared in 1750. Then, after a delay of eight years – allegedly the result of Baumgarten's failing health – under pressure from the publisher Baumgarten submitted a manuscript for a second volume, uncertain whether he would live to finish the project.[20] Upon Baumgarten's death in 1762, a large section of the *Aesthetics* remained unpublished and almost certainly unwritten. He had planned to discuss aesthetic philosophy under two headings, "theoretical aesthetics" (*aesthetica theoretica*) and "practical aesthetics" (*aesthetica practica*), and by the end of the second volume he had not yet concluded his discussion of theoretical aesthetics.[21] But what Baumgarten was able to publish does suggest that his ultimate aim in developing an aesthetic theory was to encourage his readers, by natural, philosophical means, to become skilled at cultivating "living cognition" in themselves and, more importantly, in the audiences to whom they addressed themselves.

Developing this skill, according to Baumgarten, requires achieving aesthetic philosophy's explicit aim: the "perfection of sensate cognition as such" (*perfectio cognitionis sensitivae, qua talis*).[22] This perfection, or "beauty" (*pulchritudo*), Baumgarten describes along lines familiar to any reader of Christian Wolff.[23] It is a harmonious relationship (*consensus, Übereinstimmung*) between parts of a whole, functioning together in such a way as to promote the purpose of the whole, or as Wolff sometimes explained it, functioning together in conformity with the nature of the whole.[24] In the case of the lower cognitive faculties, responsible for sensate

---

[19] A student's dictates of lectures Baumgarten gave, apparently on his already-published *Aesthetica* (from which Poppe infers that the dictates correspond to lectures given in the 1750–51 academic year), were transcribed by Bernhard Poppe and published in 1907 as *Kollegium über die Ästhetik*, in Poppe, *Alexander Gottlieb Baumgarten*.

[20] Abbt, *Leben und Charakter*, 228–31; Meier, *Alexander Gottlieb Baumgartens Leben*, 43; A. G. Baumgarten, *Aesthetica*, II.praefatio.

[21] A. G. Baumgarten, *Aesthetica*, I.synopsis, §13.   [22] A. G. Baumgarten, *Aesthetica*, §14.

[23] The following discussion refers to A. G. Baumgarten, *Aesthetica*, §§14–26; and *Metaphysica*, §§94, 662: "*Beauty* is perfection as phenomenon, i.e., [perfection] observable to 'taste' in the broad sense of the word [*Perfectio phenomenon, s[eu] gustui latius dicto observabilis, est PULCRITUDO*]." Cf. H. G. Peters, *Die Ästhetik Alexander Gottlieb Baumgartens* (Berlin: Junker, 1934), 17, 23–25; and, addressing some of the interpretive difficulties in Baumgarten's account of beauty, Beiser, *Diotima's Children*, 146. Cf. also Christian Wolff's more general definition of beauty as the "observability of perfection" (*observabilitas perfectionis*) in C. Wolff, *Psychologia empirica* (Leipzig, 1738; repr., Hildesheim: Olms, 1968), §545; and elucidations on it in Beiser, *Diotima's Children*, 48–53; and Guyer, *A History of Modern Aesthetics*, I.306, 328.

[24] The purpose or nature of this whole, referred to by Baumgarten as the "focus of perfection" (*focus perfectionis, ratio perfectionis determinans*) (*Metaphysica* §94), is difficult to identify. Baumgarten says virtually nothing about it in his *Aesthetics*, which has led H. G. Peters to identify it, on the strength

cognition, the "whole" is the "entirety" (*complexus*) of ideas[25] that are clear but not distinct, and its "parts" are the individual ideas themselves. When the parts themselves and their relationships to each other are not perceived distinctly, the harmonious relationship among them can be called beauty. Baumgarten specifies three kinds of beauty, or indistinctly perceived harmonious order, that these individual ideas must have in order for sensate cognition itself to be beautiful: the beauty of each individual idea, the beauty of the sequence in which the individual ideas are arranged, and the beauty of the signs (e.g., words, images, or sounds) used to express the ideas.[26] In the case of both sensate cognition as a whole and the individual ideas that constitute its parts, the beauty arises from the presence of six ideal qualities: richness (*ubertas* or *Reichtum*), greatness (*magnitudo* or *Adel*), truth (*veritas* or *Wahrheit*), clarity (*lux, claritas*, or *Licht*), certainty (*certitudo, Gewissheit*, or *Gründlichkeit*), and life (*vita, Lebendigkeit*, or *Leben*).[27]

The means by which the lower cognitive faculties and the ideas they generate can be made more beautiful are twofold: performing practical exercises and acquiring theoretical knowledge. Baumgarten prescribes both. The former, which Baumgarten calls "*askēsis*" or "aesthetic exercise" (*exercitatio aesthetica*),[28] relies upon a "connate" or inborn "natural

---

of Baumgarten's *Meditationes*, as the sensate representation of a "theme." One alternative to this view would be to see the perfection of the lower faculties not as a measure of their fulfillment of a particular goal, but as a "heightening" of their powers. Peters calls this a "functional" as opposed to a "purposive" definition of *perfection*. Peters, *Die Ästhetik Alexander Gottlieb Baumgartens*, 17–18, 30; Bäumler, *Das Irrationalitätsproblem*, 227. Cf. Beiser, *Diotima's Children*, 5, 64–67, 148, insisting on Wolff's and Baumgarten's accommodation of nonpurposive wholes in their definitions of perfection; and Schwaiger, *Alexander Gottlieb Baumgarten*, 158–65, arguing that Baumgarten abandons Wolff's emphasis on purposiveness. Buchenau, *The Founding of Aesthetics*, e.g., 56–58, 218–22, appears tacitly to reject Beiser's and possibly also Schwaiger's position. Cf. above, Chapter 1, note 24.

[25] The words Baumgarten uses, all of which in various contexts appear to denote the same thing, include *repraesentatio, perceptio, cogitatio, Vorstellung, Gedanke*, and *Erfindung*.

[26] For discussion of the correspondence of these three types of beauty with the ancient Roman classification of rhetoric into three parts, *inventio, dispositio*, and *elocutio*, as explained by Quintilian: M.-L. Linn, "A. G. Baumgartens 'Aesthetica' und die antike Rhetorik," *Deutsche Vierteljahrsschrift für Literaturwissenschaft und Geistesgeschichte* 41.3 (August 1967): 427; and P. Guyer, "18th Century German Aesthetics," in *Stanford Encyclopedia of Philosophy*, Fall 2008 ed., ed. Edward N. Zalta, cited 29 June 2009. On the two sets of things that Baumgarten describes as capable of harmony, i.e., (1) *inventio, dispositio*, and *elocutio*, and (2) the six qualities of ideas, cf. Peters, *Die Ästhetik Alexander Gottlieb Baumgartens*, 25.

[27] A. G. Baumgarten, *Aesthetica*, §22. On the Ciceronian origins of these terms: Buchenau, *The Founding of Aesthetics*, 139–40. As Guyer notes (*A History of Modern Aesthetics*, I.331–32), *Lebhaftigkeit* and *Lebendigkeit* are not the same; the former appears to denote *lux* or "clarity," whereas the latter usually denotes *vita* or "life." To avoid ambiguity, I refer to the former as "vividness" or "liveliness," and reserve "life" and "living" for cognates of the latter.

[28] A. G. Baumgarten, *Aesthetica*, §47.

disposition of the whole mind to think beautifully."²⁹ The two components of this general inborn disposition, Baumgarten identifies as "a good
head and a good heart":³⁰ (1) a talent for exercising the various lower and
higher faculties of the mind, and (2) an inborn eagerness to "strive for worthy and moving perception" and to attain the highest degrees of virtue –
which Baumgarten calls an "inborn aesthetic temperament."³¹ These two
components need to be maintained, enlarged, and trained, such that their
possessor actually becomes able to "think beautifully" and does not allow
his inborn predispositions to wither.³² Nor can the head be trained at
the expense of the heart, or vice versa. Anyone without trained cognitive
faculties – both sensate and rational – will be unable to avoid "errors" in
the operation of his sensate perception and expression. Likewise, anyone
who has trained only his cognitive faculties, i.e., only his "head," may be
able to produce beautiful expressions, but without a convincing display
of the beautiful thoughts that he has purported to express. Like the hypocrite, who "can perhaps give a prayer that is beautiful as far as the words
are concerned" but that will never be beautiful to those who know the
person saying the words and who therefore "detect an inner bitterness,"
anyone who neglects his heart in favor of training his cognitive faculties
will display "very many pseudo-virtues" (*Scheintugenden*). Pseudo-virtues,
when they are detected as such, betray "an ignoble heart" and cannot be
considered beautiful.³³ Perfecting one's lower cognitive faculties therefore
requires developing a genuine love of the perfection of those faculties,
which is to say, a love of the beautiful mind, referred to by Baumgarten as
"greatness of heart" (*Größe des Herzens, magnitudo pectoris*).³⁴

So the head and the heart – the cognitive faculties and the desire for their
perfection – must be cultivated in tandem. To this end, Baumgarten proposes a set of exercises that he says must be repeated continually so that the
cognitive abilities and desires they foster become habitual. The cognitive

---

²⁹ A. G. Baumgarten, *Aesthetica*, §28:

> Ad characterem felicis aesthetici generalem supponendo generaliora, §27, requiritur I) AES-
> THETICA NATURALIS CONNATA, §2 (φύσις, natura, εὐφυΐα, ἀρχέτυπα, στοιχεῖα
> γενέσεως), dispositio naturalis animae totius ad pulcre cogitandum, quacum nascitur.
>   C.f. A. G. Baumgarten's reference to some children's natural disposition to seek
> harmonious order in their games, in *Kollegium*, §55.

³⁰ A. G. Baumgarten, *Kollegium*, §44.
³¹ A. G. Baumgarten, *Aesthetica*, §§44–45; A. G. Baumgarten, *Kollegium*, §45.
³² A. G. Baumgarten, *Aesthetica*, §§47–48; A. G. Baumgarten, *Kollegium*, §§47–48.
³³ A. G. Baumgarten, *Kollegium*, §§50–51.
³⁴ A. G. Baumgarten, *Aesthetica*, §§45, 59; on which, see D. Mirbach, "*Ingenium venustum* und *magnitudo pectoris*: Ethische Aspekte von Alexander Gottlieb Baumgartens *Aesthetica*," *Aufklärung* 20
(2008): esp. 199–218.

faculties, on the one hand, are to be trained by exercises in creating things, whereby a teacher points out the ways in which each attempt at creation has or has not achieved the kind of harmonious order that, when it is perceived indistinctly, constitutes beauty.[35] The love of beauty, on the other hand, is to be cultivated by the repeated, guided observation of "beautiful" actions:

> The one who is supposed to train the beautiful mind must lead it, right at the very beginning, so that it learns to identify and, as it were, add up the beauty and ugliness in actions. In the depths of the soul, all ideas that can later become desires must be directed immediately toward what is beautiful with respect to the heart, and all the similar cases that [the beautiful mind] sees must be shown to it as they are.[36]

What these types of exercises rely on, both the exercises meant to cultivate the perception of beauty by the lower cognitive faculties and the exercises meant to cultivate a love of that beauty, is the repeated observation and imitation of examples of beauty. "[W]hen I read beautiful writings, see beautiful paintings, and convincingly think, 'that is beautiful, that is pleasing,'" Baumgarten explains, "I am already training myself."[37] The training is still more useful when the observations are immediately accompanied by closer consideration of what exactly makes this or that beautiful and pleasing. The same advice applies to the more difficult exercises of writing, painting, or otherwise giving expression to thoughts of one's own.[38] The result of undertaking such exercises, which in conjunction with careful observation should reveal one's own natural limits and thereby reveal where more exercise would be most beneficial, is that thinking beautifully becomes ever more habitual.[39]

But exercises alone do not suffice to produce good habits. Baumgarten insists that if one's lower cognitive faculties and the love of indistinctly perceived harmony are to reach the highest naturally possible degree of perfection, the *askēsis* or exercises he prescribes must be accompanied by a

---

[35] A. G. Baumgarten, *Kollegium*, §49.
[36] A. G. Baumgarten, *Kollegium*, §54:

> Wer den schönen Geist bilden soll, muß ihn gleich anfangs darauf führen, daß er das Schöne und Häßliche in den Handlungen wahrnehmen und gleichsam abzählen lerne. Im Grunde der Seele müssen alle Vorstellungen, die hernach zu Begierden werden können, sogleich auf das Schöne in Ansehung des Herzens gerichtet werden, und alle ähnlichen Fälle, die er siehet, müssen ihm gezeigt werden, wie sie sind.

[37] A. G. Baumgarten, *Kollegium*, §56: "[W]ann ich schöne Schriften lese, schöne Gemälde sehe und dabei überzeugend gedenke: das ist schön, das gefällt, so übe ich mich schon."
[38] A. G. Baumgarten, *Kollegium*, §§56–58.
[39] A. G. Baumgarten, *Aesthetica*, §§59–61; A. G. Baumgarten, *Kollegium*, §§60–61.

concerted effort to acquire theoretical knowledge, which Baumgarten calls *"mathēsis"* or "aesthetic instruction" (*disciplina aesthetica*).[40] This *mathēsis* has two parts: (1) careful study of the things about which one intends to think beautifully, in order to develop a knowledge that Baumgarten calls "beautiful learning" (*pulcra eruditio, schöne Gelehrsamkeit*);[41] and (2) an orderly demonstration of the "rules of thinking beautifully" (*regulae pulcre cogitandi*). The latter is what Baumgarten proposes to undertake in the remainder of his textbook:

> A moment ago, . . . I asserted that it is scarcely sufficient for nature, talent, character, exercise, or the cultivation of the mind to be obtained without any learning, as a practical knowledge of the rules of thinking beautifully. I have proven that this practical knowledge truly only serves well if it is, at least in relation to its chief and most important elements, a science. Now once again I am asserting that those exercises, discussed [earlier],[42] are more correct and more reliable when no day is spent without doing something. Without exercises, what they call rules are on their own lifeless and speculative, yet should you not take advantage of them, they will never, I insist, be in fact beneficial to the full extent that they should be. After some further remarks, I will not assert much more [than this].[43]

In this elliptical but valuable statement of purpose, Baumgarten explains the importance of the rules to whose description he devotes most of his *Aesthetics*. Alone, they are "lifeless and speculative." No one who merely knows the rules will be able to think beautifully. The rules are beneficial only when they are applied in a regimen of aesthetic exercises, without which the natural cognitive abilities and desire to perfect those abilities tend to wither away. But by explaining the fundamental, general rules of beautiful thinking, Baumgarten purports to make those exercises more beneficial. The rules, as Baumgarten explains in his lectures on aesthetics, are meant to "support" (*unterstützen*) the exercises.[44]

---

[40] A. G. Baumgarten, *Aesthetica*, §62.
[41] A. G. Baumgarten, *Aesthetica*, §63; A. G. Baumgarten, *Kollegium*, §§63, 68.
[42] A. G. Baumgarten, *Aesthetica*, §58.
[43] A. G. Baumgarten, *Aesthetica*, §77:

> Iam postulavi, ante theoriam eiusmodi, naturam, ingenium, indolem, exercitia, culturam ingenii nunc sine aliqua eruditione vix satis impetrandam, regularum pulcre cogitandi peritiam, quam unice probavi vere praestare, si sit prima saltim et primaria sua ex parte scientia. Nunc denuo postulo correctiora ac certiora illa exercitia, de quibus §58, in quibus nulla dies sine linea, sine quibus mortuas ipse speculativasque, quas vocant, regulas, utiles quidem, quibus tamen non utaris, nunquam edico profuturas, eo, quo maxime debent. Nec ita multa post plura postulabo.

[44] A. G. Baumgarten, *Kollegium*, §62.

They do this by virtue of being a science (*Wissenschaft* or *scientia*), which is to say, by virtue of being known distinctly and therefore with certainty. Their "support" for the exercises appears to rely on a mechanism that Baumgarten leaves to his readers' imaginations, but that most readers of Wolff would have inferred: the creation of a natural obligation to seek perfection, by presenting that perfection as distinctly as possible. The rules for perfecting the lower cognitive faculties, when perceived distinctly and with certainty, are like the ethical maxims described in Wolff's *German Ethics*. They stimulate the rational appetite in proportion to the distinctness with which they are perceived, and they thereby engage the will to seek the perfection of the lower faculties by the means they prescribe, namely, aesthetic exercises.

Baumgarten does not explain this mechanism in any detail, but he does hint that it is what he has in mind. He frequently refers to the rules he is about to lay down as "laws" (*leges*), and he explicitly states that the purpose of laying out the general "laws" of beautiful thinking, even if they do not give specific guidance about specific genres of beautiful thinking – that is, about "rhetoric, poetry, music, etc." – is to reveal the "essence" (*Inbegriff*) from which the more specific laws of each genre can be derived, and thereby to "place the strength of those same [more specific laws] manifestly enough before one's eyes."[45] As a result, Baumgarten predicts, aesthetic exercises will no longer be seen as primarily an activity for children; they will seem "worthy of men, and will even move them either to dare something new and excellent in their aesthetic exercises" or at least to be "more competent judges" of the application of aesthetic rules.[46] For Baumgarten, in other words, laying out the general rules or "laws" of thinking beautifully, in the form of a science, could not only help his audience improve their judgment of the beauty of ideas produced by the lower cognitive faculties but could also engage their wills, such that they would attempt to improve their own lower cognitive faculties by engaging in aesthetic exercises. As Siegmund Jacob Baumgarten explained more directly in a summary of the main achievements of his brother's *Meditationes* in 1735, "every art can be joined to a science if its rules are demonstrated so as to avoid exception," and the purpose of demonstrating the rules of an art is to help that art "form an effective *habitus* by means of reason."[47] Exposition and demonstration of the general rules of thinking beautifully, provided by Baumgarten's textbook, should therefore be considered an aid to the

---

[45] A. G. Baumgarten, *Aesthetica*, §69, 71–73. [46] A. G. Baumgarten, *Aesthetica*, §76.

[47] S. J. Baumgarten, *Programmata*, ed. G. C. Bakius (Halle, 1740), 302–3.

mathēsis that Baumgarten hoped would in turn stimulate his students to undertake and to perfect the *askēsis* from which the habit of thinking beautifully would ultimately derive its strength. This, in general terms, was the ostensible purpose of Baumgarten's *Aesthetics*.[48]

Within the parameters set by this general purpose, Baumgarten ascribed special importance to the cultivation of ideas' "life," although this importance would have been more obvious if Baumgarten had lived to complete his *Aesthetics*. The published sections, unfortunately, include only the set of rules for judging the beauty of the ideas themselves, not the rules for judging the beauty of their sequence or of the signs used to express them, and even this first set of rules remains incomplete. Of the six qualities of beautiful ideas, Baumgarten finished his accounts of richness, greatness, truth, clarity, and certainty, but not the final quality, life: the essential quality of "living cognition" and the quality that denotes an idea's power to move the human will. He nonetheless gives indications that of all the six qualities, life was in several respects the most important, and its cultivation the ultimate aim of aesthetic philosophy. Not only does Baumgarten refer to life as "the chief gift of beautiful cognition" (*pulcrae cognitionis dos primaria*)[49] and "the sweetest beauty of beautiful cognition" (*venustae cognitionis dulcissima pulcritudo*);[50] he even suggests that the production of life is the ultimate function of the other five qualities. Perception is perfect, Baumgarten explains, when richness and greatness together produce clarity, when clarity and truth produce certainty, and when all the qualities together produce life.[51]

The priority that Baumgarten gives to life also makes itself felt in Baumgarten's continual assertions that a human being who has perfected his lower cognitive faculties and thereby developed a "beautiful mind" aims to generate ideas that move the will. In explaining why sensate perception can only be beautiful if its possessor has a powerful imagination and uses it to envision future events, for example, Baumgarten notes that

---

[48] A fuller exposition of Baumgarten's *Aesthetics* as a stimulus to the practice of aesthetic exercises can be found in G. Trop, "Aesthetic Askesis: Aesthetics as a Technology of the Self in the Philosophy of Alexander Baumgarten," *Das achtzehnte Jahrhundert* 37.1 (2013): 56–73. Cf. Buchenau, *The Founding of Aesthetics*, 148–50.

[49] A. G. Baumgarten, *Aesthetica*, §188.   [50] A. G. Baumgarten, *Aesthetica*, II.praefatio.

[51] A. G. Baumgarten, *Aesthetica*, §22; but cf. A. G. Baumgarten, *Kollegium*, §22, where *vita* appears to be glossed in terms of vividness and is not obviously elevated above the other qualities. Cf. also the discussion of "the practical utility of philosophy" in A. G. Baumgarten's posthumously published lectures on "general philosophy," *Philosophia generalis* (Halle, 1770; repr., Hildesheim: Olms, 1968), §232. On the supreme importance of *vita* in Baumgarten's *Aesthetics*, cf. F. Piselli, "Ästhetik und Metaphysik bei Alexander Gottlieb Baumgarten," *Aufklärung* 20 (2008): 111; and Guyer, *A History of Modern Aesthetics*, I.331–32, I.339.

something that is supposed to be beautiful must be moving [*bewegen*]; this is a characteristic of beautiful cognition. Anything meant to move me has to generate desires in me. But desires can arise in no other way than on account of a future good, and so because a beautiful mind [*schöner Geist*] should cause movement [*bewegen soll*], it must also see into the future.[52]

What Baumgarten here postulates the beautiful mind must do, namely, "cause movement," depends on generating desires by generating the idea of a future good, which is to say, the judgment that something attainable in the future has a high degree of perfection.[53] This is what Baumgarten later in the same lecture calls "speaking the language of the heart," a metaphor for "being stirring" (*rühren*), which requires "arousing desires" in oneself and in those to whom one presents one's thoughts.[54] The utterances of a beautiful mind must be "strong enough to set us into motion, into sorrow and sympathy."[55]

Nor does Baumgarten argue that the mind is most beautiful simply when its ideas' life allows it to move the will in any way at all; rather, he suggests that it must move the will in the direction of virtue rather than vice. Admittedly, his suggestions to this effect are ambiguous and indirect. On the one hand, he issues repeated reminders that a beautiful mind necessarily adopts a morally virtuous persona. It must present itself as "virtuous, well-brought-up, engaged in noble thoughts"; must "choose subjects that only a virtuous person would think of";[56] and must present things in a way that does not violate moral laws.[57] A poem in praise of money, for example, could never be considered beautiful because it would seem to betray "an ignoble heart."[58] Just as a mind cannot be beautiful unless the character of its possessor appears to be virtuous, so a work of art cannot be beautiful

---

[52] A. G. Baumgarten, *Kollegium*, §31:

> Denn, was schön sein soll, muß bewegen, dies ist eine Eigenschaft der schönen Erkenntnis. Was mich bewegen soll, muß Begierden in mir hervorbringen, Begierden aber können nicht anders als wegen eines zukünftigen Gutes entstehen, da nun ein schöner Geist bewegen soll, so muß er auch in die Zukunft sehen.

[53] Cf. A. G. Baumgarten, *Metaphysica*, §§663–71; *Metaphysik*, §§489–95.

[54] A. G. Baumgarten, *Kollegium*, §36.

[55] A. G. Baumgarten, *Kollegium*, §39: "Seine Erdichtungen müssen z.B. so stark werden, daß sie uns in Bewegung, in Trauer und Mitleid setzen."

[56] A. G. Baumgarten, *Kollegium*, §§195, 435.

[57] A. G. Baumgarten, *Kollegium*, §433. Baumgarten's assertion that a beautiful mind can think beautifully about vicious and otherwise evil things (*Kollegium*, §§203–4) suggests that the beautiful mind may present things that themselves violate moral laws, but it cannot present them in a *manner* that violates a moral law. Vice and virtue, it would seem, must be presented in such a way as to communicate love of the former and aversion to the latter. Cf. A. G. Baumgarten, *Kollegium*, §§193, 397.

[58] A. G. Baumgarten, *Kollegium*, §51.

unless it displays things in the way that someone with a virtuous character would want to display them. That is to say, things a virtuous person would desire must be presented as desirable and praiseworthy, and things a virtuous person would avoid or condemn must be presented as blameworthy.[59]

On the other hand, Baumgarten does not clearly indicate that improving one's own will and becoming more virtuous is a necessary precondition for successfully cultivating the morally virtuous persona requisite for a beautiful mind. On the one hand, he asserts that a beautiful mind must possess a "good heart."[60] And just as in the example of the hypocrite whose prayers are not beautiful to anyone aware that his apparent virtuousness is in fact a façade,

> as soon as here and there some lazy ignorance or some crude behavior shows through from beneath the mask, the game is up. You will be condemned by the opinion of highly fit judges as someone covering up your shamefulness in a shameful way.[61]

On the other hand, if the façade of virtue is impenetrable, even if vice in fact lies behind it, then there is no valid criterion by which the beauty of the mind in question can be judged to be anything but beautiful:

> If it were granted that someone, because of a powerful tendency to dissimulate, is capable of posing as a good man, so that not even the least defect of mind or soul were apparent in the ordering of his thinking, would anyone refrain from terming him a good man on grounds of both aesthetics and likelihood, unless the opposite were proven?[62]

For someone with a vicious character it is possible, though admittedly very difficult and therefore unlikely, to cultivate a mind that doesn't betray its possessor's vicious character and therefore at least seems genuinely beautiful. The morally bad man, in other words, can appear aesthetically good.[63]

---

[59] Cf. the similar conclusion drawn from Baumgarten's *Meditationes* in H. J. Lasius, Review of *Meditationes*, by A. G. Baumgarten, in *Critischer Versuch zur Aufnahme der Deutschen Sprache* 6 (Greifswald, 1742), 580ff.

[60] A. G. Baumgarten, *Kollegium*, §360.

[61] A. G. Baumgarten, *Aesthetica*, §362:

> Quam primum ibi non nihil supinae ignorantiae, hic inconditorum morum sub vulpe latentium pellucet: peracta res est, et ex iudicum maxime competentium sententia turpitudinem turpius tegens condemnaris.

[62] A. G. Baumgarten, *Aesthetica*, §362:

> [S]i detur aliquem, ingentem simulandi per habitum, posse virum bonum ita mentiri, ut ne minima quidem in eius cogitandi ratione transpareat mentis animique pravitas, quis vetat, eum virum bonum aesthetice verisimiliterque dicere, donec constet contrarium?

[63] An important qualification of the thesis in Mirbach, "*Ingenium venustum* und *magnitudo pectoris*," 203, i.e., that for Baumgarten, "the perfection of one's desiring faculties and the direction of those

In this case, it would seem that beauty of mind is a quality not of a virtuous character itself, but rather of the "manner of thinking" that constitutes the sign of a virtuous character. In light of this fact, it is difficult to imagine that Baumgarten considered the cultivation of beauty in the minds of his readers – ostensibly the aim in whose service he developed his aesthetic theory – to be a necessary means of helping them cultivate their own living cognition in the moral sense of that term as Zimmermann, Wolff, and many others used it. But Baumgarten must have considered the cultivation of beauty in the minds of his readers a useful means of helping them cultivate a morally edifying, living cognition in their own audiences – that is, the audiences to whom they themselves would present their minds through artistic media.

One part of the evidence for this inference comes from Baumgarten's discussion of persuasion (*persuasio*), the quality that he calls the precondition (*conditio antecedens*) of an idea's life.[64] The crucial point is this: by *persuasion*, Baumgarten does not mean simply the success of an idea in creating certainty about something – and therefore perhaps a willingness to do something – in an audience. Rather, he means only "true persuasion" (*persuasio vera*), the success of an idea in creating certainty by giving an audience "indistinct and sensate knowledge of the truth" (*indistincta et sensitiva veritatis conscientia*) rather than by presenting falsehoods.[65] The implication, of course, is that an oration that aims at persuading an audience to violate a moral law cannot be beautiful, because in presenting such a violation as praiseworthy it would be presenting a falsehood. Only virtue, after all, can accurately be presented as praiseworthy.

Another part of the evidence comes from Baumgarten's discussion of that other crucial quality of beautiful ideas, namely, their aesthetic "magnitude" or "greatness" (*magnitudo*). Here, Baumgarten indicates that in the case of presenting virtue and vice, giving audiences knowledge of the "truth" means creating a desire for the former and an aversion to the latter. The very fact that Baumgarten calls "praise of the divinity" the greatest subject of a poem, rather than merely divinity itself, suggests this.[66] Baumgarten makes the point still more explicitly in addressing the question of whether

---

faculties toward moral goodness is indispensible for the perfection of sensate cognition and its representation in art." On Baumgarten's reluctance to concede the point of this discussion: H. R. Schweizer, *Ästhetik als Philosophie der sinnlichen Erkenntnis* (Basel: Schwabe, 1973), 29–32; and, in reference to Schweizer, Mirbach, ed., *Aesthetica*, by A. G. Baumgarten, II.968. Cf. Guyer, *A History of Modern Aesthetics*, I.335.

[64] A. G. Baumgarten, *Aesthetica*, §829.

[65] A. G. Baumgarten, *Aesthetica*, §832.   [66] A. G. Baumgarten, *Kollegium*, §183.

vice and evil can be a great subject for a work of art. His answer is that they can, but only if they are presented in such a way as to excite an audience's aversion to them and affection for virtue:

> There has been controversy over whether evil, vices, and malice can belong to greatness. . . . This much we can state with certainty: malice as such can never be great, and vices always remain small, when one considers their inner composition. Evil alone we consider from another perspective, namely in so far as it provides an opportunity for greatness in thinking, for portraying virtue as its opposite in a great way and producing no enthusiasm about vice. To this extent, vice and malice also belong to greatness. The vice of a tyrant who represses people is great, in so far as I can think in a great way about the juxtaposed gentleness of a king.[67]

In sum, beauty requires greatness, and greatness requires portraying virtue and vice as such. This does not mean, for Baumgarten, that the criteria of beauty and the criteria of moral goodness are the same, nor that the one can be derived from the other.[68] Baumgarten moreover avoids drawing upon the conclusions of moral theology, reminding his readers that he does not want to deduce the necessity of aesthetic greatness "from the more severe and higher laws of the blessed life or entirely from the holiest revelations of true Christianity," as if he were "crossing into another genre" or as if his "sickel were being sent into someone else's field."[69] But he does make moral demands on orators, poets, and other artists on the basis of purely aesthetic principles. That is to say, Baumgarten can – and does – make some degree of moral edification a criterion of beauty, (1) without deriving the criteria of beauty from the criteria of moral perfection, (2) without deriving the obligation to perfect the lower cognitive faculties from any other moral obligation, and (3) without eliding the distinction between moral and aesthetic judgment.

All these indications that Baumgarten conceived his aesthetic theory as a means of helping his readers and auditors learn how to cultivate living

---

[67] A. G. Baumgarten, *Kollegium*, §203:

> Man hat darüber gestritten, ob das Böse, die Laster und die Bosheit mit zu dem Großen gehören könnten. . . . So viel können wir gewiß bestimmen, Bosheit als Bosheit kann nie groß sein und die Laster bleiben allezeit klein, wann man auf ihre innere Beschaffenheit siehet; allein betrachten wir das Böse aus einem anderen Gesichtspunkte, nämlich insofern es Gelegenheit geben kann groß zu denken, die Tugend als das Gegenteil groß zu schildern und vom Laster keine Begeisterung zu geben, insofern gehören Laster und Bosheiten auch mit zum Großen. Das Laster eines Tyrannen, der Menschen würgt, ist groß, insofern ich von der entgegengesetzten Sanftmut eines Regnaten groß denken kann.

[68] Cf. Peters, *Die Ästhetik Alexander Gottlieb Baumgartens*, 55–56.

[69] A. G. Baumgarten, *Aesthetica*, §183.

cognition in their own audiences may seem sparse, indirect, and therefore inconclusive. For this the blame should almost certainly fall on the circumstances that prevented Baumgarten from finishing the sections of his *Aesthetics* in which he planned to discuss the "life" of a beautiful idea and "practical aesthetics." Fortunately, however, another text can serve in these missing sections' stead: the published version of the inaugural lecture Baumgarten delivered in May 1740, shortly after arriving in Frankfurt (Oder) to take up his professorship.[70] This lecture foreshadowed Baumgarten's *Aesthetics* in significant ways, probably because in composing it, as in composing his *Aesthetics*, Baumgarten was drawing on ideas about aesthetic philosophy that he had been developing at least since 1735. More than any other of Baumgarten's surviving texts, it lays explicit emphasis on the importance of producing living cognition in one's audience.

One of the central arguments in the lecture is that everyone who speaks before an audience is obliged to engage the audience's lower cognitive faculties, not only their intellects. After announcing that he has been officially charged with helping the university flourish and improving its reputation, Baumgarten purports to devote his lecture to explaining the most appropriate means to that end. Within a couple of minutes, Baumgarten has brought himself by means of several rapid logical maneuvers to familiar aesthetic terrain: (1) "observant and rational applause" (*sehender und vernünfftiger Beyfall*) contributes at least a small amount to the well-being of an academic institution,[71] (2) this "applause" consists of the pleasure students take in attending a professor's lectures,[72] and (3) the applause is "observant and rational" when it is the result of the students having correctly perceived the good qualities of the lecture.[73] Anticipating the basic structure of his *Aesthetics*, Baumgarten describes these good qualities, or perfections, with reference to the standard rhetorical division of the orator's tasks into three parts: (1) *inventio*, (2) *dispositio*, and (3) *elocutio*. The most perfect lecture, according to Baumgarten, communicates (1) "the best things, in the most proper order, by means of the most fitting words" (i.e., *inventio*), (2) "joined together in the most exquisite ways" (i.e.,

---

[70] A. G. Baumgarten, *Gedancken vom Vernünfftigen Beyfall auf Academien*, 2nd ed. (Halle, 1741). In this second edition, Baumgarten apparently expanded the original lecture to almost three times its original length, from sixteen to forty-five pages. Cf. A. Aichele, introduction to *Gedancken vom Vernünfftigen Beyfall auf Academien*, by A. G. Baumgarten, ed. A. Aichele, in *Aufklärung* 20 (2008), 282; U. Niggli, ed., *Die Vorreden zur Metaphysik*, by A. G. Baumgarten (Frankfurt (Main): Klostermann, 1998), 226. I thank Alexander Aichele for alerting me to the importance of this text.

[71] A. G. Baumgarten, *Gedancken vom Vernünfftigen Beyfall auf Academien*, §1.

[72] A. G. Baumgarten, *Gedancken vom Vernünfftigen Beyfall auf Academien*, §2.

[73] A. G. Baumgarten, *Gedancken vom Vernünfftigen Beyfall auf Academien*, §3.

dispositio), (3) "with a most beautifully harmonious eloquence of the body" (i.e., *elocutio*).[74] Given his duty to promote the well-being and reputation of his university by producing "observant and rational applause," a lecturer is morally obliged to deliver as perfect lectures as he can, which means lectures that excel in precisely these three elements. In the case of the first and most important of a lecture's perfections, the communication of "the best things," this means choosing and verbalizing the contents of the lecture in such a way as to produce perceptions in the audience that are "true, clear, certain, and living or practical" (*wahr, klar, gewiss und lebendig oder practisch*).[75] In his choice of the contents of this list, and in his definition of certainty (*Gewissheit*) as "the clear perception of the truth" (*klare Erkenntnis der Wahrheit*),[76] Baumgarten reveals that he has brought the systematic, polemical thrust of his metaphysics to bear on the subject of university lecturing, just as he would later bring it to bear on his *Aesthetics*. As in the *Metaphysics*, Baumgarten here portrays the obligation to distinctness of cognition as secondary to the more general obligation to clarity.

This is not to say that in omitting distinctness from his list of a lecture's perfections and subsuming it under the term "clear" (*klar*), Baumgarten disparages distinct ideas as inappropriate to a perfect lecture; quite to the contrary. There are certain things, Baumgarten reminds his audience, whose importance demands that we try to think of them distinctly and with as little confusion as possible. "Therefore," he explains,

> when an academic teacher has to explain things . . . like those that arise in the sciences, the most vivid sensory treatment will not suffice. Not only sensation, imagination, and everything else we associate with the lower cognitive faculties of souls should be engaged, but the intellect should also be occupied, and reason soothed and convinced.[77]

At the same time, Baumgarten by no means urges that a lecturer, obliged though he is to resist the temptation to present difficult things

---

[74] A. G. Baumgarten, *Gedancken vom Vernünfftigen Beyfall auf Academien*, §4:

> Folglich wäre der vollkommenste mündliche Vortrag, der die besten Sachen in der geschicktesten Ordnung durch die bequemsten Worte, nach ihren auserlesensten Zusammenfügungen, mit einer schönsten harmonisierenden Beredsamkeit des Leibes andern beybrächte.

[75] A. G. Baumgarten, *Gedancken vom Vernünfftigen Beyfall auf Academien*, §5.
[76] A. G. Baumgarten, *Gedancken vom Vernünfftigen Beyfall auf Academien*, §8.
[77] A. G. Baumgarten, *Gedancken vom Vernünfftigen Beyfall auf Academien*, §7:

> Hat demnach ein academischer Lehrer Dinge von dieser Art, wie in Wissenschaften vorkommen, zu erklären, so will die lebhaffteste Sinnlichkeit noch nicht hinreichen. Nicht nur Empfindung, Einbildung, und was wir sonst zu denen untern Erkenntnis-Vermögen der Seelen zählen, soll unterhalten, sondern auch der Verstand beschäfftigt, die Vernunfft beruhigt und überzeugt werden.

simplistically, omit all use of examples and other sensory devices in his discussions of things that need to be treated distinctly; the use of sensory perceptions alone simply "does not suffice."

In fact, Baumgarten emphasizes the danger of omitting sensate ideas from a lecture. Even in the case of a lecture whose chief aim is to communicate distinct perceptions, "a good lecturer cannot completely forget about vividness." Presenting the multiplicity of distinguishing characteristics that allow an audience to identify sensory objects is what keeps an audience alert and awake, makes the time seem short, and gives the audience pleasure. "A thousand little touches, even cheerfulness in the eyes, a lit-up face, and appropriate modulations of the voice all work together," Baumgarten explains, "to combine solidity with beauty as well as possible."[78] Nor should a lecturer restrict himself to vividness alone:

> Whatever we learn must be useful. Whatever is supposed to be useful must be used. Whatever is used has influence in action. A good lecture is not only vivid, but also stirring, stimulating, moving, living – this one more, that one less, this one more presently, that one farther off, but always practical.[79]

In other words, a lecturer should aim ultimately to exert a positive moral influence on the audience and move them to action. This is what it means to instill living cognition in one's audience. That it requires an appeal to the audience's lower cognitive faculties justifies, in short, the lecturer's study of aesthetic philosophy.

It would of course require severely selective reading of Baumgarten's long and detailed aesthetic writings to insist that he had only a single purpose in composing them.[80] Yet the importance that Baumgarten laid on the use of aesthetic theory as an instrument for the cultivation of living cognition makes two interrelated contemporary discussions seem likely to have been among those to which Baumgarten intended his aesthetic theory to contribute. The more directly practical of these discussions concerned the training of pastors and the spiritual and moral education of the congregations in their charge; while the more theoretical discussion concerned

---

[78] A. G. Baumgarten, *Gedancken vom Vernünfftigen Beyfall auf Academien*, §6: "Tausend Kleinigkeiten, selbst der Augen Heiterkeit, ein aufgeklärt Gesicht, der Stimme gehörige Veränderungen stimmen hie zusammen, das gründliche mit schönen nach bestem Vermögen zu verbinden."

[79] A. G. Baumgarten, *Gedancken vom Vernünfftigen Beyfall auf Academien*, §9:

> Was wir lernen, muß nützlich seyn. Was nützlich seyn soll, muß gebraucht werden. Was gebraucht wird, hat in Thun und Lassen seinen Einfluß. Ein guter Vortrag ist nicht nur lebhafft, sondern auch rührend, reitzend, bewegend, lebendig, der mehr, jener weniger, der näher, jener entfernter, aber allezeit practisch.

[80] As observed by E. Witte, *Logik ohne Dornen* (Hildesheim: Olms, 2000), 15–17.

the underlying disagreement about the foundation of morality that had resulted in Wolff's departure from Halle.

Aesthetics and the Problem of "Wolffian" Pedagogical Style

Baumgarten's aesthetic theory represented a concrete solution to a pedagogical problem that had begun to preoccupy the Halle Theology Faculty by 1736. That was the year in which Siegmund Jacob Baumgarten's colleagues politely but firmly brought to his attention their disapproval of his "Wolffian" teaching style.[81] On the evening of 11 March, a letter signed by Christian Benedict Michaelis, Johann Heinrich Michaelis, Joachim Lange, and Gotthilf August Francke was delivered to Siegmund Jacob Baumgarten, presenting him with a series of concerns that reflected – as he must have known – several weeks of deliberation on their part. The first of the concerns raised in the letter was Baumgarten's failure to submit various dissertations by his students, as well as his own textbook on moral theology, to the faculty censor before publication, and this concern Baumgarten quickly put to rest by agreeing to comply in the future.[82] The rest of the faculty's concerns – above all that Baumgarten had based his textbook of moral theology on "the Wolffian philosophy" and had thereby rendered his own teaching less effective and in some respects disadvantageous to his students – were more difficult to address.

The principal worry was not that Baumgarten had deviated in any way from what they regarded as Lutheran orthodoxy. On this issue, the faculty implicitly accepted the verdict of Johann Heinrich Michaelis, who claimed to have "found no heterodoxy" in Baumgarten's textbook.[83] Rather, the faculty worried that Baumgarten's method of teaching theology was, in Christian Benedict Michaelis's words, "overly philosophical," and made excessive reference to the principles of "Wolffian philosophy."[84] Vaguely invoking "the objections of our predecessors" – by which they almost certainly meant

---

[81] The most direct evidence of the investigation of Siegmund Jacob Baumgarten's teaching by the other members of the Theology Faculty in Halle is contained in a file entitled, "Einige Scripturae, des Hn. Prof. Baumgartens philosophische Lehrart betreffend / de anno 1736. d. 19 Febr. bis 29 April" and preserved in the archive of the Franckesche Stiftungen in Halle, AFSt /H E7. The title on the cover is in the hand of Christian Benedict Michaelis, who appears to have assembled the file. The most detailed and illuminating recent discussion of the affair is Martin Schloemann's, in *Siegmund Jacob Baumgarten*, 38–50. Less illuminating but still useful, in part because of the documents they preserve, are F. A. Tholuck, *Geschichte des Rationalismus*, v. 1 of 2 (Berlin, 1865; repr., Aalen: Scientia, 1990), I.31, I.135ff.; and Schrader, *Geschichte der Universität Halle*, I.293, II.462–63.

[82] "Einige Scripturae," AFSt /H E7, fols. 2v, 3r, 19r.

[83] "Einige Scripturae," AFSt /H E7, fols. 11v–12r.   [84] "Einige Scripturae," AFSt /H E7, fol. 3r.

those colleagues of theirs who had criticized Wolff in the previous decade but had since died, including August Hermann Francke, Joachim Justus Breithaupt, and Johann Liborius Zimmermann[85] – the faculty explained their objection to an overly philosophical teaching method in terms of the order in which theology students should be presented with various ways of communicating divine truths.

In several key respects, it was a problem familiar from the older conflict with Wolff. Buddeus and Zimmermann had happily granted that philosophical principles could reveal truths about God to those who had never seen the text of the Bible, but they had also insisted that the persuasive force of those principles alone could not carry anyone all the way through the entire process of moral development. Moral reform ultimately required that two conditions be met. First, only knowledge of God's will as such could facilitate the necessary transition from "worldy man" to life under the law and the earnest attempt to reform one's own corrupt will. Second, the transition from life under the law to life according to the gospel required the kind of exercises that led to *aisthēsis*: hymn-singing, meditation on the wounds of Christ, and above all, meditation on the text of the Bible, with the aim of experiencing the presence of the Holy Spirit.[86]

In their letter to Baumgarten, the Halle theological faculty emphasized the second of these two conditions. On the one hand, they allowed that logical deduction, an essential part of the method appropriate to philosophical instruction, was by no means to be shunned. "Philosophical principles," the faculty noted, are "a gift from God."[87] But they worried that the excessive use of Wolffian philosophical principles in theological instruction was causing theology students to "make this philosophy their chief task" and "lose all their taste [*Geschmack*] for God's word":[88]

> Of course we have to start getting concerned about our students, when we see that they formerly attended lectures on the Old and New Testaments so eagerly and often, but that by contrast, from the moment one got so

---

[85] "Einige Scripturae," AFSt /H E7, fols. 3r–3v:

> Ob ~~nun~~ aber die Wolffische Philosophie, ~~welche in~~ ~~der~~ Ihrer Theol. Moral allenthalben durchscheinet, ~~eine~~ [3v] so unanstössige ~~Philosophie~~ sey, ~~worauf~~ ^daß man eine theologische Moral darauff bauen könne, müssen wir so viel mehr zweifeln, als unsere Facultät, unter Einstimmung unserer gottseligen und nunmehro im Herrn ruhenden Vorfahren, dagegen ^vormals gezeuget gewarnet hat.

In this as in other quotations of handwritten drafts, underlining preceded by a caret indicates that the underlined words were inserted later.

[86] See above, Chapter 1, pp. 30–32, 41–44.   [87] "Einige Scripturae," AFSt /H E7, fol. 5r.

[88] "Einige Scripturae," AFSt /H E7, fol. 4r.

strongly involved in philosophizing, they let us for the most part lecture to empty benches, and are disgusted by the dear word of God (from which they should in fact be taught exclusively and at some point should instruct others in holiness through faith in Jesus Christ) as though it were a defective text.[89]

What made this contempt for the language of the Bible dangerous among theology students, the faculty continued, was in large part its deleterious consequences for the instruction of the laity:

No wonder, then, that our students (examples of whom have unfortunately become known both here and in other places), when they step into the pulpit, instead of using the simple, clear and pure word of God, philosophize – devoid of zest and power, giving offense and irritation to their consciences – and speak of possible, coincidental, simple things, of specification of one's behavior, of distinct ideas, of concepts, of a later condition based on a prior one, and of other things like this, which to the common man and to children come across like the names of Bohemian villages[90] – and after their characters have been filled solely with ideas like this, they can hardly do otherwise – and they thereby enervate the gospel rather than planting it in the heart with proof of the Spirit and its power.[91]

In asserting that Baumgarten's excessive use of a Wolffian vocabulary in the auditorium was contributing to a real problem in the pulpit,[92] the

---

[89] "Einige Scripturae," AFSt /H E7, fols. 4r–4v:

> Es muß uns billich wegen unserer Studiosorum ein Kummer ankommen, ^wenn wir sehen, daß da ^sie ehedem die Collegia über die h. Schrifft A.[?] und N. Testaments mit solcher Begierde und Frequentz besuchet haben, ~~wir~~ sie hingegen von der Zeit an, da man in das Philosophiren so starck eingegangen ^ist ~~haben wahrnehmen müssen, wie wir~~ [4v] ^uns guten Theils in solchen Collegiis ~~gutenteils~~ denen leeren Bäncken ~~haben~~ ^haben gelesen ~~müssen~~ ^haben lassen, und ~~denen Studiosis~~ ^ihnen vor dem lieben Wort Gottes (~~vor~~ aus ^welchem ~~sie~~ doch ^allein sie sollen unterrichtet werden, und ~~auch~~ andere ^mal dereinst ^wieder unterweisen ~~wol sollen~~ zur Seligkeit, durch den Glauben an Christo J̅esu) als vor einer losen Schrift eckelt.

[90] That is, things no one has heard of.

[91] "Einige Scripturae," AFSt /H E7, fol. 4v:

> Wunder ist es denn nicht, daß unsere Studiosi, (wie ~~uns~~ dergleichen Exempel, so wol an hiesigen, als an andered Orten leider! bekant worden sind) wenn sie auff die Kantzel kommen, statt des einfaltigen, lauteren und reinen Worts Gottes, safft- und krafftloß, zum Anstoß und Ärgerniß derer Gewissen, philosophiren, und lauter möglichen, zufälligen, einfachen ^Dingen, von Bestimmung des Verhaltens, deutlichen Vorstellungen, ^Begriffen, folgendem Zustand in den vorhergehenden gegründet, und anderen dergleichen Sachen, welche dem ~~armen~~ gemeinen Mann und den Kindern als Böhmische Dörffer vorkommen, zu reden wissen, ^ ^auch nachdem ihre Gemüther mit lauter solchen Ideen angefüllet werden, kaum anders können; dadurch aber das ~~andere~~ [?] herrliche Evangelium vielmehr enerviren, als mit ~~Krafft~~ Beweisung des Geistes und der Krafft an die Hertzen legen.

[92] This problem, which Baumgarten's colleagues clearly perceived as widespread, has been described at much greater length as the "controversy about the philosophical sermon" in A. Straßberger, *Johann*

faculty were drawing on presuppositions familiar from the arguments that Buddeus and Zimmermann had advanced against Wolff. A human being's transition to "holiness" required "faith in Jesus Christ," and only the language of the Bible, by virtue of its having been inspired by the Holy Spirit, had the force sufficient to effect that transition. Nor did it derive its force from its appeal to the intellect. Inculcating "distinct ideas" about the "nexus of things" by means of a philosophically precise vocabulary was likely to leave the "common man" and children unmoved. A good preacher was therefore well-advised to rely on the power of the biblical text in his sermons, which meant that Halle's professors – who had evidently become known for "dressing up the clear Bible with unclear Wolffian language" – should be inculcating theology students with a "taste" (*Geschmack*, *Goût*) for God's word and, in an attempt to facilitate their students' conversion, should appeal to the power of the examples of Christ and the apostles rather than the power of "human wisdom."[93] In reference to the anti-Wolffian history of philosophy drawn on by Buddeus and Zimmermann, the theology faculty referred to the former as the "ancient method" of education revived by Johann Arndt and championed by Pietism, and the latter, by contrast, as a return to "Scholasticism."[94]

Upon receiving his colleagues' letter and reading their concerns about his use of Wolffian philosophical terms in his teaching, Siegmund Jacob Baumgarten offered a set of responses which, while appropriate and correct, did not squarely address the faculty's worry about the deleterious consequences his teaching might have on Halle theology students' conversion and their effectiveness as preachers. On the one hand, he contested his colleagues' portrayal of the facts: there were many parts of his teaching, he asserted, in which he did not rely heavily on Wolff's philosophical vocabulary. On the other hand, Baumgarten claimed that in the limited number of places where he did make use of Wolffian terms, he did so because philosophical terms were necessary for the purposes of giving a coherent lecture.[95] It was a prudent response. In offering this second answer, Baumgarten was evidently appealing to a division in the faculty

---

Christoph Gottsched und die "philosophische" Predigt (Tübingen: Mohr Siebeck, 2010), 145–53, 346–51, 384–89, 399, 430–51, 481, 491–93.

[93] "Einige Scripturae," AFSt /H E7, fol. 9r. Cf. Thomas Abbt's caricature of this prescription, above, Chapter 2, p. 70. On the significance of the concept of "taste" in this context: S. Grote, "Vom geistlichen zum guten Geschmack? Reflexionen zur Suche nach den pietistischen Wurzeln der Ästhetik," trans. C. Drese, in *Schönes Denken: A. G. Baumgarten im Spannungsfeld zwischen Ästhetik, Logik und Ethik*, ed. A. Allerkamp and D. Mirbach (Hamburg: Meiner, 2016).

[94] "Einige Scripturae," AFSt /H E7, fols. 5v–6r.

[95] "Einige Scripturae," AFSt /H E7, fols. 29r–30r.

on precisely the question of whether philosophical terminology should be entirely excluded from theological lectures. In the deliberations over what concerns should be brought to Baumgarten's attention, Johann Heinrich Michaelis had declined to endorse Baumgarten's pedagogical method in its entirety, but he had clearly defended Baumgarten's use of Wolffian philosophical terms, especially since Baumgarten had been using them selectively rather than ubiquitously. It was Joachim Lange, the member of the faculty who had for years expressed private irritation about the popularity of Baumgarten's lectures among students, and who had in fact already brought formal complaints against Baumgarten before the Theology Faculty three times between 1733 and 1736,[96] who took a more radical position, insisting that theological lectures exclude philosophical terminology.[97] In flatly disagreeing with Lange on this point, Baumgarten did not risk alienating his other colleagues. But to the question of whether theology students who attended university lectures laced with philosophical terms were likely to adopt similar terms while preaching in a parish church, Baumgarten gave no direct answer.

He must have felt some pressure to do so, though, since King Friedrich Wilhelm I, in his answers to Lange's and Baumgarten's appeals for royal support in the conflict, made it clear that the question was important to him. Though the king urged Lange to refashion himself into a "useful example of Christian calmness" (*ein nützliches Exempel einer Christlichen Gelassenheit*) and expressed a skepticism that Wolff's ideas could be suppressed either by force or by refutation, he also reaffirmed his hope that the Theology Faculty would work harmoniously toward the goal that Lange and his colleagues had worried was being endangered by Baumgarten's pedagogical method:

> that theology students be led to true, living Christianity and to genuine competence in serving God usefully as preachers, so that many upright preachers may become of them.[98]

To Baumgarten, the king expressed a similar hope, if in different terms. He reminded Baumgarten

---

[96] Tholuck, *Geschichte des Rationalismus*, I.135.

[97] "Einige Scripturae," AFSt /H E7, fols. 32r–35v.

[98] Friedrich Wilhelm I to J. Lange, 22 September 1736, in Schrader, *Geschichte der Universität Halle*, II.462:

> dass die Studiosi Theologiae zum wahren Lebendigen Christenthum und rechtigen [richtigen?] Tüchtigkeit Gott in Predigt Amt nützlich zu dienen, angeführet werden, damit ferner viele rechtschaffene Prediger aus ihnen werden mögen.

that you will do well by your own conscience, and will recommend yourself to me, if you withdraw from all incomprehensible philosophical absurdities, which neither improve nor edify and only give innocent and simple characters opportunity for error, and instead stick with what is real in theology, and teach it in the same way that it was taught by the blessed Breithaupt and Francke, and lead your listeners to a true, active Christianity.[99]

Unsurprisingly, given the king's explicit concern, Siegmund Jacob Baumgarten did not wait long to address directly the alleged danger of his lectures to the spiritual development and homiletic skill of his students. In printed form, Baumgarten's response survives in his introduction to the 1738 edition – probably the first complete edition – of the moral theology textbook that had worried his colleagues on the Theology Faculty in 1736, when it had not yet been printed in its entirety.[100] According to Baumgarten, three of the four criticisms raised against the book relate in some way to its exaggerated appeal to the human intellect. His critics claim (1) that he considers arguments derived from naturally perceived truths to be indispensable to a correct understanding of revealed truths; (2) that he thinks the truths contained in scripture should be accepted only insofar as they are "rational" (*vernünftig*); and (3) that he claims that spiritual improvement and conversion depend on the human intellect and the "sharpness of proof," and are within the power of humans themselves.[101] But the criticism that Baumgarten describes first, and the criticism that he addresses first and at greatest length, is the one his colleagues in fact dwelt on in their discussion of his lectures: that his moral theology textbook is unconducive to the spiritual edification of his students and leads them to give dry sermons. In response, Baumgarten appeals to the intended purpose of the book. "If the capacity of a book to edify depends on its mode of presentation being vivid, moving, stimulating, and designed genuinely to touch

---

[99] Friedrich Wilhelm I to S. J. Baumgarten, 22 September 1736, in Schrader, *Geschichte der Universität Halle*, II.463:

> dass Ihr sowohl vor Euer Gewissen wohl thun, als auch Euch bei Mir recommendiren werdet, wann Ihr von allen dergleichen unverstendlichen Philosophischen Fratzen, so weder bessern noch erbauen, unschuldigen und einfeltigen Gemüthern aber nur Gelegenheit zu Irwegen geben, hinführo abstrahiret, dagegen bei dem reellen in der Theologie bleibet, und solche auf gleiche Arth, als sie von den Seel. Breithaupt und Francken dociret worden, lehret, auch Eure Zuhörer auf ein Wahres thätiges Christenthum führet.

[100] S. J. Baumgarten, *Unterricht vom rechtmässigen Verhalten eines Christen oder Theologische Moral* (Halle, 1738), Vorbericht. According to Ludovici, sections of the work had already been printed in February 1736 and formed the basis for a review in the fourteenth installment of the *Hamburgische Berichte von Gelehrten Sachen* of that year. Ludovici claimed in 1736 to have seen "only ten sheets" (*nur 10. Bogen*). Ludovici, *Ausführlicher Entwurf*, II.§472.

[101] S. J. Baumgarten, *Unterricht vom rechtmässigen Verhalten eines Christen*, Vorbericht [xxi].

the soul [*Gemüth*]," he explains, "then I admit that this cannot be found here." But such edification is not his purpose; rather, he intends "to teach and convince the reader," which should not be dismissed as irrelevant to spiritual edification. Rational persuasion of theological truths may not suffice on its own, but neither do the nonrational means that Francke and Breithaupt had stressed. "The mere awakening of sensate emotions in the soul," Baumgarten points out, "if it is detached from adequate persuasion, is just as insufficient for fundamental and long-lasting improvement."[102] As for the alleged danger that the rational persuasion of theology students in the classroom will lead them to use the same, dry pedagogical technique in the pulpit, Baumgarten calls this "an unnecessary misuse" of his textbook, which contradicts the very rules of good preaching asserted in it.[103] In Siegmund Jacob Baumgarten's view, the rational persuasion aided by his allegedly "Wolffian" teaching style could be an effective means of teaching students to give vivid, spiritually edifying sermons in a less "philosophical" style. His brother, Alexander, took the same position.

On the one hand, Alexander Baumgarten shared the Theology Faculty's concern about philosophizing in the pulpit. In his lectures on aesthetics, Baumgarten explicitly recommended to aspiring homiletes the study of aesthetic philosophy, with its explanation of how to develop and appeal to the lower cognitive faculties of one's audience by employing clear and confused ideas to describe things that the "common man" would not understand if they were expressed distinctly. By means of aesthetics, Baumgarten says, "a theologian will become a good homilete."[104] In fact, Baumgarten later notes, the very word *theology* once denoted "nothing more than thinking about God and godly things in a beautiful way," and this aspect of theology must be preserved for "the great mass" of people who depend on it. "One can prove God's existence philosophically, but one can also do it beautifully."[105] Similarly telling is a footnote that Baumgarten inserted in the 1741 edition of his inaugural lecture at Frankfurt (Oder), after mentioning a lecturer's obligation to clarity (*Klarheit*):

> It would be good if the discipline of pedagogy were in general somewhat more commonly known, and still better if it were more frequently put into practice. Several parts of it, under the name of catachism and homiletics, have frequently had to endure serious abuse, yet they have finally also had the good fortune to be treated solidly by learned people who understand art. But when it comes to how adults are to be instructed in any fields of

---

[102] S. J. Baumgarten, *Unterricht vom rechtmässigen Verhalten eines Christen*, Vorbericht [xxiv–xxv].
[103] S. J. Baumgarten, *Unterricht vom rechtmässigen Verhalten eines Christen*, Vorbericht [xxvi].
[104] A. G. Baumgarten, *Kollegium*, §3.   [105] A. G. Baumgarten, *Kollegium*, §126.

learning, most logics are completely silent, and a few say a little and are not widely known.[106]

Poor or absent instruction in pedagogy, in Baumgarten's view, was a problem that teachers of logic had not solved and could not solve. Even a professor of philosophy had to give lectures that, for all the necessity of occasionally using distinct ideas to treat especially difficult and important subjects, were "not only vivid, but also stirring, stimulating, moving, living":

> Even the doctrine of fear of God, which is useful in all things, can be propounded in a dead and lifeless way. It is even easier [to do so] in other truths, but it is not therefore more proper.[107]

The Halle Theology Faculty's self-proclaimed dismay at the spread of preaching "devoid of zest and power" finds an unmistakable echo in Baumgarten's evocation of the danger of dry lectures – even on subjects as obviously stirring as the fear of God – as a warning to lecturers to make their lectures on all subjects vivid, moving, and of practical consequence.

On the other hand, of course, although Baumgarten deplored dry and overly theoretical preaching, he clearly did not entirely share his brother's colleagues' fear of the deleterious effects of a "Wolffian" lecture style. His own lectures were by no account the least bit dry, but his Latin textbooks were notoriously turgid,[108] and both his textbooks and lectures on aesthetics made full use of the conceptual vocabulary and method of demonstration that Wolff had championed. Baumgarten himself was thereby implicitly demonstrating that the use of philosophical language in textbooks and in the auditorium – albeit in lectures on philosophy, not theology – could in fact be a powerful means of discouraging the exclusive use of such language

---

[106] A. G. Baumgarten, *Gedancken vom Vernünfftigen Beyfall auf Academien*, §4:

> Es wäre guth, wenn die Didactik oder Lehr-Kunst überhaupt etwas gemeiner bekannt, und noch besser, wenn sie häuffiger ausgeübet würde. Einige Theile derselben haben unter dem Nahmen der Catechetik und Homiletik sich zwar öffters höchlich mißhandeln lassen müssen, doch auch endlich das Glück gehabt, von kunstverständigen Gelehrten gründlich abgehandelt zu werden. Wie aber Erwachsene in jeden Theilen der Gelehrsamkeit zu unterrichten seyen, davon schweigen die meisten Logiken gantz, wenige sagen wenig, und sind wenig in Händen.

[107] A. G. Baumgarten, *Gedancken vom Vernünfftigen Beyfall auf Academien*, §9: "Da selbst die Lehre der zu allen Dingen nützlichen Gottesfurcht todt und lebloß vorgetragen werden kan: so ist es noch leichter in andern Wahrheiten, aber deswegen eben nicht rechtmäßiger." Cf. [A. G. Baumgarten], *Philosophische Brieffe*, 12.

[108] On the difficulty of Baumgarten's Latin: C. Denina, *La Prusse littéraire sous Frederic II*, v. 1 of 3 (1790; repr., *DBA*), s.v. "Baumgarten (Alexandre Théophile)"; and G. F. Meier, introduction to *Metaphysik*, by A. G. Baumgarten, trans. G. F. Meier (Halle, 1783), ed. Dagmar Mirbach (Jena: Schleglmann, 2004), 3. More generally on Baumgarten's style: Gawlick and Kreimendahl, introduction to *Metaphysica*, by A. G. Baumgarten, XL–XLVI.

in the pulpit. The logical force of his words, he hoped, would convince students to undertake the exercises necessary for them to refine their taste – that is, their ability to use their lower cognitive faculties to judge whether a given thing is beautiful[109] – and thereby become good preachers, moving an audience to action by the beauty of their ideas and their words. Put more generally, Baumgarten employed pedagogical techniques whose excessive use in theological instruction concerned the Halle Theology Faculty, but he did so in order to persuade students to develop the kind of taste the faculty feared was lacking in its graduates and urgently wanted to inculcate in them primarily by other means, namely, by meditation on the text of the Bible.[110] Moreover, like the members of the Theology Faculty who had criticized his brother, and like those who had criticized Wolff, Baumgarten saw the development of taste as crucial not only to instruction in homiletics but also to students' moral and spiritual education more generally. His aesthetic theory therefore offered a solution not only to the problem of poor instruction of Halle theology students in homiletics but also to a problem much broader in its scope and in its immediate social significance: the alleged undermining of the foundation of morality by Christian Wolff.

Aesthetics and the Foundation of Morality

On the one hand, Baumgarten clearly disagreed with Wolff's critics about the question at the heart of their debate, namely, whether people who have neither encountered the Bible nor developed any awareness of the will of God are capable of genuine moral improvement, or whether moral improvement necessarily begins with an awareness of divine law and a fear of divine punishment. Like Wolff, Baumgarten consistently asserted that there is such a thing as natural moral obligation, and that this obligation arises from the perception of perfection – not necessarily the perception of a law in the strict sense – by the human conscience. On the other hand, although Baumgarten did not concede that the reform of the will needs to begin with fear of God, he not only conceded but even insisted that moral obligation necessarily arises in part from clear and confused ideas, and not in fact or even ideally from distinct ideas alone. Baumgarten wanted to preserve, in other words, the sensory part of moral education that Wolff's critics regarded as essential, and whose absence in Wolff's program of moral education they had taken as grounds for accusing him of Scholasticism. In

---

[109] A. G. Baumgarten, *Metaphysica*, §§606–9.
[110] For an elaboration on this conclusion, see Grote, "Vom geistlichen zum guten Geschmack?"

terms of the divisions of university education, this project by Baumgarten belonged to the realm of moral philosophy and natural law, but it left marks on most of Baumgarten's writings, including his aesthetic writings, which described for the benefit of writers, orators, homiletes, and other practitioners of the "fine arts" the rules for cultivating the kind of cognition that needed to be applied in the specific area of moral education.

The abundant and incontrovertible evidence that Baumgarten fundamentally agreed with Wolff about the existence and effectiveness of natural obligation can be found primarily in his writings on moral philosophy. Pride of place belongs to his *Initia philosophiae practicae primae* (Elements of first practical philosophy), a textbook he began writing long before 1760, the year he finally published it after considerable delays owing primarily to poor health.[111] The book's very purpose, as Baumgarten's explication of its title reveals, was to explain how to acquire, without faith, a fundamental knowledge of human obligations, which is to say, a knowledge of those general principles of obligation from which one can deduce the more specific principles of obligation relevant to every other, more specialized "practical discipline."[112] Baumgarten's agreement with Wolff comes to light in the book's most basic principles. Obligation, Baumgarten explains, can be distinguished according to how it arises. Whereas *positive* or *external* obligation has its source in the will of someone other than the obligated actor, *natural* or *internal* obligation has its source in the nature of an actor or an action.[113] Like Wolff, Baumgarten describes the actions from which internal obligation arises as morally good insofar as they tend to increase perfection.[114] Human beings, he asserts, including atheists, are naturally obliged to live as closely in accordance with their own nature as possible, which is to say, to seek their own perfection to as great an extent as they can.[115]

Baumgarten's agreement with Wolff about the subjection of atheists to natural moral obligation, unsurprisingly, can be traced to his agreement with Wolff about the human conscience. Moral obligation, he explains, exerts force on the human will when the human conscience subsumes the

---

[111] A. G. Baumgarten, *Initia philosophiae practicae primae* (Halle, 1760), praefatio; Meier, *Alexander Gottlieb Baumgartens Leben*, 44.

[112] A. G. Baumgarten, *Initia philosophiae practicae primae*, §§1, 6.

[113] A. G. Baumgarten, *Initia philosophiae practicae primae*, §29.

[114] A. G. Baumgarten, *Initia philosophiae practicae primae*, §36. Baumgarten does not specify whose or what perfection a morally good action must tend to promote, an ambiguity familiar to readers of Wolff. On Baumgarten's position with regard to this ambiguity, and on his reformulation of Wolffian perfection-oriented ethical principles in terms of obligation: Schwaiger, *Alexander Gottlieb Baumgarten*, 129–39, 155–65.

[115] A. G. Baumgarten, *Initia philosophiae practicae primae*, §§43–48.

idea of a particular action under a "moral law," and this law need not be a law in the strict sense (*lex stricte dicta*). Law in the strict sense – also called positive law (*lex positiva*) or external law (*lex externa*) – is the law whose application by the conscience creates external or positive obligation, whereas the law whose application creates internal or natural obligation is natural law (*lex naturalis*), otherwise known as a recommendation or counsel (*consilium*), internal law (*lex interna*), or law in the broad sense (*lex late dicta*).[116] Baumgarten does not deny that all natural laws are in fact also divine positive laws, with their origin in the will of God, but he insists that their application by the conscience can create internal moral obligation even in people who reject that origin. A "theoretical atheist,"[117] Baumgarten asserts, in spite of denying God's existence, "can be persuaded about many things rightly claimed of natural law spoken of in a broad sense, or of practical philosophy, independently of his atheism or those assumptions that he denies, or that at any rate must be supposed of him, as an atheist." At the same time, Baumgarten adds,

> Nevertheless, having established this, it is not admitted that (1) the law of nature in a broad sense, or practical philosophy, would exist even if God's existence were not granted; (2) it is wholly independent from God; (3) it can be derived from the will of God with no reason at all; (4) it can be understood equally by an atheist and by someone who is an agnostic about divine being. For the atheist's law of nature, or practical philosophy, as it is understood by one who persists in his error, lacks the following things: (1) breadth and abundance, (2) dignity of its matter, (3) truth, (4) clarity, (5) certainty, and (6) life, the capacity for which belongs to natural law for someone who accepts divine existence.[118]

---

[116] A. G. Baumgarten, *Initia philosophiae practicae primae*, §§60–66. Baumgarten introduces parallel sets of terms for almost every important element of his textbook – e.g., he notes that "norm" (*norma*) is another word for *law* – but for the sake of clarity and concision I confine my summary to a single set of terms.

[117] That is, atheists who display their disbelief in God's existence through what they teach, as distinct from "practical atheists," those who display their disbelief through how they live. Cf. Walch, *Philosophisches Lexikon*, s.v. "Atheisterey," 136.

[118] A. G. Baumgarten, *Initia philosophiae practicae primae*, §71:

> Hinc si ius naturae athei asseritur hoc sensu, existentiam divinam qui neget, eum tamen de bene multis assertis iuris naturae late dicti, s[eu] potius philosophiae practicae ... convinci posse, independenter ab eius atheismo, aut illis praemissis, quas negat, qua atheus, utique ponendum est. Neque tamen hoc posito admittitur: 1) ius naturae late dictum s[eu] philosophia practica esset, etiam si non daretur deus ... 2) prorsus est independens a deo ... 3) ex voluntate dei nulla ratione omnino derivari potest ... 4) aeque bene cognosci potest ab atheo, ac ab agnoscente divinam existentiam. Nam ius naturae athei s[eu] philosophia practica, quam in suo errore perseverans cognoscere potest, destituitur ea 1) latitudine et copia, 2) dignitate materiae[,] 3) veritate, 4) luce, 5) certitudine[,] 6) vita,

In this discussion of the obligation of atheists to obey the precepts of natural law, Baumgarten explains his position elliptically but with a care that reveals his awareness of the state of the debate in which he is implicitly engaging. That atheists would be obliged to obey natural law even if God did not exist was an assertion of Wolff's that had drawn criticism from Gundling, and Baumgarten explicitly avoids it. Like Walch, he moreover steers clear of the view that natural law, whose continuing existence he agrees depends on the will of God, is the product of God's arbitrary will, uninformed by reason.[119] Like Wolff, though perhaps more obviously than Wolff, he also grants that one who denies God's existence – a "theoretical" atheist – cannot be obliged by natural law to the extent that a believer can, since natural law's scope, dignity, truth, clarity, and life are diminished for him. But Baumgarten nonetheless asserts the obligatory force of the reasoning that an atheist can engage in. The capacity for reasoning that the atheist shares with all other human beings, believers or not, is presumably the capacity to reason about which actions best contribute to his own perfection, and this capacity is what allows natural law to exert the force of moral obligation on him.

Baumgarten advances the same view in the textbook on ethics that he first published in 1740.[120] The first significant indication of his agreement with Wolff about the effectiveness of natural, internal moral obligation for atheists comes in the preface and synopsis of the first edition, where we learn that, like many authors of textbooks on ethics, Baumgarten will devote the vast majority of his textbook to discussing the three types of obligations: obligations to oneself, to others, and to God.[121] Baumgarten places the obligations to God first. This represents a reversal of the order of obligations in Wolff's *German Ethics*, but Baumgarten explains his decision to reverse the order by appealing to an argument made by Wolff himself. The obligations to God come first "not so much on account of the excellence of the most perfect [being]" (*non tam ob excellentiam perfectissimi*), but rather "because they contain the most majestic bonds of the remaining obligations" (*quia reliquarum obligationum augustissima vincula*

cuius capax est ius naturae late dictum s[eu] philosophia practica existentiam divinam admittentis.

119 Cf. A. G. Baumgarten, *Initia philosophiae practicae primae*, §69; [A. G. Baumgarten], *Philosophische Brieffe*, 65–68. Cf. above, Chapter 1, pp. 40–41.

120 A. G. Baumgarten, *Ethica philosophica* (Halle, 1740); A. G. Baumgarten, *Ethica philosophica*, 3rd ed. (Halle, 1763; repr., Hildesheim: Olms, 1969); Meier, *Alexander Gottlieb Baumgartens Leben*, 41–43. All citations of A. G. Baumgarten's *Ethica philosophica* follow the 1763 edition.

121 Cf. Wolff, *Deutsche Ethik*. Baumgarten calls the treatment of the three categories of obligation *ethica generalis*, leaving only the last sixty pages of his 326-page book to *ethica specialis*, an outline of obligations not shared by all human beings as such. A. G. Baumgarten, *Ethica*, §§400–500.

continent).[122] Wolff, too, had indicated that the obligation to obey the natural law can be deduced from the obligation to further God's honor (which includes the obligation to piety),[123] an apparently apologetic point around which Baumgarten now purports to shape his whole book. Meanwhile, while emphasizing this apologetic argument in his preface, Baumgarten unsurprisingly refrains from drawing explicit attention to his still more substantive agreement with Wolff on the point that had drawn criticism from Lange and Zimmermann in the first place: namely, that the natural obligation to piety can itself be deduced from the obligation to perfect oneself. *This* chain of reasoning is in fact what occupies Baumgarten's seventy-four-page discussion of the obligations to God. Having unabashedly ended the book's prolegomena by declaring a moral maxim much like the one in Wolff's *German Ethics* ("Perfect yourself in your natural state, as much as you can"),[124] Baumgarten proceeds to argue systematically that as human beings, we are naturally obliged to acts of piety and to true knowledge of God's perfections because they perfect us.[125]

Aware of the offense this argument could cause, Baumgarten included in his 1740 preface a gesture of self-defense, embedded in an extraordinary passage, one of the relatively few statements that sheds more than a faint glimmer of direct light on a contemporary polemic in which he must have imagined himself to be engaged:

> For me cognition was always the most enjoyable pleasure of philosophical knowledge – if there is any in me. Little tender-minded folk, in their narrow pursuit of a good mind, shudder at anything more burdensome or annoying. Yet all that which the sacred prophecies of our Saviour bid be taken into consideration has not been established by some blind will, much less as something that is evil to good men, but as being so closely consistent with a truly blessed life, so intimately related to the beautiful requirements [*nexibus*] of our salvation, that even a weakened rational faculty, such as men possess, would be sufficient whatever its extent, and remains wholly at rest in the will of our most loving Father when joyously perceiving their wondrous interconnection. For this reason, although it is something usually left unspoken, it is a particularly bitter grief for me when I see that even honest men, the kind of men from whom a more exact consideration of things is to be expected, oppose themselves to moral philosophy because they believe

---

[122] A. G. Baumgarten, *Ethica*, praefatio [1740], 3r.   [123] Wolff, *Deutsche Ethik*, §§654–55, 670–71.

[124] A. G. Baumgarten, *Ethica*, §10: "Ergo *perfice te in statu naturali*, QUANTUM POTES." On the significance of Baumgarten's addition of "as much as you can" to Wolff's formula: Schwaiger, *Alexander Gottlieb Baumgarten*, 135–36.

[125] A. G. Baumgarten, *Ethica*, §§11–149.

that it fosters the error named after Pelagius. We must perform as much religious devotion through the powers of our corrupt nature as the most sacred
deity demands from us. Only philosophers vow that they will be led to religious devotion by the hand, as it were, completely by their own proofs, and
they boast that they will arrive at it without faith.[126]

Without naming names, Baumgarten alludes to the foundation-of-
morality controversy, just as he would twenty years later in his *Initia*, and
clearly indicates his side. As in the *Initia*, Baumgarten expresses dissatisfaction with the view that moral principles are decreed by God's "blind will"
rather than by his reason, a view that Wolff had attributed to Buddeus
and that Walch, in reply, had dismissed as an unfair caricature.[127] He also
takes issue with the charge of Pelagianism, leveled against philosophers for
purporting to inculcate moral obligation, including obligations to God, by
natural means. That such a purpose involved minimizing the value of faith
and, by extension, the revealed word of God and the penitential struggle,
was of course the general charge that Zimmermann and Buddeus had leveled against Wolff. Baumgarten's description of his own, alternative position is also reminiscent of Wolff's. Human beings are naturally capable, by
virtue of their own reason, of insight into the "wonderous interconnection"
of "the beautiful requirements of our salvation": that is, the decree by God,
the "most loving Father," that the behavior he enjoins in scripture for the
sake of salvation does not contradict the behavior whose goodness can be
observed naturally, without scripture's help.

That Baumgarten was directing his comments specifically at Wolff's critics in the foundation-of-morality controversy becomes still clearer – uncan-
nily so – in his defense against the charge that the philosophical exposition
of moral obligations fosters Pelagianism. The defense consists primarily

---

[126] A. G. Baumgarten, *Ethica*, praefatio [1740], 3v–4r:

> Iucundissimus mihi semper, cognitionis si quid est in me philosophicae, fructus eiusdem
> ille fuit, perspicere, quicquid onerosius aut molestius in angusto bonae mentis tramite
> horrent delicatuli, quod iniungitur tamen in sacris nostri sospitatoris oraculis, illud omne,
> non caeco quodam arbitrio stabilitum, multo minus, ut male sit viris bonis, excogitatum
> esse, sed tam arcte cum vita vere beata cohaerere, tam pulcris insinuari saluti nostrae nex-
> ibus, ut satis etiam infirma ratio, qualis est hominum, quanta quanta [*sic*] sit, possit tamen
> mirabilem eorum concatenationem penetrans hoc lubentius in indulgentissimi patris vol-
> untate conquiescere. Quam ob rationem, licet tacitum plerumque, tamen amarius est mihi
> cordolium, ubi video, probos etiam viros, a quibus tamen accuratior esset exspectanda
> rerum ponderatio, philosophiae morum sese opponere propter hanc caussam, quia fovere
> credunt eum errorem, quem a Pelagio dicunt, quantam sanctissimum numen a nobis reli-
> gionem postulat, tantam corruptae naturae viribus esse praestandam, ad hanc se manu
> quasi ducturos omnino per suas demonstrationes unice polliceri philosophos, ad hanc eos
> sine fide se perventuros gloriari.

[127] See above, Chapter I, pp. 40–41.

of an illustrative example of a very similar type of educational exposition, conducted by the critics themselves, in which the charge of Pelagianism is patently unfair. The example Baumgarten chooses is biblical exegesis:

> Suppose that in the theology that we call *revealed*, someone has taught the most weighty chapters of the law, as distinguished from the gospel; has especially insisted upon a meaning for it that they call *spiritual*, and has related the entire scope of the decalogue sufficiently richly and rigorously. Suppose that while the same person is at a point where he might pass to an interpretation of the gospel for increasing the strengths [of his argument], objections are raised (as I noted above) by philosophers that make it erroneous. What do you think he will reply, or what would you yourself reply if you had to take up his case?[128]

This final question – Baumgarten takes his response no further – is of course rhetorical. Inferring what Baumgarten expected the answer to be requires filling in some ellipses in his train of thought. Baumgarten clearly takes biblical exegesis to be similar to moral philosophy, and the key to understanding why is supplied by August Hermann Francke's handbook on biblical hermeneutics, which Baumgarten encountered either directly or indirectly as a student in Francke's schools.[129] The charge of Pelagianism that Baumgarten says has been raised against teachers of moral philosophy could equally be turned against theologians expounding upon the Bible, insofar as theologians routinely explain the spiritual meaning of the text of the law to people who have not had the *aisthēsis* – that is, spiritual knowledge inspired by the Holy Spirit – that Francke himself insisted was requisite for a full understanding of that spiritual meaning. If moral philosophers are guilty of believing, falsely, that the demonstrations they use to teach moral principles can lead students, without the help of faith, to reach the highest degree of piety and general moral rectitude that God requires, then surely theologians must be guilty of believing, equally falsely, that the rhetorical means they use to convince their audience of the spiritual meaning of the text of the law can lead that audience to adopt a spiritual moral *habitus* without intervention by the Holy Spirit. But since

---

[128] A. G. Baumgarten, *Ethica*, praefatio [1740], 4r:

> Fac in theologia, quam revelatam nuncupamus, docuisse non neminem gravissima capita legis, qua distinguitur ab evangelio, sensum illius, quem spiritualem appellant, inculcasse praecipue, totumque decem verborum ambitum satis ubertim absolvisse, satis rigide: fac eidem, dum est in procinctu, quo transeat ad evangelii vires largientis interpretationem, obiici, quae philosophis vitio verti supra notavi: quid regesturum eum opinaris, aut quid ipse caussam ipsius suscepturus regereres?

[129] See above, Chapter 2, pp. 74–78, 87.

theologians are presumably innocent of this charge – so Baumgarten's example implies – then the same must be true of moral philosophers. To accuse them of Pelagianism is unfair.

The actual proof of the theologians' innocence, which supplies by analogy a defense of moral philosophers, Baumgarten leaves to his reader's imagination. But Francke's descriptions of biblical exegesis and moral education offer a clue. *Aisthēsis* may have been ultimately unavailable to anyone who lacked the experience of inspiration by the Holy Spirit, in Francke's view, but this did not mean that discussing the spiritual meaning of the law among such people was pointless; quite to the contrary. An awareness of the law's spiritual meaning, even without any corresponding change in one's own character, was presumably a useful preparation for such a change. On Francke's account, one could affirm the usefulness of human theological education while at the same time, without inconsistency, affirming that moral regeneration was impossible without faith, and that faith required the collaboration of the Holy Spirit. By analogy, one could affirm the usefulness of a philosophical education in the principles of ethics while at the same time denying that the highest degree of moral obligation could arise in the absence of the "supernatural knowledge" of moral obligation that only the faithful could acquire. It was therefore not "Pelagian" of Baumgarten to describe the aim of philosophical ethics as "certainty of internal obligations in a natural state"[130] and thereby to affirm both that atheists were capable of the certainty that philosophical ethics could provide, and that natural, internal moral obligation could have an effect on them. Francke's own method of instruction, Baumgarten implied, gave the lie to Wolff's critics' attack.

But Baumgarten did not simply repeat Wolff's arguments. He followed neither Wolff's defense of natural obligation as a function exclusively of the rational appetite, nor Wolff's program for moral education, with its warning against engaging the human affections and its heavy emphasis on training the human conscience to construct syllogisms whose terms are as distinct as possible. The most pervasive suggestion of Baumgarten's deviation from Wolff can be found in his style of teaching ethics, which corresponded to his public declaration, in Frankfurt (Oder) in 1740, that a good lecturer is obliged to engage an audience's lower cognitive faculties. The textbook he had written for the use of his students was admittedly little more than an outline: dry, terse, and brief. Baumgarten intended it to be a strictly logical treatment of the subject, appealing exclusively to his

---

[130] A. G. Baumgarten, *Ethica*, §3.

students' intellects.[131] The aesthetic treatment of the subject, on the other hand, which would appeal to students' imaginations and sensory faculties, Baumgarten included in his spoken lectures, where he promised to "expound more copiously" on the topics in the book.[132] As Baumgarten explained to prospective auditors, he did not want his lectures to be simply an exercise in transcription:

> Would that in expounding upon ethics one didn't have to take refuge in your hands and pens! It is quite a sweet task for me to exercise minds, stimulate the nerves of thinking, and keep the reason engaged of those who listen to me. To exhaust their hands and fill their pages is something that I not only do not strive for but in fact avoid as much as I can.[133]

What Baumgarten hoped to engage was not solely his auditors' reason, but their minds more generally and their "nerves of thinking" (*nervi cogitandi*). He meant "to place the beauty of [the virtues] before their eyes."[134] Nor could this aesthetic treatment of ethics be dispensed with: "A book of this kind," Baumgarten explained in reference to his textbook, "is never really perfected and must have all its rhythms polished, but then finally acquires perfect unity when the living voice and speaking style of a commentator, in a carefree manner, come together as one."[135]

Given these suggestions that Baumgarten followed his own aesthetic precepts in lecturing on ethics, it comes as no surprise that in the arguments

---

[131] Baumgarten clearly intended the book to be used by students listening to his lectures on ethics, which he began giving at the University of Halle in Spring 1738 and Winter 1739, the semester in which he received the call to Frankfurt (Oder). It superseded the handwritten outlines of Baumgarten's ethics that appear to have been in use among Halle students already in 1738. (The mention of a "very brief" text in the advertisements for Baumgarten's 1738 and 1739 lectures on ethics in Halle suggests that his textbook or something like it was already available before 1740 in some form. *Catalogi lectionum . . . publicati in Academia Fridericiana*, Spring 1738, Winter 1739.) Cf. Gawlick and Kreimendahl, introduction to *Metaphysica*, by A. G. Baumgarten, XL–XLVI; and [A. G. Baumgarten], *Philosophische Brieffe*, 17.

[132] *Catalogi lectionum*, Spring 1738, Winter 1739.

[133] A. G. Baumgarten, *De ordine in audiendis philosophicis per triennium academicum . . .* (Halle, 1738), §XXIII:

> Utinam in ethica pertractanda non iterum confugiendum esset ad manus vestras et calamos! Animos exercere, cogitandi nervos adstringere, occupatam tenere rationem eorum, qui me audiunt, oppido mihi dulce est: fatigare dextras et chartas implere non solum non laboro, sed et fugio, quantum possum.

[134] A. G. Baumgarten, *De ordine*, §XXIII: "earumque [virtutum] pulchritudinem ponat ob oculos"; cf. [A. G. Baumgarten], *Philosophische Brieffe*, 14.

[135] A. G. Baumgarten, *Ethica*, praefatio nova:

> Liber eiusmodi nunquam recte completum et suis numeris iam omnibus absolutum opus est, sed tunc demum perfectam unitatem nanciscitur, quando viva vox et sermo commentantis in eundem liberior accesserit.

themselves, Baumgarten asserts that human beings are naturally obliged to cultivate their lower cognitive faculties; that natural moral obligation itself arises in part from the exercise of those faculties; and that inculcating clear ideas of perfection, rather than necessarily distinct ideas, is the overriding concern of moral education. These assertions, all of which represented deviations from Wolff's *German Ethics*, depended on Baumgarten's redefinition of "living cognition" in his *Metaphysics*. One sign of this comes from Baumgarten's account of his purposes in lecturing on ethics in the first place, published in an essay containing an extended advertisement of his lectures during the coming semester – summer 1738 – in Halle:

> It has been a while since I recalled how it was by my friends that I was asked also to touch upon ethical subject matter at some point in my teaching, and when I did so I tried to remove the stain that the murmerings of ill-intentioned people advance as an unreasonable claim against the lovers of metaphysics when they assert that this subtle and thorny type of inquiry, as it seems to them, brings with it an aversion to the practical sciences, and thereby they maintain that it turns out to be a rare occurance for anyone from that sect (which they condemn) to explain the doctrine of the virtues and place their beauties before their eyes.[136]

Baumgarten claims to have tried to show that metaphysics need not be kept separate from the teaching of ethics, and that a metaphysician, too, could convey the beauty of the virtues to his auditors. The identity of the "ill-intentioned people" whose "unreasonable claim" Baumgarten wished to contradict is not obvious. They may have included those members of the Halle Theology Faculty who two years earlier had voiced concern that his brother was ruining theology students' "taste" for the morally edifying word of God by basing his moral theology on "Wolffian philosophy," particularly Wolff's ethics and the metaphysics on which the ethics were based. In any case, Baumgarten's *Ethics* does make frequent and regular reference to his *Metaphysics*, and in fact the very structure of most arguments in his *Ethics* derives from the contents of his *Metaphysics*. The essential attributes of things, as described in the *Metaphysics*, become in the *Ethics* the attributes that human beings are obliged to cultivate or "heighten" in order to perfect

---

[136] A. G. Baumgarten, *De ordine*, §XXIII:

> Dudum est, ex quo solicitari me ab amicis memini, ut ethicam etiam doctrinam aliquando docendo tangam, et meo quoque facto tentem abstergere maculam, quam metaphysices amatoribus inustam eunt, nescio quae malevolorum admurmurationes, dum, subtile et spinosum speculandi genus quod illis videtur, fastidium practicarum scientiarum secum ferre autumant, et inde contendunt evenire, ut raro quis ex ea, quam contemnunt, familia doctrinam virtutum expediat, earumque pulchritudinem ponat ob oculos.

the things themselves.[137] We learn in Baumgarten's *Metaphysics*, for example, that "intellect" refers to the human mental capacity for "attention,"
"abstraction," "reflection," and "comparison," among other things. These
are therefore the powers that, under the heading of "cultivation of the intellect" in his *Ethics*, Baumgarten specifically asserts human beings are morally
obliged to cultivate.[138] Likewise, in accordance with Baumgarten's conclusion in the *Metaphysics* that perceptions are perfected by being made living, which requires clarity rather than necessarily distinctness, Baumgarten
argues in the *Ethics* that human beings are obliged to cultivate the clarity
of their perceptions, and not solely the distinctness.

In the specific case of the conscience, so central to the dispute between
Wolff and Zimmermann, Baumgarten therefore avoids Wolff's insistence
that distinctness of cognition is the highest aim. On the one hand, distinctness sometimes cannot be attained, in which case Baumgarten warns
against neglecting the *analogon rationis* or "analog of reason" – a label
for the lower cognitive faculties.[139] On the other hand, and more powerfully, Baumgarten argues that applying the lower faculties in the exercise
of conscience generates desires and aversions that – contra Wolff – can be
morally salutary. For one thing, the lower faculties' perceptions of good and
bad strengthen the bonds of moral obligation, which Baumgarten says is
stronger (*fortior*) when cognition is "truer, clearer, more certain, and more
ardent," and not only when cognition is more distinct.[140] The "ardor" of
the ideas that generate moral obligation, which Baumgarten consistently
uses as a synonym for "life" in his list of ideas' ideal qualities, is a measure
of the degree of pleasure or pain associated with imagining a given thing
to be good or bad, perfect or imperfect. Because sensate ideas of perfection and imperfection, and not just distinct ideas, generate such pleasure,
they should be cultivated rather than avoided.[141] Moreover, the desires and
aversions generated by the lower cognitive faculties – which Baumgarten
classifies as instincts and appetites rather than volitions, or acts of the will –
are necessary to supply a motivation to behave virtuously when the will cannot be rationally engaged. This means that to one degree or another, they
are always necessary. "Since willing and not willing follow from a more

---

137 Baumgarten deploys the same argument in his *Meditationes*: a poem is defined as "perfect sensate
     discourse" (*oratio sensitiva perfecta*), and from this definition Baumgarten deduces the obligation
     to make the poem as "sensate" as possible. On the basic concept of perfection as a "heightening"
     (*Steigerung*) of a thing's essential attributes, see above, note 24.
138 A. G. Baumgarten, *Metaphysica*, §§625–26; A. G. Baumgarten, *Ethica*, §221.
139 A. G. Baumgarten, *Ethica*, §182.
140 A. G. Baumgarten, *Initia philosophiae practicae primae*, §17.
141 A. G. Baumgarten, *Ethica*, §226.

perfect cognition than the appetites and the affections," Baumgarten writes, "seek them as much as possible in your attractions and aversions." But, he continues,

> because you are not obliged to impossible things, you are not obliged (1) to will or not will anything purely. Aether is purer, but here one will have to consume air; (2) to will all things that you desire, or to not will all things you should avoid.[142]

Desiring and avoiding things in a "sensate" way (*appetere vel aversari sensitive*), in other words, is almost always necessary, and sometimes sufficient, to produce action, and it should not be categorically condemned.[143]

The consequences of these claims for Baumgarten's program of moral education are not especially clear in Baumgarten's *Ethics*, since Baumgarten focuses his attention there on logically deducing the moral obligations, rather than explaining the more sensate means by which students ought to increase the force of those obligations in themselves. Those means are the province, rather, of Baumgarten's *Aesthetics*, where the moral-educational function of aesthetic exercises is nonetheless only dimly visible. The clearest link between the aesthetic exercises and moral education can be found in a single text, brief and precious: a dissertation on "the force and efficacy of ethical philosophy" written under Baumgarten's supervision by one of his first students in Frankfort (Oder), Samuel Wilhelm Spalding, in 1741, a year after the publication of Baumgarten's *Ethics* and a year before Baumgarten began lecturing on aesthetics.[144] Drawing from Baumgarten's *Ethics* and *Metaphysics*, Spalding explicitly argues what Baumgarten's *Ethics* leaves implicit: when we perceive in a confused way that our perfection is promoted by the kind of virtuous actions to which Baumgarten's *Ethics* demonstrates we are naturally obliged, we acquire a "sufficient reason" for the various appetites and aversions, or "instincts," that prompt us to perform those actions.[145] This fact implies that moral education must involve more than just training the conscience to construct syllogisms whose terms are distinct

---

[142] A. G. Baumgarten, *Ethica*, §246:

> Quum volitiones nolitionesque perfectiorem cognitionem sequantur, quam instinctus et affectus, M. §. 690. eas potissimum in omnibus tuis appetitionibus aversationibus appete, §.237. sicut in elateribus animi motiva prae stimulis, M. §.690. Quia tamen non obligaris ad impossibilia, §. 7, non obligaris 1) ad quicquam pure volendum nolendumve. Aether purior est, tamen aëre vescendum heic erit. 2) ad omnia, quae appetenda tibi sunt, volenda, omnia aversanda tibi nolenda M.§.692.

[143] A. G. Baumgarten, *Ethica*, §246. Cf. above, note 124.
[144] Spalding, *De vi et efficacia ethices philosophiae*. Cf. Schwaiger, *Alexander Gottlieb Baumgarten*, 83.
[145] Spalding, *De vi et efficacia ethices philosophiae*, §19.

as possible; it must also involve the study of the kinds of texts whose perfections Baumgarten outlines in his *Aesthetics*. According to Spalding, morally edifying "stories, histories, comedies, tragedies, rules, proverbs, homilies, and so on" help us develop "good instinctive desires and aversions." By producing in us ideas that are clear and vivid but not distinct, these stories increase the "magnitude" and "force" of our cognition and impel us to act in a way that conduces to our own perfection.[146]

In essence, Spalding was bringing philosophical rigor to a sentiment expressed in a poem published by Baumgarten in 1741, the same year as Spalding's dissertation. Ostensibly sent by "Musophilus" to Aletheophilus in Baumgarten's *Philosophische Brieffe* (Philosophical letters), the poem implicitly rejects the error conventionally attributed to the Stoics:

> Reason and Virtue make souls
> sublime, noble, great, and free,
> quick in thinking and clever in choosing,
> but one thing still is lacking.
> Here, souls live in bodies.
> Whatever moves [body], moves [soul] too,
> and it is the body that often takes the first step
> toward ensuring the [soul's] complete well-being.[147]

For this reason, the poem continues, even a philosopher, a lover of reason and virtue, cannot live happily unless he feels true love – the "tug of the heart," the "obscure stimuli [*dunckle Triebe*]" with which "Nature" moves the human soul to a higher degree of love. "Beauty moves the breast" and brings "pleasure [*Vergnügen*]" even to the wise man.[148] In the language of Baumgarten's *Ethics* and *Metaphysics*, as employed by Spalding, the wise man is obliged to cultivate virtue by allowing himself to take pleasure in genuine beauty, or indistinctly perceived perfection.

---

[146] Spalding, *De vi et efficacia ethices philosophiae*, §23–24. On the source of these concepts in Baumgarten's *Metaphysics*, see p. 104–5.

[147] [A. G. Baumgarten], *Philosophische Brieffe*, 90:

> Vernunft und Tugend macht zwar Seelen
> Erhaben, edel, groß und frey,
> Geschwind im Denken, klug im Wählen,
> Allein es fehlt noch einerley.
> Die Seelen wohnen hier im Leibe,
> Was diesen rührt, das rührt die mit,
> Und daß ihr Wohlstand sorglos bleibe,
> Wagt dieser oft den ersten Schritt.

[148] [A. G. Baumgarten], *Philosophische Brieffe*, 92.

Spalding's defense of the importance of indistinct ideas in moral education brings the connection between Baumgarten's aesthetic theory and the controversies over homiletics and the foundation of morality into sharp focus. In developing his aesthetic theory, Baumgarten was trying to incorporate into the philosophical curriculum of the university a science that could help students cultivate in themselves and in others a living cognition of good and evil by natural means – a natural *aisthēsis*, in other words – and that did not fall afoul of the anti-Scholastic polemic directed against Wolff by Zimmermann, Buddeus, and Gundling, among others, in the dispute over the foundation of morality. Baumgarten unambiguously took Wolff's side on the question of whether natural obligation, generated by the judgment that a particular action tends toward the perfection of the actor, was an effective moral compass. But he also insisted, by contrast with Wolff, that this judgment could and should be at least partly sensate. Moral education required not only the cultivation of the higher cognitive faculties, as taught by logic, but also the cultivation of the lower cognitive faculties, as taught by aesthetics. The reform of the will, in other words, depended not only on the reform of the intellect but also on the reform of the cognitive faculties associated with the sensory experience of good and evil. If this adjustment of Wolff's ethics did not represent a capitulation by Baumgarten to Wolff's critics' insistence that wisdom must begin with fear of God and that philosophy should therefore aim primarily to inculcate such fear, it nonetheless represented an acceptance of those critics' underlying view that moral regeneration depended ultimately on experience and, speaking more broadly, on the exercise of the senses and the sense-related faculties of the mind. Siegmund Jacob Baumgarten's critics could rest assured that teaching students the basic principles of Wolffian philosophy would not necessarily diminish their homiletic skill, and Wolff's critics could rest assured that philosophical instruction in ethics, even instruction that drew on some of Wolff's basic principles, would not necessarily undermine the foundation of morality.

Conclusion

This assessment of the argumentative force of Baumgarten's aesthetics, admittedly, does not find support in the kind of specific evidence that one might most hope to find: personal testimony by Baumgarten himself that he had a high opinion of any of the arguments advanced against Wolff by Buddeus, Zimmermann, Gundling, or anyone else. The assessment does find support, however, in Baumgarten's obvious sensitivity to the anti-Scholastic polemic that echoes throughout their attacks on Wolff. This sensitivity is worth a moment of attention, if only as a suggestive coda to the argument that has preceded it here.

Baumgarten was intimately familiar with Buddeus's anti-Scholastic schema of the history of philosophy. He used Buddeus's *Compendivm historiae philosophicae* (Compendium of philosophical history) as the textbook for his own lectures on the history of philosophy in the summer and winter semesters of 1738 in Halle.[149] Of course, this alone cannot be taken as evidence that Baumgarten agreed with Buddeus about any essential point. One student attending Baumgarten's lectures in Frankfurt (Oder) in the mid 1740s recalled that in correcting the authors of the textbooks on which he based his lectures, Baumgarten showed no mercy.[150] But Baumgarten's own surviving sketch of the history of philosophy indicates that if he did not agree with Buddeus in every respect, he nonetheless did not engage in wholesale revision; quite to the contrary.

At the start of his lectures on aesthetics, as the one surviving set of student dictates indicates, Baumgarten presented a brief history of philosophy whose aim, he explained, was to prove that explaining aesthetics as a science might be new, but that thinking beautifully was not new at all. From its very beginnings, philosophical thinking had made use of clear and confused ideas, rather than restricting itself to the clear and distinct. Baumgarten's parade of aesthetically inclined philosophers, beginning with Egyptian philosophers who had communicated their thoughts with "hieroglyphic pictures" and proceeding through the Greeks and Romans, came to a halt with Seneca, who, like Cicero, was "a better *aestheticus*[151] than philosopher." Next came an interruption:

> In the Scholastic times, when all sciences were in a state of barbarism, not a single one was as neglected as aesthetics. This is now the only period where one saw only thick theologies and legal tracts, and it completely cast aside – and also had no knowledge of – the aesthetic.[152]

---

[149] J. F. Buddeus, *Compendivm historiae philosophicae*, ed. J. G. Walch (Halle, 1731); *Catalogi lectionum . . . publicati in Academia Fridericiana* (Halle, Summer 1738 and Winter 1738).

[150] M. Frontius, "Baumgarten und die *Literaturbriefe*: Ein Brief aus Frankfurt/Oder an Louis de Beausobre in Berlin," *Deutsche Vierteljahrsschrift für Literaturwissenschaft und Geistesgeschichte* 80.4 (December 2006): 571–72.

[151] That is, one who is accomplished in thinking beautifully, as instructed by aesthetics.

[152] A. G. Baumgarten, *Kollegium*, §1 (p. 69):

> In den scholastischen Zeiten, wo alle Wissenschaften in der Barbarei lagen, wurde keine einzige so sehr verbäumet als die Ästhetik. Dies jetzt ist der einzige Punkt, wo man nur dicke Theologien und Traktate von Jure sah, das Ästhetische aber gänzlich verwarf und auch gar nicht kannte.

In this passage, Baumgarten's agreement with Buddeus appears not simply in his use of the word *Scholastic* to describe a defective period in the history of philosophy, but also in his singling out as a notable defect the Scholastics' inattention to the aesthetic rules of thinking and writing, and by extension their inattention to the beauty of what they thought and wrote – a problem closely akin to the one upon which Buddeus had expounded at great length in print.[153] Where Baumgarten departs from Buddeus is in the next phase of his history. For him, "Scholastic times" had not persisted into the eighteenth century in the person of Christian Wolff. According to Baumgarten, Peter Ramus (1515–72) inaugurated the return of aesthetic thinking, which found noteworthy practitioners in Descartes, Leibniz, Bilfinger, and Wolff. Bilfinger and Wolff, in comparison with Leibniz ("aesthetically a great mind [*ein ästhetisch großer Kopf*]"), "are no less aesthetically beautiful."[154] Buddeus had attacked Wolff by revealing in him the same emphasis on the perfection of the higher cognitive faculties that Buddeus found offensive among the Scholastics. Baumgarten, on the other hand, expresses his esteem for Wolff not by rehabilitating Scholasticism, but rather by presenting Wolff as having departed from it. This portrayal of Wolff contrasts with Buddeus's, to be sure, but it also reflects Baumgarten's appreciation of Scholasticism's dangers.

That Baumgarten's attempt to save Wolff from the charge of Scholasticism moreover involved modifying Wolff's moral psychology and program of moral education in light of that charge, rather than simply refuting the charge and reasserting Wolff's position, is reflected by the quarrels that arose between Baumgarten and Wolff's other admirers in the wake of Baumgarten's forays into aesthetic philosophy. The earliest explicit, printed attack on Baumgarten can be found in an essay by Theodor Johann Quistorp (b. 1722), whose admiration for Wolff, unlike Baumgarten's, involved no soft-pedaling of those principles that had drawn anti-Scholastic criticism. Quistorp was a former student of a follower of Wolff at the University of Leipzig, Johann Christoph Gottsched (1700–66), who had published several philosophy textbooks in use in Halle. Quistorp's essay, an early salvo in a controversy that would come to be known as the "little war of poets" (*kleiner Dichterkrieg*) between friends of Baumgarten and Georg Friedrich Meier in Halle on the one side and friends and students of Gottsched in Leipzig on the other side, appeared in Gottsched's journal, *Neuer Büchersaal der schönen Wissenschaften und freien Künste* (New library

---

[153] See above, Chapter 1, note 114.   [154] A. G. Baumgarten, *Kollegium*, §1 (p. 70).

of the fine sciences and liberal arts), in 1745.[155] The question most fundamentally at issue for Quistorp, reminiscent of the controversy addressed by
August Hermann Francke and Johann Jakob Rambach in their discussions
of *aisthēsis*, was whether moral education and, ultimately, human happiness
requires the suppression of human affections. Quistorp assumed that it did,
and by way of explaining the consequences of this assumption for the happiness of poets, he set his sights on Baumgarten's *Meditationes*, which may
have been brought to his attention by a complimentary review published in
1742.[156] Baumgarten's definition of a poem as *oratio sensitiva perfecta* (perfect sensate discourse), Quistorp explains, implies that a poet is obliged to
"enslave" his will to the whims of his "fleshly desires" (*sinnliche Lüste*) and
affections.[157] As has often been pointed out, Quistorp misunderstood or
deliberately misrepresented Baumgarten's position in many respects. He
translates Baumgarten's definition of a poem as "vollkommen sinnliche
Rede" (perfectly sensate discourse) rather than "vollkommene sinnliche
Rede" (perfect sensate discourse), and he unfairly attributes to Baumgarten
the view that the words and ideas in a poem should be as obscure as possible, rather than as "extensively clear" as possible.[158] Quistorp was nonetheless correct in recognizing Baumgarten's argument that poets are obliged to
employ words and ideas that tend to arouse human affections as strongly
as possible. Baumgarten may not have specified, as Quistorp did, that the
affections of poets themselves were among those that needed to be aroused,
but Quistorp's interpretation was not obviously outside the realm of possibility, and his objection did apply to the argument Baumgarten had in fact
made.

What Quistorp objected to was precisely the position that appears most
obviously to distinguish Baumgarten from Christian Wolff: Baumgarten's
insistence that clear but confused ideas of good and bad, conceived and
presented in perfect accord with the rules laid out in his *Aesthetics*, operate
on the will in a salutary way, motivating virtuous action by arousing the
affections rather than by stimulating the rational appetite. In Quistorp's
view, the danger of arousing affections is that they deprive the human will
of freedom. Taking Wolff as his authority on this point, Quistorp writes,

[155] T. J. Quistorp, "Erweiß, daß die Poesie schon für sich selbst ihre Liebhaber leichtlich unglückselig
machen könne," repr. in *Frühe Schriften zur ästhetischen Erziehung der Deutschen*, v. 2 of 3, ed. H.-
J. Kertscher and G. Schenk (Halle: Hallescher, 1999), 20–32. On the *Kleiner Dichterkrieg* and the
background of Quistorp's text: Kertscher and Schenk, *Frühe Schriften*, II.173–83, II.195–97.
[156] I.e., Lasius, Review of *Meditationes*. Cf. Kertscher and Schenk, *Frühe Schriften*, II.14, II.190–91.
[157] Quistorp, "Erweiß," 28–29, 31–32.
[158] On Quistorp's errors: G. Waniek, *Gottsched und die deutsche Litteratur seiner Zeit* (Leipzig, 1897),
516; Kertscher and Schenk, *Frühe Schriften*, II.191, II.195–97.

Everyone will willingly grant that the moral or spiritual slavery, as I shall describe – or the dominion of the senses, the imagination, and the affections, which put the soul, with its freedom and its will, into a state of slavery – is both a source and the most essential part of human unhappiness. For, our excellent philosopher, Herr Chancellor Wolff, with whom alone our Germany can stand up to all her neighbors, demonstrated in his [*German Metaphysics*] . . . that because a human being in a state of affection doesn't consider what he is doing and accordingly no longer has control over his actions, he is forced to do and to avoid what he otherwise would not do or avoid if he distinctly grasped what it was. . . . This great philosopher of ours demonstrates still more distinctly in his [*German Ethics*] . . . that this slavery of the will is an obstacle, such that a human being doesn't obey the law of nature (nor divine nor earthly laws, for the same reason), and consequently neglects his own happiness – and, on the contrary, makes himself unhappy.[159]

Quistorp's choice of passages from Wolff's ethics and metaphysics could not have indicated more aptly the position of Wolff's that Baumgarten had sought to modify. Baumgarten's responses to criticisms like Quistorp's, which appear at the beginning of his *Aesthetics*, reaffirm his repudiation of the fear, discernible in Wolff and Quistorp, that the affections are almost invariably an obstacle to the effectiveness of natural obligation. In response to the objection that "the inferior faculties, [i.e.] the flesh, ought to be vanquished rather than excited and strengthened," Baumgarten writes,

> (1) Dominion over the inferior faculties, not tyranny, is required. (2) In so far as this can be accomplished by natural means, aesthetics leads to it, as it were, by the hand. (3) In so far as they are corrupt, the inferior faculties should not be excited and strengthened by the *aesthetici*, but rather should

---

[159] Quistorp, "Erweiß," 22:

> Genug, daß ein jeder mir willig einräumen wird, daß die sittliche oder geistliche Sklaverey, wie ich schreiben soll; oder die Herrschaft der Sinnen, der Einbildungskraft, und der Affecten, welche die Seele mit ihrer Freyheit und ihrem Willen in eine Sklaverey setzen; so wohl eine Quelle, als auch der wesentlichste Theil der menschlichen Unglückseligkeit ist. Denn so beweiset unser vortrefflicher Weltweiser, der Herr Kanzler Wolf, mit dem unser Deutschland schon allein allen seinen Nachbarn Trutz biethen kann, bereits in seinen Vernünftigen Gedanken von Gott, der Welt, und der Seele des Menschen, im 491sten §. daß, weil der Mensch bey den Affecten nicht bedenket, was er thut; und er demnach seine Handlungen nicht mehr in seiner Gewalt hat; er gleichsam gezwungen wird, zu thun und zu lassen, was er sonst nicht thun und lassen würde, wenn er deutlich begriffe, was es ware. . . . Noch deutlicher aber beweist eben dieser unser großer Weltweiser in seinen Vernünftigen Gedanken von der Menschen Thun und Lassen, im 183. §. daß diese Sklaverey des Willens eine Hinderniß sey, daß der Mensch das Gesetz der Natur, (und aus eben dem Grunde so, wie dieses, auch die göttlichen und weltlichen Gesetze) nicht beobachtet, und folgends seine Glückseligkeit verabsäumet; dahingegen sich unglückselig machet.

Cf. above, Chapter 1, p. 26.

be directed by them, so that they are not further misled by harmful exercises, or that the advantage of a divinely granted talent is not taken away on the weak pretext of avoiding abuses.[160]

Baumgarten's reminder that the inferior faculties and their capacity to produce affections are a "divinely granted talent" recall unmistakably August Hermann Francke's and Johann Jakob Rambach's defense of poetry as a means by which God communicates with human beings and stimulates their wills. That the suppression of the affections is not the prerequisite of moral improvement, and that the affections *per se* do not stand in the way of obedience to divine and human laws, was precisely what Francke and Rambach had argued, what Wolff had denied, and what Baumgarten aimed, in producing his aesthetic theory, to reassert.

---

[160] A. G. Baumgarten, *Aesthetica*, §12:

> Obi. 10) Facultates inferiores, caro, debellandae potius sunt, quam excitandae et confirmandae. Rsp. a) Imperium in facultates inferiores poscitur, non tyrannis. b) Ad hoc, quatenus naturaliter impetrari potest, manu quasi ducet aesthetica. c) Facultates inferiores non, quatenus corruptae sunt, excitandae confirmandaeque sunt aestheticis, sed iisdem dirigendae, ne sinistris exercitiis magis corrumpantur, aut pigro vitandi abusus praetextu tollatur usus concessi divinitus talenti.

CHAPTER 4

Francis Hutcheson at the Margins of the Scottish Enlightenment

By the mid 1730s, as Alexander Baumgarten began to formulate an aesthetic philosophy in the aftermath of Christian Wolff's explosive debate with Halle's Pietist theologians about the foundation of morality, Francis Hutcheson had already spent a decade publishing and defending his own reflections on beauty for an English-reading audience amid a series of similar – and similarly explosive – controversies within the Church of Scotland. To the extent that the Scottish controversies resembled the debate in Halle, Wolff's role in those dramas was played by a larger cast: a group of Presbyterian clergymen and university professors, now conventionally regarded as the vanguard of the Scottish Enlightenment, who sought to reform Presbyterian theology and the moral philosophy curricula in Scottish universities along lines laid down by Anthony Ashley Cooper, third Earl of Shaftesbury (1671–1713).[1] These reformers agreed with one another in at least one general principle: simply put, the Christian Church and the university should acknowledge and promote human virtue, and the reigning orthodoxy was stifling it. Among the doctrines they targeted for blame was one that Lutheran, Presbyterian, and other varieties of Reformed Orthodox theology had in common, and that Wolff's own moral philosophy had ostensibly fallen afoul of: the doctrine that original sin had left human beings naturally incapable of transcending their own depravity without help from a divine act of regenerative grace, and that the only possible instrument for promoting virtue among the unregenerated was knowledge of divine law and of the rewards and punishments attached to its observance or transgression. Like Wolff, these Presbyterian reformers denied that fear of God is invariably the beginning of wisdom. They asserted instead that human beings naturally contained within themselves

---

[1] Representative of the state of the field in this regard is D. Daiches, "The Scottish Enlightenment," in *A Hotbed of Genius*, ed. D. Daiches, P. Jones, and J. Jones (Edinburgh: Edinburgh University Press, 1986), 12–14.

the means of virtue, granted to them by God in order that they might find happiness in this world.

Francis Hutcheson – long identified as founder, "father," or forefather of the Scottish Enlightenment[2] – was one of the oldest, most prolific, institutionally well-placed, and intellectually committed members of this group. There can be no doubt that he exerted considerable influence and developed most of his systematic philosophical thinking, including his moral philosophy and what has come to be known as his aesthetic theory, in support of the movement's aims. And yet even in Hutcheson's lifetime, younger contemporaries of his – not to mention Hutcheson himself – publicly acknowledged what has seldom been recognized since then: Hutcheson had diverged from Shaftesbury in important ways.[3] By the 1740s and 1750s, these younger contemporaries had publicly decided to prefer Shaftesbury to Hutcheson. The evidence of this preference can be found not only in their own direct attestations but also in their moral-philosophical writings and in their written contributions to the history of aesthetic theory, namely, their analyses of the human mental faculties involved in the perception of beauty and the contemplation of art. Those writings reveal that although both Hutcheson and many of his Scottish contemporaries developed aesthetic theories for the purpose of engaging in debates over the foundation of morality, as Alexander Baumgarten was doing in Brandenburg-Prussia, the main stream of aesthetic engagement in the Scottish debate – and the stream that bears closest resemblance to Alexander Baumgarten's own engagement – was flowing unmistakably from Shaftesbury, with Hutcheson standing at the margins.

The Shaftesburian Reform of Scottish Presbyterianism

The Presbyterian reformers' program, which would develop into what became known in the nineteenth century as moderate Presbyterianism, had long roots in a number of theological and philosophical traditions, including traditions of opposition to religious persecution, of insistence upon the right of private judgment in religious matters, and of antipathy toward creeds. The sources of these traditions included the dissenting churches of

---

[2] E.g., T. D. Campbell, "Francis Hutcheson: 'Father' of the Scottish Enlightenment," in *The Origins and Nature of the Scottish Enlightenment*, ed. R. H. Campbell and A. Skinner (Edinburgh: John Donald, 1982), 165–85; P. Wood, "Introduction: Dugald Stewart and the Invention of 'the Scottish Enlightenment,'" in *The Scottish Enlightenment: Essays in Reinterpretation* (Rochester, NY: University of Rochester Press, 2000), 1–20, esp. 4–5, 15.

[3] Discussion of this divergence begins on p. 161.

Ireland as well as pietistic currents within Scottish Episcopalianism.[4] Much of the reformers' direct inspiration and many of their central ideas, however, were also to be found in the writings of Shaftesbury, published in 1711 under the title, *Characteristics of Men, Manners, Opinions, Times*.[5] In Shaftesbury's *Characteristics* the Presbyterian reformers discovered, ready-made, an elaborate description of human nature and an educational program designed to challenge the moral authority of the Established Church.[6]

Shaftesbury himself had designed his *Characteristics* specifically as a sustained critique of positions he ascribed to his former tutor, John Locke, whom he associated – an absence of references to him in the *Characteristics* notwithstanding – with Thomas Hobbes in denying that virtue was natural to human beings.[7] In Shaftesbury's view, Locke, like Hobbes, had argued that moral principles and the motivation to obey them are by their very nature the creation of an arbitrary act of will by a lawgiver with the power to reward obedience and punish disobedience.[8] Morality must therefore,

---

[4] Ahnert, *Moral Culture*, esp. Chapters 1–2, provides a synthetic account of the Scottish theological context of the reformers' program; see also J. Moore, "Presbyterianism and the Right of Private Judgment: Church Government in Ireland and Scotland in the Age of Francis Hutcheson," in *Philosophy and Religion in Enlightenment Britain*, esp. 141–52. On the classification of Hutcheson and his fellow reformers as forerunners or founders of "moderate Presbyterianism" and as "new lights": Ahnert, *Moral Culture*, Chapter 3; R. Sher, *Church and University in the Scottish Enlightenment* (Princeton, NJ: Princeton University Press, 1985), 16–17; and H. Sefton, "'Neu-lights and Preachers Legall': Some Observations on the Beginnings of Moderatism in the Church of Scotland," in *Church Politics and Society: Scotland 1408–1929*, ed. N. MacDougall (Edinburgh: John Donald, 1983), 186–96.

[5] A version of Shaftesbury's *Inquiry Concerning Virtue or Merit*, which is contained in the 1711 *Characteristics*, had also been published in 1699 by John Toland, possibly without Shaftesbury's approval. D. Walford, introduction to *An Inquiry Concerning Virtue, or Merit*, by Anthony Ashley Cooper, third Earl of Shaftesbury (Manchester: Manchester University Press, 1977), ix–x; and Rivers, *Reason, Grace, and Sentiment*, II.14.

[6] This formulation borrows heavily from Lawrence Klein's interpretation of Shaftesbury's larger program, in *Shaftesbury and the Culture of Politeness: Moral Discourse and Cultural Politics in Early Eighteenth-Century England* (Cambridge: Cambridge University Press, 1994), esp. 1–14. The remainder of the present chapter incorporates revised sections from S. Grote, "Shaftesbury's Egoistic Hedonism," *Aufklärung* 22 (2010): 135–49. Reused with permission of Felix Meiner Verlag.

[7] The vast body of modern scholarship endorsing this interpretation includes, in reverse chronological order, D. Carey, *Locke, Shaftesbury, and Hutcheson: Contesting Diversity in the Enlightenment and Beyond* (Cambridge: Cambridge University Press, 2006), 129–41; Rivers, *Reason, Grace, and Sentiment*, II.89–91, II.127–30; R. Voitle, *The Third Earl of Shaftesbury* (Baton Rouge: Louisiana State University Press, 1984), 65–66, 69, 118–22, 125, 154–55, 230, 339; J. A. Dussinger, "'The Lovely System of Lord Shaftesbury': An Answer to Locke in the Aftermath of 1688?" *Journal of the History of Ideas* 42.1 (1981): 151–58; J. Aronson, "Critical Note: Shaftesbury on Locke," *American Political Science Review* 53.4 (1959): 1102–4; and E. Tuveson, "The Importance of Shaftesbury," *English Literary History* 20.4 (1953): 279–80.

[8] Cf. Carey, *Locke, Shaftesbury, and Hutcheson*, 129–33; Rivers, *Grace, Reason, and Sentiment*, II.127; Voitle, *Third Earl of Shaftesbury*, 118–21; Tuveson, "The Importance of Shaftesbury," 279. Note that although Carey describes Shaftesbury as having "resisted Locke's moral philosophy because it resolved everything into diversity" (135), much of his own account also explicitly supports the standard view

as Shaftesbury explained with explicit reference to Hobbes, be imposed by "our governors,"[9] human or divine. The "law" of custom, which Locke asserted to be the source of human opinions about virtue and vice – though not the source of genuine moral principles – appeared to Shaftesbury no less arbitrary.[10] Shaftesbury himself, by contrast, asserted that society was "natural" to human beings. In the absence of external coercion of any kind, human beings do not necessarily engage in war, and morality does not need to be imposed. Moral principles are eternal and immutable; they exist and can be discerned independently of a sovereign's will. Moreover, the motivation to obey them can and should have its source in human beings' awareness of virtue's "natural advantages," rather than in their awareness of any rewards and punishments that a sovereign, such as God, may have attached to virtue and vice. To assert otherwise, in Shaftesbury's view, leads to appalling conclusions. Denying that "*Justice* and *Injustice*, *Truth* and *Falsehood*, *Right* and *Wrong*" exist independently of God's will, he repeatedly insists, renders the very words meaningless when applied to God and suggests that God himself must be regarded as a being merely of supreme power rather than of "the highest goodness and worth."[11] Likewise, insisting that virtue must be motivated by a desire for divine rewards and a fear of divine punishments only has the effect of strengthening crass self-love at the expense of the more generous affections toward others.[12]

Evidence that this was the essential substance of Shaftesbury's disagreement with Locke, and that the refutation of Locke was a significant part of the impetus behind his development and public exposition of an alternative moral philosophy, abounds.[13] It can be epitomized by a pair of quotations: an assertion by Locke and a critical response from Shaftesbury. The first, from Locke's *Essay Concerning Human Understanding*, represents the kind of assertion that Shaftesbury clearly found objectionable:

> That God has given a Rule whereby Men should govern themselves, I think there is no body so brutish as to deny. He has a Right to do it, we are his Creatures: He has Goodness and Wisdom to direct our Actions to that

---

(represented by Tuveson, Voitle, and Rivers) that Shaftesbury resisted Locke's moral philosophy because it resolved moral principles into arbitrary divine laws.

9 Shaftesbury, *Characteristics of Men, Manners, Opinions, Times*, ed. L. E. Klein (Cambridge: Cambridge University Press, 1999), 42. Cf. Christian Wolff's similar critique of Johann Franz Buddeus and Samuel Pufendorf, above, Chapter 1, p. 40.

10 Cf. Carey, *Locke, Shaftesbury, and Hutcheson*, 129–30, 133.

11 Shaftesbury, *Characteristics*, ed. Klein, 182.   12 Shaftesbury, *Characteristics*, ed. Klein, 177–92.

13 Carey and Rivers offer collections of Shaftesbury's well-known published and unpublished references to Locke (and in Carey's case at least one hitherto unknown reference) and discuss them in the context of relevant passages from Locke's works: Rivers, *Reason, Grace, Sentiment*, II.126–28; and Carey, *Locke, Shaftesbury, and Hutcheson*, 129–36.

which is best: and he has Power to enforce it by Rewards and Punishments, of infinite weight and duration, in another Life: for no body can take us out of his hands. This is the only true touchstone of *moral Rectitude*; and by comparing them to this Law, it is, that Men judge of the most considerable *Moral Good* or *Evil* of their *Actions*; that is, whether as *Duties, or Sins*, they are like to procure them happiness, or misery, from the hands of the ALMIGHTY.[14]

The vision of God suggested here – the explicit lawgiver with dominion over man, whose goodness and wisdom are inscrutable, and whose enforcement of his laws by means of rewards and punishments after death is both the "only true touchstone of moral rectitude" and, by implication, the only respectable incitement to moral rectitude – is precisely the target of Shaftesbury's repeated criticisms of Locke.[15] The best known of these criticisms and the second quotation, cited by virtually every modern commentator, is Shaftesbury's remark, in a letter of 3 June 1709, that Locke "threw all order and virtue out of the world, and made the very idea of these (which are the same as those of God) unnatural, and without foundation in our minds."[16] That is to say, Locke made morality a matter of divine law; he asserted that divine law is the source of moral distinctions, that knowledge of moral principles can only be derived reliably from knowledge of divine law (if not exclusively than at least primarily as recorded in scripture),[17] and that because human beings are naturally egoistic hedonists, seeking their own pleasure above all else, the only reliable source of motivation for human beings to behave in accordance with moral principles is an awareness that God has attached rewards and punishments to his laws.[18] Shaftesbury, by contrast, aimed to show that the idea of virtue is in fact natural and has a "foundation in our minds,"[19] in the sense that it can be attained with reference in the first instance not to divine law, but to what is observable in the world by those who have no awareness of God's will.

The transmission of Shaftesbury's ideas and concerns into Scotland is a complex story.[20] As the story is currently understood, the principal

---

[14] J. Locke, *An Essay Concerning Human Understanding*, ed. P. H. Nidditch (Oxford, 1975), II.xxviii.8, also qtd. in Rivers, *Reason, Grace, and Sentiment*, II.127.

[15] As cited, e.g., in Carey, *Locke, Shaftesbury, and Hutcheson*, 132–36.

[16] Shaftesbury to M. Ainsworth, 3 June 1709, in *The Life, Unpublished Letters, and Philosophical Regimen of Anthony, Earl of Shaftesbury*, ed. B. Rand (London, 1900), 403.

[17] Cf. Voitle, *Third Earl of Shaftesbury*, 121; Tuveson, "The Importance of Shaftesbury," 279; Carey, *Locke, Shaftesbury, and Hutcheson*, 137.

[18] Cf. Rivers, *Reason, Grace, and Sentiment*, II.129; Carey, *Locke, Shaftesbury, and Hutcheson*, 137.

[19] Shaftesbury to Ainsworth, in *Life, Unpublished Letters, and Philosophical Regimen*, 403.

[20] Parts of it have been thoroughly investigated and sketched in detail by M. A. Stewart. See "John Smith and the Molesworth Circle," *Eighteenth-Century Ireland* 2 (1987): 89–102; "Rational Dissent in Early Eighteenth-Century Ireland," in *Enlightenment and Religion*, ed. K. Haakonssen (Cambridge: Cambridge University Press, 1996), 42–63; "Berkeley and the Rankenian Club," in *George*

vehicle of dissemination was a general program for educational and religious reform, largely inspired by the writings of a friend and disciple of Shaftesbury's: Robert, first Viscount Molesworth (1656–1725), a wealthy merchant, landowner, and member of the Irish and the English parliaments who retired to Dublin in 1722 after losing his seat in the House of Commons.[21] Molesworth had attracted the attention of Shaftesbury with the publication of his *Account of Denmark, as it was in the Year 1692*, occasioned by his ambassadorial mission to the Danish court in that same year. Parts of the book might as well have been written by Shaftesbury himself. According to Molesworth, philosophical and moral education was the guardian of political liberty. The people of Denmark and the other nations of Europe had lost "the precious jewel *Liberty*" because their education had been turned over to clerics in the service of the monarchy, and Protestant England was in serious danger of following their example. " '[T]is plain," Molesworth wrote,

> the Education of Youth, on which is laid the very Foundation Stones of the Publick Liberty, has been of late years committed to the sole management of such as make it their business to undermine it.[22]

As a result, Molesworth continued, children are presented with "obscure and subtle notions," and the principle of blind and passive obedience to authority,

> whilst the weightier Matters of true Learning, whereof one has occasion every hour; such as good Principles, Morals, the improvement of Reason, the love of Justice, the value of Liberty, the duty owing to one's Country and the Laws, are either quite omitted, or slightly passed over.[23]

Molesworth's Shaftesburian association of the promotion of virtue with the elimination of clerical authority over education found a great sympathizer in William Wishart (1692–1753), preacher in Edinburgh and later principal of Edinburgh University, who in 1722 engaged Molesworth in a

Berkeley: Essays and Replies, ed. D. Berman (Dublin: Irish Academic Press, 1986), 25–45; "Academic Freedom: Origins of an Idea," *Bulletin of the Australian Society of Legal Philosophy* 16.57 (1991/1992): 1–31; and "George Turnbull and Educational Reform," in *Aberdeen and Enlightenment*, ed. J. Carter and J. Pittock-Wesson (Aberdeen: Aberdeen University Press, 1987), 97–105. See also Moore, "Presbyterianism and the Right of Private Judgment," 147–48. A detailed account of Shaftesbury's influence in England and Scotland can be found in Rivers, *Reason, Grace, and Sentiment*, II.153–99.

[21] *DNB*, s. v. "Molesworth, Robert," by D. W. Hayton.

[22] R. Molesworth, *An Account of Denmark, as it was in the Year 1692* (London, 1794; repr., Copenhagen: Rosenkilde and Bagger, 1976), b3r.

[23] Molesworth, *Account of Denmark*, b3v.

nine-month-long correspondence on precisely that topic.[24] Francis Hutcheson also had contact with Molesworth, but of a closer kind: in the early 1720s after retiring to Dublin, Molesworth became his literary patron and a valuable source of ideas, as Hutcheson acknowledged in the preface to his first book, *An Inquiry into the Original of our Ideas of Beauty and Virtue.*[25]

For the most part, of course, the transmission of Shaftesburian ideas was not strictly linear; the ideas were in the air, as it were, within a decade of the publication of the *Characteristics*, disseminated in part by the social clubs that were becoming an important fixture of the Scottish intellectual landscape.[26] The Rankenian Club was one example, founded in Edinburgh in 1717 by a number of professors and soon-to-be professors for the sake of "mutual improvement by liberal conversation and rational enquiry."[27] A number of the club's members – including William Wishart – had Shaftesburian sympathies, which unsurprisingly found their way into the classroom. In several essays from the 1730s, 1740s, and 1750s by students of John Stevenson (1695–1775), professor of logic and metaphysics at Edinburgh from 1730 to 1775 and a Rankenian himself, the Shaftesburian sentiments are unmistakable, with some essays containing whole sentences extracted directly from Shaftesbury's *Characteristics.*[28]

The general climate of interest in Shaftesbury within academic and clerical circles in Edinburgh, as well as its influence on the intellectual formation of Edinburgh students in the 1720s and 1730s, is well-illustrated by the career of William Leechman (1706–85).[29] Leechman was more than twelve years younger than Hutcheson and Wishart, and it is almost certain that he had no direct contact with Molesworth, but by the time he became old

---

[24] The other participant in this correspondence was George Turnbull (1698–1748). The occasion was a student uprising at Glasgow University over abuses of authority by the university principal. M. A. Stewart, "Academic Freedom," 17; and "Berkeley and the Rankenians," 27, 31–34.

[25] F. Hutcheson, preface to *An Inquiry into the Original of Our Ideas of Beauty and Virtue*, 1st ed. (London, 1725; repr., Hildesheim: Olms, 1971), x. Cf. W. R. Scott, *Francis Hutcheson* (Cambridge: Cambridge University Press, 1900), 18–36; and M. Brown, *Francis Hutcheson in Dublin, 1719–30: The Crucible of His Thought* (Dublin: Four Courts Press, 2002), 25–50.

[26] Daiches, "The Scottish Enlightenment," 34–38; and, more thoroughly, D. D. McElroy, *Scotland's Age of Improvement: A Survey of Eighteenth-Century Literary Clubs and Societies* (Pullman: Washington State University Press, 1969).

[27] These are the words of one of the club's founding members, George Wallace, quoted in P. Jones, "The Scottish Professoriate and the Polite Academy, 1720–46," in *Wealth and Virtue: The Shaping of Political Economy in the Scottish Enlightenment*, ed. I. Hont and M. Ignatieff (Cambridge: Cambridge University Press, 1983), 99.

[28] Jones, "The Scottish Professoriate," 99–100; essays by students of John Stevenson, EUL MS Dc.4.54. See also below, pp. 182–83.

[29] Daiches identifies William Leechman and William Wishart as the most important voices of moderatism in the early eighteenth century. Daiches, "The Scottish Enlightenment," 13.

enough to be their colleague, he, too, had adopted Shaftesburian principles. In 1724, while Wishart was preaching in Glasgow and discussing Shaftesbury with members of the Glasgow Trinamphorian Club,[30] and while Hutcheson was running a dissenting academy in Dublin and exchanging ideas with the circle of young men who had gathered themselves around Robert Molesworth, William Leechman was beginning his training in divinity at Edinburgh under the guidance of William Hamilton (1669–1732).[31] What Hamilton taught in his divinity classes is not known except through meager second-hand accounts, which suggest an aversion to religious persecution and perhaps a certain diffidence about orthodox Presbyterian redemption theology, but no explicit connection with Shaftesbury.[32] Some exposure, however, was inevitable, and in Leechman's case it would seem that at least the seeds of sympathy had been sown. Twenty years after studying with Hamilton, having left Edinburgh to become a private tutor and then a minister, Leechman joined the Shaftesburian fold. He was elected professor of theology at Glasgow in 1743 with the active support of Francis Hutcheson, with whom he had become acquainted many years earlier, and whose lectures he had attended after leaving Edinburgh.[33] Hutcheson, who had himself secured the Glasgow chair of moral philosophy with the help of William Wishart in 1729, became a close friend of Leechman, who he believed would "put a new face upon Theology in Scotland."[34] This meant, of course, that Leechman would reform theology along the lines of the new Presbyterianism promoted by Hutcheson and Wishart.

Hutcheson's, Wishart's, and Leechman's theologies accommodated ideas articulated by Shaftesbury in connection with (1) his objections to understanding moral principles as laws issued by God either arbitrarily or for reasons that cannot be discerned or evaluated by human beings, and (2) his conviction that human beings have a natural capacity to

---

[30] The club was renamed "Sophocardian" ("wise-heart") in honor of Wishart's arrival. Stewart, "John Smith and the Molesworth Circle," 95–96.

[31] Stewart, "John Smith and the Molesworth Circle," 95–96; Scott, *Francis Hutcheson*, 30–33; J. Wodrow, "The Life of Dr. Leechman, with Some Account of His Lectures," in W. Leechman, *Sermons*, v. 1 of 2 (London, 1789), 1–19.

[32] I infer Hamilton's diffidence from a story about his treatment of the Trinity, retold in Sefton, "Neulights and Preachers Legall," 189–90. Cf. T. D. Kennedy, "William Leechman, Pulpit Eloquence and the Glasgow Enlightenment," in *The Glasgow Enlightenment*, ed. A. Hook and R. B. Sher (Phantassie: Tuckwell, 1995), 60; and below, Chapter 5, p. 189.

[33] Wodrow, "The Life of Dr. Leechman," 1–10; R. L. Emerson, "The 'Affair' at Edinburgh and the 'Project' at Glasgow: The Politics of Hume's Attempts to Become a Professor," in *Hume and Hume's Connexions*, ed. M. A. Stewart and J. P. Wright (Edinburgh: Edinburgh University Press, 1994), 17–18.

[34] Francis Hutcheson to Thomas Drennan, [1743], GUL MS Gen 1018.

act genuinely virtuously, independent of their knowledge of divine law. In opposition to many of their Presbyterian colleagues, whom modern scholarship has classified as upholders of orthodoxy, they asserted the unbounded goodness of God, insisting that Calvinist voluntarism had rendered "goodness" meaningless by equating it with the will of God, and that God's conformity to an independent, immutable, and eternal standard of goodness – namely, a disinterested desire to promote human happiness – is what makes him meaningfully good.[35] In accordance with his supreme wisdom and goodness, moreover, God had implanted in all human beings the means of achieving happiness in this world: an innate faculty for the perception of good and evil and an innate attraction to good and aversion to evil, independent of all considerations of reward or punishment in a future state. The implication of this view, namely, that even non-Christians are capable of a considerable degree of genuine virtue, is as evident in the reformers' writings as the principles from which it follows.[36]

The most vivid illustrations both of Hutcheson's, Wishart's, and Leechman's espousal of these positions, and of the heated controversies in which they consequently became embroiled, can be found in several incidents in which their careers were endangered by accusations of heresy. The three men's books, sermons, and lectures revealed unambiguously that they found much to admire in Shaftesbury. Unsurprisingly, the accusations they endured from Presbyterian ministers in Edinburgh and Glasgow resembled those that Shaftesbury, made famous in part by his followers, was also receiving at the hands of such Irish and Scottish ministers as John Leland (1691–1766), George Berkeley (1685–1753), John Witherspoon (1723–94), and Philip Skelton (1707–87): they seemed to be false Christians, espousing deism and Socinianism under the cloak of true piety.[37] They allegedly denied the necessity of revelation or knowledge of Christ; they denied the natural depravity of mankind and insisted upon the possibility of salvation without divine regeneration; they attempted to exclude matters of religious orthodoxy from the province of civil authority; and from their "heathen religion of nature" they deduced moral principles that contradicted the Westminster Confession of Faith and the word of God as expressly stated in the holy scriptures.

---

[35] E.g., F. Hutcheson, *An Inquiry into the Original of our Ideas of Beauty and Virtue*, 4th ed. (London, 1738; repr., Westmead, England: Gregg International, 1969), 275; and W. Wishart, *The certain and unchangeable Difference betwixt Moral Good and Evil* (London, 1732).

[36] E.g., W. Leechman, "Observations on the Truth of the Christian Religion," GUL MS Gen 884, fols. 144–45.

[37] On Shaftesbury's mid-century critics: Rivers, *Reason, Grace, and Sentiment*, II.15–18, II.187–90.

In the case of William Wishart, elected principal of Edinburgh University by the Town Council in 1737, the Edinburgh presbytery stood in the way of his appointment to minister in any Edinburgh church, and then to represent the university at the 1738 General Assembly of the Church of Scotland, ultimately on the grounds that two sermons he had delivered in 1731 and 1732 contained principles contrary to the Bible and the Westminster Confession and thereby threatened the "purity and peace" of the Church.[38] According to the author of a contemporary pamphlet ostensibly written to convince two skeptical ministers of the validity of the presbytery's complaints, Wishart demonstrated more familiarity with Shaftesbury's *Characteristics* than with the Bible.[39] Copying the teachings of "Shaftesbury, and other Patrons of Deism," he had denied "the perfection and perspicuity of the sacred scripture" by reducing all Christian virtue to charity and moderation, and by dismissing all the "peculiar" Christian doctrines that seemed to enjoin uncharitable actions, such as the punishment of sin.[40] By objecting to the use of "awe of future rewards and punishments" as a means of instilling virtue in children, moreover, he had implicitly denied the natural depravity of all human beings, including children, together with the necessity of divine regeneration and knowledge of the revealed word of God for salvation.[41]

In the case of Leechman, suspicions of deism were also accompanied by suspicions of Socinianism – namely, suspicions that Shaftesburian Christianity tended toward the denial of the essential divinity of Jesus Christ. In the aftermath of Leechman's hotly contested election to the professorship of divinity at Glasgow University in January 1744, the Glasgow presbytery refused to allow him to subscribe to the Confession of Faith, which was necessary for him to begin teaching. The bitter controversy that ensued ended in Leechman's favor, but only after reaching the General Assembly. Citing an allegedly unorthodox sermon he had published in 1743, entitled "The Nature, Reasonableness, and Advantages of Prayer,"[42] the Glasgow

---

[38] [G. Lindsay], *Some Observations on these Two Sermons of Doctor Wishart's, Which have given Offense to the Presbytery of Edinburgh* (Edinburgh, 1737), dedication. The whole set of incidents can be reconstructed on the basis of a combination of existing secondary and primary documents, including A. Bower, *The History of the University of Edinburgh; chiefly compiled from original papers and records, never before published,* v. 2 of 3 (Edinburgh, 1817), 137; *Protest by Mr. Robert Stewart Professor of natural phylosophy, and Mr. John Ker professor of Humanity in the university of Edinburgh by Commission from the University,* NLS MS 3431, fols. 70–71; Report of the Presbytery of Edinburgh, 19 April 1738, NLS MS 3431, fols. 74–75; and Wishart, *The certain and unchangeable Difference betwixt Moral Good and Evil.*

[39] *Some Observations,* 3.   [40] *Some Observations,* 16–17.   [41] *Some Observations,* 33.

[42] C. H. Gordon and J. Williamson, *Memorial for the Reverend Mr William Leechman* ([Glasgow?], 1744), NCL APS 3.84.34. See also N. Morren, *Annals of the General Assembly of the Church of Scotland,*

presbytery claimed Leechman had denied the necessity of divine revelation for knowledge of God, and that he had substituted God for Christ as the object of prayer, failing to mention the intercession and the merits of Christ at all.[43] A pamphlet published in Glasgow in 1746, two years after the General Assembly dismissed the charges against Leechman, reaffirmed those charges and expanded the case to include William Wishart and all other ministers who, like Leechman, seemed to be contributing to an ominous trend: an increase in the preaching of sermons "without Christ, and consisting of Morality, without that relation to the Gospel of Christ (that alone can render it acceptable in the Sight of God)."[44] Leechman and Wishart had allegedly struck at the heart of true Christian doctrine, asserting – as Leechman put it in the formal apology that prompted the General Assembly to dismiss the case against him – "that the Merits and Propitiation of Jesus Christ are not the only Grounds of a Sinner's Acceptance with God, and of his obtaining the Forgiveness of Sin."[45] They seemed to have let their insistence upon God's benevolence and mankind's natural capacity for virtue cast a shadow over the necessity of Christ's intercession on mankind's behalf, even suggesting that the faculty by which human beings perceived moral principles was sufficient for salvation without knowledge of the word of God.[46]

Francis Hutcheson faced similar accusations, and his theological position remained a liability for him throughout his career in Glasgow. Shortly after joining the faculty of the university, he noted to his friend, Thomas Drennan, that his reputation had already begun to cause difficulties for his friends and associates there:

> I think it altogether proper you should not mention my name to your Brethren, but conceal it. I am already called new light here. I don't value it for my self, but I see it hurts some ministers here who are most intimate with me.[47]

---

from the *Final Secession in 1739, to the Origin of the Relief in 1752*, v. 1 of 2 (Edinburgh: John Johnstone, 1838), 46–61. For the controversy within Glasgow University preceding Leechman's election, see Emerson, "The 'Affair' at Edinburgh," 17.

[43] Morren, *Annals*, 47–60.

[44] *An Essay to Prevent the Dangerous Consequences of the Moral Harangues, Now so common in Scotland* (Glasgow, 1746), iv. The quotation was taken from an account of the proceedings against Leechman, written by John Robe.

[45] Quoted in J. Robe, *An Appendix to Mr. Robe's Historical and Remarking Paper; Vindicating the Late Act of Assembly, concerning Mr. Leechman's Affair* (Edinburgh, 1744), 10.

[46] On Benjamin Whichcote, the other culprit named in the pamphlet: Rivers, *Reason, Grace, and Sentiment*, II.87; and F. Beiser, *The Sovereignty of Reason* (Princeton, NJ: Princeton University Press, 1996), 159–65, 177–79.

[47] Hutcheson to Drennan, GUL MS Gen 1018.

In 1738, Hutcheson's situation became more dire when the presbytery of Glasgow prosecuted him, in the words of his biographer W. R. Scott,

> for teaching to his students in contravention to the Westminster Confession the following two false and dangerous doctrines, first that the standard of moral goodness was the promotion of the happiness of others; and second that we could have a knowledge of good and evil, without, and prior to a knowledge of God.[48]

The substance of the controversy, which was ultimately resolved in Hutcheson's favor, can be discerned from a pamphlet that appeared in the midst of the ferment excited by the prosecution. Titled *Shaftesbury's Ghost conjur'd*, it takes the form of a letter accusing Hutcheson of conspiring with Shaftesbury to undermine Christianity along deist lines. Hiding his infidelity under the cloak of reverence for a supremely benevolent God – so the anonymous author asserted – Hutcheson pretended that human beings could have "Knowledge of Moral Good and Evil" without knowing anything of "the Being of a God" or of "Divine Law," though it was clearly inconceivable, not to mention inconsistent with the first commandment, that anyone could have knowledge of a law without knowing a thing about the lawgiver.[49] Equally objectionably, from the false premise that virtue consists of nothing more than the tendency of an action to promote other people's happiness, Hutcheson had deduced that disobeying the divine prohibitions against suicide, lying, and gambling could under some circumstances be virtuous.[50] Like Shaftesbury, Hutcheson treated human beings' so-called innate sense of virtue and vice as the highest arbiter in matters of conduct, leaving no real need for God's revealed word. Along similar lines, the author of the pamphlet alleged, Hutcheson had contradicted scripture by asserting that human beings are naturally capable of virtue and that a majority of mankind would be

---

[48] Scott, *Francis Hutcheson*, 84. Scott quotes this summary almost directly from John Rae's *Life of Adam Smith* (London, 1895), 12–13. Rae, however, does not cite any source, and I have been unable to find one.

[49] [H. Heugh], *Shaftesbury's Ghost conjur'd, or, a Letter to Mr. Francis Hutcheson, Professor of Moral Philosophy in the University of Glasgow* ([n.p.], 1738), 6–7. On the details of the controversy and the author's identity as Hugh Heugh, a former student of Hutcheson's: J. Moore, "Evangelical Calvinists versus the Hutcheson Circle: Debating the Faith in Scotland, 1738–1739," in *Debating the Faith: Religion and Letter Writing in Great Britain*, ed. A. Dunan-Page and C. Prunier (Dordrecht, Netherlands: Springer, 2013); and D. Carey, "Francis Hutcheson's Philosophy and the Scottish Enlightenment: Reception, Reputation, and Legacy," in *Scottish Philosophy in the Eighteenth Century*, v. 1, ed. A. Garrett and J. A. Harris (Oxford: Oxford University Press, 2015), 61–65.

[50] [Heugh], *Shaftesbury's Ghost conjur'd*, 8–20.

saved, including the "heathens," led to eternal happiness by the light of nature.[51]

Among the common threads running through all three controversies was the issue of the foundation of morality, on which Shaftesbury had taken a stand against Locke. This was also the issue that proved most obviously intractable. Hutcheson and his colleagues found ways of evading the more extreme accusation of "deism" and its implication that they had declared divine revelation superfluous in human beings' moral education; they simply asserted that God had indeed needed to reveal his law in the distant past, when mankind's "gross ignorance and corruption" had made extreme measures necessary, and that even in "the present enlightened age of the world" the threat of divine punishment could help create an aversion to vice in people whose vicious passions were otherwise uncontrollable.[52] But Hutcheson and his colleagues had no intention of denying the charges that they had elevated charity above all the other Christian virtues and had asserted human beings' capacity for genuine virtue without the aid of divine regeneration and knowledge of divine law. In fact, they consistently responded to such charges by simply restating the assertions that had come under attack and continuing to draw on the presuppositions about human nature that their critics had called into question.[53]

The stalemate on this issue appears particularly vividly in the 1737 pamphlet containing anonymous objections to the sermons of William Wishart's that had drawn criticism from the Edinburgh presbytery. In his sermon on "The certain and unchangeable Difference betwixt Moral Good and Evil," Wishart had remarked that "the Awe of future Rewards and Punishments" – at least "as they are made Use of, without ever explaining the Nature and Justice of them" – can contribute no more to promote a liberal Piety and Virtue, a Relish for true Goodness, and Savour

---

[51] [Heugh], *Shaftesbury's Ghost conjur'd*, 22–26.

[52] Leechman, "Observations on the Truth of the Christian Religion," fols. 144–45; F. Hutcheson, *Inquiry into the Original of our Ideas of Beauty and Virtue*, ed. Wolfgang Leidhold (Indianapolis, IN: Liberty Fund, 2004), 269; cf. Shaftesbury, *Characteristics*, ed. Klein, 185–86; Ahnert, *Moral Culture*, 42–44, 60–61. Except where otherwise noted, page references for Hutcheson's *Inquiry* refer to the original pagination and text of the second edition (London, 1726), as indicated by Leidhold.

[53] See, e.g., William Wishart's anonymous defense of Shaftesbury from George Berkeley's *Alciphron: or, the Minute Philosopher* (London, 1732): *A Vindication of the Reverend D—— B——y, from The scandalous Imputation of being Author of a late Book, intitled, Alciphron, or, the minute Philosopher* (London, 1734). A detailed description of the pamphlet and its attribution to Wishart can be found in M. A. Stewart, "William Wishart, Early Critic of *Alciphron*," *Berkeley Newsletter* 6 (1982/83): 5–9.

of Honesty in the Mind, than *Whips* and *Sugar-Plumbs.*[54] To this point, the pamphlet-writer responded:

> Is it possible the Doctor can think, that the Hope of eternal Happiness will have no more Influence upon a rational Creature, possessed of a Desire of Immortality, to engage him to the Practice of Holiness, than the Hope of a Sugar-plumb? Or does he imagine, that the Fear of eternal Misery will be of no greater Weight to deter him from Sin, than the Fear of a Whipping?[55]

These rhetorical questions demonstrate that the writer of the pamphlet misunderstood Wishart in a way that illuminates the point of contention. Of course Wishart had not considered the appeal to people's hopes and fears to be an ineffectual method of inculcating obedience to divine commandments. He had disparaged whips and sugarplums not because he thought them insufficient instruments of terror and temptation, but rather because of their effectiveness. It was quite as revolting, he thought, that people should behave virtuously out of hope for eternal bliss and fear of eternal damnation, as it was that they should behave virtuously out of hope for sugarplums and fear of being whipped. Both pairs of instruments merely coerced outward conformity to moral principles, promoting hypocrisy rather than sincere virtue. Instead of inculcating a love of virtue and an aversion to vice, they inculcated a love of reward and an aversion to punishment. Wishart's critic simply did not see this, because he considered obedience to the letter of divine law to be the standard of virtue and took for granted that human beings, in their natural state, were incapable of acting out of any motive other than the two "inner springs" of hope and fear. That was simply the condition of postlapsarian man; only the grace of God could bring any human being out his natural condition of depravity. As the author of *Shaftesbury's Ghost conjur'd* declared to Hutcheson,

> If our Eyes were opened to see the original Corruptness of our Natures, whereby we are utterly indisposed, disabled and made opposite to all Good, and wholly inclined to all Evil, we would readily agree with our Saviour, that *a corrupt Tree cannot bring forth Fruit.*[56]

More simply put, "*there is none that doth Good, no not one.*"[57] This was the picture of human nature that Hutcheson, like Wishart and Leechman, rejected.

---

[54] Wishart, *The certain and unchangeable Difference betwixt Moral Good and Evil,* 34.
[55] *Some Observations on these Two Sermons of Doctor Wishart's,* 31.
[56] [Heugh], *Shaftesbury's Ghost conjur'd,* 22.   [57] [Heugh], *Shaftesbury's Ghost conjur'd,* 22.

Hutcheson's Divergence from Shaftesbury

Hutcheson may have taken the Shaftesburian side in the basic debate over the foundation of morality within early-eighteenth-century Scottish Presbyterianism, but when it came to some of the crucial details, he was hardly a Shaftesburian through and through.[58] The contrary view, that Francis Hutcheson was in fact the most faithful exponent and defender of Shaftesbury's moral philosophy, has a long history, beginning at least as early as the publication in 1725 of Hutcheson's *Inquiry into the Original of our Ideas of Beauty and Virtue, in which the principles of the late Earl of Shaftesbury are Explain'd and Defended, against the Author of the Fable of the Bees: and the Ideas of Moral Good and Evil are establish'd, according to the Sentiments of the Antient Moralists.*[59] In support of Hutcheson's claim to have defended Shaftesbury's principles, Thomas Fowler wrote in 1882 that

> Hutcheson acted quite rightly in connecting his name on the title-page with that of Shaftesbury. There are no two names, perhaps, in the history of English [*sic*] moral philosophy, which stand in a closer connexion.[60]

Nor has the view that Hutcheson's and Shaftesbury's philosophies bear close resemblance to each other ended with Fowler; it can be found in more recent classifications of the two men as members of the "sentimentalist" school of moral philosophy, allegedly founded by Shaftesbury and supplied by Hutcheson with a more elaborate and precise defense. According to this classification, Hutcheson and Shaftesbury agreed, in opposition to the school of "rationalists" or "intellectualists," that the perception of moral principles and the motivation of moral actions was "ultimately a matter of feeling rather than of knowledge."[61]

---

[58] The following section of this chapter incorporates revised sections from S. Grote, "Hutcheson's Divergence from Shaftesbury," *Journal of Scottish Philosophy* 4.2 (2006): 159–72. Reused with permission from Edinburgh University Press.

[59] On Hutcheson's critique of Mandeville, see below, Chapter 5, p. 200.

[60] T. Fowler, *Shaftesbury and Hutcheson* (London, 1882), 183.

[61] This last phrase is J. B. Schneewind's, in *Moral Philosophy from Montaigne to Kant* (Cambridge: Cambridge University Press, 2003), 504. For standard descriptions of Hutcheson and Shaftesbury as sentimentalists, see L. A. Selby-Bigge, introduction, *British Moralists*, ed. Selby-Bigge (Oxford: Oxford University Press, 1897; repr., New York: Bobbs-Merrill, 1964), xliv, l–li, lxvi; and D. D. Raphael, *The Moral Sense* (Oxford: Oxford University Press, 1947), 2. Cf. below, Chapter 5, pp. 185–87. The view that Hutcheson worked Shaftesbury's suggestive writings into a coherent system can be found in, among others, Raphael, *Moral Sense*, 17; and J. Martineau, *Types of Ethical Theory*, 2 v. (Oxford: Oxford University Press, 1901), II.514, as cited in S. Darwall, *The British Moralists and the Internal "Ought"* (Cambridge: Cambridge University Press, 1995), 207n1.

On the other hand, the view that Shaftesbury's and Hutcheson's philosophies differ quite considerably from one another has an equally long history. Recent commentators have challenged the classification of Shaftesbury as a sentimentalist, and not without good reason,[62] but the longer pedigree belongs to another characterization of the major difference, one that in fact appears to have the strongest claim, stronger even than Fowler's view, to the authority of Hutcheson and many of his contemporaries. It can be found in a review of Hutcheson's posthumously published *System of Moral Philosophy*, printed anonymously in 1755 in the first volume of the short-lived *Edinburgh Review*, and for clarity and incisiveness, it seems never to have been bettered.[63] Henry Sidgwick suggests it with some hesitation in his *Outlines of the History of Ethics*, and A. O. Aldridge notes it with less hesitation and less precision in his 1951 study of Shaftesbury,[64] but whereas Sidgwick and Aldridge interpret it as a modification or extension of Shaftesbury's philosophical system by Hutcheson, it is in fact quite a substantial difference. In the words of William Leechman's preface to Hutcheson's *System*, from which the reviewer of the *System* appears to have taken many cues, "the difference is the greatest imaginable."[65] It lies in their respective conceptions of "the supreme principle of human nature," and it corresponds to fundamental differences not only in their moral philosophies but also in their aesthetic theories.

According to Hutcheson's reviewer, probably the Edinburgh minister and later professor of rhetoric and *belles-lettres*, Hugh Blair (1718–1800),[66]

---

[62] One particularly bold version of this view can be found in Darwall, *British Moralists*, esp. 210; cf. D. McNaughton, "Shaftesbury, third Earl of (Anthony Ashley Cooper) (1671–1713)," in *Routledge Encyclopedia of Philosophy*, ed. E. Craig, v. 8 of 10 (London: Routledge, 1998), esp. 731–32. Isabel Rivers offers a more detailed description of the ambiguities in Shaftesbury's writings that make definitive classification difficult, in *Reason, Grace, and Sentiment*, II.122–34.

[63] [Hugh Blair?], Review of *A System of Moral Philosophy*, by F. Hutcheson, *Edinburgh Review* 1 (1755): 15–16.

[64] H. Sidgwick, *Outlines of the History of Ethics for English Readers*, 6th ed. (London: Macmillan, 1931; repr., Bristol: Thoemmes, 1996), 202–3; A. O. Aldridge, "Shaftesbury and the Deist Manifesto," *Transactions of the American Philosophical Society* 41 (1951): 314.

[65] Qtd. in W. Leechman, preface, *A System of Moral Philosophy*, by F. Hutcheson (Glasgow, 1755), xlvi. Whether Leechman himself is the author of this passage is not clear.

[66] In the 1818 reprint of the *Edinburgh Review*, the originally anonymous review is attributed to Hugh Blair, but Richard Sher follows Leslie Stephen in demurring to state unreservedly that Blair is the author. Blair or not, the author of the review appears more or less to have taken his comments about Hutcheson's relation to Shaftesbury, with some paraphrase, from William Leechman's preface to Hutcheson's *System*. See L. Stephen, s.v. "Blair, Hugh," *Dictionary of National Biography*, ed. L. Stephen and S. Lee (Oxford: Oxford University Press, 1922); R. Sher, s.v. "Blair, Hugh," *Dictionary of National Biography*, ed. H. C. G. Matthew and B. Harrison (Oxford: Oxford University Press, 2004); and J. Mackintosh, "Preface to a Reprint of the Edinburgh Review," in *Miscellaneous Works of the Right Honourable Sir James Mackintosh*, v. 2 of 3 (London, 1854), 466.

both Shaftesbury and Hutcheson assert that human beings are naturally capable of disinterested affections, affections directed toward others and not toward themselves:

> The ground-work of our author's philosophy is the same with that of Lord Shaftesbury.... Both agree in asserting a distinct order of kind affections in our nature, which have the happiness of others for their ultimate object, without reference to our own interest.

When it comes to the question of the origin of such "kind affections," however, Blair notices a "remarkable difference in opinion between Mr. Hutcheson and that noble author":

> But when, all passions apart, we calmly consider what is the wisest regulation of human conduct; when the question is put, For what reason we ought to pursue virtue, and to cultivate the friendly and benevolent affections, rather than the selfish? the answer returned by Lord Shaftesbury is, Because virtue is the chief happiness, and vice the ill or misery of every one; because we experience the purest and sublimest joy in the gratification of the generous emotions. Thus, according to that philosopher, the calm desire of our own happiness, is the leading, the supreme principle of human nature. Whereas, according to our author, the desire of our own happiness is not the supreme principle in the soul. But, independent of this, and independent of all particular affections; there is a calm desire of the happiness of all rational beings; which is not only co-ordinate with, but even of superior authority to, the desire of our own happiness: insomuch that, should an opposition betwixt these principles fall out, the moral sense would declare in favour of the former; and would authorise and require the entire sacrifice of our own happiness to the happiness of the rational system.[67]

Whatever ambiguities one may detect in Blair's comparison of Hutcheson with Shaftesbury, such as the absence of any reference to Shaftesbury's view of the moral sense by contrast with Hutcheson's, one thing could hardly be clearer: Blair distinguishes their philosophical systems by the desire they identify as the "principle of human nature" that, in the course of calm consideration of the "wisest regulation of human conduct," leads human beings to pursue virtue and cultivate benevolent affections. For Shaftesbury, it is the calm desire for one's own happiness, and for Hutcheson it is an additional calm desire, the calm desire for the happiness of others. In the words of Leechman's preface, Shaftesbury differs from Hutcheson in "taking it for granted, that there can be but one ultimate end of the agent's cool and deliberate pursuit, viz. his own highest interest or personal happiness,"

---

[67] [Blair?], Review of *A System of Moral Philosophy*, 15–16.

which is therefore necessarily the "determiner of his choice" to gratify his own benevolent affections.[68]

In the case of Shaftesbury, what may appear self-contradictory in Blair's description – namely, that human beings are led by a desire for their *own* happiness to gratify affections that nonetheless have *others'* happiness as their ultimate object – is in fact born out by Shaftesbury's own description of those affections. He associates them with goodness and virtue solely on account of their objects, and with no regard to the desire that leads to their gratification. A creature is *good*, according to Shaftesbury, insofar as its affections are directed immediately toward the "public good," the good of the larger "system" of which it is a part. A human being is *virtuous* insofar as its affections – a second order of affections – are directed immediately toward good affections and actions, as an object of mental reflection.[69] Affections directed immediately toward "self-good" and only accidentally toward the public good cannot be called good, and affections directed toward goodness not "for its own sake, as good and amiable in itself," but rather for the sake of some "reward," cannot be called virtuous.[70] Even where Shaftesbury readily admits that some affections that have self-good as their object are entitled to be called *good*, such as the affection toward self-preservation, he only includes those self-directed affections which are "not only consistent with public Good, but in some measure contributing to it" and in that sense also have the good of the larger system as their immediate object.[71]

This definitional injunction against the direction of good and virtuous affections toward self-good and toward rewards by no means excludes the gratification of good and virtuous affections for the sake of the private happiness they afford. The problem with seeking rewards may seem to be simply that rewards are a species of private happiness, but in fact the

---

[68] Qtd. in Leechman, preface, xlv.

[69] Shaftesbury, *Characteristics*, ed. Klein, 167–77. It is difficult to use cognates of the terms *good* and *virtue* with precision and consistency. Shaftesbury himself, unfortunately, does not always set a perfect example. The problem chiefly arises from the need to avoid clumsy verbiage while distinguishing four things: (1) actions, (2) a first order of affections toward objects of sensation, (3) a second order of affections directed toward the first order of affections as an object of reflection, and (4) an animal or human being who does or has one or more of the preceding three. Specifying a particular referent, unfortunately, greatly increases the chance of misrepresenting Shaftesbury, who often uses the terms ambiguously. With as much consistency as possible, I use *goodness* and *good affections* to refer to affections directed toward the good of the larger system, and I use *virtue* and *virtuous affections* to refer to the affections of a virtuous person – i.e., good affections as well as the second order of affection directed toward those good affections as an object of reflection.

[70] Shaftesbury, *Characteristics*, ed. Klein, 188.   [71] Shaftesbury, *Characteristics*, ed. Klein, 170.

problem must be that gratifying good affections for the sake of rewards implies a second-order affection that is not directed toward those good affections. The truly virtuous, after all, do show regard for a different species of private happiness, one that Shaftesbury calls the *natural advantages* of virtue and identifies with "the intrinsic worth or value of the thing [i.e., virtue] itself."[72] These are the "mental enjoyments" or "speculative pleasure" attendant upon the contemplation of one's own virtuous affections, and the "mental pleasure" (or "happiness" or "mental enjoyment")[73] that arises from the "natural effects" of virtuous affections.[74] That the pursuit of this happiness does not in itself imply the directing of one's affections toward self-good, Shaftesbury makes particularly clear in a critique of Duc François de la Rochefoucauld's (1613–80) *Maxims*, one of various "modern" attempts to "new-frame the Human Heart" and "reduce all its Motions, Ballances and Weights, to that one Principle and Foundation of a cool and deliberate *Selfishness*":

> You have the very same thought spun out a hundred ways and drawn into mottoes and devices to set forth this riddle, that 'act as disinterestedly or generously as you please, *self* still is at the bottom, and nothing else'. Now if these gentlemen who delight so much in the play of words, but are cautious how they grapple closely with definitions, would tell us only what self-interest was, and determine happiness and good, there would be an end of this enigmatical wit. For in this we should all agree – that happiness was to be pursued and in fact was always sought after. But, whether found in following nature and giving way to common affection or in suppressing it and turning every passion towards private advantage, a narrow self-end, or the preservation of mere life, this would be the matter in debate between us. The question would not be, 'who loved himself or who not?' but 'who loved and served himself the rightest and after the truest manner?'[75]

In explaining that Rochefoucauld's argument depends upon a specious identification of the pursuit of happiness with not only self-interest but also selfishness and therefore vice, Shaftesbury unambiguously distinguishes the pursuit of happiness from the directing of affections solely toward oneself. Whereas the latter constitutes vice, the former cannot be taken as the measure of vice or virtue at all. The difference between vice and virtue is the difference between two ways of pursuing happiness, one by "giving way to" affections directed toward "private advantage," and the other by giving

---

[72] Shaftesbury, *Characteristics*, ed. Klein, 46.
[73] Shaftesbury employs all these terms apparently interchangeably.
[74] Shaftesbury, *Characteristics*, ed. Klein, e.g., 192–93, 200–204.
[75] Shaftesbury, *Characteristics*, ed. Klein, 56.

way to affections directed toward the common good. Shaftesbury draws a distinction, in other words, between the *object* or *direction* of an affection and what might safely be called – though not on Shaftesbury's authority – the affection's *motivation*.[76] In Shaftesbury's view, the motivation that leads human beings to "give way" to an affection is invariably a desire for private happiness. Virtuous affections, therefore, are those which have the good of others as their ultimate object,[77] and which human beings give way to, motivated by a desire for the private happiness such affections afford. In this way, to borrow Henry Sidgwick's classification, Shaftesbury's moral philosophy is a refined variety of *egoistic hedonism*. At least with respect to motivation, it takes the proper aim of human action to be the happiness or pleasure (*hedonism*) of the individual actor (*egoistic*).[78]

Accordingly, Shaftesbury describes moral education as the process by which naturally egoistic and hedonistic human beings discover – without immediate reference to God's will – that the greatest or truest happiness or pleasure, even in this life, is in fact to be found in the pursuit of virtue.[79] It is also a process of aesthetic education, insofar as the virtue at which moral education aims is a love of contemplating the greatest possible beauty, motivated by the pleasure naturally afforded by that contemplation.

Shaftesbury does not always make this motivation clear. He frequently describes the process by which we learn to discern beauty simply as a discovery of order in the objects of our contemplation. Order, Shaftesbury explains, refers to the "perfection" (or "unity") of a thing, which in turn refers to the "sympathizing" of a thing's parts, such that together the parts

---

[76] Whether this distinction is in fact plausible may be open to question, but it is at any rate one which Robert Voitle, in his efforts to defend Shaftesbury from the charge of egoism, appears at least implicitly to reject. See R. Voitle, "Shaftesbury's Moral Sense," *Studies in Philology* 52 (1955): 23; and Voitle, *The Third Earl of Shaftesbury*, 130. The distinction bears some resemblance to a distinction between the *immediate* objects and the *intentional* objects of an affection, drawn by G. Trianosky in "On the Obligation to Be Virtuous: Shaftesbury and the Question, Why Be Moral?," *Journal of the History of Philosophy* 14.3 (1978): 291–93.

[77] "Ultimate object" is the phrase used by Hutcheson's reviewer. In this context, to say virtuous affections have the good of others as their "ultimate object" means simply that the second-order affection of a virtuous person is directed toward first-order affections which have the good of other people as their object.

[78] H. Sidgwick, *The Methods of Ethics* (Indianapolis, IN, 1981), 6–11.

[79] Shaftesbury's frequent injunctions against seeking happiness in "mere pleasure" or in "whatever pleases me" refer not to the danger of seeking pleasure itself, but rather to the danger of allowing one's unregenerate appetites, rather than "reason," to dictate where pleasure is to be sought. The "true" or "real" pleasure that virtue affords and that reason enjoys may be "too refined for our modern Epicures," and Shaftesbury often refers to it in various contexts as "joy," "happiness," "advantage," or "real self-interest," but he does not deny that it is a form of pleasure. On Shaftesbury's distinction between true and false pleasures, cf. *Characteristics*, ed. Klein, e.g., 138–39, 250, 332; Shaftesbury, *Second Characters*, ed. B. Rand (Cambridge: Cambridge University Press, 1914), 32, 114.

serve the purpose (or "good") of the thing itself or "whole." The purpose of the whole, in turn, is to serve the purpose of the larger whole of which it is only a single part.[80] In the case of any material object, the "real relation" of parts and the purpose they serve persist despite any changes in the matter of which the object consists, and Shaftesbury describes the "uniting principle" responsible for this persistence as the object's "form" or "nature": an immaterial and immortal substance that all wholes of a single type (whether all individual human beings, all types of animals, all types of inhabitant in the world, or all worlds in the universe) have in common.[81] Human beings are able to perceive order and the nature or form responsible for it by means of perceptive faculties that they naturally possess. The discovery of a purposive whole by the examination of the coherence among its parts, and the judgment of the degree to which those parts serve the purpose of the whole – that is, the judgment of how orderly or perfect a thing is – Shaftesbury attributes variously to "imagination," "common sense," and "internal sensation."[82] The judgment itself, according to Shaftesbury, consists of a perception of a thing's parts, followed by an "anticipation" or "presensation" of the thing's form, and finally a measurement of the degree of perfection of the thing itself by comparison with the full perfection of its form.[83] If Shaftesbury's equation of the beautiful with the good[84] can be taken at face value, then *beauty* is another name for order,[85] a name that Shaftesbury tends to employ in the context of referring to the instinctive human preference of order to disorder, and to the love that human beings instinctively feel when they contemplate order.[86]

From this bare description, it is hardly obvious that the act of perceiving orderliness requires any significant motivation at all, let alone that the prospect of deriving pleasure from the contemplation of order is what sets the perceptive faculties in motion. But judging the degree of order and therefore beauty in any given thing can be difficult, and the difficulty

---

[80] Shaftesbury, *Characteristics*, ed. Klein, 273–74, 299–301. On Christian Wolff's employment of nearly identical concepts, see above, Chapter 1, pp. 24–25. Cf. Guyer, *A History of Modern Aesthetics*, I.30, I.47–48.

[81] Shaftesbury, *Characteristics*, ed. Klein, 274–75, 299–303.

[82] Shaftesbury, *Characteristics*, ed. Klein, e.g., 63, 67, 274, 353.

[83] Shaftesbury, *Characteristics*, ed. Klein, 178, 273, 282, 326, 329, 408, 429; Carey, *Locke, Shaftesbury, and Hutcheson*, 110–19.

[84] Shaftesbury, *Characteristics*, ed. Klein, e.g., 254–55, 320.

[85] Cf. R. Glauser, "Aesthetic Experience in Shaftesbury," pt. I, *The Aristotelian Society* suppl. vol. 76 (2006), 26–27.

[86] Shaftesbury, *Characteristics*, ed. Klein, 320–21, 326.

increases with the scale and complexity of the whole under consideration. In the case of particular plants, for example, the real relations between the parts, and the degree to which those parts function together coherently, are easy to discern.[87] In the case of the universe as a whole, many of whose parts are inaccessible to us, conclusive judgment is impossible.[88] Judging the universe to be orderly would seem to depend on the inference that what is true of all the known parts is likely to be true of the whole: if the known parts of the universe are orderly by virtue of their forms or uniting principles, then the universe as a whole is almost certainly orderly by virtue of its uniting principle. To quote Theocles, one of two participants in Shaftesbury's philosophical dialog, *The Moralists*: if matter is

> compounded and put together in a certain number of such parts as unite and conspire in these frames of ours and others like them, if it can present us with so many innumerable instances of particular forms, who share this simple principle, by which they are really one, live, act and have a nature or genius particular to themselves and provident for their own welfare, how shall we at the same time overlook this in the whole and deny the great and general One of the world?[89]

Theocles's conversation partner, Philocles, assents relatively quickly to Theocles's arguments,[90] but Shaftesbury clearly did not regard the discovery of forms and of the orderliness they convey as a matter of rational demonstration. Shaftesbury repeatedly indicates that the observation of orderliness in material objects does not lead immediately to the discovery of their forms and the perception of those forms' orderliness; and the discovery of order in the universe is a much more challenging feat.[91] As in the arts of architecture, painting, and music, Theocles points out, "it is not instantly we acquire the sense by which these beauties are discoverable. Labour and pains are required and time to cultivate a natural genius ever so apt or forward."[92] Theocles is referring to what Shaftesbury describes in the *Miscellanies* as "the labour and pains of criticism," which necessarily precede the development of a taste for what is truly beautiful.[93] More obviously than the apparently simple act of perceiving order, this labor requires motivation.

[87] Shaftesbury, *Characteristics*, ed. Klein, 273.
[88] Shaftesbury, *Characteristics*, ed. Klein, 279, 298, 305–6, 315.
[89] Shaftesbury, *Characteristics*, ed. Klein, 301, cf. 305.
[90] Shaftesbury, *Characteristics*, ed. Klein, 279–80, 305–7.
[91] Shaftesbury, *Characteristics*, ed. Klein, e.g., 279, 298, 305–6.
[92] Shaftesbury, *Characteristics*, ed. Klein, 320.
[93] Shaftesbury, *Characteristics*, ed. Klein, 408, cf. 409.

That the motivation to undertake the labor consists necessarily of the prospect of pleasure afforded by the contemplation of beauty, appears especially vividly in Shaftesbury's description of the discovery of beauty as a gradual process that can fruitfully begin with the contemplation of works of art. Shaftesbury clearly considers the contemplation of art, not to mention the production of art, an aid to the discovery of forms. The best art aims not at the reproduction of the details of any particular object, but rather at "the reduction of a thing to its species" or form, which Shaftesbury calls the communication of "plastic truth."[94] The "virtuoso" or "gentleman of fashion" who admires "what is naturally graceful and becoming," and who seeks to perfect his judgment of the beauty of works of art, implicitly accepts that there are such truths and that the correct representation of a given thing's form is not merely a matter of opinion.[95] Consequently, according to Shaftesbury, John Locke would not have philosophized as he did – which is to say, he would not have thrown "all virtue and order out of the world" and reduced moral principles to acts of divine legislation – if he had been a virtuoso.[96] Shaftesbury moreover proposes that the love of art characteristic of the "virtuoso," which derives from a delight in contemplating the forms represented by works of art, can provide the motivation necessary to cultivate one's love of forms such that one progressively acquires a taste not ultimately for works of art, but rather for minds, then for communities of minds, and ultimately for the mind that directs the universe. This progressive acquisition of a taste for ever-higher degrees of order[97] relies on the virtuoso's persistent desire for pleasure. In an appeal to "the grown youth of our polite world," Shaftesbury makes no effort to hide this fact:

> Whoever has any impression of what we call gentility or politeness is already so acquainted with the decorum and grace of things that he will readily confess a pleasure and enjoyment in the very survey and contemplation of this kind. Now if in the way of polite pleasure the study and love of beauty be essential, the study and love of symmetry and order, on which beauty depends, must also be essential in the same respect.[98]

The path of the argument can already be foreseen: lovers of beauty in material objects and external behavior can be convinced, by appeal to the

---

94 Shaftesbury, *Characteristics*, ed. Klein, 67; Shaftesbury, *Second Characters*, 98–102.
95 Shaftesbury, *Characteristics*, ed. Klein, e.g., 62.
96 Shaftesbury to Ainsworth, in *Life, Unpublished Letters, and Philosophical Regimen*, 403 (qtd. in Carey, *Locke, Shaftesbury, and Hutcheson*, 132), 416.
97 Shaftesbury, *Characteristics*, ed. Klein, 415–16n25.   98 Shaftesbury, *Characteristics*, ed. Klein, 414.

fact that what gives them pleasure is the contemplation of symmetry and order, to seek to admire symmetry and order in minds.

This appeal does not rely on a superficial analogy between spatial symmetry in material objects and well-ordered affections in minds.[99] Rather, in both cases the symmetry refers to the perfection of the thing under consideration, which is to say, the suitability of the thing's parts to serve the purpose or "good" of the whole. In the case of the "imitative or designing arts," Shaftesbury explains,

> the truth or beauty of every figure or statue is measured from the perfection of nature in her just adapting of every limb and proportion to the activity, strength, dexterity, life and vigour of the particular species or animal designed.
> Thus beauty and truth are plainly joined with the notion of utility or convenience, even in the apprehension of every ingenious artist, the architect, the statuary or the painter.

The same point, Shaftesbury continues, can be made about the health of the human body:

> Natural health is the just proportion, truth and regular course of things in a constitution. It is the inward beauty of the body. And when the harmony and just measures of the rising pulses, the circulating humours and the moving airs or spirits are disturbed or lost, deformity enters and, with it, calamity and ruin.

It only remains for Shaftesbury to assert that the human mind can be understood in the same way:

> Is there nothing which tends to disturbance and dissolution? Is there no natural tenor, tone or order of the passions or affections? No beauty or deformity in this moral kind? Or allowing that there really is, must it not, of consequence, in the same manner imply health or sickliness, prosperity or disaster? Will it not be found in this respect, above all, that what is beautiful is harmonious and proportionable, what is harmonious and proportionable is true, and what is at once both beautiful and true is, of consequence, agreeable and good?[100]

This rehearsal of the steps by which a lover of beauty in material things can be convinced to love moral beauty is more complex than it may seem. Shaftesbury is not simply restating the argument, well known from his *Inquiry Concerning Virtue or Merit*, that virtue is in every human being's self-interest. Here, he explicitly describes "utility or convenience" not as simply an attribute or effect of beauty, but rather as the measure of beauty; we measure a statue's beauty by determining the degree to which its parts – that is, "every limb and proportion" – are portrayed as adapted to promote the natural good of the creature represented in the statue. In other words, the beauty of a statue corresponds to the degree to which the sculptor has portrayed his subject in its perfect state, or achieved the "reduction of a thing to its species."[101] Anyone who acknowledges this can be convinced that the same principle applies to living bodies and to minds. Just as the "inward beauty" of a body is inseparable from the body's "natural health," so is the beauty of a mind dependent on the "natural tenor, tone or order of the passions or affections." The search for beauty of mind, Shaftesbury continues, can only succeed with the help of philosophy. Through this series of realizations, the virtuoso blithely following the "way of polite pleasure," as Shaftesbury calls it, can be led to engage in philosophy for the purpose of seeking still greater pleasure in contemplating internal order. This conclusion is the context in which Shaftesbury poses his well-known rhetorical question: "Who can admire the outward beauties and not recur instantly to the inward, which are the most real and essential, the most naturally affecting and of the highest pleasure as well as profit and advantage?"[102]

Nor does the pleasure of contemplating order cease for those who have proceeded to where Shaftesbury suggests the virtuoso can ultimately be led,[103] namely, to the contemplation of ever-higher degrees of inward beauties in ever-larger associations of human beings, and ultimately the highest degree of order: "that which fashions even minds themselves" and "contains in itself all the beauties fashioned by those minds and is consequently the principle, source and fountain of all beauty."[104] Consider Philocles's visionary description of Palemon as an accomplished lover of beauty in the *Moralists*. Philocles begins by indicating Palemon's general tendency, as someone "experienced in all the degrees and orders of beauty, in all the mysterious charms of the particular forms," to "rise to what is more general and, with a larger heart and mind more comprehensive, . . . generously [to] seek that which is highest in the kind." Philocles proceeds to illustrate Palemon's ascent, step by step, beginning with the transfer of his attention from an individual work of art to the mind of its maker:

---

[101] See above, p. 169. Cf. Shaftesbury, *Characteristics*, ed. Klein, 417n25.
[102] Shaftesbury, *Characteristics*, ed. Klein, 416. For a description of this process on a national scale, cf. Shaftesbury, *Second Characters*, 20.
[103] Shaftesbury, *Characteristics*, ed. Klein, 416–17n25.
[104] Shaftesbury, *Characteristics*, ed. Klein, 324, cf. 332.

> Not captivated by the lineaments of a fair face or the well-drawn proportions of a human body, you view the life itself and embrace rather the mind which adds lustre and renders chiefly amiable.

Next comes the transition from contemplating the mind of that individual to contemplating the minds collected in human communities:

> Nor is the enjoyment of such a single beauty sufficient to satisfy such an aspiring soul. It seeks how to combine more beauties and by what coalition of these to form a beautiful society. It views communities, friendships, relations, duties and considers by what harmony of particular minds the general harmony is composed and commonweal established.

Palemon's soul then turns from a single society to all mankind:

> Nor satisfied even with public good in one community of men, it frames itself a nobler object and with enlarged affection seeks the good of mankind. It dwells with pleasure amid that reason and those orders on which this fair correspondence and goodly interest is established. Laws, constitutions, civil and religious rites (whatever civilizes or polishes rude mankind!), the sciences and arts, philosophy, morals, virtue, the flourishing state of human affairs and the perfection of human nature – these are its delightful prospects, and this the charm of beauty which attracts it.

From mankind, Palemon's soul then advances to contemplation of the universe itself and to the universe's creator:

> Still ardent in this pursuit (such is its love of order and perfection), it rests not here nor satisfies itself with the beauty of a part but, extending further its communicative bounty, seeks the good of all and affects the interest and prosperity of the whole. True to its native world and higher country, it is here it seeks order and perfection, wishing the best and hoping still to find a just and wise administration.
>
> And since all hope of this were vain and idle if no universal mind presided, since without such a supreme intelligence and providential care the distracted universe must be condemned to suffer infinite calamities, it is here the generous mind labours to discover that healing cause by which the interest of the whole is securely established, the beauty of things and the universal order happily sustained.[105]

Palemon's search for ever-higher degrees of beauty – which proceeds from bodies to minds, from particular forms to more general forms, from the beauty of individual minds to the beauty of ever-larger and more complex human societies, from all humanity to the universe itself, and ultimately to

---

[105] Shaftesbury, *Characteristics*, ed. Klein, 243–44.

the intelligence governing the universe – is motivated explicitly by a "love of order and perfection." Dissatisfaction with a lower degree of perfection leads Palemon to seek to contemplate a higher degree. To discover the desire for pleasure behind Palemon's longing to contemplate ever-higher degrees of order and perfection does not require imagining – however plausibly – that Shaftesbury, in invoking "dissatisfaction," has tacitly adopted Locke's conception of the human will as determined by an "*uneasiness* of the mind for want of some absent good,"[106] and with it Locke's classification of all goods and evils as species of pleasure and pain.[107] Shaftesbury himself suggests the motivation more plainly than this. Palemon's "aspiring soul" is attracted explicitly by the "delightful prospects" and "the charm of beauty" in the "orders" responsible for the good of mankind. His soul "dwells" on them "with pleasure." There seems to be no reason to doubt that the prospect of pleasure in contemplating beauty draws Palemon's soul to contemplate the higher beauties as well.[108]

The contrast between this egoistic and hedonistic conception of an aesthetic moral education and Hutcheson's, as Hugh Blair noted, could hardly be more stark. In general terms, of course, the two conceptions served similar aims. Shaftesbury's aim in criticizing Hobbes and Locke resembles Francis Hutcheson's professed aim in refuting a position to which he attaches the names of Hobbes and Samuel Pufendorf: to establish that virtue is natural to man. In an article of 1724 in the *London Journal*, a preview to the first edition of his *Inquiry into the Original of our Ideas of Beauty and Virtue*, Hutcheson declares his intent to establish that the "foundations of all virtue" are not self-interest.[109] In his inaugural lecture as professor of moral philosophy at the University of Glasgow, Hutcheson purports to show that human beings have a "natural inclination" to benevolence toward the public, without aiming at "favours" or at private advantage.[110] In both the 1724 *London Journal* article and the 1730 inaugural lecture, Hutcheson ascribes to Hobbes and Pufendorf the view he wishes to refute – namely, the view that human beings behave virtuously with the sole aim of attaining private advantage. "Many of our moralists, after Mr. Hobbs [*sic*]," Hutcheson writes,

---

106 Tuveson, "The Importance of Shaftesbury," 281; Locke, *Essay Concerning Human Understanding*, II.xxi.31.
107 Locke, *Essay Concerning Human Understanding*, II.xxi.41–42.
108 Cf. Glauser, "Aesthetic Experience in Shaftesbury," 51–53.
109 F. Hutcheson, "Reflections on the Common Systems of Morality," in *On Human Nature*, ed. T. Mautner (Cambridge: Cambridge University Press, 1993; repr., 1995), 97–98.
110 F. Hutcheson, *De naturali hominum socialitate*, in *On Human Nature*, ed. Mautner, §20.

> tell us that men are to each other what wolves are to sheep; that they are all injurious, proud, selfish, treacherous, covetous, lustful, revengeful: Nay, the avoiding the mischiefs to be feared from each other, is . . . the sole motive in this life of any external good offices which they are to perform.[111]

In his inaugural lecture, Hutcheson describes Pufendorf along similar lines:

> Pufendorf, and most recent writers, advocate the doctrine once proposed by the Epicureans, that is, that self-love alone, or everyone's search for his own pleasure or advantage, is the spring of all actions.[112]

In opposition, Hutcheson proposes the answer recommended by "the excellent Lord Shaftesbury, a man combining nobility of mind with that of birth, who gave the best and most elegant account of this matter." On Shaftesbury's account, Hutcheson explains, "human nature is also in itself, directly and in a primary sense benevolent, kind and sociable, even in the absence of any calculation of advantage or pleasure to oneself," and "there are implanted by nature in man many kind and benevolent affections and passions which, both immediately and in the longer view, have regard to the happiness of others."[113]

This homage to Shaftesbury in Hutcheson's inaugural lecture notwithstanding, Hutcheson's defense of virtue as natural to man in fact differed from Shaftesbury's along precisely the lines indicated by Hugh Blair. Hutcheson could agree that, as Shaftesbury had asserted, human beings were capable of affections that were not directed toward self-good, but he could not agree with Shaftesbury that those affections themselves flowed in any way from a desire for private happiness, in the form of the pleasures immediately attendant upon virtue itself. It was no accident that his critique of Pufendorf and the Epicureans for claiming "everyone's search for his own pleasure" to be "the spring of all actions" could have applied equally well to Shaftesbury. Moreover, for all his clarifications, inconsistencies, and changes of emphasis from one work to the next, Hutcheson clearly diverged from Shaftesbury on this issue from the very beginning. In the introduction to the second half of his 1725 *Inquiry*, Hutcheson explicitly sets out to distinguish himself from two groups of moralists who assert that human beings pursue virtue out of self-interest, and the second of these groups bears a striking resemblance to Shaftesbury:

---

[111] Hutcheson, "Reflections," 97–98. [112] Hutcheson, *De naturali hominum socialitate*, §21.
[113] Hutcheson, *De naturali hominum socialitate*, §24.

> Some other moralists suppose "an immediate natural Good in the Actions call'd Virtuous; that is, that we are determin'd to perceive some Beauty in the Actions of others, and to love the Agent, even without reflecting upon any Advantage which can any way redound to us from the Action; that we have also a secret Sense of Pleasure accompanying such of our Actions as we call Virtuous, even when we expect no other Advantage from them." But they alledge at the same time, "That we are excited to perform these Actions, even as we pursue, or purchase Pictures, Statues, Landskips, from Self-Interest, to obtain this Pleasure which accompanys the very Action, and which we necessarily enjoy in doing it."[114]

Notice Hutcheson's conscientious allusion to the distinction, found in Shaftesbury, between public affections that are ultimately self-directed and therefore vicious, and public affections that are directed immediately toward their object and are therefore – according to Shaftesbury – good or virtuous. What Hutcheson proceeds to repudiate is Shaftesbury's supposition that even these virtuous affections are necessarily motivated by a desire for the pleasures they afford.

Unlike Shaftesbury, Hutcheson refuses to admit any fundamental distinction between affections directed toward private interest and affections toward which we are led by a desire for the pleasures of virtue itself. Insofar as both types have as their end the attainment of pleasure, however sublime, Hutcheson considers them both self-interested. In the introduction to the second half of his *Inquiry*, Hutcheson establishes this connection in his definitions of *immediate good* and *advantage*:

> The Pleasure in our sensible Perceptions of any kind, gives us our first Idea of natural Good, or Happiness; and then all Objects which are apt to excite this Pleasure are call'd immediately Good. Those Objects which may procure others immediately pleasant, are call'd Advantageous: and we pursue both Kinds from a View of Interest, or from Self-Love.[115]

The pleasures of perceiving harmony in paintings, accordingly, Hutcheson associates with the pleasures of eating and drinking.[116] By extension, Hutcheson argues that the distinction between "rewards" and the immediate pleasures of virtue, a distinction on which Shaftesbury's distinction between virtue and vice ostensibly rests, is merely a matter of degree. In a rebuttal to the argument that virtuous affections are excited by the prospect of the pleasurable perceptions of one's own virtue, Hutcheson asserts that if virtuous affections really did aim at immediate or "concomitant" pleasures,

---

[114] Hutcheson, *Inquiry*, 2nd ed., 115–16.
[115] Hutcheson, *Inquiry*, 2nd ed., 113. [116] Hutcheson, *Inquiry*, 2nd ed., 114.

they would share a foundation with vicious affections, and since it is this – selfish – foundation that makes vicious affections vicious, any affections that rest upon it cannot be called virtuous:

> [W]e do not by an Act of Will raise in ourselves that Benevolence which we approve as virtuous, with a View to obtain future Pleasures of *Self-Approbation* by our Moral Sense. Could we raise Affections in this manner, we should be engaged to any Affection by the *Prospect of an Interest* equivalent to this of *Self-Approbation*, such as Wealth or sensual Pleasure, which with many Tempers are more powerful; and yet we universally own, that *that* Disposition to do good Offices to others, which is raised by these Motives, is not virtuous: how can we then imagine, that the virtuous Benevolence is brought upon us by a Motive equally *selfish*?[117]

To Hutcheson, the pleasures of self-approbation, wealth, sensual pleasure are all species of self-interest – which is to say, selfishness – and therefore impossible candidates for the desires that motivate virtuous affections.

Hutcheson offers two reasons for rejecting these self-interested desires. On the one hand, it is simply implausible that they motivate the affections we regard as virtuous. In a discussion of whether the love of benevolence is motivated by "nice views of self-interest" – that is, whether the "very frame of our nature" disposes us to pursue virtue for the sake of the pleasures it affords us – Hutcheson argues in the negative, asserting that not all virtue is in fact pleasant: we often expose ourselves to pain, voluntarily, for the sake of other people.[118] Moreover, the very theory that appears to underlie the argument that all passions must be self-interested, the theory that passion itself is a form of "uneasiness" whose satisfaction necessarily brings pleasure and indeed aims at that pleasure, Hutcheson dismisses as contrary to experience: the passions of sorrow, anger, jealousy, and pity give us merely pain.[119] Then there is the difficulty that, although Shaftesbury's explanation of virtue's foundations implies otherwise, we do not in fact approve of actions motivated in any sense by self-interest as virtuous:

> To acknowledge the several generous ultimate affections of a limited kind to be natural, and yet maintain that we have no general controlling principle but self-love, which indulges or checks the generous affections as they

[117] Hutcheson, *Inquiry*, 4th ed., 141–42.

[118] Hutcheson, *Inquiry*, 2nd ed., 142, 152–53. In the fourth edition of his *Inquiry*, Hutcheson reorganizes and expands this discussion by fourteen pages.

[119] Hutcheson, *Inquiry*, 2nd ed., 153. On Locke's theory of the will as determined invariably by "some (and for the most part the most pressing) uneasiness a Man is at present under" (Locke, *Essay Concerning Human Understanding*, II.xxi.31), cf. above, p. 173.

conduce to, or oppose, our own noblest interest, . . . is a scheme which brings indeed all the powers of the mind into one direction by means of the reference made of them all to the calm desire of our own happiness, in our previous deliberations about our conduct. . . . But the feelings of our heart, reason, and history, revolt against this account: which seems however to have been maintained by excellent authors and strenuous defenders of the cause of virtue.[120]

Still more vividly, Hutcheson writes, "[T]hat disposition of mind must upon this scheme be approved which coolly sacrifices the interest of the universe to its own interest. This is plainly contrary to the feelings of our hearts."[121]

Nor is implausibility Hutcheson's only objection to Shaftesbury's scheme. Suggesting that human beings do in fact approve of fundamentally self-interested affections as virtuous, warns Hutcheson, also implies that we cannot distinguish a good God from an evil one. Since God's private advantage cannot depend upon the good of some greater system of which he is merely a part, and unless it can be proven that his happiness depends upon his creatures' happiness, we have no reason to suppose that the God whom we approve as virtuous is not in fact a "Manichean Evil God," aiming at our unhappiness.[122]

As an alternative to Shaftesbury's scheme, therefore, Hutcheson proposed the scheme summarized by the reviewer of his *System*: that human beings possess a "calm desire for the happiness of others," and that the regulation of the affections in accordance with *this* desire is what the moral sense approves. This is precisely what Hutcheson sets out to show in the second half of his *Inquiry*. While readily asserting, as does Shaftesbury, that virtuous actions give immediate pleasure to the actor, Hutcheson promises to show precisely what Shaftesbury does not:

> That what excites us to these Actions which we call Virtuous, is not an Intention to obtain even this sensible Pleasure; much less the future Rewards from Sanctions of Laws, or any other natural Good, which may be the Consequence of the virtuous Action; but an entirely different Principle of Action from Interest or Self-Love.[123]

Hutcheson's words do not correspond precisely to his reviewer's; where Hugh Blair gives us *calm desire*, a term that becomes prominent only in

---

[120] Hutcheson, *System*, I.iv.12, 75.   [121] Hutcheson, *System*, I.iv.12, 76.
[122] Hutcheson, *Inquiry*, 2nd ed., 151.   [123] Hutcheson, *Inquiry*, 2nd ed., 116.

Hutcheson's later writings,[124] in the *Inquiry* Hutcheson offers *principle of action*. The referent, however, is the same. It is an inclination or *instinct* toward benevolence, existing previous to all rational deliberation but nonetheless guided and strengthened by it, whose motivation of affections toward other human beings constitutes the necessary condition of the moral sense's approval and is therefore the criterion of genuine virtue.[125]

Accordingly, Hutcheson describes the cultivation of a virtuous character *not* as the progressive discovery that one's greatest pleasure comes from the contemplation of the greatest beauty, but rather as the progressive strengthening of one's own natural, instinctive benevolence. In the fourth edition of his *Inquiry*, in an explication of the "many places of Plato, Aristotle, Cicero, and others of the Antients, when they speak of 'natural Instinct or Disposition in each Being, toward his own Preservation and highest Perfection, as the Spring of Virtue,'" Hutcheson gives voice to his own conception of virtue as the perfection of particular instincts:

> 'Tis acknowledged by all, that we have such an Instinct, which must operate very indistinctly at first, till we come to consider our Constitution, and our several Powers. When we do so, we find, according to them, the natural Principles of Virtue, or the φυσικαί ἀρεταί [natural virtues], implanted in us: They appear to us the noblest Parts of our Nature; such are our Desires of Knowledge, our Relish for Beauty, especially of the Moral Kind, our Sociable Affections. These upon Reflection we find to be natural Parts of our Constitution, and we desire to bring them to Perfection from the first-mentioned general Instinct.[126]

Hutcheson does not explain in much greater detail how precisely these virtuous instincts are to be brought to perfection, but in the 1742 edition of his *Essay on the Nature and Conduct of the Passions and Affections*, he offers a more detailed account in the case of instinctive benevolence, which he calls a *calm* or *general desire* for the happiness of other people, or *calm universal*

---

[124] J. D. Bishop, "Moral Motivation and the Development of Hutcheson's Philosophy," *Journal of the History of Ideas* 57 (1996): 292–93.

[125] Hutcheson, *Inquiry*, 4th ed., 191–92; F. Hutcheson and G. Burnet, *Letters between the Late Mr. Gilbert Burnet and Mr. Hutchinson, concerning the True Foundation of Virtue or Moral Goodness* (London, 1735), 50; F. Hutcheson, *An Essay on the Nature and Conduct of the Passions and Affections*, 3rd ed. (London, 1742; repr. Gainesville, FL: Scholars' Facsimiles and Reprints, 1969), 28–30; Bishop, "Moral Motivation," 285; Darwall, *British Moralists*, 224–28. Hutcheson occasionally appears to have used the term *instinct* with some reservation, because its connotation of a mental function characteristic of animals had provoked resistance from some of his contemporaries, including John Gay and John Balguy. Greene, "Instinct of Nature," 195–98. On Balguy, see below, Chapter 5, pp. 210–11.

[126] Hutcheson, *Inquiry*, 4th ed., 197–98.

benevolence. Drawing explicitly on Nicolas Malebranche's (1638–1715) distinction of *affections* from *passions*, Hutcheson describes *calm general desire* as the desire of some good that appears "to our reason or reflection," and that "alone would incline us to pursue whatever objects were apprehended as a means of good." According to Hutcheson himself, the calm desire for any good upon which we reflect is not invariably enough to incline us to pursue it, since calm desire tends to be overridden by desires of "objects presented immediately to some sense," which Hutcheson calls *particular passions*, and which, when they are attended by bodily pleasure or pain, can "prevent all deliberate reasoning about our conduct." It is by a process of habituation, "through frequent reflection" on good and evil, that calm desire can be made stronger than the particular passions and thereby capable of inclining us consistently toward what we apprehend as good.[127]

By contrast with Shaftesbury's conception of moral education, Hutcheson's has hardly any clearly aesthetic component at all. He does, to be sure, devote most of the first half of his 1724 *Inquiry into the Original of our Ideas of Beauty and Virtue* to a defense of the existence of an innate sense of beauty, and this text has come to be regarded as a founding text in the history of aesthetic theory. But it is relatively brief, and it comprises only one of many arguments Hutcheson adduces in defense of the existence of human beings' instinctive benevolence and the moral sense by which they perceive and approve of benevolence.

Beauty, according to Hutcheson, is an idea derived from our perception of "uniformity amidst variety" in the objects of our external senses.[128] This uniformity amidst variety takes many forms, depending on whether we are contemplating a theorem (a unity from which an infinite number of varied truths can be deduced), a work of art (a unitary whole whose varied parts are capable of having a uniform proportion among themselves and between themselves and the whole), or some other object or set of objects.[129] What all these species of uniformity amidst variety have in common is that by virtue of an internal sense, distinct from all the external ones, they produce in us the sensation of beauty: a pleasurable sensation whose pleasure comes neither from any knowledge we may have of the things we are contemplating, nor from any way in which we may anticipate using the things to gratify our self-interest.[130] Nor, contra John Locke and other "opponents

---

[127] Hutcheson, *Essay*, 28–30.
[128] Hutcheson, *Inquiry*, 1st ed., 15. On the charge that Hutcheson plagiarized his definition of beauty from Jean-Pierre de Crousaz, see Raynor, "Hutcheson's Defence," 177–81.
[129] Hutcheson, *Inquiry*, 1st ed., 27, 33.   [130] Hutcheson, *Inquiry*, 1st ed., 10–12.

of innate ideas," is this pleasurable sensation simply the effect of custom or education; Hutcheson insists that custom and education can alter our aversions and appetites but are incapable of generating in us a new sense. The sense of beauty must be natural to human beings, and antecedent to custom, education, and all considerations of advantage, including considerations of pleasure.[131]

These arguments compose the moral-philosophical core of Hutcheson's aesthetic theory, insofar as Hutcheson asserts that the same arguments apply to our instinctive attraction to, and sense of, benevolence. In fact, as Hutcheson explains in his preface to the joint *Inquiry*, his very purpose in asserting and defending the existence of a sense of beauty is to make his portrayal of the moral sense easier to accept:

> If the Reader be convinc'd of such Determinations of the Mind to be pleas'd with Forms, Proportions, Resemblances, Theorems, it will be no difficult matter to apprehend another superior Sense natural to Men, determining them to be pleas'd with Actions, Characters, Affections.[132]

More precisely, what Hutcheson purports above all to show is that, like the human sense and relish of beauty, the moral sense and the attraction to benevolence operate independently of all considerations of any advantage one hopes to derive from the thing one is contemplating, and they are as inborn as any of the external senses.

Hutcheson's system of moral philosophy therefore differed from Shaftesbury's in a fundamental way. Whereas Shaftesbury held virtue to be natural in the sense that, in contradistinction to Locke's view, human beings were able to develop a desire for the private happiness specifically afforded by it, by recourse merely to the exercise of their innate affection for beauty and the cultivation of their powers of rational contemplation, Hutcheson abandoned Shaftesbury's aesthetic account of moral education and its egoist and hedonistic implications. His references to virtue as a species of beauty were casual and infrequent. His very occasional references to beauty as in some cases the idea of harmony among the parts of a whole were far overshadowed by his insistence that most ideas of beauty were derived from "uniformity amidst variety," a formulation nowhere to be found in Shaftesbury's writings.[133] He sharply dismissed the view, proposed unabashedly by Shaftesbury, that the pleasure we derive in contemplating beauty arises from any perception of utility whatsoever. He explicitly and categorically

---

[131] Hutcheson, *Inquiry*, 1st ed., 82–84.   [132] Hutcheson, *Inquiry*, 1st ed., viii.
[133] Cf. Raynor, "Hutcheson's Defence," 181; and, cited by Raynor, C. D. Thorpe, "Addison and Hutcheson on the Imagination," *English Literary History* 2 (1935): 215–34.

rejected the possibility that the desire for the pleasure of contemplating beauty should be the ultimate motivation of virtuous action. Hutcheson's primary purpose in discussing beauty at all was to reinforce the plausibility of his account of virtue as natural in the sense that human beings were naturally endowed with an instinctive benevolence and moral sense that, if properly cultivated, allowed them to pursue virtue without any regard whatever to the happiness it afforded them.

From the perspective of a disinterested observer, of course, Hutcheson's defense of natural virtue merely differs from Shaftesbury's; he makes a similar point in response to adversaries whom he gives similar names, but he invokes a different conception of human nature and a different criterion of virtue. From Hutcheson's perspective, however, Shaftesbury could hardly have deserved to be called a defender of virtue at all, since his defense and his scheme of an aesthetic moral education whose success depended on an innate desire for pleasure presupposed what Hutcheson considered a view of human beings as fundamentally selfish, a view he alleged to be fundamentally no different from Pufendorf's and the Epicureans'.

Conclusion

Hutcheson's departure from Shaftesbury's account of moral education as fundamentally aesthetic and unmistakably egoistic did not reflect the mainstream, even among Hutcheson's collaborators in the project of reforming Scottish Presbyterian theology and educational practice to reflect human beings' natural capacity for virtue. One important piece of evidence for the marginality of Hutcheson's view can be found in Hugh Blair's 1755 review of Hutcheson's *System of Moral Philosophy*. On the one hand, Blair finishes his review on a complimentary note:

> On the Whole, Whatever objections may be made to some few particularities of Mr Hutcheson's scheme, yet, as a system of morals, his work deserves, in our judgment, considerable praise. He shows a thorough acquaintance of the subject of which he treats. His philosophy tends to inspire generous sentiments and amiable views of human nature. It is particularly calculated to promote the social and friendly affections; and we cannot but agree with the author of the preface, that it has the air of being dictated by the heart, no less than the head.[134]

On the other hand, Blair's "On the whole" registers a certain unease. Among the objections he himself insinuates is the very divergence from

---

[134] [Blair?], Review of *A System of Moral Philosophy*, 23.

Shaftesbury by Hutcheson that he takes pains to describe in detail. The tendency of Hutcheson's system to inspire "amiable views of human nature" may be praiseworthy in itself, but it probably departs slightly from the truth. By contrast with Shaftesbury's moral philosophy, Blair writes, Hutcheson's

> must indeed be allowed to be the highest strain of the benevolent system. But how far it is consonant to human nature, is a question of fact which we shall leave to our readers to judge of for themselves.[135]

The presence of this last sentence suffices to indicate Blair's own reservations.

Nor was Blair alone in suspecting Hutcheson of having gone slightly astray. He was merely one member of a generation of students at Edinburgh University who, guided in their reading of Shaftesbury by Professor John Stevenson over the course of a forty-five-year career, appear to have felt similarly.[136] The surviving collection of essays by Stevenson's students, written between 1735 and 1750,[137] display not only close familiarity with Shaftesbury's *Characteristics* but also an unquestioning acceptance of precisely the egoistic hedonism that Hutcheson had rejected in Shaftesbury's aesthetic conception of moral education. The students commonly took for granted that moral education depends on harnessing a person's innate desire for the mental pleasures attendant on contemplating beautiful material things, such that one learns to take pleasure in the contemplation of higher orders of beauty in individual minds, communities of minds, and ultimately the divine mind governing the entire universe for the good of the whole.

Not every one of the student essays discusses topics in which the psychology of moral education plays a role, but some do. The position rejected by Hutcheson finds unambiguous expression in two of them: "On the Nature and Origin of Poetry," copied down in May 1740 by Robert Clerk, and "De pulchro," copied down in April 1739 by Gilbert Elliot, son of a friend and patron of Hutcheson's.[138] Clerk's discussion of moral education comes in the course of his description of poetry's two ends: to please and, above all, to reform mankind.[139] The proper means to both ends, Clerk explains, "is by

---

135 [Blair?], Review of *A System of Moral Philosophy*, 16.

136 On Stevenson, see above, p. 153, and below, Chapter 5, p. 190.

137 Essays by Students of Professor John Stevenson, 1737–50, EUL MS Dc.4.54; and on the essays' contents, Jones, "The Scottish Professoriate," 99.

138 M. A. Stewart, *The Kirk and the Infidel* (Lancaster: Lancaster University Press, 1995, rev. 2001), 9.

139 R. Clerk, "On the Nature and Origin of Poetry," in Essays by Students of Professor John Stevenson, fol. 143.

exciting passion."[140] By way of justifying this assertion, Clerk remarks that "everyone who is pleased is moved," and that "we are moved by pleasure, which is happiness, to do every thing we do," from which follows the conclusion – or so Clerk proposes – that poetry ought to please us by presenting us with the prospect of attaining further pleasures. Poetry likewise ought to "reform our minds" by "mak[ing] vice odious & virtue lovely," which causes us to expect pleasure from virtue.[141] Poetry functions as an effective instrument of moral education, Clerk adds, because it "makes the very violence of our passions contribute to our reformation."[142] What Hutcheson found anathema, namely, that virtue be inculcated by appeal to the human desire for pleasure, even the pleasure of contemplating beautiful objects, Clerk states as a matter of fact. In Gilbert Elliot's essay, the Shaftesburian egoism and hedonism are even more obvious. Human beings are drawn to virtue by its loveliness, he asserts, once they realize that the "symmetry and proportion" of which virtue partakes "are most conducive to our happiness."[143]

Therefore, while it is fair to say that Hutcheson formulated an aesthetic theory in order to support a position in the foundation-of-morality controversy that many reformers of Presbyterianism and fellow admirers of Shaftesbury shared, it is not fair to call Hutcheson's theory, or its function in his moral philosophy, either representative of an early or mid-eighteenth-century Scottish mainstream or especially suitable for comparison with Alexander Baumgarten's. That title belongs rather to an aesthetic theory of moral education more like Shaftesbury's, proposed by Baumgarten's near-exact contemporary, William Cleghorn.

[140] Clerk, "On the Nature and Origin of Poetry," fol. 144.
[141] Clerk, "On the Nature and Origin of Poetry," fols. 144–45.
[142] Clerk, "On the Nature and Origin of Poetry," fol. 145.
[143] G. Elliot, "De pulchro," in Essays by Students of Professor John Stevenson, fols. 61–62.

CHAPTER 5

William Cleghorn and the Aesthetic Foundation of Justice

If anything is generally known about William Cleghorn the man, it is a single fact: he bested a far better known and far greater philosopher, David Hume, in a contest for the chair of moral philosophy at the University of Edinburgh in 1745.[1] About Cleghorn the moral philosopher, still less is generally known, doubtless because he died at the young age of thirty-five, nine years after his appointment to the chair, without having published anything substantial on his subject. Even the most extensive published treatments of Cleghorn's thought to date have delved only deep enough into the few unpublished records of his ideas to afford a vague and fragmentary summary. According to Douglas Nobbs, author of the first and only published essay specifically on Cleghorn, Cleghorn expounded a theory of political obligation unlike Francis Hutcheson's and with frequent reference to ancient Greek and modern English republican authors.[2] According to J. C. Stewart-Robertson, Cleghorn drew upon and criticized Cicero's *De officiis* (On duties) and *De finibus* (On ends) in his moral philosophy lectures.[3] According to Richard Sher, the circumstances surrounding Cleghorn's election to the chair of moral philosophy can be taken as evidence that he "held acceptable views in religion and politics and possessed a suitably didactic, moralistic conception of the function of moral philosophy."[4] The picture that emerges of Cleghorn's philosophical system, in other words, remains colorless and dim. The only ray of light

---

[1] The following chapter consists largely of revised extracts from S. Grote, *The Moral Philosophy of William Cleghorn*, MPhil diss. (Cambridge University, 2005).

[2] D. Nobbs, "The Political Ideas of William Cleghorn, Hume's Academic Rival," *Journal of the History of Ideas* 26.4 (1965): 575–86; and, following Nobbs, A. du Toit in *DNB*, s.v. "Cleghorn, William." Nobbs expressly refrains from all interpretive claims about Cleghorn's moral philosophy.

[3] J. C. Stewart-Robertson, "Cicero among the Shadows: Scottish Prelections of Virtue and Duty," *Rivista Critica di Storia della Filosofia* 38.1 (January–March 1983): 29–34.

[4] R. Sher, "Professors of Virtue: The Social History of the Edinburgh Moral Philosophy Chair in the Eighteenth Century," in *Studies in the Philosophy of the Scottish Enlightenment*, ed. M. A. Stewart (Oxford: Oxford University Press, 1990), 106–9.

cast by virtually every commentator would seem to be this: Cleghorn criticized Francis Hutcheson's theory of the moral sense and espoused instead a "rationalist" theory of moral perception.[5] Even this observation, however, while strictly correct, does not clearly illuminate Cleghorn's moral-philosophical system or his philosophical aims, for it assumes that moral rationalism and its implied opposite, moral "sentimentalism," constitute two sides of a significant eighteenth-century moral-philosophical controversy.

The division of the so-called British moralists into rationalists and sentimentalists is not new. In English-language scholarship, it can be found in a particularly influential form as early as 1897, in L. A. Selby-Bigge's two-volume anthology, *British Moralists*. Selby-Bigge identifies two "principal lines of thought" among British moral philosophers of the seventeenth and eighteenth centuries. He calls them the "intellectual" and the "sentimental" schools and asserts that they are "primarily distinguished by their adoption of reason and feeling respectively as the faculty which perceives moral distinctions."[6] Representatives of the intellectual school, according to Selby-Bigge, include Ralph Cudworth (1617–88), Samuel Clarke (1675–1729), Richard Price (1723–91), and John Balguy (1686–1748), while representatives of the sentimentalist school include Shaftesbury, Francis Hutcheson, Joseph Butler (1692–1752), David Hume, and Adam Smith (1723–90).[7] Nor has respect for this dichotomy ended with Selby-Bigge; D. D. Raphael and Jerome Schneewind observe it as well, and Isabel Rivers has shown its applicability to a far wider range of authors than those treated by Schneewind, Raphael, and Selby-Bigge.[8] In the case of William Cleghorn, its continuing usefulness seems obvious; it allows the addition of color and focus to the otherwise indistinct picture of his ideas, by identifying him as a philosophical adversary of Francis Hutcheson and David Hume.[9]

That Hutcheson and Hume can be classed together as sentimentalists and mutual opponents of moral rationalism – as found, for example, in Samuel Clarke's second Boyle Lecture and William Wollaston's

---

[5] Nobbs, "Political Ideas," 575; Sher, "Professors of Virtue," 106–7; *Dictionary of Eighteenth-Century British Philosophers*, ed. J. W. Yolton, J. V. Price, and J. Stevens (Bristol: Thoemmes, 1999), s.v. "Cleghorn, William."

[6] Selby-Bigge, *British Moralists*, l. Cf. above, Chapter 4, p. 161.

[7] Selby-Bigge, *British Moralists*, e.g., li–lxxxiv.

[8] Raphael, *The Moral Sense*, 2; J. B. Schneewind, *Moral Philosophy from Montaigne to Kant* (Cambridge: Cambridge University Press, 2003), 483, 504.

[9] Along the lines suggested by Sher, "Professors of Virtue," 106–7.

(1660–1724) *Religion of Nature Delineated* – is beyond question.[10] The substance of Hutcheson's arguments against rationalist critiques of his 1724 *Inquiry into the Original of our Ideas of Beauty and Virtue* can be found in the text of David Hume's *Treatise of Human Nature.* Both Hume and Hutcheson deny that ideas of virtue and vice arise from the operation of human reason, discovering relations between moral propositions and the judgments that inform actions, and they both insist to the contrary that ideas of virtue and vice arise from sensations internal to the mind of the beholder.[11] In 1740, Hume himself acknowledged this similarity between his view and Hutcheson's in a letter to Hutcheson, noting that "Morality, according to your Opinion as well as mine, is determin'd merely by Sentiment."[12] Cleghorn's unmistakable critique of Francis Hutcheson's sentimentalism, therefore, would seem to set him opposite Hutcheson and Hume.

In the case of the rationalist-sentimentalist dichotomy, however, its tight grip on the historiography of eighteenth-century moral philosophy notwithstanding, there is compelling evidence to suppose that its unfortunate implication – that it not only describes real patterns of division among eighteenth-century philosophical systems but also served as a source of deep and heated controversy among the exponents of those systems – falls short of the truth. The case of Francis Hutcheson and his relationship with David Hume, in fact, indicates that controversy over moral rationalism and sentimentalism was subordinate to the very different controversy over the foundation of morality, the broad outlines of which appear in the heated exchanges between Shaftesbury's reform-minded Presbyterian sympathizers – such as Hutcheson, William Wishart, and William Leechman – and their critics. At issue in this controversy was not whether human beings perceive moral qualities by reason or sensation, but rather, as we have seen, the extent to which human beings are by nature capable of genuine virtue. Both Hume and Hutcheson took the Shaftesburian position, agreeing that human beings are indeed naturally capable of disinterested benevolence

---

[10] Mainly by virtue of arguments issued by N. K. Smith, *The Philosophy of David Hume: A Critical Study of Its Origins and Central Doctrines* (London: Macmillan, 1941), esp. 23–51; and endorsed by D. D. Raphael, as described in J. Moore, "Hume and Hutcheson," in *Hume and Hume's Connexions*, ed. M. A. Stewart and J. P. Wright (Edinburgh: Edinburgh University Press, 1994), 23–24. See also D. F. Norton, "Hume and Hutcheson: The Question of Influence," in *Oxford Studies in Early Modern Philosophy* 2 (2005), 211–12; and *Routledge Encyclopedia of Philosophy*, s.v. "Francis Hutcheson," by D. F. Norton.

[11] D. Hume, *Treatise of Human Nature*, ed. D. F. and M. J. Norton (Oxford: Oxford University Press, 2000), II.3.3, III.1.1, esp. ¶26; Hutcheson, *Essay*, 250–79.

[12] D. Hume to F. Hutcheson, 16 March 1740, *HL*, Letter 16.

toward others, but they disagreed about the extent to which such benevolence is responsible for the formation and cohesion of human societies. From recent research into the details of Hume's failed campaign for the Edinburgh chair of moral philosophy, it has become clear that Hutcheson, despite his agreement with Hume about the implausibility of moral rationalism, opposed Hume's candidacy largely on the grounds that Hume considered justice, the supreme social virtue and the principle of large-scale social cohesion, to be an artificially cultivated form of human self-interest rather than an enlargement of the human instinct of benevolence.[13] Further evidence of the subordination of the rationalism-sentimentalism disagreement to the controversy over the foundation of morality can be found in Francis Hutcheson's critiques of adherents to moral rationalism, including especially Gilbert Burnet (1690–1726) and John Balguy, in which Hutcheson evinces a suspicion that moral rationalism is not only incoherent but also a cloak for the view that human beings are simply incapable of disinterested benevolence.

It is to this loosening of the sentimentalism-rationalism straitjacket and, simultaneously, to the elucidation of the role of aesthetic theory in the mid-century Scottish debate about the foundation of morality, that an analysis of William Cleghorn's moral philosophy can contribute. The bright light cast on Cleghorn's ideas by examining them against the backdrop of Francis Hutcheson's disputes with David Hume and his earlier critics, moral rationalists included, reveals that Cleghorn aimed to address the problems of human benevolence and the nature of justice over which Hutcheson and Hume had been wrangling, and that he was employing a rationalist theory of moral perception, conjoined with an aesthetic theory of moral education much like Shaftesbury's, as an instrument to that effect. As a representative of those Shaftesbury-sympathizers such as Hugh Blair, who thought Hutcheson had deviated too far from Shaftesbury, and of John Stevenson's students, who accepted without comment the egoism and hedonism in Shaftesbury's aesthetic account of moral education, Cleghorn was striking what, loosely speaking, could be regarded as a middle position between Hutcheson's and Hume's, one that

---

[13] The results of this research can be found primarily in Stewart, *The Kirk and the Infidel*; Moore, "Hume and Hutcheson"; and, with greater emphasis on issues of ideology and institutional politics, Sher, "Professors of Virtue," esp. 102–8; and Emerson, "The 'Affair' at Edinburgh." A more detailed elaboration of Moore's view, though not reliable in all its details, can be found in S. Grote, *The Rejection of David Hume*, AB diss. (Harvard College, 2001). The older interpretation of Hutcheson's opposition to Hume's candidacy, now superseded, is E. Mossner's, in *The Life of David Hume*, 2nd ed. (Oxford: Oxford University Press, 1980), esp. 157–60.

acknowledged the difficulties with Hutcheson's position as indicated by Hume, but that aimed to explain how, in contradistinction to Hume's position, justice could be regarded as a form of disinterested benevolence.

Cleghorn's Life

In the attempt to understand this intellectual project, knowing all that can be known about William Cleghorn the man provides unfortunately only a modicum of help. The surviving details of Cleghorn's life allow for a biography that, if occasionally illuminated by the bright light of contemporary anecdote, remains in large part tantalizingly vague.[14] He was born in Edinburgh in 1719, the eldest child of Hugh Cleghorn and Jean Hamilton.[15] His father, who would die in 1734, was heir to a successful brewery and comfortable house close to the site currently occupied by the National Museum of Scotland, and his mother was the eldest daughter of William Hamilton, five-time moderator of the General Assembly of the Church of Scotland, and professor of divinity at the university from 1709 until becoming principal nine months before his death in 1732.[16] Jean's fifteen younger siblings, some of whom lived at various points in the Cleghorn family home, included several models of professional success. William's uncle Gavin Hamilton (1704–67) opened a book-selling business in 1729 and a printing business in 1739 that became the most important in Edinburgh for the next two decades. Between 1732 and 1745, Gavin Hamilton also served on the Edinburgh Town Council, wielding considerable political power by virtue of his office and his loyalty to the interest of the "Squadrone" faction, led by John Hay, fourth Marquess of Tweeddale (1695–1762).[17] Another uncle of Cleghorn's, Alexander Hamilton (1712–56), studied medicine at Edinburgh and traveled to Annapolis, Maryland, where he

---

[14] References to many of the documents in which these details appear can be found in A. Clark, *An Enlightened Scot: Hugh Cleghorn, 1752–1837* (Duns: Black Ace, 1992), 1–11; and in Nobbs, "Political Ideas," 575–77.

[15] Hugh Cleghorn and Jean Hamilton were married 6 July 1718, as recorded in H. Paton, *Scottish Record Society, Register of Marriages for the Parish of Edinburgh 1701–1750* (Edinburgh, 1908), 105. The year of Cleghorn's birth is not absolutely certain; it must be extrapolated from accounts of his age at the time of his death on 23 August 1754. An obituary in the *Edinburgh Evening Courant* of 26 August 1754, notes his age as thirty-six; but his nephew, Hugh, who had obviously read the obituary with great care, refers to William as having died at the age of thirty-five. Hugh Cleghorn to John Lee, 25 July 1836, NLS MS 3441, fols. 122–23; Clark, *Enlightened Scot*, 7.

[16] A. Dalzel, *History of the University of Edinburgh from its Foundation*, ed. D. Laing, 2 v. (Edinburgh, 1862), II.332; Clark, *Enlightened Scot*, 3; *DNB*, s.v. "Hamilton, William (1669–1732)," by L. A. B. Whitley.

[17] *DNB*, s.v. "Hamilton, Gavin (1704–1767)," by W. MacDougall; Emerson, "The 'Affair' at Edinburgh," 3, 11.

established a successful medical practice and became a prolific writer of social and political commentary.[18] Nor was it unusual for a Hamilton to train for the ministry. Cleghorn's uncle Gilbert Hamilton received his preaching license in 1736 and his D.D. in 1760, and his uncle Robert received his license in 1730 and became professor of divinity at Edinburgh in 1754.[19] If the distinguished example of Cleghorn's grandfather and namesake can be taken as a guide, the family's Presbyterianism was hardly conservative; William Hamilton, the teacher of William Leechman,[20] has been identified as a major force for moderation, liberalism, and doctrinal relaxation within the early-eighteenth-century Presbyterian church.[21]

The evidence of William Cleghorn's own ideas and activities firmly suggests that he ought to be associated with the group of his better-known contemporaries influentially described by Richard Sher as "Christian Stoics," identifiable by their conservative whiggish defense of the mixed constitution, their profession of an ethic of self-sacrifice for the sake of the public good, their view of preachers and professors as teachers of virtue, and their support of the Shaftesburian program for the reform of Presbyterianism pursued by Hutcheson, Leechman, and Wishart. On Sher's account they included, among others, Hugh Blair, John Home (1722–1808), Alexander Carlyle (1722–1805), and Adam Ferguson (1723–1816).[22] The earliest evidence of Cleghorn's association with this group comes from his education at the University of Edinburgh, beginning in 1731 at the age of twelve, a year before his grandfather's promotion to principal, and following closely in the footsteps of his uncles Gilbert, Gavin, and Alexander.[23] For the years 1731, 1732, and 1733, Cleghorn and Hugh Blair matriculated as students of Adam Watt, professor of humanity.[24] Shortly after Watt's death

---

[18] *DNB*, s.v. "Hamilton, Alexander (1712–1756)," by E. G. Breslaw. Cf. A. Hamilton, *Hamilton's Itinerarium*, ed. A. B. Hart (Saint Louis, MO: William K. Bixby, 1907).

[19] *Fasti Ecclesiae Scoticanae*, v. 1, by H. Scott (Edinburgh: Oliver and Boyd, 1915), 11, 12, 46, 81.

[20] See above, Chapter 4, p. 154.

[21] Sefton, "Neu-lights and Preachers Legall," 188–90. Robert Wodrow would later recall that William Hamilton himself, evidently a very popular lecturer, demurred to insist on belief in the doctrine of the Trinity and was thought more generally by some to have "departed from the Calvinisticall doctrine." R. Wodrow, *Analecta, or Materials for a history of remarkable providences mostly relating to Scotch ministers and Christians*, ed. M. Leisman, 4 v. (Edinburgh: Maitland Club, 1842–43), IV.139; J. Wodrow, "The Life of Dr Leechman, with some Account of his Lectures," in W. Leechman, *Sermons*, v. 1 of 2 (London, 1789), 1–19; Hutcheson to Drennan, [1743], GUL MS Gen 1018.

[22] Sher, *Church and University*, 37–38, 175–212.

[23] *Matriculation Roll of the University of Edinburgh, Arts, Law, Divinity*, transcribed by A. Morgan, v. 1 of 4, 1623–1774, EUL Special Coll. Reading Rm., 192, 199.

[24] Unfortunately little appears to be known about Adam Watt. According to Alexander Bower, Watt was the son of an old friend of his predecessor, Laurence Dundas, and Dundas made Watt's

in March 1734 – the same year in which Cleghorn's father died – his and Blair's names appear on the list of students of John Stevenson.[25] What Watt taught, unfortunately, cannot be identified with any certainty; if the standard progression is any guide, Cleghorn and Blair studied Latin and Greek authors.[26] Stevenson, whose teaching has been better documented, taught a number of works which would later make an appearance in Cleghorn's lectures as well.[27] Alexander Carlyle, in a sentiment shared by William Robertson (1721–93), among others, would recall having "received greater benefit from that class than from any other."[28] The volume of essays by Stevenson's students, which reveals so vividly his importance as a disseminator of Shaftesburean aesthetic and moral-philosophical ideas, begins in 1737, unfortunately, three years too late to include an essay by Cleghorn.[29]

How Cleghorn spent his remaining years in the university is somewhat less clear. Like Carlyle, Home, Ferguson, and Blair, he almost certainly began training for the ministry. Henry Mackenzie, biographer of John Home, refers to Cleghorn as a member of the "circle" of Home's "fellow churchmen"; Douglas Nobbs has found in the Sasine Register a reference to Cleghorn as a "student of Divinity"; and a charter granted to Cleghorn's mother in 1760 refers to her late son as a "preacher of the Gospel."[30] This implies that Cleghorn probably took instruction in the scriptures and in Bénédict Pictet's (1655–1724) *Christian Theology* from professor of divinity John Gowdie (1682–1762), memorably described by Alexander Carlyle as "dull and Dutch and prolix."[31] He is also likely to have attended lectures

appointment a condition of his retirement in 1727. "He is represented," Bower writes, "as having been a young man of promising talents, and the favourite pupil of Mr Dundas." A. Bower, *History of the University of Edinburgh*, v. 2 of 3 (Edinburgh, 1817), 262.

[25] *Matriculation Roll*, 204.

[26] A. Grant, *Story of the University of Edinburgh during its first three hundred years*, 2 v. (London, 1884), I.264; C. Shepherd, *Philosophy and Science in the Arts Curriculum of the Scottish Universities in the Seventeenth Century*, PhD diss. (University of Edinburgh, 1974), introduction.

[27] A record of Stevenson's teaching can be found not only in anecdotes by admiring students but also in an invaluable "Short Account of the University of Edinburgh" in the *Scots Magazine* of August 1741, which indicates that Stevenson taught Johann Gottlieb Heineccius' *Elementa Philosophiae Rationalis*; John Locke's *Essay*; Gerard De Vries's *Ontologia*; histories of philosophy by Heineccius, Diogenes Laertius, Thomas Stanley, and Johann Jakob Brucker; Longinus's *On the Sublime*; and Aristotle's *Poetics*. See "A Short Account of the University of Edinburgh," *Scots Magazine* 3 (August 1741): 373.

[28] A. Carlyle, *The Autobiography of Dr. Alexander Carlyle of Inveresk, 1722–1805*, ed. J. H. Burton (London: T. N. Foulis, 1910; repr., Bristol: Thoemmes, 1990), 48; Grant, *Story of the University of Edinburgh*, II.329.

[29] On Stevenson and the student essays, see above, Chapter 4.

[30] H. Mackenzie, *Account of the Life and Writings of John Home*, in *Works*, by J. Home (Edinburgh, 1822), 12; Nobbs, "Political Ideas," 576; Clark, *Enlightened Scot*, 7.

[31] "A Short Account of the University of Edinburgh," 371; Carlyle, *Autobiography*, 63–64; Grant, *Story of the University of Edinburgh*, I.336–37.

in pneumatics and moral philosophy by the unoriginal and uninspiring John Pringle (1707–82).[32] In any case, it is clear that he received his MA in 1739 under unusual circumstances. Cleghorn and four classmates – again including Hugh Blair – had agreed with Principal Wishart to revive a custom that had fallen into disuse since the advent of the professorial system, namely, to publish and publicly defend Latin theses.[33] On this occasion, the students seem to have chosen the subjects; in Cleghorn's case, the result was a thirteen-page dissertation on natural philosophy, dedicated to James Douglas, Earl of Morton.[34] The last record of Cleghorn's attendance at the University occurs in the Commonplace book of Charles Mackie (1688–1770), professor of history from 1719 until 1765, who notes Cleghorn's attendance in 1740 at his two sets of lectures, on universal history and on "Roman antiquities," describing him as having entered the household of Sir John Nisbet as a tutor to his son, Henry.[35]

A somewhat more colorful picture of Cleghorn emerges from the evidence of his academic career, which appears to have begun in 1742. That summer, John Pringle had been appointed physician to the Earl of Stair and taken a leave of absence to join the British army commanded by Stair in Flanders. His substitutes, according to the minutes of the Academic Senate, were Cleghorn and George Muirhead, a student of Francis Hutcheson's at Glasgow who had studied divinity at Edinburgh and taken his MA in

[32] Pringle is known to have made use of Cicero's *De officiis*, Bacon's *Novum organon*, Pufendorf's *De officio hominis et civis*, Marcus Aurelius's *Meditations*, and Harrington's *Oceana*, among others. "A Short Account of the University of Edinburgh," 373; Bower, *History of the University*, II.291; A. Kippis, *The Life of John Pringle*, in *Six Discourses*, by J. Pringle (London, 1783), vii; J. Pringle, Lectures from Cicero, taken down by a student, Edinburgh, 1741, EUL MS Gen 74D.

[33] Shepherd, *Philosophy and Science*, 13; Grant, *Story of the University*, I.277–78. The five graduands were Cleghorn, Hugh Blair, John Witherspoon, William Mackenzie, and Nathaniel Mitchell, all of whom defended their theses before a large crowd in the "Common Hall" on the morning of 23 February 1739. According to John Stephens, Cleghorn took his MA in 1735, but I can find no authority for this; Cleghorn's name appears in the Edinburgh University Matriculation Book under the year 1739. See *Dictionary of Eighteenth-Century British Philosophers*, ed. J. W. Yolton et al. (Bristol: Thoemmes, 1999), s.v. "Cleghorn, William," by J. Stephens.

[34] W. Cleghorn, *Dissertatio philosophica inauguralis, de analogia et philosophia prima* (Edinburgh, 1739); *DNB*, s.v. "Douglas, James," by A. Guerrini. Morton was first president of the Edinburgh Philosophical Society and patron of the University of Edinburgh's astronomical observatory. Though the Philosophical Society was founded in 1737 and included several Edinburgh professors among its members, including John Stevenson and Charles Mackie, there is no evidence that Cleghorn ever became a member. R. L. Emerson, "The Philosophical Society of Edinburgh, 1737–1747," *The British Journal for the History of Science* XII.2.41 (July 1979): 154–62, 189–91.

[35] Grant, *Story of the University*, II.367; C. Mackie, "Alphabetical List of those who attended the Prelections on History and Roman Antiquities from 1719 to 1744 inclusive," in Commonplace Book, EUL Dc.5.24, v. 2, 206; Nobbs, "Political Ideas," 576–77; *Book of the Old Edinburgh Club* (Edinburgh, 1908), I.121–22. Nobbs describes Cleghorn as tutor to Henry Nisbet in 1739 as well as 1740, but I have found no authority for this.

the spring before Pringle's departure. Pringle had counted on being able to return to Edinburgh when his service in Flanders ended. As long as the Edinburgh Town Council and the presiding provost, John Coutts (1699–1750) – who together controlled academic appointments to the university – agreed to extend his leave, Cleghorn and Muirhead's appointment as his substitutes continued to be renewed.[36] In June 1744, however, with the war in Flanders showing all signs of escalation, Pringle declared in a letter to Provost Coutts that he was prepared to resign, whence began a long and hard-fought contest over who was to be appointed to the soon-to-be-vacant chair of moral philosophy. The contest grew more heated as Pringle equivocated about his intentions and stalled for time. On one side, Coutts and his friends inside and outside the Town Council, under the patronage of Archibald Campbell, third Duke of Argyll (1682–1761), had arranged to back the candidacy of David Hume. On the other side was a mixed group of Hume's philosophical and clerical enemies and Provost Coutts's political rivals, including notably Cleghorn's uncle, Gavin Hamilton, acting to promote the Squadrone interest.[37] After many months of frustrating negotiations with Pringle had come to an end with Pringle's resignation in March 1745, the Town Council declared the chair of moral philosophy vacant and confirmed Cleghorn as Pringle's acting successor.[38] It is clear that by the middle of April, having attempted and failed to appoint Francis Hutcheson to the chair, Gavin Hamilton and his allies on the Town Council were actively promoting Cleghorn's candidacy at the expense of Hume's reputation, and with great success on both counts.[39] Even after the Edinburgh clergy had voted to withhold their approval from Hume, prompting Coutts to nominate as a substitute candidate William Wishart – who only "early last Winter," in Wishart's words, had agreed with Gavin Hamilton to support Cleghorn instead of seeking the chair himself – Coutts could not overcome the opposition organized by Hamilton.[40] On 5 June, the Town Council elected Cleghorn to the chair of moral philosophy by a majority of nineteen votes to Wishart's twelve.[41] The Academic Senate admitted him

---

36 Stewart, *The Kirk and the Infidel*, 4, 6–12; *DNB*, s.v. "Muirhead, George," by R. Sher.
37 *DNB*, s. v. "John Hay, fourth marquess of Tweeddale (1695–1762)," by R. Scott; R. Sedgwick, *The House of Commons 1715–1754*, v. 1, *The History of Parliament* (London: HMSO, 1970), 159–60; J. S. Shaw, *The Management of Scottish Society, 1707–1764* (Edinburgh: John Donald, 1983), 48–55.
38 TCM, 27 March 1745; Academic Senate Minutes, 1733–1811, EUL Dup. 436, 26 March 1745.
39 Alexander Arbuthnot to Tweeddale, 16 April 1745, NLS MS 7065, fols. 157–58.
40 W. Wishart, "Copy [of] Letter, or Speech, intended: and Letter to John Forrest. June 5, 1745," transcribed and expanded by M. A. Stewart as "The Wishart Speedhand," in Stewart, *The Kirk and the Infidel*, 27.
41 TCM, 5 June 1745.

five days later, and after a year's postponement he delivered his inaugural lecture on 11 February 1748.[42]

Surviving testimony indicates without exception that Cleghorn's reputation as a teacher and philosopher, before and after his appointment to the chair, was very good. Francis Hutcheson had recommended him as one of several possible candidates in a letter of 4 July 1744 to a friend of John Coutts, noting that although he did not know Cleghorn as well as he knew the other men he'd suggested for the position, he had met him in person and "judged him a very acute man from some few days conversation."[43] Colin MacLaurin (1698–1746), professor of mathematics at Edinburgh from 1725 until his death in 1746, was still more impressed; he described Cleghorn in a letter of the same year as "a great Moral Philosopher."[44] Nor was a positive impression of Cleghorn's abilities restricted to these two luminaries. One of Tweeddale's agents in Edinburgh, Alexander Arbuthnot, noted in a letter shortly after Pringle's resignation that Cleghorn had taught the moral philosophy class "for three years past . . . with great approbation."[45] Four years after Cleghorn's promotion to the professorship of moral philosophy, Gilbert Hamilton reported in a letter to his brother Alexander that their nephew continued to enjoy this approbation. Almost eighty years later, Cleghorn's nephew, Hugh, would recall reports that Cleghorn had filled his classroom with students and townspeople "of all ages and of the most Liberal Professions."[46] These reports suffice to distinguish Cleghorn from the alleged dreariness of his less popular predecessor, Pringle, and his successor, James Balfour (1705–95), who within six years of his appointment was urged to step down because the size of

---

[42] A record of Cleghorn's inaugural lecture, probably indecipherable, survives among Wishart's papers in the Edinburgh University Library. Academic Senate Minutes, 10 June 1745, 12 December 1746, 7 December 1747, 25 February 1748; M. A. Stewart, "Principal Wishart (1692–1753) and the Controversies of His Day," *Records of the Scottish Church History Society* 30 (2000): 67.

[43] Francis Hutcheson to Gilbert Elliot, Lord Minto, July 4, 1744, NLS MS 11004, fol. 57r–v.

[44] Colin MacLaurin to the Earl of Morton, 5 May 1744, Scottish National Archives (previously Scottish Record Office), GD 150/3486/3.

[45] Alexander Arbuthnot to Tweeddale, 16 April 1745, NLS MS 7065, fols. 157–58.

[46] Gilbert Hamilton to Alexander Hamilton, qtd. in Clark, *Enlightened Scot*, 10–11:

William has the reputation of a fine scholar; he is a well bred man, keeps the best company in Town and as he is the Professor of Moral Philosophy in the College of Edinburgh, so he teaches it with deserved applause.

See also Hugh Cleghorn's remark to John Lee (13 March 1836, NLS MS 3441 fols. 84–85), that he had heard

from many Eminent men, most of them not unknown to you, particularly from the late Sir William Pulteney, and from Andrew Stuart (a name Inferior to none) that his [William Cleghorn's] Lectures were universally esteemed and numerously attended by men of all ages and of the most Liberal Professions.

his class had dwindled almost to nothing.[47] If Cleghorn's whiggish politics and passionate defense of freedom of religious judgment were sources of irritation to some, such as Thomas Ruddiman (1674–1757), well-known Jacobite and printer to the university during Cleghorn's years as a student, they certainly did not keep students and unmatriculated auditors from filling his classroom.[48]

Cleghorn's whiggish politics must have been common knowledge. Writing almost sixty years after the Jacobite Rebellion of 1745, John Home would remember Cleghorn as "one of the most zealous volunteers" among the students who had enlisted in the so-called College Company to defend Edinburgh from Prince Charles Edward Stuart's (1720–88) approaching army. According to Home, it was Cleghorn who volunteered to "stand forth at the proper time" and lead his young companions in an eastward march toward the likely battleground, should the order come that Edinburgh was to be surrendered.[49] Alexander Carlyle would recall that Cleghorn and John Home had tried to persuade a group of their friends to march out of the city and join the Hanoverian army under Sir John Cope, and that Cleghorn, William Robertson, and Carlyle himself in fact made such an attempt.[50] There is also the evidence of a pamphlet attributed to Cleghorn, described by Hugh Cleghorn in 1834 as "the Address to some Gentlemen immediately after the Rebellion"[51] and identified by some catalogers as *The Spirit and Principles of the Whigs and the Jacobites compared: Being the substance of a discourse delivered to an audience of gentlemen at Edinburgh, December 22, 1745*, printed in 1746 in Edinburgh and, with some alterations, in London.[52]

---

47 Sher, "Professors of Virtue," 112, 114–15; Grant, *Story of the University of Edinburgh*, II.338–39.
48 On Cleghorn's detractors: George Chalmers observed that the Edinburgh Town Council chose Cleghorn over Hume for the professorship of moral philosophy, "sagely considering that . . . a deist might probably become a Christian, but a jacobite could not possibly become a Whig." Chalmers appears to have taken his cue partly from a comment allegedly by Thomas Ruddiman:

> Inquiring once of the Reverend Robert Walker, who was then his amanuensis, what classes he had been attending at the college of Edinburgh; and being told, that he had that morning heard a lecture on *Liberty* and *Necessity*, Ruddiman said, "Well: does your professor make us free agents or not?" To which Mr. Walker answered, "He gives us arguments on both sides, and leaves us to judge." "Very well," rejoined Ruddiman; "*The fool has said in his heart there is no God*; and the professor will not tell you, whether the fool be right or wrong."

G. Chalmers, *Life of Thomas Ruddiman* (London, 1794), 275–76. For Cleghorn's defense of freedom of judgment, see W. Cleghorn, Lectures, taken down by W. Dalgleish, EUL MS Dc.3.3–6, I.367–75.
49 J. Home, *History of the Rebellion in the Year 1745* (London, 1802), 85–91.
50 Carlyle, *Autobiography*, 121, 130–31, 134, 138–41.
51 Hugh Cleghorn to John Lee, 25 July 1836, NLS MS 3441 fol. 122r.
52 [W. Cleghorn?], *A Comparison of the Spirit and Principles of the Whigs and the Jacobites: Being the substance of a discourse delivered to an audience of gentlemen at Edinburgh, Dec. 24, 1745* (Edinburgh, 1746); and [W. Cleghorn?], *The Spirit and Principles of the Whigs and the Jacobites compared: Being the substance of a discourse delivered to an audience of gentlemen at Edinburgh, December 22, 1745*

The argument of the pamphlet favors the Whigs, identifying their aim as the promotion of "the interests of all mankind" through the instrument of limited monarchy, and attacking the Jacobites as a self-interested faction.[53]

The most obvious evidence not only that Cleghorn belongs among Richard Sher's whiggish "Christian Stoics" but also that his philosophy deserves serious attention, comes from Cleghorn's relationship with Adam Ferguson, who almost certainly heard Cleghorn lecture, possibly during his brief time in Edinburgh as a divinity student from 1743 to 1745, and with whom Cleghorn clearly grew to be on very close terms.[54] Upon becoming seriously ill in the last year of his life,[55] Cleghorn tried to arrange for Ferguson to assume the chair of moral philosophy, but to no avail. His efforts attest to his friendship with Ferguson and his respect for Ferguson's abilities. "[W]hen the able and accomplished Mr Cleghorn was on his death-bed," John Lee wrote in 1824,

> he urged his young friend to apply for the office, which, in his apprehension, no man was more capable of adorning. Mr Cleghorn, after expressing his regret at having no such influence with the patrons as to secure such an arrangement, added, as Mr Ferguson sometimes related with much emotion, "I can only say of you, as Hamlet did of Fortinbras, *He has my dying voice.*"[56]

Ferguson would have to wait ten years before assuming Cleghorn's professorship. For all his nephew's efforts, Gavin Hamilton could not be persuaded to use his influence in Ferguson's favor and give up support for his brother-in-law and partner in the printing business, James Balfour; in fact, quite to the contrary. Under pressure from his uncle, Cleghorn resigned his professorship two days before his death, whereupon Balfour was elected to it.[57] Cleghorn's helplessness notwithstanding, Ferguson's gratitude and

---

(London, 1746). One basis for attributing the pamphlet to Cleghorn, in addition to Hugh Cleghorn's description of it and occasional verbal echoes between the pamphlet and Cleghorn's moral philosophy lectures, is an inscription on the title page of the copy of the Edinburgh edition in the British Library (Classmark BL 8142.b.59(1)), which reads, "By W. C." According to M. A. Stewart, this inscription is in the hand of David Fordyce, whose acquaintance with the Wisharts during the time he spent in Edinburgh as a preacher in 1742 would have put him in a good position to know that Cleghorn had written the pamphlet. M. A. Stewart to Richard Sher and Mark Box, 30 April 2005, electronic mail in the possession of M. A. Stewart.

[53] [W. Cleghorn?], *The Spirit and Principles of the Whigs and the Jacobites compared*, 12–17.

[54] *DNB*, s.v. "Ferguson, Adam (1723–1816)" by F. Oz-Salzberger.

[55] According to Hugh Cleghorn, Cleghorn made a trip to Lisbon on account of his health shortly before his death, but to no avail. Hugh Cleghorn to John Lee, 13 March 1836, NLS MS 3441, fol. 84r.

[56] *Supplement to the Fourth, Fifth, and Sixth Editions of the Encyclopaedia Britannica.* v. 4 of 6 (Edinburgh, 1824), s.v. "Ferguson (Adam, LL.D.)," 240–41.

[57] Hugh Cleghorn to John Lee, 13 March 1836, NLS MS 3441, fol. 84v. This election, like Cleghorn's in 1745, was of some political import; Balfour, it seems, was the favorite not only of Gavin Hamilton

affection toward him persisted. Eighty years after Cleghorn's death, Hugh Cleghorn would report that in his efforts to learn more about his "most Respectable relation," he had heard "many anecdotes concerning him from our friend Dr A. Ferguson who retained to the last the most affectionate remembrance of his Talents and his Virtues."[58] Hugh himself suspected that Ferguson had written the obituary that appeared in the *Edinburgh Evening Courant* on Monday, 26 August 1754:

> The same Day died here, in the 36th Year of his Age, after a tedious Illness, Mr WILLIAM CLEGHORN, Professor of Moral Philosophy in the University of Edinburgh. For several Years he had filled that Station to the public Advantage and his own Honour, deservedly admired for singular Beauty of Genius, Richness of Imagination, and Fertility of Invention. Esteemed as a Philosopher, he was no less beloved as a Man and a Friend. Never indeed did anyone possess a greater Fund of innate Worth and Goodness. His whole Character was a bright Example of these moral Virtues he taught others. Fill'd with Sincerity and Candour; simple in his Manners; warm in his Friendships; disinterested in his Views; his strongest Passion was to be useful to the World. So worthy a Man cut off in the Prime of Life, gives Occasion to deep and lasting Regret in all who knew him.[59]

"It is the work of no ordinary hand," wrote Hugh. "I have no authority for ascribing it to Dr Ferguson but it resembles his best style and breathes the veneration and affection with which He always mentioned his name."[60]

A careful comparison of the two men's philosophical systems would no doubt reveal that Ferguson owed another, intellectual debt to Cleghorn, beyond his personal affection for Cleghorn and Cleghorn's professional support for him. The most immediate evidence for such a debt comes from Ferguson's testament to it, in an incomplete draft of a philosophical dialog, possibly completed in 1799, in which Ferguson assigns Cleghorn a major part, ascribes to him a concept of beauty like the one which Ferguson himself proceeds to expound, has him explicitly endorse Ferguson's own belief that "the soldier[']s glory for which life is exposed a thousand times and

---

but also of the faction on the Town Council opposed to then-Provost George Drummond. William Alston, observing the Council's business on behalf of Andrew Fletcher, Lord Milton, wrote confidently to Milton in a letter of 20 August 1754, "Professor Cleghorn cannot live long, so that Mr Balfours Prospect is very near." William Alston to the Right Honorable Lord Milton, Edinburgh 20 August 1754, NLS MS 16685, fol. 65r. See also Sher, "Professors of Virtue," 109.

58 Hugh Cleghorn to John Lee, 13 March 1836, NLS MS 3441, fol. 84r.

59 *Edinburgh Evening Courant*, no. 5958, Monday 26 August 1754, [3]. In the *Scots Magazine*, v. 16 (August 1754), 404, appeared the following announcement of Cleghorn's death: "23. [August] At Edinburgh, in the 36th year of his age, after a tedious illness, Mr William Cleghorn, Professor of Moral Philosophy in the University of Edinburgh."

60 Hugh Cleghorn to John Lee, 13 March 1836, NLS MS 3441, fol. 84r.

often sacrificed" is the most pleasurable gratification of the human mind, and refers to Cleghorn as one of a company "from whom I had taken in my first draughts of moral science."[61]

Of course, Adam Ferguson's dialog cannot be depended upon for an account of Cleghorn's character or a clear and authoritative summary of his ideas; it is brief and fragmentary, and Ferguson completed it almost half a century after Cleghorn's death. For a clearer and far more detailed picture of Cleghorn's mind than either Ferguson or Cleghorn's biography can supply, we must turn to the only surviving evidence of those details: three sets of dictates of his lectures on moral philosophy.

The most important of these is a set of four notebooks in the Edinburgh University Library, one of which bears the title, "The Heads of Professor Cleghorn's Lectures,"[62] and all of which bear the name of William Dalgleish of Linlithgow, who appears to have matriculated as a student of John Ker in 1740, of Robert Law in 1741, and of John Stevenson in 1742.[63] The set is incomplete,[64] but the surviving volumes preserve at least two-thirds of the lectures given by Cleghorn in the 1746–47 academic year, and they occupy almost six hundred pages. They also have the marks of being relatively faithful dictations or "dictates" of a then-common type: taken down as a lecturer spoke, aiming at an exact record of his words, each sitting lasting about an hour per day, from Monday through Friday.[65] The accuracy of Dalgleish's dictates is not easy to gauge, but he appears more often than not to have made a conscientious effort at recording Cleghorn word-for-word.[66] Throughout the dictates, places emerge where

[61] A. Ferguson, "An Excursion in the Highlands: Discourse on Various Subjects," in *Collection of Essays*, by A. Ferguson, ed. Y. Amoh (Kyoto: Rinsen, 1996), 310, 45–46, 39.

[62] W. Cleghorn, Lectures, EUL, II.[i].

[63] *Matriculation Roll of the University of Edinburgh*, 13 February 1740, 18 March 1741, 12 February 1742.

[64] The spines are numbered as if the first of five original volumes were missing, and the 1861 auction catalogue of manuscripts in the possession of Hugh Cleghorn's friend, John Lee, indicates that this set of lecture dictates, when Lee possessed it, was composed of five volumes. The lectures themselves, moreover, begin with 22 December 1746, more than a month after other courses at the university appear normally to have begun. (In 1741, at any rate, most "colleges" began in the beginning or middle of November.) It is also possible, though probably impossible to confirm, that the final lecture in the set, from 28 April 1747, was not the final lecture in the course. See Amoh, introduction to *Collection of Essays*, by A. Ferguson, xiv, xxvii–xxviii; and "An Account of the University of Edinburgh," 371–74.

[65] Shepherd, *Philosophy and Science*, 4–8.

[66] Often the dictates display corrections to minor phrases and words, and occasionally Dalgleish seems to have marked (with an "X" or an asterisk) places in the dictates where he had not caught everything Cleghorn had said, sometimes adding the missing sentences or further explanatory remarks in the margins later, though other times not. He seems to have missed less and less as the year progressed, eventually marking an "X" very seldom and still more seldom adding any missing sections in the margins.

the spoken quality of Cleghorn's words makes itself distinctly felt.[67] The absence of the first volume, however unfortunate, is partly compensated by the two other surviving sets of dictates, each of which consists of a small notebook containing a section of the lectures entitled, "Plan of the Whole Course of Moral Philosophy," likely delivered by Cleghorn at the very beginning of the course.[68]

These documents, however incomplete, are of course invaluable; they are the only known, reliable record of the mind of a man whose moral philosophy and aesthetic theory otherwise could only remain a mystery. With their help, we need not rest content with the generic view of William Cleghorn as a theologically moderate, whiggish republican, nor with the existing analyses of his thought and their emphasis on the factually correct but incomplete description of Cleghorn as a moral rationalist and critic of Francis Hutcheson's moral sense theory. Rather, we can begin to examine the more detailed reality of Cleghorn's use of moral rationalism and aesthetic moral education to engage with Hutcheson on an issue of greater moment to them both.

Hutcheson and Hume on the Foundation of Justice

That Hutcheson played a central role in fomenting opposition to Hume's candidacy for the moral philosophy chair was certainly clear to Hume

---

[67] E.g., W. Cleghorn, Lectures, EUL, I.369–75, II.327.

[68] The first of these, taking up seventy-five pages in a small notebook which appears to have belonged to one Neill Duncanson, records the "plan" from Cleghorn's lectures in 1752. (The year 1752 appears at the end of the plan, and Neill Duncanson's name appears on the first unnumbered page of the notebook.) Duncanson has been identified in the St. Andrews catalog as a schoolmaster. It is perhaps possible, though unlikely, that he is the same person whose name appears in the matriculation list of students of George Steuart at Edinburgh University in 1750. (*Matriculation Roll of the University of Edinburgh*, 15 March 1750.) Duncanson's notebook, like the set of lectures taken down by Dalgleish, appears to have been in the possession of John Lee and put up for auction in 1861. (See Amoh, introduction to *Collection of Essays*, by A. Ferguson, xiv, xxvii–xxviii.) The other copy of the "plan" fills seventy-two pages of a still smaller notebook, written in an unknown hand and bearing no date. The two plans are in many parts identical, but the presence of obvious differences – a different introductory paragraph and some occasional differences in phrasing, for example – imply that they were not taken down in the same year. In any case, Dalgleish's copy of this plan has not been found, and the two versions of it provide a useful supplement to his lectures, especially because Cleghorn often made references to it as he spoke. See, e.g., W. Cleghorn, Lectures, EUL, e.g., I.81, I.365; W. Cleghorn, "A plan of the whole course of moral philosophy," taken down by N. Duncanson, Edinburgh University 1752, StAndUL, MS BJ 1021.C6 (formerly MS 1951); and W. Cleghorn, "Plan of the whole Course of Moral Philosophy," taken down by an unknown hand, [n.d.], StAndUL, Cleghorn Papers, MS dep. 53/Box 3/3. There also survives, in addition to these three sets of lecture dictates, a 366-page commonplace book by Cleghorn, apparently from the years 1738–1740, entitled *Adversariorum Methodus, Promptuarium, seu Loci communes, Tomus [Pri]mus* (StAndUL, Cleghorn Papers, MS dep. 53/Box 3/1).

himself. In the summer of 1744, Hume reported as much, with some astonishment, to his friend William Mure:

> The accusation of Heresy, Deism, Scepticism, Atheism &c &c &c. was started against me; but never took, being bore down by the contrary Authority of all the good Company in Town. But what surprizd me extremely was to find that this Accusation was supported by the pretended Authority of Mr Hutcheson & even Mr [William] Leechman, who, tis said, agreed that I was a very unfit Person for such an Office. This appears to me absolutely incredible, especially with regard to the latter Gentleman. For as to Mr Hutcheson, all my friends think, that he has been rendering me bad Offices to the utmost of his Power. And I know, that Mr Couts, to whom I said rashly, that I thought I coud depend upon Mr Hutcheson's Friendship & Recommendation; I say, Mr Couts now speaks of that Professor rather as my Enemy than as my Friend. What can be the Meaning of this Conduct in that celebrated & benevolent Moralist, I cannot imagine.[69]

Given the difficulties that Hutcheson and William Leechman themselves had faced over the previous decade, fending off accusations of "deism" and "heresy," it is hard to imagine that the various slurs reported by Hume represented the real basis of their opposition to him. That real basis, however, cannot be discerned with any clarity from documents contemporary with Hume's campaign for the Edinburgh professorship. Rather, it must be inferred from two earlier sources: Hume's side of an epistolary exchange with Hutcheson five years earlier, in which an area of intellectual disagreement related to the third book of Hume's *Treatise of Human Nature* came quite clearly to the surface, and a review of that third book, which in the spring of 1741 appeared anonymously in the *Bibliothèque Raisonnée* but is known to have been assembled by a friend of Hutcheson's and appears to incorporate criticisms evident in the Hume-Hutcheson correspondence. The substance of Hutcheson's criticisms, as evinced by these two sources, is that Hume treats justice, the supreme social virtue whose exercise provides human societies with a principle of cohesion, not as an expression of instinctive disinterested benevolence toward other human beings, but rather as an artificially cultivated species of self-interest.

The difference between Hutcheson's and Hume's positions on the nature of justice can hardly appear more clearly than in their respective critiques of Bernard Mandeville, who in his *Fable of the Bees* had described justice as a product of the artificial cultivation of self-interest. What appeared to be a genuine desire for the public good, Mandeville had argued, was in fact

---

[69] David Hume to William Mure of Caldwell, 4 August 1744, *HL*, Letter 24.

a self-interested restraint of socially destructive passions, self-interested in that it arose from individuals' vain desire to be seen to be virtuous.[70] What appeared a virtue, in other words, had its roots in vice. Hutcheson's vituperative rebuttal followed from his basic view, also evident in his veiled critiques of Shaftesbury, that virtue must by definition be a species of disinterested benevolence. A desire for the public good, in Hutcheson's view, could not arise from the artificial cultivation of vanity: "We might have form'd the metaphysical Idea of *publick Good*, but we had never desir'd it, farther than it tended to our own *private Interest*, without a Principle of *Benevolence*."[71] Hume criticized Mandeville on precisely the opposite grounds. It made no sense, Hume observed in his 1754 essay, "Of Refinement in the Arts," to describe self-interest as a vice, when it produced so many public benefits:

> Is it not very inconsistent for an author to assert in one page, that moral distinctions are inventions of politicians for public interest; and in the next page maintain, that vice is advantageous to the public? And indeed it seems upon any system of morality, little less than a contradiction in terms, to talk of a vice, which is in general beneficial to society.[72]

For Hume, the prospect of a human society whose cohesion and prosperity depended upon the indulgence of private desires, rather than on fundamentally benevolent affections, was by no means disconcerting.

Indeed, as far as Hume was concerned, there could be no other explanation for social cohesion and prosperity. For one thing, there was simply no such thing as "public benevolence."[73] To be sure, human beings were naturally capable of instinctive, disinterested, generous affection, as Hutcheson had long insisted, but it appeared only among members of the same family, and it could by no means be made to extend to mankind as a whole.[74] Far from serving as a foundation for social life on a larger scale, it produced an antisocial clannishness:

> But 'tho this generosity must be acknowledg'd to the honour of human nature, we may at the same time remark, that so noble an affection, instead of fitting men for large societies, is almost as contrary to them, as the most narrow selfishness. For while each person loves himself better than any other single person, and in his love to others bears the greatest affection to his

---

[70] B. Mandeville, *Fable of the Bees*, ed. F. B. Kaye, 2 v. (Oxford: Oxford University Press, 1924), esp. I.43–44.

[71] Hutcheson, *Inquiry*, 4th ed., 229.

[72] D. Hume, "Of Refinement in the Arts," in *Essays Moral, Political, and Literary*, ed. E. Miller (Indianapolis, IN: Liberty Fund, 1985), 280.

[73] Hume, *Treatise*, III.2.1, ¶12–13.   [74] Hume, *Treatise*, III.2.1, ¶12.

relations and acquaintance, this must necessarily produce an opposition of passions, and a consequent opposition of actions; which cannot but be dangerous to the new-establish'd union.[75]

As a substitute for instinctive benevolence as the foundation of social cohesion, Hume proposed a principle of human nature that could be made to check those excesses of self-interest which posed a danger to social life and to the external advantages that social life existed to secure. This substitute, which could not be explained as a form of benevolence, was the principle of *sympathy*.

According to Hume, sympathy is the foundation of human beings' esteem and respect for justice. It is the principle by which human beings partake in the passions of others, and it serves as a principle of social cohesion insofar as it causes us to feel unease at the thought that an injustice is being done to someone else, even when that injustice has no bearing at all upon our own private interests. In a long and famous passage from the third book of his *Treatise*, Hume describes sympathy's operation as follows:

> After men have found by experience, that their selfishness and confin'd generosity, acting at their liberty, totally incapacitate them for society; and at the same time have observ'd, that society is necessary to the satisfaction of those very passions, they are naturally induc'd to lay themselves under the restraint of such rules, as may render their commerce more safe and commodious. To the imposition then, and observance of these rules, both in general, and in every particular instance, they are at first mov'd only by a regard to interest; and this motive, on the first formation of society, is sufficiently strong and forcible. But when society has become numerous, and has encreas'd to a tribe or nation, this interest is more remote; nor do men so readily perceive, that disorder and confusion follow upon every breach of these rules, as in a more narrow and contracted society. But tho' in our own actions we may frequently lose sight of that interest, which we have in maintaining order, and may follow a lesser and more present interest, we never fail to observe the prejudice we receive, either mediately or immediately, from the injustice of others; as not being in that case either blinded by passion, or byass'd by any contrary temptation. Nay when the injustice is so distant from us, as no way to affect our interest, it still displeases us; because we consider it as prejudicial to human society, and pernicious to every one that approaches the person guilty of it. We partake' of their uneasiness by *sympathy*; and as every thing, which gives uneasiness in human actions, upon the general survey, is call'd *vice*, and whatever produces satisfaction, in the same manner, is denominated *virtue*; this is the reason why the sense of moral good and evil follows upon justice and injustice.[76]

[75] Hume, *Treatise*, III.2.2, ¶6.   [76] Hume, *Treatise*, III.2.2, ¶24.

Hume's repudiation of Hutcheson in this passage is radical. Whereas Hutcheson understands instinctive benevolence to be the social virtue that the moral sense approves and positively identifies as virtuous, Hume understands the "sense of moral good and evil" to respond to a form of private pleasure and pain. Though this form of pleasure and pain does not depend upon a sense of immediate and narrow private interest, by the effect of sympathy it comes to depend upon the sense that one's private interest is intimately connected with the welfare of a larger society whose order redounds indirectly to one's own benefit. Fundamentally, what Hume thought the "moral sense" approved – in other words, that quality of a person's character which Hume thought gave pleasure to someone contemplating it – was not benevolence *per se*. It was rather the "usefulness" or simply "agreeableness" of the quality in question, either to the contemplator or to its possessor.[77]

To this conception of justice, Hutcheson appears to have responded negatively. If Hutcheson's response indeed made its way into an anonymous review of Book III of Hume's *Treatise* in the *Bibliothèque Raisonnée*, as seems likely,[78] then the response was very negative indeed: Hume had merely presented "Hobbes's system . . . in a new form."[79] The details of Hutcheson's negative response appear still more clearly and authoritatively in four surviving letters from Hume to Hutcheson between 1739 and 1743.[80] It is clear from the first of these, dated 17 September 1739, that Hume had sent Hutcheson a draft of the third book of the *Treatise*, and that Hutcheson had replied with a number of criticisms. Of these, Hume mentions three, the first of which vividly establishes the theme of the rest. "What affected me most in your Remarks," Hume writes, "is your observing, that there wants a certain Warmth in the Cause of Virtue."[81] This well-known comment has been interpreted in various ways,[82] but what Hume proceeds to write makes its meaning relatively clear:

> There are different ways of examining the Mind as well as the Body. One
> may consider it either as an Anatomist or as a Painter; either to discover its

[77] Hume, *Treatise*, III.3.1, ¶30.

[78] J. Moore, "A Scots-Irish Bookseller in Holland: William Smith of Amsterdam (1698–1741)," *Eighteenth-Century Scotland: The Newsletter of the Eighteenth-Century Scottish Studies Society* 7 (Spring 1993): 8–11; J. Moore and M. A. Stewart, "William Smith and the Dissenters' Book Trade," *Bulletin of the Presbyterian Historical Society of Ireland* 22 (April 1993): 21–26.

[79] Review of *A Treatise of Human Nature*, Book III, by D. Hume, *Bibliothèque Raisonnée* 26.2 (April–June 1741): 425, trans. J. Fieser, in *Early Reponses to Hume's Moral, Literary and Political Writings, I. Hume's Moral Philosophy* (Bristol: Thoemmes, 1999), 10.

[80] David Hume to Francis Hutcheson, *HL*, Letters 13, 15, 16, 19.

[81] David Hume to Francis Hutcheson, 17 September 1739, *HL*, Letter 13.

[82] Most notably by Sher, "Professors of Virtue," 102–3; and Moore, "Hume and Hutcheson," 35–38.

most secret Springs & Principles or to describe the Grace & Beauty of its Actions. I imagine it impossible to conjoin these two Views. Where you pull off the Skin, & display all the minute Parts, there appears something trivial, even in the noblest Attitudes & most vigorous Actions: Nor can you ever render the Object graceful or engaging but by cloathing the Parts again with Skin & Flesh, & presenting only their bare Outside.[83]

Hutcheson had very likely suggested what he clearly believed, namely, that the inner principles of human action necessarily appear as "beautiful" as the actions themselves – in other words, that virtuous motives lie behind virtuous actions. In the case of justice, of course, this meant that behind the "skin" of promoting the public good without regard to one's own narrow interest, there must lie an equally disinterested, benevolent motive, not something "trivial" such as a mere love of others' utility to oneself. The remaining philosophical criticisms, as they appear from Hume's responses, merely extend this theme. Hutcheson had objected to Hume's description of justice as artificial rather than natural, to Hume's inclusion of "natural abilities" among the virtues despite their remoteness from benevolence (which Hutcheson seemed to regard as the only genuine virtue), and to Hume's assertion that sympathy, rather than a moral sense that approved of benevolence, was the source of human beings' esteem for justice. The echoes of Hutcheson's criticisms of Pufendorf and the "Epicureans" in his inaugural lecture are unsurprisingly unmistakable;[84] in response, Hume claims the authority of Pufendorf as he endorses Horace's maxim that utility is "properly the mother of the just and equitable man"![85]

Whether the dispute between Hutcheson and Hume can be summarized with any fairness as a revival of debates between the Stoics and the Epicureans is open to dispute,[86] but it cannot be denied that just as Hutcheson criticizes Hume for errors that he associates with Epicureanism, Hume responds to Hutcheson by pointing out the weakness of the Stoic position, as he finds it in the fourth book of Cicero's *De finibus*, that virtue is the only genuine good. As a postscript to his letter of 17 September 1739, Hume writes to Hutcheson:

---

[83] David Hume to Francis Hutcheson, 17 September 1739, *HL*, Letter 13.
[84] See also above, Chapter 4, p. 174.
[85] David Hume to Francis Hutcheson, 17 September 1739, *HL*, Letter 13.
[86] James Moore presents the seminal exposition of this revival in "Hume and Hutcheson," 25–35. David Fate Norton has criticized Moore's arguments, taking issue with the application of the terms "Stoic" and "Epicurean" and restating the case that Hutcheson and Hume should be regarded as moral sentimentalists, but he does not engage with Moore's principal claim, that the issue dividing Hume and Hutcheson was the nature of justice. Norton, "Hume and Hutcheson," 211–56.

You are a great admirer of Cicero as well as I am. Please to review the 4th Book, *de finibus bonorum & malorum*; where you find him prove against the *Stoics*, that if there be no other Goods but Virtue, tis impossible there can be any Virtue; because the Mind woud then want all Motives to begin its Actions upon: And tis on the Goodness or Badness of the Motives that the Virtue of the Action depends. This proves, that to every virtuous Action there must be a Motive or impelling Passion distinct from the Virtue, & that Virtue can never be the sole Motive to any Action. You do not assent to this; tho' I think there is no Proposition more certain or important.[87]

Hume's point may seem limited, but in fact it can be taken as a reference to the nub of his disagreement with Hutcheson over the nature of justice. The difficulty with the Stoic identification of the ultimate good with virtue alone, according to the critique rehearsed by Cicero, is that the Stoics overlook the fact that human beings are composed of bodies and minds, rather than minds alone. To insist that the only good is "morality of life," as Zeno does, contradicts the Stoics' own maxim that the greatest good is "life in harmony with nature" – since nature "strongly recommends" bodily goods such as health and freedom from pain as necessary for any animal, human beings not excepted, to reach its supreme and happiest state.[88] More specifically, since bodily goods are the "springs of conduct" and the very things that excite desire, to reject them as irrelevant to the attainment of the supreme good is to reject the only means by which human beings can have any hope of attaining that good.[89] In referring to a "Motive or impelling Passion distinct from the Virtue," therefore, Hume insinuates that the motive to virtue must be something capable of arousing desire by appeal to bodily interests, and that this motive should not be dismissed as alien or opposed to virtue. With reference to the error of the Stoics, in other words, Hume is redirecting his criticism of Mandeville against Hutcheson: justice is no less a virtue for arising out of self-interest.

Hutcheson against the Rationalists

The concurrent controversy over moral sentimentalism and moral rationalism, to borrow Selby-Bigge's terms, may seem at first glance to have been

---

[87] David Hume to Francis Hutcheson, 17 September 1739, *HL*, Letter 13. On the central importance of this observation to Book III of Hume's *Treatise*, see M. A. Stewart, "The Stoic Legacy in the Early Scottish Enlightenment," in *Atoms, Pneuma, and Tranquillity*, ed. M. Osler (Cambridge: Cambridge University Press, 1991), 284.

[88] Cicero, *De finibus bonorum et malorum*, ed. and trans. H. Rackham (London: Heinemann, 1914; repr., 1951), 329–33.

[89] Cicero, *De finibus*, 353.

quite a separate issue from the substance of Hutcheson's quarrel with David Hume, not least of all because Hume and Hutcheson can with good reason be grouped together as moral sentimentalists.[90] Hutcheson himself, however, did not see it this way. In fact, he clearly considered the rationalism-sentimentalism controversy to be intimately related to the question of whether natural benevolence was the source of human sociability.

The *locus classicus* for Hutcheson's view of rationalism is his epistolary exchange with Gilbert Burnet in the *London Journal* of 1725, published in 1735 as *Letters between the Late Mr. Gilbert Burnet and Mr. Hutchinson, concerning the True Foundation of Virtue or Moral Goodness.*[91] The two men's dispute lasted almost twenty years. It began with a pseudonymous letter printed in the *London Journal* of 1725, in which Burnet expressed dissatisfaction with the theory of the moral sense advanced by Hutcheson in the recently published *Inquiry*, and it ended with Hutcheson's final responses to Burnet's criticisms, first in his 1728 *Illustrations on the Moral Sense*, and then, arguably, in additions to the 1745 edition of his *Inquiry*. Over the course of the original epistolary exchange between Burnet and Hutcheson, the basic questions at issue between them became clear: what are moral good and moral evil, by means of what mental faculty do human beings discern them, and what is the source of the obligation to act in accordance with good and not evil? By the end of the exchange, the incompatibility between Burnet's and Hutcheson's answers to those questions had become equally evident.

According to Burnet, the moral goodness of an action consisted of what he called its "reasonableness," "fitness," and "conformity to truth," and the discovery of this quality by the faculty of reason produced a moral obligation to perform the action.[92] Burnet borrowed these terms, and likely many of the tacit arguments behind his position, from the man whose principles he recommended above Hutcheson's as the "true and solid foundation" of virtue, Samuel Clarke. In his 1705 Boyle Lecture, *A Discourse on the Unalterable Obligations of Natural Religion*, Clarke had argued, ostensibly in opposition to Hobbes, that the source of moral obligation was to be found neither in compacts, nor in the power of a lawgiver to attach sanctions to laws, nor in any considerations of advantages, rewards, and punishments, but rather in the "natural and necessary difference between

---

[90] See above, p. 186.

[91] B. Peach, "The Correspondence between Francis Hutcheson and Gilbert Burnet: The Problem of the Date," *Journal of the History of Philosophy* VIII.1 (January 1970): 87–91.

[92] Burnet and Hutcheson, *Letters*, 11–12, 34, 37–39, 43.

Good and Evil."[93] Moral obligation, he explains, is like the obligation to assent to a mathematical truth, insofar as it, too, is a "dictate of judgment," albeit one that our "brutish lusts" often compel us to disobey.[94] In the case of action, the type of truth to which our judgment commands assent consists of the conformity between a proposition about what kind of action is good or evil, and the idea of some prospective action. If we will an action that our judgment has informed us is evil, then we are acting in accordance with a proposition that contradicts the one presented by our judgment. In this sense, Clarke declares, we are guilty of a "contradiction."[95]

On the question of the source of moral obligation, Burnet is less explicit than Clarke; he is content to assert that reason is "[t]hat which lays the *proper*, and indeed, strictly speaking, the *only Obligation* upon us to act in a certain manner."[96] On the further question of how we arrive at these propositions about good and evil that allow us to judge our own actions by an act of comparison, Burnet makes his position clearer than Clarke's. As an example, he takes the case of acting for the public good:

> If the Question be, *Why should I in my Actions regard Publick Good?* – The proper and first Answer is, "Because it is the *Fit* means of obtaining the *Publick Good*, that every constituent Member of that *Publick* should regard it." But if it be further demanded – *Why ought the Publick Good to be sought after?* – Then the right Answer is, – "Because it is *Fit* for the accomplishing the wise *End* of our Creator, to make all his Creatures Happy, that it should be so." And if it be further urged – "Why is that *End* to be regarded?" The Answer is – "Because it is a *wise* and *reasonable* End."[97]

In order to judge whether an action is good, therefore, one must discover whether an action is reasonable – which, it seems, does not necessarily depend upon discovering the will of God, since God's ends, too, can be judged reasonable or unreasonable. When pressed by Hutcheson to explain the meaning of "reasonable" and the way in which reasonableness can be perceived, Burnet has recourse to psychology. An end is *reasonable*, he explains, if human reason (which he calls "the Sense of the Agreement or Disagreement of our Simple Ideas, or of the Combinations of them, resulting from their Comparison") perceives it to be best. The proposition "that it is in it self Best that All should be Happy" is "immediately perceivable by

---

[93] S. Clarke, *A Discourse concerning the Being and Attributes of God, the Obligations of Natural Religion, and the Truth and Certainty of the Christian Revelation*, in *A Discourse concerning the being and attributes of God . . . being Sixteen Sermons*, 3rd ed. (London, 1711), II.58, II.72.

[94] Clarke, *Discourse*, II.53.   [95] Clarke, *Discourse*, II.51.

[96] Burnet and Hutcheson, *Letters*, 43.   [97] Burnet and Hutcheson, *Letters*, 39–40.

all rational Natures."[98] It is a "self-evident Axiom" analogous to the mathematical equality of a whole with all its parts, an "unmoveable *Truth*" that we perceive "intuitively" and that "will bear all the Weight we can lay upon it."[99] Moral perception, therefore, is an act of reason, comparing an intuitively perceived, supremely reasonable end with the end of a prospective action, and it is from this act of perception that moral obligation flows.[100]

The problem with Hutcheson's scheme of moral perception as the function of a "moral sense," by contrast, seemed to Burnet to be twofold. First, Burnet registers dissatisfaction with the notion that good and evil are discernible only by a sensation of pleasure arising from perceptions by a sense whose truthfulness cannot be verified except by appeal to the authority of God, the author of human nature.[101] Second, he finds it implausible that the sensation of pleasure following the perception of "beauty" in a human action, which on Hutcheson's account appears to constitute moral approbation, should precede a rational judgment about whether the action is in fact virtuous. The "inward pleasure" of such approbation must follow and depend, he insists, upon the activity of reason.[102] After all, he adds, "Things do not seem to us to be True or Right, because they are beautiful, or please us; but seem beautiful, or please us, because they seem to us to be true or right."[103] Even if it should be objected that "the Sense of Beauty or Pleasure moves faster than the Sense of Truth or Right," in that the latter only operates "after a long Deduction of Reasoning," this can be explained by the fact that we often "imagine" beauty in an object about which we have not yet formed a demonstrative judgment. It does not mean that we can take our sense of beauty to be the criterion of beauty itself, since if we examine the object further and discover that we have initially judged wrong, "the Beauty immediately vanishes away, and a Sentiment of the contrary succeeds."[104] In examining morally good actions, as in examining beautiful objects, human beings discern the moral goodness by an act of reasoning, and the pleasure of approbation follows. Even if, as Burnet admits, the sensation of pleasure is what ultimately motivates virtuous actions, this sensation nonetheless cannot be the ultimate arbiter of an action's goodness or rightness.[105]

According to Hutcheson, on the other hand, Burnet's scheme has crippling problems of its own. The most fundamental of these is that the

---

[98] Burnet and Hutcheson, *Letters*, 11. 61.   [99] Burnet and Hutcheson, *Letters*, 61–62, 66–68.
[100] On Burnet's affinities with Wolff in this matter, see below, Conclusion.
[101] Burnet and Hutcheson, *Letters*, 9–11.   [102] Burnet and Hutcheson, *Letters*, 11.
[103] Burnet and Hutcheson, *Letters*, 12.   [104] Burnet and Hutcheson, *Letters*, 14.
[105] Burnet and Hutcheson, *Letters*, 59.

faculty of reason simply cannot do what Burnet expects of it; that is, it cannot identify ends of action, for this is in fact the province of the will. To assert otherwise, Hutcheson warns, is to forget that reason or intellect – Hutcheson uses the two words interchangeably – presents "the natures and relations of things," whereas "affection, volition, desire, action" depend on the will. "But the will is forgot of late," he writes,

> and some ascribe to the *Intellect*, not only *Contemplation* or Knowledge, but *Choice, Desire, Prosecuting, Loving.* Nay some are grown so ingenious in uniting the Powers of the Soul, that *contemplating with Pleasure,* Symmetry and Proportion, an Act of the *Intellect* as they plead, is the same thing with *Goodwill* or the virtuous *Desire* of publick Happiness.[106]

To claim that some actions or ends of action are simply "reasonable," and that this reasonableness can be discovered through an act of contemplation quite distinct from any desire or pleasure that may happen to accompany the discovery, is to ignore that this desire or accompanying pleasure is precisely what prompts us to identify an action or an end as reasonable.

To prove this point, Hutcheson turns to Grotius's *De jure belli et pacis* (On the law of war and peace) for a bipartite classification of reasons for action.[107] Reasons, he declares, are either *exciting reasons* or *justifying reasons.* Although they both comprise "truths" in the form of propositions about the fitness of an action to achieve some end, neither constitutes an ultimate end of action; exciting reasons must refer ultimately to desires or instincts, and justifying reasons must refer ultimately to sensations of approval, which is to say, to the activity of an internal or "moral" sense. Otherwise, we have no choice but get caught in an infinite regress. As an authority for this observation, and for the apparent corollary that all reasons must terminate in a desire or a sensation of approval, Hutcheson cites Aristotle:

> But are there not *Exciting Reasons* even antecedent to any *End*, moving us to propose one *End* rather than another? To this Aristotle long ago answered, that there are *Ultimate Ends*, not desired with a view to anything further; and *Subordinate Ends*, desired with a view to something further. There are *Exciting Reasons*, or *Truths*, about subordinate Ends, shewing their Tendency toward the *Ultimate End*; but as to the *Ultimate Ends*, there is no Truth or Reason exciting us to pursue them. Were there *Exciting Reasons* for all Ends, there could be no *Ultimate End*; but we should desire One thing for the Sake of Another in an infinite Series.[108]

---

[106] Hutcheson, *Essay*, 220.   [107] Burnet and Hutcheson, *Letters*, 48–49; Hutcheson, *Essay*, 218.
[108] Burnet and Hutcheson, *Letters*, 49–50.

Hutcheson would later expand the significance of this observation, interpreting Aristotle's assertion of the necessary existence of ultimate ends as a full-scale endorsement of his own moral sense theory.[109] Here, however, he refers to Aristotle by way of showing that Burnet's position must be regarded as incoherent. The absolute "fitness" and "reasonableness" of actions, to which Burnet so insistently refers, necessarily presuppose an instinctive desire and a moral sense. It is on the basis of this fact that Hutcheson connects moral rationalism with Epicureanism.

Strictly speaking, of course, such a connection seems incredible. Hutcheson's argument against Burnet appears not to bear at all on the question of whether human beings ultimately desire the good of others and approve as virtuous only acts of disinterested benevolence. Even Hutcheson himself does not assert that rationalist theories of moral perception necessarily presuppose an instinctive desire for private pleasure or a moral sense that approves of selfishness or utility as virtuous; they must simply presuppose *some* instinctive desire and *some* moral sense. Either they can be equated with the system of "Hobbes and Rochefoucault [*sic*]," according to which all desires and sensations of moral approval are "reducible to self-love," or they can be equated with Hutcheson's own system, according to which some affections are genuinely benevolent and the moral sense approves of them alone.[110]

On the other hand, for all Hutcheson's apparent neutrality, he clearly suspects that theories of virtue as "reasonableness" perceptible by intellect are in many cases mere cloaks for selfish theories. This suspicion is vaguely detectable in his epistolary responses to Burnet, in which he insists that in the absence of the presupposition of a moral sense, "reasonable" can only refer to the fitness of an action to serve one's private interest.[111] It appears far more clearly in the corrections and additions to the fourth edition of Hutcheson's *Inquiry*, which appeared in 1745, after Hutcheson had ostensibly finished his dispute with Burnet and had turned his attention to two other sources of criticism.

---

[109] F. Hutcheson, *Philosophiae moralis institutio compendiara* [= *Compend*], 2nd ed. (Glasgow, 1745), I.6, I.103n. This reference to Aristotle in the *Compend*, in which Hutcheson explicitly follows Henry More's comment to the same effect in his *Enchidirion*, is explained by James Moore in his preface to Hutcheson's *Logicae compendium*, ed. J. Moore and M. Silverthorne (Indianapolis, IN: Liberty Fund, 2006), xxv–xxvi.

[110] Hutcheson, *Essay*, 207–13, 232–33. Hutcheson observes a similar dichotomy in the case of moral obligation: either obligation is explained as a function of the selfish affections or as a function of the approbation of a moral sense.

[111] E.g., Burnet and Hutcheson, *Letters*, 21–23.

At first glance, it would seem that these two critics whom Hutcheson appears to have had in mind as he prepared the fourth edition of his *Inquiry*, John Balguy and John Clarke of Hull (d.1734), had attacked him from quite opposite directions.[112] Balguy, in his 1728–29 *Foundation of Moral Goodness, or, a Further Inquiry into the Original of our Idea of Virtue*, had assailed Hutcheson for "inverting the frame of our nature" and "transferring supremacy from the highest principle to the lowest" by identifying the foundation of virtue not as the faculty of reason but as an instinctive benevolence, something that human beings share with animals, and an apparently arbitrarily constituted moral sense.[113] Largely following "that excellent, that inestimable, Dr Samuel Clarke's Boyle Lectures," Balguy asserts that the foundation of virtue is "truth," that virtue itself can be described as "fitness," that the faculty of reason is sufficient to perceive the agreement and disagreement of "moral ideas," and that it is by an act of reason that moral obligation arises. Moral obligation – which he calls "internal," as opposed to the "external obligation" that follows from considerations of private pleasure – is "a state of mind into which [one] is brought by the perception of a plain reason for acting, or forbearing to act, arising from the Nature, Circumstances, or Relations of Persons or Things."[114] With the exception of his terminology, his emphasis on the dignity of reason as opposed to instinct, and his omitting to lay stress on the intuitive nature of moral perception, Balguy does not deviate far from the line taken by Burnet three years earlier.

He goes farther than Burnet, however, and arguably farther even than Samuel Clarke, in his defense of reason as the "foundation" of morality. Whereas Burnet is willing to concede that reason cannot actually motivate action, that it merely presents an end to the mind and relies upon the pleasure of moral approbation to motivate the pursuit of that end, Balguy insists that moral approbation itself can motivate action. To the question whether "affections arise necessarily from rational apprehensions of good or evil," Balguy answers in the affirmative.[115] Hutcheson's "exciting" and "justifying" reasons, in other words, are identical.[116] In this sense,

[112] *DNB*, s.v. "Clarke, John (bap. 1687, d. 1734)," by R. S. Tompson; and *DNB*, s.v. "Balguy, John (1686–1748)," by I. Rivers. On the differences between Balguy's and Clarke's critiques: e.g., Carey, "Francis Hutcheson's Philosophy and the Scottish Enlightenment," 43–48.

[113] J. Balguy, *Foundation of Moral Goodness, or a Further Inquiry into the Original of our Idea of Virtue* (London, 1728–29), 7–8, 14.

[114] Balguy, *Foundation of Moral Goodness*, 22–23, 31, 47–48, 57.

[115] Balguy, *Foundation of Moral Goodness*, 43–44.   [116] Balguy, *Foundation of Moral Goodness*, 45.

Balguy opposed Hutcheson with a more thoroughgoing rationalism even than Gilbert Burnet's.

John Clarke, on the other hand, had attacked Samuel Clarke's second Boyle Lecture as unconvincing, for the same reason advanced by Hutcheson against Burnet: "fitness" was unintelligible without the presupposition of some ultimate end that could only be explained in terms of an individual's desire for happiness. Unlike Hutcheson, however, John Clarke insisted that this desire could not have as its ultimate object the happiness of other people; it could only refer ultimately to the happiness of the individual, in the form of pleasure or the absence of pain. "Reasons and relations," he declared in his 1726 *Foundation of Morality in Theory and Practice Considered*, "will no more be able to stand it against pleasure and pain, than dust before a whirlwind."[117] When it came to Hutcheson's theory of virtue as a thoroughly disinterested, instinctive benevolence, therefore, John Clarke was not convinced. He insisted that the only thing that could motivate human action was the prospect of pleasure, at the very least the pleasure that constituted moral approbation. Hutcheson had aimed to overturn precisely this view at the beginning of his *Inquiry*, and it was to this aim that John Clarke took exception.[118] On the one hand, he argued, it clearly contradicted the teachings of Paul,[119] and on the other hand, the anatomy of the human mind made it impossible. Borrowing explicitly from John Locke's theory of the will, Clarke argued that "everything but pain and pleasure is indifferent to the mind, since the mind can be at ease without those things." After all, he explained, "the desire of, or inclination for any thing, is nothing but an uneasiness for the want of it," and the prospect of pleasure is what creates the sensation of unease and thereby raises an affection or produces a disposition to act.[120] Clarke's implication, of course, was that all desires are by their very nature self-interested. Even the parental affection toward children, which Hume and Hutcheson had agreed was a form of irreducible generosity, Clarke considered self-interested, since it involves parents "taking pleasure" in their children's happiness.[121] To Clarke, this did not mean that parental affection was not genuinely benevolent, but of course to Hutcheson it did. As far as Hutcheson was concerned, John Clarke could be categorized as an Epicurean.

---

[117] J. Clarke, *The Foundation of Morality in Theory and Practice considered, in an examination of the learned Dr. Samuel Clarke's opinion, concerning the original of moral obligation; as also of the notion of virtue advanced in a late book, entituled* [*sic*], An Inquiry into the Original of our Ideas of Beauty and Virtue (York, 1726), 8.

[118] Clarke, *Foundation of Morality*, 43–44.   [119] Clarke, *Foundation of Morality*, 50.

[120] Clarke, *Foundation of Morality*, 27, 53.   [121] Clarke, *Foundation of Morality*, 61.

Moreover, in Hutcheson's view, Balguy's and John Clarke's positions amounted more or less to the same thing. John Clarke had simply made explicit what Balguy necessarily – though tacitly – presupposed: that human actions are driven by an instinctive self-love, previous to all rational deliberation. Balguy's position suffered from the same incoherence as Burnet's, namely, the presupposition that reason can discover an ultimate end of action in the form of a true proposition, without reference to any sensation of moral approbation. Balguy fell into the additional trap of thinking that this true proposition can motivate action. In fact, like Burnet, he had no choice but presuppose that all exciting reasons terminate in a desire or instinct. In Hutcheson's words:

> Some will not allow that Virtue can spring from Passions, Instincts, or Affections of any Kind. . . . They tell us, That "Virtue should wholly spring from Reason;" as if Reason or Knowledge of any true Proposition could ever move to Action where there is no End proposed, and no Affection or Desire toward that End.[122]

The problem with Balguy, however, was that his aversion to the indignity of admitting that the moral nature of human beings consists of an instinct, rather than the faculty of reason, implied an unwillingness to admit that instincts could be anything but selfish. Otherwise, there could be no reason for him to deny that human beings might possess two instincts, one toward private happiness and the other toward public.[123]

John Clarke's theory of concomitant pleasures, therefore, represented a formidable defense of a position to which Hutcheson believed Balguy's could be reduced: the position that human beings cannot be genuinely benevolent. It can be no accident that in the fourth edition of the *Inquiry*, Hutcheson inserted his veiled refutation of Balguy immediately preceding the place where, in the previous editions, he had reiterated his refutation of the Lockean theory of desire wielded so destructively by John Clarke. As in those editions, though at greater length and shifted into a new fourteen-page discussion of the various ways of "deducing benevolence from self-love," Hutcheson attacks the supposition that without a sensation of uneasiness, human beings are incapable of desire:

> We may be uneasy while a desired Event is in Suspence, and yet not desire this Event only as the *Means* of removing this Uneasiness: Nay, if we did

---

[122] Hutcheson, *Inquiry*, 4th ed., 195–96. On the reference of this passage to Balguy, to whom Hutcheson appears to refer as "an ill-natur'd Adversary" in an accompanying footnote, see Greene, "Instinct of Nature," 195–98.

[123] Hutcheson, *Inquiry*, 4th ed., 195–96.

not desire the Event without view to this *Uneasiness*, we should never have brought the Uneasiness upon ourselves by *desiring* it. So likewise we may *feel Delight* upon the Existence of a desired Event, when yet we did not desire the Event only as the Means of obtaining this Delight.[124]

Desire, in other words, does not arise from unease; unease arises from desire, such that pleasure may follow the satisfaction of a desire without being the desire's object. The extension of this argument, which Hutcheson articulates in his *Essay*, is that the desire of the good of others is *entirely* unconnected with the sensations of pleasure and pain that arise from the satisfaction of desires for material things; even the pleasure that arises from the contemplation of moral goodness, Hutcheson describes as more akin to joy than to "immediate" bodily sensations.[125]

Hutcheson's debates with Gilbert Burnet, John Balguy, and John Clarke, therefore, constitute a second context – the first is Hutcheson's disagreement with Hume about the foundation of justice – in which he asserted and defended his theory of disinterested benevolence as the only source of virtue. This was the vortex, as it were, that William Cleghorn attempted to navigate. He used a rationalist theory of moral perception, adapted to conform with Hutcheson's strictures against the crypto-Epicureanism of moral rationalism, and conjoined to a scheme of aesthetic moral education akin to Shaftesbury's, as a way of acknowledging Hume's insistence on justice's artificiality while nonetheless maintaining Hutcheson's insistence that it is a species of benevolence.

Cleghorn's Alternative

That Cleghorn sided with Hutcheson's rationalist critics on the general issue of how human beings perceive moral good and evil could not be clearer. In his lectures, he singles out Hutcheson's theory of the moral sense for explicit criticism, and he invokes arguments advanced to the same end by Gilbert Burnet. The arena in which he chooses to lay out his criticisms is aesthetic, the particular question being how the beauty that constitutes moral goodness is perceived. "Now beauty," Cleghorn begins, "consists of proportions etc. which can only be perceived by the understanding. Hence the more conversant the understanding power is about these objects, the more knowledge will it gain."[126] Cleghorn then begins to examine "the question whether these perceptions are communicated to the mind by a

---

[124] Hutcheson, *Inquiry*, 4th ed., 149–50.   [125] Hutcheson, *Essay*, 3rd ed., 61–64.
[126] W. Cleghorn, Lectures, EUL, I.219.

certain impulse, sense, or instinct superadded by the Deity," in a manner reminiscent of Burnet's treatment of Hutcheson.[127] Moral sense theorists, Cleghorn explains, are forced into the position of having to appeal to the authority of God to justify relying on the moral sense's approbation as the standard of moral goodness, since they insist that the perception of beauty is immediate, prior to any act of judgment by the faculty of reason:

> Some deny the understanding to have any part here, and say that these per-ceptions are communicated by an implicit sense analogous to the sense of the body. If they are asked whence they have it, they answer, "from the Deity." This is said in consequence of that famous question, whether the perception of beauty is prior to the knowledge of the proportions which constitute the beauty. We would here choose to take the negative side. But the other is espoused by severals [sic]. Therefore we must take notice of the reasons by which they support their scheme. 1. They say that our perceptions of this kind are instantaneous, and are perceived in the same way as the sweetness in honey etc. are. Hence, say they, there is a power of sensation in the mind as well as in the body.[128]

To this, Cleghorn immediately offers a retort:

> That this perception of beauty is immediate in all simple and ordinary cases we will readily allow. But unless it be so also in instances less common and more complex, in which a great variety of proportions are to be traced out, the hypothesis will not be agreeable to appearances. 'Tis certain that some species of beauty don't strike so much at the first as afterwards, and admi-ration always rises in proportion to our knowledge of the proportions on which beauty depends. If we attend to the reason of sudden perception, there will be no need to run to a moral sense to account for it. 'Tis plain that in simple and common instances [it] arises from obvious and habitual associations.[129]

The question of whether the sensation of beauty precedes judgment of proportions is one that both Cleghorn and Burnet answer in the neg-ative, on similar grounds. Just as Burnet insists that the sensation of beauty in an action depends on the judgment that the action is "right," Cleghorn observes that the sensation of beauty in a thing increases with the knowledge of the thing's harmonious proportions. Likewise, just as Burnet attributes sudden perceptions of beauty to a predeliberative and

---

[127] W. Cleghorn, Lectures, EUL, I.219.   [128] W. Cleghorn, Lectures, EUL, I.219.
[129] W. Cleghorn, Lectures, EUL, I.219–21. Cf. D. Clerk, "Taste," May 1740, in Essays by Students of Professor John Stevenson, fols. 122–23.

nonrational process – namely, an act of imagination – Cleghorn attributes sudden perceptions of beauty to "obvious and habitual associations."[130]

In proposing an alternative to Hutcheson's moral sense, however, Cleghorn does not follow Burnet's example. Whereas Burnet ostensibly concedes Hutcheson's division of reasons into *exciting* and *justifying*, rendering his position vulnerable to the specter of the infinite regress that Aristotle supposedly observed in his discussion of ultimate ends, Cleghorn makes no such concession. For one thing, he denies that Aristotle's discussion of ultimate ends constitutes an endorsement of Hutcheson's moral sense theory.[131] What's more, he refuses to accept Hutcheson's division of reasons into exciting and justifying:

> 'Tis said farther that reason can never be the faculty by which we perceive good; for, say they, 'tis either justifying or exciting, but both of these kinds presuppose an ultimate end or good. Indeed if there is no other kind [of reason] but these, the conclusion is good. But if there be a faculty superior to any of these, this distinction of theirs will be found to be ineffectual.[132]

There is a type of reason, it would seem, that does not presuppose an ultimate end. For all his conciliatory rhetoric, of course, Burnet had implied as much in his endorsement of reason as a faculty that could identify the self-evident, axiomatic propositions that allegedly guided God. But Cleghorn's approach differs from Burnet's not only rhetorically but also in substance. Having distinguished between two distinct types of reason earlier in his lectures, he jettisons the one that corresponds most closely to Burnet's description, *intellect* or *intuitive reason*, favoring instead *discursive reason* as the only realistic answer to Hutcheson's accusation that reason by its very nature is incapable of identifying ultimate ends:

> Another consideration worthy of our attention is that they form too narrow a notion of the mind. The description is taken in its imperfect sense. We may recollect that intellect was divided into two kinds, intuitive and discursive. Now there is a great difference between these, that is, between intellect and reason. Reason may be called imperfect intellect and intellect perfect reason. Now there is scarce anything in the world that is thus intuitive unless axioms, wherefore intellect can be competent to such a limited creature as man only in a weak degree and reaches a very few truths. But the mind cannot intuitively view the ideas of good and beauty. This only belongs to the deity. However, from this discursive faculty we may learn some imperfect hints and anticipations of that ultimate good

---

[130] On Cleghorn's association of habits and habituation with the imagination, see below.
[131] W. Cleghorn, Lectures, EUL, I.223–25. [132] W. Cleghorn, Lectures, EUL, I.223.

comprehended by the intellect or the Deity, in whom they are perfect. Yet these serve to guide us to the understanding of the ultimate good.[133]

As a testament to the importance of recognizing that intellect need not be accepted as the rational faculty of moral perception, Cleghorn adds, "On this difference between intellect and reason the whole controversy depends."

Having discarded intellect as the faculty of moral perception, Cleghorn also discards Burnet's description of the identification of moral goodness as an instantaneous act of apprehension, analogous to the apprehension of mathematical axioms. Rather, he describes it as an act of forming the idea of the "supreme end" or "ultimate good" of the universe itself, by means of the principal activities of which discursive reason is capable: the comparison of ideas, the discovery of relations, and the formation of the idea of a whole and its parts. In most cases, Cleghorn admits, the discovery of a whole by the examination of its parts and their relations does not produce the idea of an end, but the universe is an exception. In the "narrow and limited systems [which] we have occasion to meet with in this world," he explains, proponents of moral sense theories insist that

> reason cannot be said to approve of them, because the end lies without them, whence it is that the good is felt. Thus it is with respect to the human body. Reason in this case can do no more than investigate all its different parts and consider it as a whole. But the end is not in itself; and therefore can no other way be perceived than by certain sensations of pleasure and advantage, which must ultimately reside in something else than reason. But notwithstanding this, it would be very false reasoning to carry this observation and draw the same conclusion with respect to the universe or general system.[134]

The universe is different because its end lies within itself, such that the conception of it as a whole necessarily involves a discovery of its end.[135] Cleghorn later restates his point in slightly more vivid and suggestive terms. Perceiving a relation between two things, he begins, is the same as perceiving a truth. The entire system of relations among the parts of a whole, he continues, constitutes the idea of a whole, which is nothing else than a "general truth." Most wholes, however, have a good that is external to themselves, in the sense that they are good for something other than themselves, something of which they are themselves parts. In the

---

[133] W. Cleghorn, Lectures, EUL, I.221–23.   [134] W. Cleghorn, Lectures, EUL, I.225.
[135] W. Cleghorn, Lectures, EUL, e.g., I.229.

case of a watch, for example, it is not difficult to perceive, by examining the relations between the spring, the chain, the balance, and so on, that the watch is a whole, and that the good of each part is connected with its relation to the other parts; but the perception of the relations of the watch's parts does not give a clear idea of the watch's relation to the larger world in which it exists as a part whose function is to tell time.[136] The watch's good, in other words, describes a relation external to the watch itself, and reason therefore cannot discover that good by an examination merely of the watch's parts. In the case of the universe, however, there are no other relations than the relations among its parts. The "general truth" of the universe, therefore, is not separate from its "good" or end, and it follows that the discovery of the relations of the parts of the universe yields an idea of the supreme end.[137] Before the discovery of all these relations, of course, the idea of the supreme end cannot be complete and stable; it must remain an "anticipation" of the supreme end.[138]

From this description of the supreme end as a "general truth" perceived – if only weakly and in the form of anticipation – by discursive reason, follows Cleghorn's account of moral approbation and moral obligation. Rather than a mere pleasurable sensation, moral approbation is a perception of the "agreement of actions with these anticipations" of the supreme end.[139] As in Burnet's letters to the *London Journal*, moral obligation for Cleghorn simply follows from the perception of the supreme end or ultimate good, and of the type of actions that would accord with it. "[W]hen our actions [are] agreeable to certain anticipations of . . . beauty, truth, and good," Cleghorn explains,

> then they are called right. Hence the nature of moral obligation takes its rise. For we mean, by saying that we ought to do such an action, [nothing other] than that 'tis right to do it.[140]

Unlike Hutcheson, therefore, who treats obligation as deriving from an idea of goodness that arises not from considerations of interest but from the pleasurable sensation of a moral sense constituted to approve of benevolence, Cleghorn hews to the line articulated by Burnet, that "only reason lays an obligation on us to act," and that the very idea of obligation

---

[136] W. Cleghorn, Lectures, EUL, I.283–87. On Christian Wolff's treatment of this analogy, see above, Chapter 1, p. 24.
[137] Cf. Shaftesbury, *Characteristics*, ed. Klein, 168–69.
[138] E.g., W. Cleghorn, Lectures, EUL, I.287.
[139] W. Cleghorn, Lectures, EUL, I.231.   [140] W. Cleghorn, Lectures, EUL, I.287.

presupposes "reason as its foundation."[141] Moral obligation arises not from a sensation, but from the perceptive activity of discursive reason.

The significance of Cleghorn's insistence upon identifying moral approbation as a function of discursive reason rather than a "super-added" internal sense, especially with regard to debates in which Hutcheson himself was involved, becomes clearer in the light of a trope that Cleghorn employs throughout his lectures: he contrasts the "Stoics" with Plato and the "Platonists," consistently taking the side of the latter. Now, it is clear from even the most cursory examination of Cleghorn's references to Platonism and Stoicism that Cleghorn did not intend simply to attach himself to an ancient school, for his professed allegiance to Plato and "Platonism" is patently incomplete. While accepting arguments for the eternity of soul, which he attributes to groups whom he names the "Pythagoreans," the "Chaldaeans," and the "Platonists," Cleghorn entertains doubts about their arguments for the "preexistence" of human souls before being associated with human bodies.[142] Nor does Cleghorn accept a related argument that he attributes to Plato, namely, that the presence of so-called common notions or *koinai ennoiai* can only be explained as a consequence of the preexistence of human souls, unearthing knowledge as an act of "remembrance" or *anamnēsis*.[143] On the issue of child-rearing, too, Cleghorn explicitly condemns Plato's view that children ought to be raised by all parents in common rather than by their own parents, and he warns against Plato's erroneous preference of polygamy over monogamous, long-lasting marriages.[144] In the ancient and famous debate over the relative merits of the active and contemplative lives, Cleghorn even takes the Stoic side, preferring their advocacy of the active life to Plato's advocacy of the contemplative, albeit taking care to describe Plato's view as a matter of his own "peculiar" taste rather than – as in the case of the Epicureans' advocacy of the contemplative life – a species of advocacy for selfishness.[145] Rather than aligning himself with Platonism over Stoicism *tout court*, Cleghorn employs praise of Platonism as a way of illustrating his position on an issue in which he thought Francis Hutcheson had taken an unrealistic and unnecessarily rigid stance against David Hume. Specifically, Cleghorn praises Platonism over Stoicism in order to draw attention to his own use of a theory of aesthetic moral education, inspired primarily by Shaftesbury, as a means of correcting Hutcheson's conception

---

[141] Hutcheson, *Inquiry*, 2nd ed., 266, 275; Burnet and Hutcheson, *Letters*, 43–45.
[142] W. Cleghorn, Lectures, EUL, I.29–31.   [143] W. Cleghorn, Lectures, EUL, I.31.
[144] W. Cleghorn, Lectures, EUL, I.679–81.   [145] W. Cleghorn, Lectures, EUL, I.595–99.

of natural sociability as fundamentally benevolent, in light of Hume's more realistic account of the artificial principle of justice that unites political societies.

To that end, Cleghorn draws repeated attention to a particular issue on which he portrays the Platonic position as superior to the Stoic one. His depiction of the two schools was by no means unique; various elements can be found in, for example, his family friend David Fordyce's (d. 1751) "Brief Account of the Nature, Progress, and Origin of Philosophy," probably delivered to students at Marischal College in 1743.[146] Nor was it original. Cleghorn appears to have built his criticism of the Stoics largely from elements of Book IV of Cicero's *De finibus*, the very section that Hume had used to insinuate a critique of Hutcheson in his letter of 17 September 1739.[147] Echoing Cicero's observation that the Stoics treat human beings as if they consisted of pure minds, rather than minds joined to bodies, Cleghorn repeatedly criticizes Stoics for ignoring human beings' "present mixed state" and "compound frame" in their discussions of the supreme good.[148]

What the Stoics did not sufficiently acknowledge, Cleghorn repeatedly points out, is that external things, which is to say, material objects, are indispensable to the cultivation of a virtuous human soul. On one level, Cleghorn says this by way of illustrating his view that sense-perception of material things plays an essential role in the psychology of a virtuous individual. In the case of motivating virtuous actions, the nature of the human being is such that affections are the only motives of actions, and reason alone cannot arouse affections; the formation of mental images of material objects, images derived in large part from the sense organs, is necessary. In the case of moral approbation, too, reason cannot be relied upon immediately; an awareness of the universal system, whose end – the ultimate end of all things – discursive reason can weakly perceive, can only be achieved by a process of contemplating smaller systems and the material things and beings that constitute them. On another level, Cleghorn criticizes the Stoics' insufficient attention to external things in order to illustrate his view that a desire for external things as goods in themselves

---

[146] D. Fordyce, "A brief Account of the Nature, Progress, and Origin of Philosophy delivered by the late Mr. David Fordyce, P. P. Marishal College, Aberdeen to his Scholars, before they begun their Philosophical course. Anno 1743/4," in *The Elements of Moral Philosophy, in Three Books, with A Brief Account of the Nature, Progress, and Origin of Philosophy*, by D. Fordyce, ed. T. Kennedy (Indianapolis, IN: Liberty Fund, 2003), xvii, 182–83.

[147] See above. On contemporary German anti-Stoic polemic, see above, Chapter 2.

[148] W. Cleghorn, Lectures, EUL, e.g., I.303, I.259; cf. W. Cleghorn, "A plan of the whole course of moral philosophy," taken down by Duncanson, 4–5.

is one of the principles of cohesion in societies larger than a single human family.

That external things play an indispensable role in the motivation of virtuous actions, Cleghorn takes to be a basic fact that follows from the anatomy of the mind and its relation to the body. Mind can only act on the body – and thereby motivate it to a particular physical action – through the mediation of the imagination, a faculty that also communicates sense impressions from the sense organs to the faculty of reason. "The body has a power of acting upon the mind, and the mind upon the body, so they mutually influence one another," Cleghorn explains, "and this is principally maintained and carried on by imagination."[149] The specifically motivational power of the imagination derives from its role in the arousal of affections, a role that Cleghorn describes as involving a two-part process of perceiving sense impressions and then attaching to them ideas that cause us to desire the objects to which the sense impressions correspond:

> The imagination operates two ways. 1. It apprehends and contemplates those objects which are conveyed to the mind by means of the organs of sense. 2. It acts upon them, that is, it associates to them ideas of its own store, such as those of beauty, order and proportion etc. In consequence of this, these things come to be more the objects of our affections.[150]

This process of attaching ideas to sense impressions of material objects, Cleghorn calls the creation of *images*.[151] It is indispensable to the motivation of actions in accordance with reason, because it creates a connection between reasoning, which can only produce abstract ideas of beauty, and the functioning of the body, which can only take place in relation to material objects. The abstract ideas generated by discursive reason's "anticipations" of the supreme good "must be associated with outward circumstances of beauty and order to give them weight and make them influence the affections, and give them the power of motives in the mind's present mixed state."[152]

The principal question, of course, is how to ensure that the imagination forms images correctly – that is, that it attaches the correct ideas to sensory impressions, arousing affections toward good and not toward evil. The power of the imagination to arouse affections without guidance from reason's view of the supreme end is clearly the source of many vices; Cleghorn notes that intemperance, avarice, ostentation, and ambition

---

149 W. Cleghorn, Lectures, EUL, I.23.   150 W. Cleghorn, Lectures, EUL, I.194.
151 W. Cleghorn, Lectures, EUL, I.194.   152 W. Cleghorn, Lectures, EUL, I.303.

result from the imagination associating various forms of sensual pleasure with the idea of genuine goodness.[153] The answer to this problem is *not*, he insists, the extirpation of the affections; this was the mistake of the Stoics.[154] The problem with the Stoic position, Cleghorn explains, was its inconsistency. On the one hand, the Stoics agreed with the "best writers of the ancients," including Plato, that because "images so much influence our affections, 'tis of great consequence to have them formed right."[155] On the other hand, they advocated doing away with all passions, such that even well-formed images could have no effect:

> The best writers among the ancients strongly inculcated this necessity; the *orthai doxai* were much insisted on by Plato and the Stoics. Which meant right notions of the external things. . . . And according to them the *pathē* depended on erronious opinions. The passions which arise from these opinions are hurtful and dangerous and therefore ought to be exterminated as much as may be, however this does not conclude that they ought to be extirpated when they proceed on a right taste or a general affection founded on a right taste. Concerning this, the Stoics seem not to have well understood their own principles.[156]

What Plato understood better than the Stoics, therefore, was that although the imagination could not be allowed simply to create images without guidance, the only solution was to train the imagination itself, not attempt to bypass it or ignore it. This meant, in Cleghorn's terms, using external things – which is to say, sense impressions of those things – to develop the proper imaginative associations. It was moreover the only way, he thought, to train oneself to act habitually in accordance with reason's anticipations of the supreme end, which was precisely the definition of virtuous action.[157] Toward the beginning of his moral philosophy lectures in 1746, Cleghorn repeatedly emphasized this observation by favorably distinguishing Plato from the Stoics:

> External things are not only of use to us as instruments of virtue; but also necessary ^useful to form us to habits of virtue, according to Plato. The Stoics maintained external things to be no way useful but as the instruments of actions, but Plato carried the thing farther and in several places seems to think them necessary to form us to the habits of virtue.[158]

[153] W. Cleghorn, Lectures, EUL, I.179–83.   [154] W. Cleghorn, Lectures, EUL, I.194.
[155] W. Cleghorn, Lectures, EUL, I.194–95.   [156] W. Cleghorn, Lectures, EUL, I.195–97.
[157] W. Cleghorn, Lectures, EUL, I.287, I.491.
[158] W. Cleghorn, Lectures, EUL, I.23. In this passage, "useful" is written immediately above "necessary," and "The Stoics . . . habits of Virtue" is inserted in the margin. Though Cleghorn does not

Developing the habits of virtue, in the language of Shaftesbury – Plato's "illustrious disciple," according to Cleghorn – means developing one's "taste" through the contemplation of corporeal things and the sense impressions they prompt.[159]

The process of using such sense impressions to form the imagination correctly, in accordance with discursive reason's anticipations of the good, is lengthy and difficult. In terms borrowed explicitly from Shaftesbury's account of aesthetic education, Cleghorn describes it as a process by which the imagination and human reason develop in tandem, such that the imagination comes to appreciate genuine beauty, beginning with the beauty of material objects and ending with the supreme beauty of the perfectly virtuous mind – the archetypal example of which is the mind of God – as expressed in the beauty of the universe. "The first objects that engage the mind," Cleghorn explains, "are sensible and external. . . . At first, it perceives the forms of beauty as the objects happen to appear before it, as in a cube, circle, etc."[160] With the development of imitative artistic ability, the ability to "communicate those ideas of beauty to other materials," comes the observation that "ideas of beauty and order are not independent of an artist."[161] Thus arises, again in terms borrowed from Shaftesbury, the notion of "design" by a "forming form," from which follows immediately the discovery – by discursive reason – of the notion of an "end" and the associated idea of a "whole," all of which are themselves susceptible of what Cleghorn calls a "second order" of beauty.[162] Hence arises further the awareness of a "third order" of beauty, the beauty of the "former of the forming forms," a mind communicating ideas of beauty to itself or other minds.[163] The ultimate aim of developing this awareness is that the imagination should associate the idea of beauty with the impression of a will that acts in accordance with the highest order of beauty, which is to say, acts in accordance with the most supreme end. In more explicitly moral terms, Cleghorn describes this process as a growing awareness of ever-more-extensive moral communities and the moral relations that they involve. A child begins by developing an awareness of its own mind and proceeds to an awareness of its nursery; the inhabitants of its house;

---

refer explicitly to any specific text by Plato, it is likely he had in mind Book IX of the *Republic*, which Hutcheson mentions in a similar context. See Hutcheson, *Essay*, 30.

[159] W. Cleghorn, Lectures, EUL, II.365, I.237. Cf. T. Young, "A Dissertation upon Taste," 11 May 1742, in Essays by Students of Professor John Stevenson, fols. 170–73.

[160] W. Cleghorn, Lectures, EUL, I.233.   [161] W. Cleghorn, Lectures, EUL, I.233.

[162] W. Cleghorn, Lectures, EUL, I.283–85, I.233, I.245–47.

[163] W. Cleghorn, Lectures, EUL, I.237. Cf. Shaftesbury, *Characteristics*, ed. Klein, 323–25.

the family members who visit it; its playfellows; its village; its country and adjacent ones; and for a person "of a philosophical turn," all mankind and the universe of all rational minds.[164]

The difficulty of this process consists in the fact that it is not simply the unfolding of an innate awareness or admiration, however faint, of moral beauty; the ascent also involves a transcendence of one's original imaginative predisposition to attach ideas of beauty and goodness to things that give "simple and unmixed sensible pleasure."[165] An attraction to genuine natural beauty, and a regard for material things as symbols of this beauty rather than mere sources of pleasure or pain, only comes later, when reason has begun to become aware of relations, parts, wholes, and design. An attraction to the "moral beauty" of the universe – which Cleghorn takes to be equivalent to "moral truth" – comes last of all.[166] The process is an enlargement and thereby a transformation of one's opinion of what is "most agreeable" to one's nature, beginning with narrow affection for one's own corporeal interests, and ending with an affection toward the good of the most expansive community of rational minds.[167] The method described by Cleghorn as necessary for this transformation, namely, the cultivation of the "inferior" virtues of temperance (which curbs the desire for sensible pleasures) and fortitude (which curbs the fear of pain), is accordingly not governed purely by any admiration of moral beauty; this was a fact that Cicero, in explaining the "foundations" of temperance and fortitude in his *De officiis*, had – in Stoic fashion – ignored. "[I]t is not this pure form [of beauty] that determines the conduct of such a mixed creature as man is in his present state," Cleghorn warned his auditors. "Therefore we may observe that Cicero is not so fit and useful for explaining and determining the real principle of human action."[168] The initial foundation of temperance and fortitude, according to Cleghorn, could be found primarily in "aversion," such that a desire to free oneself from pain could be said to be a first step toward virtue, only later superseded by a regard for moral beauty.[169]

The most concise illustration of how self-interested desire for pleasure is transcended comes from Cleghorn's treatment of the issue of concomitant

---

[164] W. Cleghorn, Lectures, EUL, II.57–61, I.279. Cleghorn is clearly echoing ancient accounts of *oikeiōsis*, some of which are preserved by Cicero. Cf. e.g., Cicero, *De finibus*, III.61; and, on *oikeiōsis* more generally, S. G. Pembroke, "Oikeiōsis," in *Problems in Stoicism*, ed. A. A. Long (London: Athlone Press, 1971), 114–49.
[165] W. Cleghorn, Lectures, EUL, I.289. [166] W. Cleghorn, Lectures, EUL, I.265–67, I.289.
[167] W. Cleghorn, Lectures, EUL, I.283, I.265. [168] W. Cleghorn, Lectures, EUL, I.327.
[169] W. Cleghorn, Lectures, EUL, I.377–79.

pleasures. On the one hand, with respect to the initial objects of desire, the external things which by virtue of giving pleasure are identified as beautiful by the imagination, Cleghorn accepts the very description of desire that Locke and John Clarke espouse and that Hutcheson condemns. "After the pleasure or sensible good is perceived by the ψυχή," he explains,

> there arises a certain uneasy sensation in the soul at the absence of it, which is immediately followed by the desire of it, so that we see there is an interme-diate principle between the perception and pursuit of sensible good. From which, we may observe that if no uneasy sensation arise after the perception of this good, the soul will be indifferent to it and will never affect or pursue it.[170]

The mark of Cleghorn's agreement with John Clarke's view is unmistak-able: the desire follows the unease rather than preceding it, such that with-out a sensation of unease there can only be indifference. This, of course, Hutcheson had taken to be the foundation of the view that the satisfac-tion of desire necessarily involves a subtle selfishness. On the other hand, Cleghorn immediately notes that the theory of unease does not apply in every case. Where the object of desire is insensible and belongs to the higher part of the soul, *nous*, the mechanism of desire is different: "In the first case, the good is external to the mind, but here it is interior to it and lodges within it; whence perceiving mental good and enjoying it are almost the same thing."[171] In other words, the intermediate principles of unease and affection, between the initial stage of perception and the final stage of enjoyment, drop out. In the case of the virtuous human being, therefore, whose admiration for sensory pleasures has given way to an admiration for moral beauty, subtle selfishness does not have a place. Like Hutcheson, Cleghorn admits that "there arises [in the mind] a pleasure from the con-templation of its own [virtuous] conduct," but he also directly contradicts John Clarke: "We don't here say what some philosophers have maintained, that the mind is drawn to virtue by its consciousness of pleasure having attended it."[172] Likewise, while the association of the idea of good with the concomitant pleasures of moral approbation may play an intermediate role in the cultivation of genuine virtue, it is ultimately superseded by a purer idea of good as the supreme end of the universe: "I have here represented good as compounded of the anticipations of moral beauty and truth, and partly of the pleasure which attends it," he says, "not that it is absolutely

---

[170] W. Cleghorn, Lectures, EUL, I.[i–ii].   [171] W. Cleghorn, Lectures, EUL, I.[ii].
[172] W. Cleghorn, Lectures, EUL, I.289.

speaking a mixed form, but only in our gradual way of acquiring the idea of it."[173]

The second aspect of Cleghorn's criticism of the Stoics' inattentiveness to the importance of external goods provides him with yet another theater for distinguishing himself from Hutcheson. This time, he criticizes the Stoics by way of making a concession to Hume's description of justice as an artificial virtue, one which cannot be regarded as an extension and codification of the benevolent affections visible within human families. Like Hume, Cleghorn views familial affection as an unreliable basis for social cohesion on a larger scale and, to a certain extent, as antithetical to it. To be sure, "tenderness and natural affection," especially in the form of that parental love which the Stoics called *storgē*, can be said to preserve the familial or "oeconomic" association.[174] The pure type of benevolence that constitutes this familial affection, however, far exceeds the benevolence of separate families toward one another, which itself exceeds by the same proportion the benevolence that exists between still larger associations, to which Cleghorn refers in this context as "political associations" or "states."[175] This confinement of natural benevolent affection to the members of one's own family, Cleghorn adds, "is one of the capital sources of human vices."[176] It is a source of harm done by individual families to one another, which Hume had described as clannishness, and which Cleghorn also identifies in the relations between separate political communities:

> Thus one who would scorn and think it below him to be parsimonious in his own individual capacity yet can endure to assume the character for the sake of his family, and thus, too, the members of a state, tho' with respect to themselves they would be far from ambition or avarice, yet rejoice at any occasion if their politic body acquire any advantage of this kind of power or riches, tho' it be to the hurt of other states.[177]

Accordingly, the principle of cohesion in "political" societies can have very little to do with *storgē*, and must be otherwise accounted for:

> [I]n states which are made up of a great number and variety of families, towns, etc., these bonds which arise from blood etc. have little place; because there is but little room ^pretence [*sic*] for operating to hold these together. There is not in nature the same foundation for affection to a fellow Britain or countryman as for a brother or son, etc. Therefore, in order to [secure?] the same subsistence of these political combinations, and to supply the defect

---

[173] W. Cleghorn, Lectures, EUL, I.291.   [174] W. Cleghorn, Lectures, EUL, II.19–21, II.159.
[175] W. Cleghorn, Lectures, EUL, II.157.   [176] W. Cleghorn, Lectures, EUL, II.157.
[177] W. Cleghorn, Lectures, EUL, II.157.

and want of natural affection and maintain the association entire, something else must be had recourse to.[178]

This "something else," which Cleghorn describes as the principle of associations "more artificial" than the family, associations which "seem to have obtained among mankind by reflexion and experience," is of course *justice*; and in describing it, Cleghorn keeps a certain distance between himself and Hutcheson by making concessions to Hume, namely, by referring to it as the principle of an "artificial" association, by incorporating into it a "sympathetic" principle, and by allowing the attainment of material possessions – things of use to the body – to be one of its ends.

The position that Cleghorn expresses a desire to refute, in declaring justice to involve a concern with bodies as well as minds, he attributes once again to the Stoics. It is "an error in the Stoic philosophy," he observes,

> "That nothing is to be regarded on its own account but virtue." Tho' this philosophically speaking is true, yet the Stoics thereby hardened their hearts against the necessities of their fellow creatures in distress. And the more so as they were solicitous to inculcate it as a fundamental maxim in their philosophy, that all those passions which implied any perturbation or were not the pure emotions of the rational soul ought to be restrained.[179]

According to the Stoics, Cleghorn continues, external evils do not constitute real suffering, and benevolence therefore cannot involve alleviating such evils. It is a case, once again, of failing to see that human beings have a "mixed frame," and that in their "present state" they must pay attention to the fact that their minds are inextricably joined to bodies. Regard for others' minds, he answers, must be regulated by a regard for others' bodies, and vice versa, lest the former fail to dictate that genuine suffering, however corporeal, be relieved.[180] Cleghorn accordingly divides the offices of justice into two classes, *liberality* and *equity*, each of which can be distinguished by the degree to which its aim and the principle of human nature from which it flows relates to bodies as well as minds. Liberality, Cleghorn explains, is of two kinds. The first is entirely disinterested; it flows from a "benevolence of a purer nature" which "seems to have its seat in a part of our constitution lower than the rational [part]," and which aims directly at "the absolute good of minds." The other kind of liberality flows from a principle of "sympathetic benevolence" and aims immediately

---

178 W. Cleghorn, Lectures, EUL, II.159. In the final sentence of this passage, Dalgleish appears to have omitted one of Cleghorn's verbs. Adding "secure" is one way of making sense of Dalgleish's "in order to the same subsistence."

179 W. Cleghorn, Lectures, EUL, I.495–97.   180 W. Cleghorn, Lectures, EUL, I.497.

at securing the means of preserving the external goods – for example, the sustenance of corporeal life – by which the union of minds is secured. In different terms, Cleghorn explains that the first kind of liberality flows from a species of benevolent affections that aims at the *communitas vitae* or "community or intercourse of life or minds," whereas the second kind of liberality flows from a species of benevolent affections that aim at the *communicatio utilitatum* or "intercourse of external things."[181] Equity, on the other hand, Cleghorn calls a "disposition to preserve the things made by God for men." It aims at the "outward order" of external goods that are "useful and agreeable" rather than "necessary" to human life. The "higher" type of equity, like both types of liberality, has as its ultimate aim the security of the union of minds; whereas the "lower" type regards external things as "good in themselves." What "moves the social affections" in the case of equity, Cleghorn notes, is "the convenience of outward things to human nature."[182] Unlike the affection that constitutes liberality, therefore, which Cleghorn denies can be considered selfish in any regard,[183] equity must be considered selfish, at least by virtue of the fact that any desire for external things involves for Cleghorn the subtly selfish mechanism of unease that Hutcheson condemned in John Clarke but that Shaftesbury took for granted. This represents a deviation from Hutcheson's strict insistence that justice be regarded as an extension of instinctive benevolence, and a partial concession to the Epicureanism that Hutcheson identified in Hume.

The reason for making such a concession, Cleghorn explains clearly and repeatedly. If justice is not admitted to be an artificial virtue, in the sense of involving a regard for external goods as ends in themselves, then the "whole foundation" of political society can be called into question. The danger of Hutcheson's position, in other words, is its implausibility. Having insisted that justice must be a natural virtue, which it clearly is not, Hutcheson effectively concedes the field to moralists of a different persuasion, who view the artificiality of justice as grounds for identifying it as mere selfishness. These philosophers, among whom Cleghorn lists not only Hutcheson's favorite Epicurean targets, Hobbes and Pufendorf, but also John Selden (1584–1654), Richard Cumberland (1631–1718), and Johann Gottlieb Heineccius (1681–1741), "have sought to weaken the real foundation of society by pretending to establish it only upon necessity, weakness, power, or arbitrary will."[184] The details of their theories differ,

---

[181] W. Cleghorn, Lectures, EUL, I.493–97, I.501.
[182] W. Cleghorn, Lectures, EUL, I.561–65.   [183] W. Cleghorn, Lectures, EUL, I.569.
[184] W. Cleghorn, "A plan of the whole course of moral philosophy," taken down by Duncanson, 54–6.

but the fundamental principle uniting them is that "moral obligation flows only from positive law from a superior," by virtue of the fact that only a superior can attach rewards and punishments to legislation, and only the prospect of rewards and punishments – that is, the prospect of acquiring or forfeiting external goods – can obligate human beings to act.[185] The alternative view, that there is an *internal* moral obligation to respect the principles of justice, independent of the *external* obligation created by the power of a superior to enforce laws,[186] would seem to require denying that justice arises from self-interest. This, of course, is Hutcheson's approach. For Cleghorn, however, the task is to explain how internal moral obligation, which arises in an individual from the perception of moral principles by the faculty of discursive reason, gains force from life in a political society, despite the fact that by its very nature, a political society depends for its existence upon its members' desire for external goods.

The linchpin of Cleghorn's answer is his argument that life in a political community, one whose principle of cohesion is in part its members' desire for material benefits, is in fact essential to the cultivation of a virtuous mind. By way of illustration, Cleghorn gives his students a translation, from Thomas Gale's (1635/6–1702) *Opuscula Mythologica*, of "a passage of an old Pythagorean philosopher preserved by Stobaeus, from which it may appear how much they considered political establishments as a necessary preparation for public virtue." In a lengthy gloss, he adds that the virtue of an individual depends on his membership in a virtuous aggregate of human beings, one to which there can be ascribed a beauty or harmony of its own, namely, a harmony of moral relations. In this sense, Cleghorn explains, "the virtue of the whole is previous to the virtue of any of the parts."[187] What this means, more precisely, is that a well-formed political community is the only school, as it were, in which the soul of the individual can be fully trained in virtue – a virtue so perfect as to render the mind "fit for other larger communities where they shall have no external interests to interfere."[188] "What a noble end then must this be," Cleghorn gushes: "This would be as it were a constant stream of minds flowing from one world to another. This then is the true scope and design human policy

---

[185] W. Cleghorn, Lectures, EUL, II.339–43.   [186] Cf. W. Cleghorn, Lectures, EUL, I.84–85.

[187] W. Cleghorn, Lectures, EUL, II.207–9. The translated passage, only one line of which is preserved in Dalgleish's dictates of Cleghorn's lectures, comes from Gale's edition of "Ocellus Lucanus," an author named in a list of Pythagoreans by Iamblichus and ostensibly preserved by Stobaeus but now considered spurious. See T. Gale, *Opuscula Mythologica* (Amsterdam, 1688), 537–38; *Oxford Classical Dictionary*, 2nd ed., ed. N. G. L. Hammond and H. H. Scullard (Oxford: Oxford University Press, 1970; repr., 1992), s.v. "Ocellus," by W. D. Ross.

[188] W. Cleghorn, Lectures, EUL, II.205.

should have in view."[189] Virtue must be the "end" of a political community, therefore, though by no means necessarily the original or only principle of its formation or cohesion.

That there is no other way for human beings to become virtuous than by living in a political community is placed beyond doubt by Cleghorn's Shaftesburian description of the mechanism by which the imagination and the reasoning faculty ascend in tandem to an awareness of the ultimate end, through the contemplation of ever-greater wholes, ending with glimpses at the "intellectual system," the universe of all rational beings. The ascent must be gradual, with the awareness of larger wholes and the moral relations associated with them proceeding gradually from one to the next; if awareness of an intermediate sphere does not develop, the ascent does not continue.[190] Cleghorn observes this fact even in the context of the order of his lectures. On 6 February 1746, long before beginning to discuss oeconomics or politics, he warns his students that the topic they are about to examine "can only be slightly touched here." "'Tis hardly possible for us to acquire any tolerable notion of the universal system and the divine being," he explains, "without taking a view of the intermediate systems and the offices of mankind."[191] The same principle holds true in the development of the human being over the longer term. Contemplating the individual mind alone, of course, is insufficient for developing an awareness of the ultimate end.[192] Nor can such an awareness be achieved if children do not become aware of the moral relations within their families; hence Cleghorn's repeated and vehement criticism of Plato's suggestion that children should be raised by all adults in common.[193] Political communities are no exception to this rule. By way of illustrating how Hutcheson falls afoul of it, Cleghorn turns once again to the Stoics.

What the Stoics understood, Cleghorn explains, is that there exists an internal, genuinely moral obligation, distinct from the external, legal obligation emphasized by Hobbes and his fellow "jurisprudential" theorists. This moral obligation arises from the exercise of the individual's faculty of moral perception, independent of any desire for external goods. The discussion of this type of obligation, Cleghorn calls "simple ethics." What the Stoics did not understand, however, is that there is another type of ethics, one more intimately connected with human associations whose principle of cohesion is in large part a desire for external goods. This, Cleghorn

[189] W. Cleghorn, Lectures, EUL, II.205.   [190] W. Cleghorn, Lectures, EUL, II.59–61.
[191] W. Cleghorn, Lectures, EUL, I.281.   [192] W. Cleghorn, Lectures, EUL, I.275.
[193] W. Cleghorn, Lectures, EUL, e.g., I.681.

identifies as "compound ethics," the type of ethics that takes account of human beings' "compound frame."[194] By treating political communities under the heading of compound ethics rather than simply jurisprudence, and by moreover deferring an examination of the universe of all rational beings until he has finished his discussion of political communities, Cleghorn purports to indicate what the Stoics didn't see: moral obligation in an individual derives force from his presence in a community whose principle of cohesion must be largely jurisprudential. Cleghorn explains this as follows:

> 'Tis a great advantage of this method that we are here enabled to distinguish the principles which operate in the moral world. In the common [method] the principles in an individual man and the intellectual system are confounded; and in bringing about this confusion the Stoics had [a] great hand. For they all along represented a virtuous man as acting from independent principles, and in these he was chiefly supported by reflection on the nature of the universe. However, these are distinct. A man indeed may be supposed capable of acting independently, to some degree, from reflecting on the principles which are in himself and on the independent powers of will and action, and also from certain sentiments of worth in action, but this is at the best but imperfect. When we suppose the individual to be a member of a system, then his obligations derive new force.[195]

The mistake of the Stoics was to suppose that an individual could become aware of the universe of all rational beings, and thereby attain at least a glimpse of the supreme good, without becoming progressively aware of ever-more-expansive moral communities and their beauty. Without making such an ascent, Cleghorn warns, one can only attain an imperfect view of the supreme end – which means that the standard by which one regulates one's imagination must be imperfect, and perfect virtue must remain very much out of reach. Hutcheson, according to Cleghorn, tended toward this error as well.

Cleghorn professes to find Hutcheson displaying this tendency in his Latin textbook, the *Compend of Moral Philosophy*, published in 1742 and 1745. Recent commentators have noticed the philosophical divergence of Hutcheson's *Compend* from his more overtly programmatic works, especially with regard to its accommodation of jurisprudential principles, and on first glance, the work bears some similarities to Cleghorn's

---

[194] W. Cleghorn, "A plan of the whole course of moral philosophy," taken down by Duncanson, 54–56.
[195] W. Cleghorn, Lectures, EUL, II.361.

lectures.[196] Contrary to his disapproval of sympathy as a subtly selfish sentiment in his *System of Moral Philosophy*, Hutcheson describes sympathy in the *Compend* as something "we naturally approve."[197] He moreover agrees with Cleghorn's condemnation of Plato's scheme of parenting.[198] Cleghorn nonetheless points out two areas in which he must take issue with the *Compend*. First, he criticizes the organization of the book for giving the impression that political and oeconomic associations are subject solely to jurisprudential principles, rather than the principles of "simple ethics":

> The Compend of Mr Hutchinson [*sic*] is an excellent treatise on this subject and will be of great use to you. His method of prosecuting it is different from ours; chiefly in this: that the first book, or simple ethics, refers only to the individual, whereas we make simple ethics to comprehend not only the individual but also a family and a state. The whole of oeconomics and politics he brings under the name of jurisprudentia, and so the natural principles are overlooked.[199]

Cleghorn refers, it seems, to the division of Hutcheson's *Compend* into three books, entitled respectively *Ethica*, *De jurisprudentia privata*, and *Oeconomices et politices elementa*.[200] In the first book, Hutcheson makes no reference to families and political associations, discussing them only after his discussion of jurisprudence. The significance of this problem to Cleghorn becomes clearer in Cleghorn's next criticism, highly reminiscent of his complaint that the Stoics ignore the importance of political associations to the development of virtue in individuals:

> Another difference betwixt the methods is this: that [Hutcheson] seems to confine the principles of the intellectual system to the individual. Ultimately, indeed, they coincide, but with respect to such creatures as we are, there is good reason to distinguish them. There is a difference betwixt those obligations which arise from our being members of the intellectual system [and] those which arise from the nature of our own mind as moral agents. Thus do we distinguish for greater clearness and accuracy betwixt the several principles which determine us to the same actions. These are the two chief reasons for varying from this author.[201]

---

[196] This philosophical divergence is the subject of J. Moore, "The Two Systems of Francis Hutcheson: On the Origins of the Scottish Enlightenment," in *Studies in the Philosophy of the Scottish Enlightenment*, ed. M. A. Stewart (Oxford: Oxford University Press, 1990).

[197] Hutcheson, *System of Moral Philosophy*, I.47–49; F. Hutcheson, *Philosophiae moralis institutio compendiaria* [= *Compend*] (Glasgow, 1742), I.i.9, I.ii.6. On Hutcheson's condemnation of sympathy: J. Moore, "Hutcheson's Theodicy: The Argument and the Contexts of *A System of Moral Philosophy*," in *The Scottish Enlightenment*, ed. Wood, 239–41.

[198] Hutcheson, *Compend*, 1742 ed., III.i.3.   [199] W. Cleghorn, Lectures, EUL, II.343.

[200] Hutcheson, *Compend*, 1742 ed., i, v, ix.   [201] W. Cleghorn, Lectures, EUL, II.343–45.

Cleghorn's use of "seems" registers the fact that Hutcheson makes no explicit reference to the "intellectual system" at all. In describing Hutcheson as having "confined" the principles of the intellectual system to the individual, he appears to refer to the fact that Hutcheson describes the improvement of the individual mind, the development of prudence, the discovery of "the true plan of life," and the discovery of the "boundless excellencies" of the divine nature, all with reference solely to the individual's investigation of human nature – that is, the nature of the individual human being as such.[202] In doing so, according to Cleghorn, Hutcheson ignores the fact that the individual's perception of the supreme end, a perception from which moral obligation arises most fully, is only made possible by life in a well-formed political society.

At last, then, in this final lecture recorded by Dalgleish, Cleghorn's critiques of Hutcheson and the Stoics visibly converge. The inadequacies of the Stoics, Cleghorn has mentioned and continually reiterated: they neglect the importance of external things to the development of virtuous habits, they insist that all affections are to be extirpated, and they deny the importance of cultivating sympathy as a part of justice. Cleghorn gives no explicit sign that any of these criticisms can be applied to Hutcheson as well, and indeed to attribute to Hutcheson an insistence that all affections are to be extirpated would require some interpretive acrobatics, to say the least.[203] On the other hand, the similarity of Cleghorn's final criticism of the Stoics to his reservations about Hutcheson's *Compend* is unmistakable: Hutcheson, like the Stoics, pays insufficient attention to the fact that the individual's development of justice in its purest, most disinterested, benevolent form requires the development of a perception of the ultimate good of the universe, which itself requires that the imagination be trained by the contemplation of the beauty of a well-formed political community, in which the beauty consists of the community's harmonious moral relations. The unified conclusion to which all these criticisms point distinguishes Cleghorn from Hutcheson with clarity. The conclusion is that self-interestedness in general, while not, strictly speaking, a virtue, is nonetheless necessary in the development of genuine virtue; it is a necessary early stage in the training of the imagination, and it is an unavoidable characteristic of the desire for external things, even

---

[202] Hutcheson, *Compend*, 1742 ed., I.vi.1.
[203] On Hutcheson's distinction between the passions and the calm desires, and on his prescription that the calm desire of benevolence be strengthened at the expense of the particular passions, see above and Chapter 4, p. 177.

as instruments of benevolence, which itself is an inextricable principle of cohesion in political communities.

This criticism of Hutcheson does not ally Cleghorn with David Hume. Rather, it could be said with fairness that Hume identified problems with Hutcheson's moral theory that Cleghorn saw as well. In what has since become a famous remark, Hume vented to Hutcheson some frustration at a section of the draft of his 1742 *Compend*:

> P. 129 & quae seq: You sometimes, in my Opinion, ascribe the Original of Property & Justice to public Benevolence, & sometimes to private Benevolence towards the Possessors of the Goods, neither of which seem to me satisfactory. You know my Opinion on this head. It mortifies me much to see a Person, who possesses more Candour & Penetration than any almost I know, condemn Reasonings, of which I imagine I see so strongly the Evidence.[204]

Hume here appears to resurrect, in a moment of uncontained frustration, the dispute over the nature of justice that arose in his 1739 correspondence with Hutcheson. Hutcheson's position that justice was simply an exercise of ultimately instinctive benevolence by individuals whose moral sense perceived only such benevolence to be virtuous, Hume once again could not accept. Whether Cleghorn drew specifically on Hume's *Treatise* for the argument that natural affection within families cannot explain social cohesion on a larger scale is probably impossible to know; at the very least, he held the same view. On the other hand, as Adam Ferguson would recall many years after Cleghorn's death, the difference between Cleghorn and Hume was great: whereas Hume asserted that the moral sense approves of justice by perceiving its utility, Cleghorn retained his rationalist conception of moral approbation as a perception of the ultimate good.[205] Moreover, though Cleghorn did not derive justice from instinctive benevolence, he insisted that, through the training of the imagination by a process of aesthetic education, and through the use of discursive reason to attain glimpses of the ultimate end of the universe, justice could reach its most supreme form, involving a benevolence which, if not instinctive, was nonetheless genuine.

Conclusion

William Cleghorn's insistence on disinterested benevolence as the purest form of justice, in the form of a love for other minds, placed him in alliance

---

[204] Hume to Hutcheson, 10 January 1743, *HL*, Letter 19.
[205] Ferguson, "An Excursion in the Highlands," 47–48, 52.

with Francis Hutcheson on an issue that Hutcheson himself had considered to be of profound importance. That this was Cleghorn's view, in any case, can be seen in his praise of Hutcheson's discussion of "simple ethics." "The Compend of Mr Hutchinson," Cleghorn told his students, "is an excellent treatise on this subject and will be of great use to you." Having proceeded to note his reservations, Cleghorn heightened his initial praise: "But this is one of the best books on the subject."[206] These are hardly the words of an antagonist.

Likewise, in his criticisms of the Stoics, Cleghorn very often noted that the Stoic view was not entirely erroneous. The Stoics were led to the conclusion that "external things of themselves had no manner of use in determining men to the practice of virtue," Cleghorn explains, by their supposition that "goods of fortune" do not "partake of the *to agathon* or good in itself."[207] In other words, while the Stoics' inference is false, their premise is true. The Peripatetics didn't understand even the premise; they said, according to Cleghorn, that external things "partook in some measure of the nature of the *to agathon*." Cleghorn adds, "But this is an inaccurate way of speaking, for nothing can partake of the nature of this but virtue, and nothing can be virtue but what belongs to the universal moral whole."[208] Similarly, Cleghorn observes that the Stoic maxim, that "nothing is to be regarded on its own account but virtue," cannot be faulted for inaccuracy; the problem is that the Stoics inferred from it an incomplete and blameworthy conception of the offices of justice, one that ignored the role of benevolence toward bodies as well as minds. Though the maxim "philosophically speaking is true," Cleghorn explains, "yet the Stoics thereby hardened their hearts against the necessities of their fellow creatures in distress."[209] In accordance with the truth of the Stoics' maxim, Cleghorn himself is careful not to suggest that the desire of external things is essential, strictly speaking, to a virtuous character; it is merely a necessary means for developing such a character. "The progression of such a finite mind as man depends ^entirely upon its union with the body in its present state," Cleghorn declares, adding, "I don't say *essentially*."[210] Toward the Stoics, as toward Hutcheson, he assumes the posture of a reviser, not an opponent.

---

[206] W. Cleghorn, Lectures, EUL, II.343–45.   [207] W. Cleghorn, Lectures, EUL, I.423.
[208] W. Cleghorn, Lectures, EUL, I.427.
[209] W. Cleghorn, Lectures, EUL, I.495. Analogously, Cleghorn states that in advocating the extirpation of all affections, the Stoics have not taken a completely false position, but rather "seem not to have well understood their own principles." W. Cleghorn, Lectures, EUL, I.197. Cf. above, p. 221.
[210] W. Cleghorn, Lectures, EUL, I.23. Emphasis added.

In introducing Plato as the exponent of a philosophical system superior to the Stoic one, Cleghorn appears to have anticipated the brief addendum to his pupil Adam Ferguson's famous account of Stoicism and Epicureanism in the late Roman republic. Having distinguished the two philosophical schools by their contrary conceptions of the good – the Epicureans resolving "the distinctions of right and wrong, of honour and dishonour, into mere appellations of pleasure and pain" and the Stoics maintaining that "a just man will ever act as if there was nothing good but what is right" – Ferguson notes the existence of other positions as well:

> Other sects affected to find a middle way between these extremes, and attempted, in speculation, to render their doctrines more plausible; that is, more agreeable to common opinions than either.[211]

For Cleghorn, Plato offered a fitting model of the more plausible middle way, having attempted to show, in the words of Andrew Michael Ramsay (1686–1743), "that the shortest way to immortality is to discharge all the duties of civil society for the love of virtue."[212] Contrary to the Epicurean or "jurisprudential" systems condemned by Hutcheson, Cleghorn's Plato considered human beings capable of becoming just, in a way that evinced disinterested benevolence toward other minds. On the other hand, contrary to the implausible adherence of Hutcheson to the ostensibly Stoic view of instinctive benevolence as the only acceptable source of justice, Cleghorn could cite Plato's suggestion – greatly elaborated upon in aesthetic terms by Shaftesbury – that the most supreme form of justice, which incorporates purely disinterested benevolence, must in fact be cultivated through a process of training the imagination. It is a process that at various stages depends for its success on fundamentally self-interested desire, as in the desire for external goods that plays such a vital role in the formation and cohesion of political communities, without whose proper functioning the development of the most supreme virtue in individuals cannot happen. Through the invocation of Plato and the adoption of much of the aesthetic conception of moral education that Shaftesbury, Plato's "illustrious disciple," had proposed, Cleghorn could acknowledge those weaknesses of Hutcheson's system to which Hume had drawn attention, while adopting a view of justice that ultimately resembled Hutcheson's far more than it did Hume's.

---

[211] A. Ferguson, *The History of the Progress and Termination of the Roman Republic*, v. 2 of 3 (London, 1783), 113–15.
[212] A. M. Ramsay, *The Travels of Cyrus, In two volumes, to which is annex'd, A discourse on the theology and mythology of the ancients*, v. 2 of 2 (London, 1727), appendix, 52.

Conclusion

An explicit comparison of Alexander Baumgarten's aesthetic theory with the theories of contemporary Scottish admirers of Shaftesbury such as William Cleghorn might have made Baumgarten's older brother blush. In a pair of book reviews from 1755 and 1756, Siegmund Jacob Baumgarten expressed unequivocal disapproval of Shaftesbury and Hutcheson. Endorsing contemporary polemics issued by two of Shaftesbury's and Hutcheson's more outspoken English-speaking critics, Baumgarten noted that Shaftesbury's philosophical system was clearly deistic, and that Hutcheson had simply added ornament to Shaftesbury's ideas.[1]

Nonetheless, if Siegmund Jacob Baumgarten's negative attitude toward Shaftesbury was hardly unusual for its time, it should not be taken as a sign that his younger brother must have had little in common with Shaftesbury's Scottish adherents. Between the 1730s and the 1750s, when Alexander was developing his aesthetic theory, some of the attention Shaftesbury received in the German-speaking world was positive. Shaftesbury had received high public praise from Jean Le Clerc and Gottfried Wilhelm Leibniz in the early 1710s and Johann Christoph Gottsched at the end of the 1720s. By the mid 1730s at the very latest, he appears to have had a readership in Halle.[2] The first published German translation of parts of Shaftesbury's *Characteristics* appeared in 1738,[3] and a decisive "theological rehabilitation" of Shaftesbury, to quote Mark-Georg Dehrmann, came in the 1740s at the

---

[1] S. J. Baumgarten, Review of *Caracteristicks* [*sic*], by Shaftesbury, *Nachrichten von merkwürdigen Büchern* 40 (April 1755), 336; S. J. Baumgarten, Review of *Inquiry*, by Hutcheson, *Nachrichten von merkwürdigen Büchern* 59 (November 1756), 440. Baumgarten quotes attacks on Shaftesbury and Hutcheson by John Leland (1691–1766) and Philip Skelton (1707–87), on whom see above, Chapter 4, p. 155.

[2] The definitive account of Shaftesbury's German reception is Dehrmann, *Das "Orakel der Deisten."* On the early reception, see Chapters 1 and 2, and on antagonism toward Shaftesbury's alleged deism, Chapter 3. Evidence of attention to Shaftesbury in Halle can be found in L. M. Kahle, praes., *Dissertatio philosophica de decoro* (Halle, 1735), ix–x.

[3] Dehrmann, *Das "Orakel der Deisten,"* 394.

hands of Johann Joachim Spalding (1714–1804).[4] By the 1750s, Siegmund Jacob Baumgarten's printed critique of Shaftesbury represented only one of several mainstream views, some of which were far more positive. Alexander's own writings suggest admiration and, at the very least, receptiveness to Shaftesbury's ideas. Calling Shaftesbury "one of the greatest arbiters of fine things,"[5] Baumgarten referred students to his "very beautifully" expressed claim in the *Characteristics* that "beauty is nothing other than truth, and a fable is only beautiful if it contains much truth."[6]

Whatever Alexander Baumgarten's precise attitude toward Shaftesbury, differences between Baumgarten's and his Scottish contemporaries' philosophies, as I have described them, certainly appear to pose obstacles to comparison. The most obvious of these is illuminated by the distinction between "rationalist" and "sentimentalist" moral theories, applied so influentially by Selby-Bigge, among many others, to the history of moral philosophy.[7] No less obvious an obstacle is the similar and equally commonplace distinction between "rationalist" (or "cognitivist") and "sentimentalist" (or "emotivist" or "empiricist") aesthetic theories. Just as moral rationalists and sentimentalists have been distinguished from each other by whether they identify the faculty of moral perception with reason or with feeling, so aesthetic rationalists have been distinguished from sentimentalists primarily by virtue of their regarding the perception of beauty as the result at least partially of reason, arriving at knowledge of a truth or an underlying order in some object of contemplation, rather than the result merely of the external and internal senses producing pleasure or some other, largely subjective, emotional response.[8] Similarly, rationalists have sometimes been distinguished from "empiricists" by their use of a primarily deductive rather than inductive method to arrive at moral and aesthetic principles.[9] By these measures, Wolff and Baumgarten have conventionally been classified as moral and aesthetic rationalists, perhaps similar in some respects to Shaftesbury but in stark contrast to Hutcheson's sentimentalism and empiricism.[10] These classifications inform the equally

---

[4] Dehrmann, *Das "Orakel der Deisten,"* 154.   [5] A. G. Baumgarten, *Aesthetica*, §556.
[6] A. G. Baumgarten, *Kollegium*, §556.   [7] See above, Chapter 5, p. 185.
[8] E.g. Guyer, *A History of Modern Aesthetics*, e.g., I.7–9, I.30–33, I.47, I.305–8; Beiser, *Diotima's Children*, 1–15; K. L. Walton, "Aesthetics: Introduction," *Grove Art Online* (Oxford University Press), cited 2 July 2015.
[9] Cf., e.g., Kant's (arguably unfounded) contrast between Baumgarten and Henry Home, Lord Kames (1696–1782) along these lines, described in Buchenau, *The Founding of Aesthetics*, 211–13; and Dugald Stewart's (1753–1828) similar distinction between British and continental philosophical traditions, mentioned in Friday, *Art and Enlightenment*, 1.
[10] E.g., Guyer, *A History of Modern Aesthetics*, I.97–98, I.100–105; Beiser, *Diotima's Children*, 61; and, as evidence of the persistence of Wolff's classification as a "rationalist," F. Copleston, *A History of*

conventional claim that, at least prior to the publication of Kant's *Critique of Judgment*, Germany and Scotland (or Britain more generally) were home to broadly unified national traditions, the German one largely rationalist and the Scottish one largely sentimentalist and empiricist.[11] And although many eighteenth-century aesthetic theories may throw into question both the homogeneity of these traditions and the possibility of classifying any theory as unambiguously rationalist or sentimentalist,[12] let alone the possibility of finding any aesthetic theory utterly divorced from empirical observation, there is no reason to doubt that in many respects Baumgarten and Hutcheson belong on different sides of these classificatory divides.

On the more microscopic scale, many details from one side of the comparison find no obvious parallel on the other side. The German, anti-Wolffian polemic against "Scholasticism" finds no obvious Scottish parallel of similar magnitude, just as William Cleghorn's invocation of Platonists produces few echoes among his German contemporaries. Neither the controversies about biblical exegesis and "philosophical preaching," so important to Baumgarten and his Pietist teachers, nor the emphasis on the moral pedagogical value of meditating on the wounds of Christ and seeking the inspiration of the Holy Spirit, finds clear parallels in the contemporary intra-Presbyterian debates as I have described them. Locke and Mandeville hardly emerge, in my portrayal of the German context, as the bugbears they clearly were for Shaftesbury and Hutcheson, respectively. Nor do German discussions of "virtue" involve an almost exclusive attention, like Hutcheson's, to the concept of unadulterated benevolence toward others.[13] The list of such mismatches, real and apparent, is endless.

The presence of these mismatches signals a still deeper obstacle to comparison, namely, the considerable degree to which Scottish and German discussions were directed toward separate, local audiences, audiences familiar with different bodies of texts and concerned with issues particular to their own communities and institutions – their own universities, their own churches, their own political regimes. The controversy over Hume's failed

---

Philosophy, v. 4, Wolff to Kant (Westminster, MD: Newman Press, 1960), 105; and I. Hunter, *Rival Enlightenments* (Cambridge: Cambridge University Press, 2001), 266.

[11] Some of the most recent adherents to such a schema include Guyer, *A History of Modern Aesthetics*, v. 1; Buchenau, *The Founding of Aesthetics*, 217; and Beiser, *Diotima's Children*.

[12] E.g., Scottish cognitivists George Turnbull (1698–1748) and Thomas Reid (1710–96), described in Guyer, *A History of Modern Aesthetics*, I.113–20, I.217–26; and Gotthold Ephraim Lessing (1729–81), described as a rationalist with "some affinity" to sentimentalism in Beiser, *Diotima's Children*, 262–66, esp. 264.

[13] Cf. S. J. Baumgarten's observation that duties to God, for example, are extraneous to Hutcheson's moral-philosophical system: Review of *Inquiry*, 449.

candidacy for the chair of moral philosophy at the University of Edinburgh, of course, was local, and although the quarrel between Christian
Wolff and his critics on the Halle Theology Faculty resounded far beyond
Halle, it, too, began locally. Of course many of the parties to these con-
flicts were defending educational projects whose horizons encompassed at
least notionally all Christendom or all humanity, but their express fears and
hopes concerned communities closer to home, and particularly the students they were training for political service, for the ministry, and for the
other professions. To explain the emergence of aesthetic theories in Scotland and Germany with reference to merely a single, transnational context would therefore seem to require overlooking the differences between
these separate communities, institutions, and projects for reform – including differences between Presbyterian and Lutheran theologies, between
church structures in Scotland and Brandenburg, between Scottish and
Brandenburg-Prussian politics, and between two distinct and in many
respects separate histories of controversy about those matters and many
others. To put the difficulty more vividly: how can Hutcheson's project to
inoculate his Scottish countrymen against moral depravity be explained in
the same way as Baumgarten's project to defend Wolffian pedagogical technique against those who worried that it was inducing theology students to
philosophize in the pulpit? The answer, of course, is that for the most part
it cannot. Many of the reasons for the development of aesthetic theories in
Scotland and Germany were local and therefore different from one another.

And yet the search for a nonteleological historical narrative that can
encompass theories in both places is not futile. Beneath the blur of differences is a pattern of broader similarities. Between the 1720s and the
1750s, similar positions were forming in similar, albeit locally inflected,
debates over the foundation of morality, and several theories we now regard
as aesthetic emerged in close connection with these debates. This fact
runs like a thread through the canonically pre-Kantian theories of Shaftesbury, Hutcheson, and Baumgarten, as well as the little-known theory of
Cleghorn. The thread's presence is clear even without extensive comparative analysis of the theories and the debates.

But even a brief comparative analysis reveals far more than this single
thread. It reveals that the debates themselves and the aesthetic theories
that emerged from them unfolded in parallel, exploiting possibilities created by the inner logic of metaphysical, ethical, psychological, and other
philosophical concepts they had in common. In both German and Scottish
contexts, we can find a distinction between two types of moral obligation:
external and *internal*. Broadly speaking, whereas the former referred to the

obligation to obey a moral principle stipulated by a lawgiver with the power
to reward obedience and punish disobedience, the latter referred to an obligation generated by a human being's own perception that a moral principle
merits obedience independent of any externally imposed rewards or punishments. We can also find in both contexts a conception of *perfection* as
the order or harmony with which parts function together for the purpose
of the whole, as well as a conception of *beauty* as the affection-arousing
aspect of perfection. Finally, we find in both contexts an assertion that the
contemplation of beauty with the sense-related perceptive faculties of the
human mind can produce a motivation to act that functions as a support
or complement to internal obligation.

Of these three shared ideas – (1) the distinction between internal and
external obligation, (2) the concepts of perfection and beauty, and (3) the
assertion that contemplating beauty can produce a motivation complementary to internal obligation – the first is the most difficult to define precisely
and produces the muddiest comparison. On the Scottish side, Shaftesbury
and Hutcheson hardly use the terms *internal* and *external obligation* at all.
On the German side, where the terms appear more frequently, the question
of how to define those terms was itself a subject of controversy. Several historians consider Christian Wolff's definition of obligation as simply motivation, for example, to be a pointed repudiation of Pufendorf's association
of obligation with the right of a lawgiver to command.[14] An illustration of
a related controversy comes from the notion, employed by Johann Liborius Zimmermann in his critique of Wolff, that lawgivers with the right
to command do not obligate in the same way that lawgivers without that
right do.[15] These examples suffice to show that asserting a shared conception of the distinction between internal and external obligation among all
the protagonists in the chapters above requires ignoring important details
of those protagonists' actual positions.

But at a high level of generality, the assertion does hold. In the background of the development of aesthetic theories in both Germany and
Scotland stood a debate at the center of simultaneous disturbances within
German Lutheranism and Scottish Presbyterianism in the early eighteenth
century. At issue in both places was the degree to which, and the ways in
which, human beings can become genuinely virtuous without being aware
of the presence of a legislator, external to the human mind, who defines
moral principles and attaches rewards and punishments to them in the
form of pleasure and pain. Shaftesbury, in texts that immediately became

----

[14] See above, Chapter 1, p. 24.   [15] See above, Chapter 1, p. 35.

central to Scottish intellectual life, defended the existence of moral principles antecedent to any divine or human act of legislation, as well the motivational effectiveness of virtue's "natural advantages," against the view allegedly espoused by Hobbes and Locke, that moral principles are created by a lawgiver and that the motivation to obey them must be supplied by external rewards and punishments.[16] Hutcheson, taking as his explicit targets not only Hobbes but also Mandeville, Pufendorf, and even Shaftesbury, equated rewards and punishments with pleasure and pain and ultimately denied that even the desire for pleasure could motivate genuinely virtuous actions.[17] Like his fellow Shaftesburian reformers of Presbyterianism, he denied that human beings in their natural state can be motivated only to external acts of virtue and only by divine law.[18] William Cleghorn, who made explicit reference to the distinction between internal and external obligation, took as his ultimate targets Hobbes, Pufendorf, Selden, and Heineccius, who he alleged had taken moral obligation to be merely external, flowing "only from positive law from a superior."[19] On the German side, Christian Wolff and Alexander Baumgarten argued against Pufendorf, Buddeus, Zimmermann, Gundling, and Walch, among others, that human beings in their natural state could become genuinely virtuous by means of internal obligation, without relying upon the promises of reward or threats of punishment by any lawgiver, human or divine.[20] These are all instances of a general debate over the foundation of morality, in which defenders of the possibility of natural virtue rejected the overriding importance of external rewards and punishments, as it allegedly had been asserted by natural jurists – including such authors as Pufendorf, common to both Scottish and German university curricula – and theologians, whether Presbyterian or Lutheran, who presupposed the natural depravity of man.

In both Germany and Scotland between the 1720s and the 1750s, defenders of natural virtue of course did not appear all at once, and to understand the parallel emergence of aesthetic theory in connection with their arguments, it helps to divide them into two phases. Francis Hutcheson and Christian Wolff constitute the first phase. What unites them is the simplicity of the natural mental faculty each of them championed as the essential and exclusive source of motivation to act virtuously. For Hutcheson, as for Wolff, virtue could only be motivated by a single, irreducible

---

[16] See above, Chapter 4, pp. 149–51, 164–66.
[17] See above, Chapter 4, pp. 173–76.   [18] See above, Chapter 4, pp. 154–55.
[19] See above, Chapter 5, pp. 227–28. Cf. Haakonssen, "Natural Jurisprudence," 267.
[20] As described above in Chapters 1, pp. 23–28, and 3, pp. 128–35.

desire, and the object of moral education was to ensure that this desire motivated one's actions as exclusively as possible. Hutcheson proposed an instinctive benevolence, which prompts human beings to prefer a course of action that aims at the good of other human beings. Wolff proposed the so-called rational appetite, which prompts human beings to prefer a course of action that experience has shown conduces to the perfection of themselves and others. Of course, benevolence is not necessarily the same as conducing to one's own or others' perfection, and Hutcheson's "instinct of benevolence" should not be conflated with Wolff's "rational appetite." But both are irreducible, natural faculties of the human mind, which have an ineradicable influence on the will, and both Hutcheson and Wolff conceived of moral education as a process of re-ordering the human mind such that the influence of these faculties would outweigh the influence of other desires. Just as Wolff proposed minimizing the influence of the human affections, Hutcheson proposed minimizing the influence of the violent passions, which he thought almost invariably involved self-interest.[21] Both Hutcheson and Wolff accepted that the threat of punishments could be used in moral education to engender salutary aversions to vice, which could then be pitted against one's older vicious desires,[22] but they also insisted that the motivation to genuine virtue had a single, simple, natural, psychological source.

The critics of Hutcheson and Wolff had far less in common, but their criticisms nonetheless shared a central theme: moral education needed to make use of self-interest to a far greater extent than Hutcheson and Wolff had admitted, and it had to engage human mental faculties that Wolff and Hutcheson had wanted to suppress. Most of Hutcheson's critics emphasized the limits of unadulterated benevolence. David Hume, unlike John Clarke and Hutcheson's most outspoken enemies within the Presbyterian clergy, happily granted that such benevolence could be observed in families, but even Hume denied that benevolence could also explain natural sociability on a larger scale; human beings' moral approval of justice, which contributed substantially to the cohesion of large societies, had to be explained as the product of a fundamentally self-interested sympathy.[23] Recalling the Stoic error relayed by Cicero's *De officiis*, Hume reminded Hutcheson still more fundamentally that "Virtue can never be the sole motive to any action."[24] Likewise, explicitly invoking a similarly anti-Stoic line of argument drawn from the same corpus of ancient texts, Wolff's

---

[21] See above, Chapter 4, pp. 172–79.   [22] See above, Chapters 1, p. 28, and 4, p. 159.
[23] See above, Chapter 5, pp. 200–202.   [24] See above, Chapter 5, p. 203–4.

critics denied the effectiveness of the alleged rational appetite. In the view of Johann Liborius Zimmermann, Johann Franz Buddeus, and Johann Georg Walch, Wolff had failed to recognize that human beings can only be purified of their vicious desires by God's grace after a period of striving to conform to divine law under the threat of punishments and the promise of rewards, and also that the preparation for this act of grace must involve arousing the affections through sensory experiences.[25] As August Hermann Francke and Johann Jakob Rambach had insisted in connection with biblical hermeneutics, at no stage were the affections to be simply extirpated.[26]

The next generation – or second phase – of defenders of natural virtue responded to these critiques not simply by restating the cases made by Hutcheson and Wolff, but by accepting the force of the arguments leveled against them, and by allowing an important place in moral education for motives that, by the standards defined by Hutcheson and Wolff, were impure. Moral education did not necessarily need to begin with a discovery of God and of divine law, the second generation maintained, but it nonetheless did need to enlist parts of the mind that exerted influence over human actions independently of the rational appetite and the instinct of benevolence. William Cleghorn and Alexander Baumgarten, representatives of this point of view, advanced aesthetic theories in order to make their respective cases.

Cleghorn devoted sustained attention to beauty and human beings' perception of it, in the course of describing an alternative to Hutcheson's program of moral education. More specifically, he delivered an account of the imagination's role in the formation of ideas of moral good and evil, as well as an account of the *oikeiōsis*-like process by which human beings gradually come to perceive the beauty of ever-greater communities around them, all under the pretense of refuting the Stoics' misguided insistence that moral education employ neither sense-images nor any self-interested desire for external goods.[27] Like Hutcheson, Cleghorn happily asserted that the very highest degree of moral obligation, the point where moral education could go no further, involved no mixed motives. But he also accepted Hume's claim that self-interest was largely responsible for large-scale human sociability.[28] Cleghorn's anti-Stoic rhetoric and his continual reminders that human beings are "mixed" creatures,[29] possessed not only of

---

[25] See above, Chapter 1, pp. 30–31, 36–38, 42–44.   [26] See above, Chapter 2, pp. 75–82.
[27] See above, Chapter 5, pp. 219–30.   [28] See above, Chapter 5, pp. 223–27.
[29] See above, Chapter 5, p. 226; cf. above, Chapter 3, p. 140.

minds but also of bodies and the self-interested desires inherent in bodies, represented a reinstatement of Shaftesbury's scheme of an aesthetic moral education and an attempt to salvage Hutcheson's defense of natural virtue by diverging pointedly from the unrealistic elements of Hutcheson's moral theory.

Baumgarten, similarly, diverged from Wolff's insistence that moral education required training the human conscience to found its judgments of moral good and evil on syllogisms whose terms were as distinct as possible. His aesthetic theory, which he conceived as one of several tools for training people to use sensate images (that is, clear and indistinct ideas) to move an audience to moral virtue, reflected his assumption that indistinct ideas can have a salutary effect on the will. In conformity with the explicitly anti-Scholastic and anti-Stoic rhetoric wielded by Wolff's critics, Baumgarten allowed that the rational appetite was not the only source of natural moral obligation, and that the affections, which Wolff had disparaged as inimical to the freedom of the will, could and should play a role. "Aether is purer," in Baumgarten's memorable words, "but here one will have to consume air."[30]

To these similar argumentative ends, Cleghorn and Baumgarten employed similar conceptual means, namely, the second and third of the three aforementioned ideas common to the German and Scottish contexts. They both understood *perfection* to refer to the order or harmony with which parts function together for the purpose of the whole, with *beauty* referring to the affection-arousing aspect of perfection. They both also maintained that the contemplation of beauty with the sense-related perceptual faculties of the human mind can produce a type of motivation complementary to internal moral obligation.[31] According to Cleghorn, internal moral obligation necessarily arises from "reason's anticipation of the supreme end" of the universe. These "anticipations" depend on the discovery of the universe's perfection; they comprise, in essence, inferences about the purpose of the largest possible whole, from an examination of its harmoniously functioning parts.[32] But until the final stages of moral development, these anticipations remain faint, and the motivation they supply remains weak. Human beings' "compound frame" requires that reason be assisted by the imagination, which enlists the affections in the cause of

---

[30] See above, Chapter 3, pp. 135–39, 145–46.

[31] Cleghorn evidently derived his conception of perfection from Shaftesbury, and Baumgarten derived his from Wolff. On Cleghorn and Shaftesbury, compare above, Chapter 5, pp. 216–17 and 222–23, with Chapter 4, pp. 166–73. On Baumgarten and Wolff, compare above, Chapter 1, pp. 24–27, with Chapter 3, pp. 106–7, 129–32.

[32] See above, Chapter 5, p. 216.

virtue by attaching ideas of beauty and ugliness to our sense impressions of material objects.[33] Baumgarten's position resembled Cleghorn's. According to Baumgarten, internal moral obligation naturally arises from rational judgments of what will best conduce to perfection,[34] judgments that rely on syllogisms whose terms are as distinct as possible.[35] But Baumgarten also held that sensate ideas of perfection, ideas that are clear but not distinct and are therefore capable of *beauty,* or indistinctly perceived harmonious order among their parts, can by virtue of their "magnitude" and "living force" produce salutary desires whose influence over human actions exceeds the influence exerted by distinct ideas of perfection.[36] Because these sensate ideas of perfection can have a morally beneficial effect, we are obliged to cultivate them in ourselves and others as a supplement to the distinct ideas that generate internal moral obligation.[37] Both Cleghorn and Baumgarten asserted that contemplating beauty, or sensate perfection, produces a motivation to be virtuous that their predecessors in the debate over the natural foundation of morality, Hutcheson and Wolff, would have regarded with suspicion. They nonetheless enlisted the contemplation of beauty as an instrument of moral education, in order to protect Wolff's and Hutcheson's essential project, the promotion of natural morality, from telling criticisms.

In light of this comparison of Baumgarten with Cleghorn, the simple parade of early-eighteenth-century stars, so common in the historiography of modern aesthetic theory, resolves itself into a double portrait that captures a more complex historical reality. In place of three big names – Shaftesbury, Hutcheson, Baumgarten – appear two full scenes, each displaying an aesthetic theorist before a lively background of older interlocutors engaged in discussions of the foundation of morality. Behind William Cleghorn appear Hume and Hutcheson, together with other Shaftesburian Presbyterian reformers and their critics. A portrait of Shaftesbury graces the wall behind them. In the other scene, Alexander Baumgarten stands before a crowd comprised of his older brother, Wolff, Christian Thomasius, Gundling, and groups of theologians from Jena and Halle – including Buddeus, Zimmermann, and August Hermann Francke. The portraits behind them include Pufendorf's. The door in the wall separating the rooms occupied by these two scenes is ajar. Kant is nowhere to be seen.

---

[33] See above, Chapter 5, pp. 219–23.
[34] This formulation registers Baumgarten's reticence about which or whose perfection is in question. See above, Chapter 3, pp. 129–32.
[35] See above, Chapter 1, pp. 25–27.
[36] See above, Chapter 3, pp. 104–5, 135–41.   [37] See above, Chapter 3, p. 138.

The value of this double portrait – Cleghorn and his intellectual milieu opposite Baumgarten and his – is that, by exposing concepts and internal dynamics that the two milieus shared, it allows the development of aesthetic theory in the early eighteenth century to be re-imagined without reference to Kant, and not at the cost of fragmenting what has long been regarded as a single historical narrative. Reconstructing and connecting several theological and philosophical debates about moral education, together with bringing hitherto obscure figures such as William Cleghorn into the light, is what allows the two scenes to cohere within themselves and reward comparison with one another even without the traditionally unifying effect of Kant's presence.

That said, although both these scenes have been arranged by the artist with care, as in most paintings not all the figures are equally detailed. Some have their heads turned away from the light, some are partly obscured by the odd table or chair, and some are so far in the background that a few brush-strokes have had to suffice to give the impression of a face. The two scenes themselves could be made far fuller than they are. Children playing outside, the future inheritors of the legacies possessed by the adults at the center of these portraits, could be presented among their older relations. Figures barely visible in the shadows could be pulled into the brightest parts of the room. The rooms themselves could be filled with more or different furniture, the walls hung with more paintings, the open doorway depicted more clearly in a state of use. Any number of alterations could enhance the portraits by bringing out aspects of each scene that now draw too little attention, or suppressing parts of each scene that draw too much.

Let that be an invitation for scholars to make those alterations, to populate the rooms with more relatives and discussants, even to add new rooms, by rereading what we have come to regard as aesthetic theories with these two scenes in mind. The chapters above exemplify one promising technique: to regard eighteenth-century theories not only as attempts to solve problems internal to and characteristic of the modern discipline of aesthetics or even the discipline as some eighteenth-century authors conceived it but also as attempts thereby to address a related problem external to the discipline, namely, the problem of the foundation of morality. From that perspective, topoi such as analyzing the cognitive and sensate aspects of aesthetic judgment, arguing about whether artistic skill can be taught, proposing solutions to the "paradox of tragedy,"[38] comparing different artistic media, and searching for an objective standard of taste,

---

[38] Guyer, *A History of Modern Aesthetics*, e.g., I.71–72.

among many others, may begin to reveal more of their theological, moral, and political implications – and not only in texts explicitly framed by their authors as contributions to disciplines other than aesthetics, such as William Cleghorn's lectures on moral philosophy. As the case of Hutcheson suffices to illustrate, not all aesthetic theories will turn out to be like Baumgarten's and Cleghorn's in locating the foundation of morality unambiguously in the perception of beauty per se.[39] But the ways in which aesthetic theories registered where their authors did in fact locate the foundation of morality, and the ways in which they thereby provided their authors with an arena in which that location could be justified, should become clearer.

Reading the eighteenth-century aesthetic canon in this way does not necessarily require rejecting interpretations of these texts from a more purely aesthetic perspective, even interpretations that require us to read between the lines of a text in order to reconstruct its author's position on questions we regard as hallmarks of the modern discipline. To the contrary, in many cases it requires elaborating upon observations that historians of aesthetics have already made about the moral aspects of various theories; reconstructing those theories' intellectual and political contexts accordingly; and incorporating into the history of aesthetics the work of scholars who have already studied canonical figures with an eye not to their aesthetic theories but rather to their pronouncements upon theological, moral, and political questions related to the foundation of morality. Many figures could in this way be inserted or afforded more prominence in the double portrait of Baumgarten and Cleghorn with relative ease. They include – to name only a small selection of plausible candidates and some suggestive scholarship – other Scottish and English followers of Shaftesbury such as George Turnbull (1698–1748) and James Harris (1709–80);[40] other interlocutors with Hutcheson such as David Hume,[41] Hugh Blair,[42] Adam

---

[39] My thanks to Dario Perinetti for impressing upon me the importance of this point.

[40] E.g., Stewart, "George Turnbull and Educational Reform"; Haakonssen, *Natural Law and Moral Philosophy*, 85–90; Guyer, *A History of Modern Aesthetics*, I.114–24; C. T. Probyn, *The Sociable Humanist: The Life and Works of James Harris, 1709–1780* (Oxford: Oxford University Press, 1991), e.g., 79–106.

[41] E.g., Caygill, *Art of Judgment*, 72–78; T. M. Costelloe, *Aesthetics and Morals in the Philosophy of David Hume* (London: Routledge, 2007); P. Guyer, "The Standard of Taste and the 'Most Ardent Desire of Society,'" in *Values of Beauty*, by P. Guyer, 37–74.

[42] E.g., T. Ahnert, "The Moral Education of Mankind: Character and Religious Moderatism in the Sermons of Hugh Blair," in *Character, Self, and Sociability in the Scottish Enlightenment*, ed. T. Ahnert and S. Manning (New York: Palgrave, 2011), 67–84; Ahnert, *Moral Culture*, Chapter 3; A. Brinton, "Hugh Blair and the True Eloquence," *Rhetoric Society Quarterly* 22.3 (1992): 30–42.

Smith,[43] Henry Home, Lord Kames (1696–1782),[44] and Jonathan Edwards (1703–58),[45] some of whose discussions of aesthetic topics are embedded in analyses of the foundation of morality; German interlocutors with Baumgarten such as Georg Friedrich Meier[46] and Moses Mendelssohn, the latter of whose forays into aesthetics have been construed as responses to Shaftesbury and Jean-Jacques Rousseau (1712-78);[47] the Swiss,[48] Italian,[49] and French[50] members of the eighteenth-century aesthetic canon, many of whose works were of course read and commented upon by the authors above; and even Kant himself.[51]

If the next comprehensive survey of eighteenth-century aesthetics presents itself as a story about early Enlightenment theology, moral philosophy, and natural jurisprudence, then this double portrait of Baumgarten and Cleghorn, waiting to be enriched by all these additions, will have served its purpose.

[43] E.g., R. Fudge, "Sympathy, Beauty, and Sentiment: Adam Smith's Aesthetic Morality," *Journal of Scottish Philosophy* 7 (2009): 133–46; C. Griswold, "Imagination: Morals, Science, and Arts," in *The Cambridge Companion to Adam Smith*, ed. K. Haakonssen (Cambridge: Cambridge University Press, 2006).

[44] E.g., Caygill, *Art of Judgment*, 62–69; *Encyclopedia of Aesthetics*, 2nd ed., ed. Michael Kelly (Oxford: Oxford University Press, 2014), s.v. "Home, Henry," by H. Caygill; Guyer, *A History of Modern Aesthetics*, I.177–94.

[45] E.g., N. Fiering, *Jonathan Edwards's Moral Thought and Its British Context* (Chapel Hill: University of North Carolina Press, 1981).

[46] E.g., Guyer, *A History of Modern Aesthetics*, I.319–21, I.324–25, I.330–32, I.337–40; Straßberger, *Johann Christoph Gottsched*, 495–506; Stöckmann, *Anthropologische Ästhetik*, 113–47.

[47] Beiser, *Diotima's Children*, 204, 238–39. Cf. Dehrmann, *Das "Orakel der Deisten,"* 246–69; Hammermeister, *German Aesthetic Tradition*, 14–19; Norton, *Beautiful Soul*, 90ff.

[48] E.g., Horlacher, *Bildungstheorie vor der Bildungstheorie*, 60–63, 144–46; S. Zurbuchen, "§65. Aufklärung in der Schweiz," in *Grundriß der Geschichte der Philosophie: die Philosophie des 18. Jahrhunderts*, v. 5, *Das heilige Römische Reich*, ed. H. Holzhey and V. Mudroch (Basel: Schwabe, 2014), 1461–64; and various essays in A. Lütteken and B. Mahlmann-Bauer, eds., *Johann Jakob Bodmer und Johann Jakob Breitinger im Netzwerk der europäischen Aufklärung* (Göttingen: Wallstein, 2009).

[49] E.g., on Vico, J. Robertson, *The Case for the Enlightenment: Scotland and Naples, 1680–1760* (Cambridge: Cambridge University Press, 2005), Chapter 5.

[50] E.g., Guyer, *A History of Modern Aesthetics*, I.73–93; Stöckmann, *Anthropologische Ästhetik*, 54–86; and E. Szécsényi, "*Gustus Spiritualis*: Remarks on the Emergence of Modern Aesthetics," *Estetika: The Central European Journal of Aesthetics* 51.1 (2014): 62–85.

[51] E.g., Kliche, "Die Institutionalisierung der Ästhetik," 330, 335; G. F. Munzel, *Kant's Conception of Moral Character* (Chicago: University of Chicago Press, 1999), 296–333; D. Henrich, "The Moral Image of the World," in *Aesthetic Judgment and the Moral Image of the World: Studies in Kant*, by D. Henrich (Stanford, CA: Stanford University Press, 1992); A. Nuzzo, *Ideal Embodiment: Kant's Theory of Sensibility* (Bloomington: Indiana University Press, 2008), 197–225; R. Zuckert, *Kant on Beauty and Biology* (Cambridge: Cambridge University Press, 2007), 370–82; and (among many other relevant discussions by the same author) Guyer, *A History of Modern Aesthetics*, I.452–58.

Bibliography

PRIMARY SOURCES

Manuscripts

Album scholae latinae (1712–29). Archiv der Franckesche Stiftungen. Halle (Saale). /S L2.

Alston, William. Letter to Andrew Fletcher, Lord Milton. 20 August 1754. National Library of Scotland. MS 16685, fol. 65.

Arbuthnot, Alexander. Letter to John Hay, fourth Marquess of Tweeddale. 16 April 1745. National Library of Scotland. MS 7065, fols. 157–58.

Baumgarten, Alexander Gottlieb. "Isagoge philosophica in theologiam theticam." Taken down by Joannes Gottfried Beneke. 3 vols. [Frankfurt (Oder)], [1748]. Berliner Staatsbibliothek. Ms theol. lat. Oct. 48. City of Edinburgh. Minutes of the Town Council. Edinburgh City Chambers.

Cleghorn, Hugh. Letters to John Lee. National Library of Scotland. MS 3441 fols. 84–85, 122–23.

Cleghorn, William. Lectures. Taken down by William Dalgleish. 4 vols. Edinburgh, 1747. Edinburgh University Library. MS Dc.3.3–6.

———. "Plan of the whole course of moral philosophy." Taken down by an unknown hand. [n.d.] St. Andrews University Library. Cleghorn Papers, MS dep. 53, Box 3/3.

———. "A plan of the whole course of moral philosophy." Taken down by Neill Duncanson. Edinburgh University, 1752. St. Andrews University Library. MS BJ 1021.C6 (formerly MS 1951).

———. *Adversariorum Methodus, Promptuarium, seu Loci communes, Tomus Primus.* 1738–39. St. Andrews University Library. Cleghorn Papers, Box 3/1.

Dalgleish, William. *Dalgleish's Lectures.* Edinburgh University Library. MS Dc.3.7.

"Einige Scripturae, des Hn. Prof. Baumgartens philosophische Lehrart betreffend/de anno 1736. d. 19 Febr. bis 29 April." Halle (Saale), 1736. Archiv der Franckesche Stiftungen. Halle (Saale)./H E7.

Essays by students of Professor John Stevenson. Edinburgh, 1737–50. Edinburgh University Library. MS Dc.4.54.

Hutcheson, Francis. Letter to Thomas Drennan. [1743]. Glasgow University Library. MS Gen 1018.

Letter to Gilbert Elliot, Lord Minto. 4 July 1744. National Library of Scotland. MS 11004, fol. 57.

Leechman, William. "Observations on the Truth of the Christian Religion, taken from the Lectures of Dr Leechman at Glasgow 1761." Glasgow University Library. MS Gen 884.

Mackie, Charles. "Alphabetical list of those who attended the Prelections on History and Roman Antiquities from 1719 to 1744 inclusive." Edinburgh University Library. MS Dc.5.24 (2).

"Index Funerareus, 29 Annorum from 11 June 1727 to June 1756." Edinburgh University Library. MS Dc.1.47.

MacLaurin, Colin. Letter to Thomas Morton. 5 May 1744. Scottish National Archives (Scottish Record Office). Edinburgh. GD 150/3486/3.

Pringle, John. Lectures from Cicero. Taken down by a student. Edinburgh, 1741. Edinburgh University Library. MS Gen 74D.

Protest by Mr. Robert Stewart Professor of natural phylosophy, and Mr. John Ker professor of Humanity in the university of Edinburgh by Commission from the University. National Library of Scotland, Edinburgh. MS 3431, fols. 70–71.

Report of the Presbytery of Edinburgh. 19 April 1738. National Library of Scotland. MS 3431, fols. 74–75.

University of Edinburgh. Minutes of the Academic Senate, 1733–1811. Edinburgh University Library. Dup.436 [formerly Mic. M. 730].

University of Edinburgh. Matriculation Roll of the University of Edinburgh: Arts, Law, Divinity. Vol. 1 of 4, 1623–1774. Transcribed by Alexander Morgan. Edinburgh University Library, Special Collections Reading Room.

University of Halle. Records of the Philosophy Faculty. Halle Universitätsarchiv. Rep. 21, III.261.

Printed Sources

Abbt, Thomas. *Alexander Gottlieb Baumgartens Leben und Character*. Halle, 1765.

    Leben und Charakter Alexander Gottlieb Baumgartens. Berlin, 1780. Reprint in *Vermischte Werke*, by T. Abbt. Vol. 4 of 6. Hildesheim: Olms, 1978.

Balguy, John. *Foundation of Moral Goodness, or a Further Inquiry into the Original of our Idea of Virtue*. London, 1728.

Baumgarten, Alexander Gottlieb. *Aesthetica*. 2 vols. Edited and translated by Dagmar Mirbach. Hamburg: Meiner, 2007.

    Dissertatio chorographica notiones superi et inferi, indeque adscensus et descensus in chorographiis sacris evolvens. Praes. C. B. Michaelis. Halle, 1735. Reprint in *Commentationes theologicae*, edited by Johann Caspar Velthusen, Christian Theoph Kuinoel, and Georg Alexander Rupert. Leipzig, 1798.

    Ethica philosophica. 3rd ed. Halle, 1763. Reprint, Hildesheim: Olms, 1969.

    Gedancken vom Vernünfftigen Beyfall auf Academien. 2nd ed. Halle, 1741.

    Initia philosophiae practicae primae. Halle, 1760. Reprint, Leiden: IDC, 2002.

Kollegium über die Ästhetik. Transcribed by Bernhard Poppe. In *Alexander Gottlieb Baumgarten: seine Bedeutung und Stellung in der Leibniz-Wolffischen Philosophie und seine Beziehungen zu Kant,* by B. Poppe. Münster, 1907.

Meditationes philosophicae de nonnullis ad poema pertinentibus. Halle, [1735]. Reprint in *Reflections on Poetry,* by A. G. Baumgarten. Translated by Karl Aschenbrenner and William B. Holther. Berkeley: University of California Press, 1954.

Metaphysica. 7th ed. Halle, 1779. Reprint, Hildesheim: Olms, 1963.

Metaphysica. Edited and translated with an introduction by Günter Gawlick and Lothar Kreimendahl. Stuttgart-Bad Cannstatt, 2011.

Metaphysik. Translated with an introduction by G. F. Meier. Edited by Dagmar Mirbach. Jena: Dietrich Schleglmann Reprints, 2004.

De ordine in audiendis philosophicis per triennium academicum . . . Halle, 1738.

Philosophia generalis. Halle, 1770. Reprint, Hildesheim: Olms, 1968.

Philosophische Betrachtungen über einige Bedingungen des Gedichtes. Translated and edited by Heinz Paetzold. Hamburg: Meiner, 1983.

Praelectiones theologiae dogmaticae. Edited by Johann Salomo Semler. Halle, 1773.

praes. *De vi et efficacia ethices philosophiae.* Resp. Samuel Wilhelm Spalding. Frankfurt (Oder), 1741.

Die Vorreden zur Metaphysik. Edited by Ursula Niggli. Frankfurt (Main): Klostermann, 1998.

[Baumgarten, Alexander Gottlieb]. *Philosophische Brieffe von Aletheophilus.* Leipzig, 1741.

Baumgarten, Siegmund Jacob. *Auslegung der Briefe Pauli an die Galater, Epheser, Philipper, Colosser, Philemon und Thessalonicher.* Edited by Johann Salomon Semler. Halle, 1767.

In funus summe rever. Jo. Liborii Zimmermanni. In *Opuscula,* by S. J. Baumgarten. Edited by Gotthilf Christoph Bake. Halle, 1746.

Öffentliche Anzeige seiner diesmaligen Akademischen Arbeit. Halle, 1734.

Programmata. Edited by Gotthilf Christoph Bake. Halle, 1740.

Unterricht vom rechtmäßigen Verhalten eines Christen oder Theologische Moral. Halle, 1744.

Unterricht von Auslegung der heiligen Schrift. Halle, 1745.

Besonders Gespräch in dem Reich derer Todten zwischen N. H. Gundling und J. F. Buddeus. Frankfurt (Main), 1731.

Bilfinger, Georg Bernhard. *Dilucidationes philosophicae de deo, anima humana, mundo, et generalibus rerum affectionibus.* Tübingen, 1725.

De triplici rerum cognitione, historica, philosophica, et mathematica. Jena, 1722.

[Blair, Hugh]. Review of *A System of Moral Philosophy.* By Francis Hutcheson. *Edinburgh Review* 1 (1755): 9–23.

Buddeus, Johann Franz. *Bedencken über die Wolffianische Philosophie mit Anmerckungen erläutert von Christian Wolffen.* Frankfurt (Main), 1724. Reprint, Hildesheim: Olms, 1980.

Compendivm historiae philosophicae. Edited by J. G. Walch. Halle, 1731.

De eo, quod in theologia pulchrum est. Jena, 1715.

Einleitung in die Moral-Theologie. Leipzig, 1719.

Elementa philosophiae practicae. 3rd ed. Halle, 1707. Reprint, Hildesheim: Olms, 2004.

Institutiones theologiae dogmaticae. Leipzig, 1723. Reprint, Hildesheim: Olms, 1999.

Institutiones theologiae moralis. Leipzig, 1727. Reprint, Hildesheim: Olms, 2007.

Burnet, Gilbert, and Francis Hutcheson. *Letters between the late Mr. Gilbert Burnet and Mr. Hutchinson, concerning the True Foundation of Virtue or Moral Goodness.* London, 1735.

Carlyle, Alexander. *Autobiography of Dr. Alexander Carlyle of Inveresk, 1722–1805.* Edited by John Hill Burton. London: T. N. Foulis, 1910. Reprint, with an introduction by Richard B. Sher, Bristol: Thoemmes, 1990.

Catalogi lectionum . . . publicati in Academia Fridericiana. Halle, 1730–39.

Catalogue of the Graduates in the Faculties of Arts, Divinity, and Law, of the University of Edinburgh, Since its Foundation. Edited by David Laing. Edinburgh: Edinburgh University Press, 1858.

Catologus bibliothecae Gundlingianae. Edited by Christian Benedict Michaelis. Halle, 1731.

Catalogus Librorum A Viro Excellentissimo Amplissimo Alexandro Gottlieb Baumgarten. Frankfurt (Oder), 1762.

Chalmers, George. *Life of Thomas Ruddiman.* London, 1794.

Cicero, Marcus Tullius. *De finibus bonorum et malorum.* Translated by H. Rackham. London: William Heinemann, 1914. Reprint, 1951.

Clarke, John. *The Foundation of Morality in Theory and Practice considered, in an examination of the learned Dr. Samuel Clarke's opinion, concerning the original of moral obligation; as also of the notion of virtue advanced in a late book, entitled, An Inquiry into the Original of our Ideas of Beauty and Virtue.* York, 1726.

Clarke, Samuel. *A Discourse concerning the Being and Attributes of God, the Obligations of Natural Religion, and the Truth and Certainty of the Christian Revelation.* In *A Discourse concerning the being and attributes of God . . . being Sixteen Sermons.* By Samuel Clarke. 3rd ed. London, 1711.

Cleghorn, William. *Dissertatio Philosophica Inauguralis, de Analogia et Philosophia Prima.* Edinburgh, 1739.

[Cleghorn, William]. *A Comparison of the Spirit and Principles of the Whigs and the Jacobites: Being the substance of a discourse delivered to an audience of gentlemen at Edinburgh, Dec. 24, 1745.* Edinburgh, 1746.

The Spirit and Principles of the Whigs and the Jacobites compared: Being the substance of a discourse delivered to an audience of gentlemen at Edinburgh, December 22, 1745. London, 1746.

Dreyhaupt, Johann Christoph von. *Pagus neletici et nudzici, oder diplomatisch – historische Beschreibung des Saal-Kreÿses.* Revised and expanded by Johann Friedrich Stiebritz. 2 vols. Halle, 1773.

Einem, Johann Justus von. *Martini Lutheri poemata.* Magdeburg, 1729.

An Essay to Prevent the Dangerous Consequences of the Moral Harangues, Now so common in Scotland. Glasgow, 1746.

Ferguson, Adam. "An Excursion in the Highlands: Discourse on Various Subjects." In *Collection of Essays*, by Adam Ferguson. Edited with an introduction by Yasuo Amoh. Kyoto: Rinsen, 1996.

⸻ *The History of the Progress and Termination of the Roman Republic.* 3 vols. London, 1783.

[Ferguson, Adam]. Obituary of William Cleghorn. *Edinburgh Evening Courant* 5958 (26 August 1754): [3].

Francke, August Hermann. *Einleitung zur Lesung Heiliger Schrift.* In *Schriften zur biblischen Hermeneutik.* Vol. 1. Edited by E. Peschke. Berlin: Walter de Gruyter, 2003.

⸻ *Instruction für die Praeceptores, was sie bei der Disciplin wohl zu beachten haben.* In *Pädagogische Schriften*, by A. H. Francke. Edited by Hermann Lorenzen. Paderborn: Schöningh, 1957.

⸻ *Kurzer und Einfältiger Unterricht wie die Kinder zur wahren Gottseligkeit und Christlichen Klugheit anzuführen sind, zum Behuff Christlicher Informatorum entworffen.* Halle, 1733.

⸻ *Lectiones paraeneticae.* Vol. 1. 2nd ed. Halle, 1730.

⸻ *Manuductio ad lectionem scripturae sacrae.* In *Schriften zur biblischen Hermeneutik.* Vol. 1. Edited by E. Peschke. Berlin: Walter de Gruyter, 2003.

Franckenstein, Jacob August. *Introduction to Discours über Buddei ... Philosophiae Practicae Pt. III. die Politic*, by N. H. Gundling. Leipzig, 1733.

Freylinghausen, Johann Anastasius, and Gotthilf August Francke. *Ausführlicher Bericht von der Lateinischen Schule des Wäysenhauses yu Glaucha vor Halle zum Dienst derer die Nachfrage zu tun pflegen.* Halle, 1736.

Fordyce, David. "A brief Account of the Nature, Progress, and Origin of Philosophy delivered by the late Mr. David Fordyce, P. P. Marishal College, Aberdeen to his Scholars, before they begun their Philosophical course. Anno 1743/4." In *The Elements of Moral Philosophy, in Three Books, with A Brief Account of the Nature, Progress, and Origin of Philosophy*, by David Fordyce. Edited by Thomas Kennedy. Indianapolis, IN: Liberty Fund, 2003.

Gale, Thomas. *Opuscula mythologica, physica et ethica.* Amsterdam, 1688.

Glassius, Salomon. *Philologia Sacra.* Leipzig, 1705.

Gordon, Charles Hamilton, and Joseph Williamson. *Memorial for the Reverend Mr William Leechman.* [Glasgow], 1744.

The Greek New Testament. Edited by Kurt Aland et al. Stuttgart: Württemberg Bible Society, 1966.

Gundling, Nicolaus Hieronymus. *Discours über Buddei ... Philosophiae Practicae Pt. III. die Politic.* Leipzig, 1733.

⸻ "Ob die natürliche Gesetze von dem Wesen der menschlichen Natur, oder von dem göttlichen Willen entstanden." *Gundlingiana* 33 (1724): 275–92.

⸻ *Philosophischer Discourse ... oder Academische Vorlesungen uber seine Viam ad veritatem moralem und Kulpisii Collegium Grotianum.* Frankfurt (Main), 1740.

⸻ *Via ad veritatem iurisprudentiae naturalis.* Halle, 1714.

[Gundling, Nicolaus Hieronymus]. *Aufrichtiges Sendschreiben eines Gundlingischen Zuhörers an Herrn Christoph August Heumann . . . darinnen er den ungezogenen Auctorem Salebrarum nach Verdiensten züchtiget. . . .* Alt-Rannstadt, 1713.

[Nicolas Veridicus Impartialis Bohemus, pseud.]. *Unpartheyisches Sendschreiben.* Wittenberg [Halle], 1724.

Hamilton, Gilbert. Letter to Alexander Hamilton. In Appendix 8 of *Hamilton's Itinerarium.* Edited by Albert Bushnell Hart. Saint Louis, MO: William K. Bixby, 1907.

Hartmann, Georg Volckmar. *Anleitung zur Historie der Leibnitzisch-Wolffischen Philosophie.* Leipzig, 1737. Reprint, Hildesheim: Olms, 1973.

Hempel, Christian Friedrich. *Nicolai Hieronymi Gundlings Umständliches Leben und Schriften.* Leipzig, [1736].

Herder, Johann Gottfried. "Entwurf zu einer Denkschrift auf Alexander Gottlieb Baumgarten, Johann David Heilmann, und Thomas Abbt" and "Von Baumgartens Denkart in seinen Schriften." In *Sämmtliche Werke*, by J. G. Herder. Vol. 32. Edited by Bernhardt Suphan. Berlin, 1899.

[Heugh, Hugh]. *Shaftesbury's Ghost conjur'd.* Glasgow, 1738.

Home, John. *Dissertatio Philosophica Inauguralis, de Respublica et Imperio Civili.* Edinburgh, 1742.

History of Rebellion in the Year 1745. London, 1802.

Hume, David. *Essays Moral, Political, and Literary.* Edited by Eugene F. Miller. Indianapolis, IN: Liberty Fund, 1985.

The Letters of David Hume. Edited by J. Y. T. Grieg. Vol. 1 of 2, *1727–1765.* Oxford: Oxford University Press, 1932.

A Treatise of Human Nature. Edited with an introduction by David Fate Norton and Mary J. Norton. Oxford: Oxford University Press, 2000.

Hutcheson, Francis. *De Naturali Hominum Socialitate.* In *On Human Nature.* Edited and translated with an introduction by Thomas Mautner. Cambridge: Cambridge University Press, 1993.

An Essay on the Nature and Conduct of the Passions and Affections, with Illustrations on the Moral Sense. 3rd ed. London, 1742. Reprint, with an introduction by Paul McReynolds. Gainesville, FL: Scholars' Facsimiles and Reprints, 1969.

An Inquiry into the Original of our Ideas of Beauty and Virtue. 1st ed. London, 1725. Reprint, Hildesheim: Olms, 1971.

An Inquiry into the Original of our Ideas of Beauty and Virtue. 4th ed. London, 1738. Reprint, Westmead, England: Gregg, 1969.

An Inquiry into the Original of our Ideas of Beauty and Virtue. Edited by Wolfgang Leidhold. Indianapolis, IN: Liberty Fund, 2004.

Letters between the late Mr. Gilbert Burnet and Mr. Hutchinson. London, 1735.

Philosophiae moralis institutio compendiara ethices et jurisprudentiae naturalis elementa continens, Lib. III. 1st ed. Glasgow, 1742.

Philosophiae moralis institutio compendiara ethices et jurisprudentiae naturalis elementa continens, Lib. III. 2nd ed. Glasgow, 1745.

Philosophiae moralis institutio compendiara ethices et jurisprudentiae naturalis elementa continens, Lib. III. Translated into English. 2nd ed. Glasgow, 1753.

"Reflections on the Common Systems of Morality." In *On Human Nature.* Edited and translated with an introduction by Thomas Mautner. Cambridge: Cambridge University Press, 1993.

A System of Moral Philosophy, in Three Books. 2 vols. London, 1755. Reprint in *The Collected Works of Francis Hutcheson.* Vols. 5 and 6. Edited by Bernhard Fabian. Hildesheim: Olms, 1969.

Kahle, Ludwig Martin, praes. *Dissertatio philosophica de decoro.* Halle, 1735.

Kippis, Andrew. *The Life of John Pringle.* In *Six Discourses,* by John Pringle. London, 1783.

König, Johann David. *Kürzester und leichtester Weg, die Grundsätze und Beschaffenheit einer grundlichen Moral und Politic zu erlernen.* Leipzig, 1723.

Lange, Joachim. *Hundert und Dreyßig Fragen aus der neuen Mechanischen Philosophie.* Halle, 1734. Reprint, Hildesheim: Olms, 1999.

Lasius, Hermann Jacob. Review of *Meditationes,* by A. G. Baumgarten. In *Critischer Versuch zur Aufnahme der Deutschen Sprache 6.* Greifswald, 1742.

Lau, Samuel. "Erbauungs- und Gedächtniß-Rede." In *Wernigerodisches Denckmal.* Wernigerode, 1734.

[Le Clerc, Jean]. *Five Letters Concerning the Inspiration of the Holy Scriptures.* London, 1690.

Parrhasiana. London, 1700.

Leechman, William. Preface to *A System of Moral Philosophy, in Three Books,* by Francis Hutcheson. London, 1755.

Leibniz, Georg Wilhelm. "Meditations on Knowledge, Truth, and Ideas." Translated and edited by Roger Ariew and Daniel Garber. In *Philosophical Essays,* by G. W. Leibniz. Indianapolis, IN: Hackett, 1989.

Philosophische Schriften. Edited by C. I. Gerhardt. 7 vols. Berlin, 1875–90.

[Lindsay, G.] *Some Observations on these Two Sermons of Doctor Wishart's, Which have given Offence to the Presbytery of Edinburgh.* Edinburgh, 1737.

Locke, John. *An Essay Concerning Human Understanding.* Edited by Peter H. Nidditch. Oxford: Oxford University Press, 1975.

[Löscher, Valentin Ernst]. Review of *Johann Jacob Rambachs geistliche Poesien. Unschuldige Nachrichten von Alten und Neuen Theologischen Sachen,* 1736.

Ludovici, Carl Gunther. *Ausführlicher Entwurf einer vollständigen Historie der Wolffischen Philosophie.* 3 vols. Leipzig, 1737–38. Reprint, Hildesheim: Olms, 2003.

Mandeville, Bernard. *The Fable of the Bees.* Edited with an introduction and notes by F. B. Kaye. 2 vols. Oxford: Oxford University Press, 1924.

Meier, Georg Friedrich. *Alexander Gottlieb Baumgartens Leben.* Halle, 1763.

Mendelssohn, Moses. Review of *Auszug aus den Anfangsgründen aller schönen Künste und Wissenschaften,* by G. F. Meier. In *Ästhetische Schriften,* by M. Mendelssohn. Edited by Anne Pollok. Hamburg: Meiner, 2006.

Michaelis, Christian Benedict. [Review of dissertation by Johann Christian Meisner.] *Wöchentliche Hallesche Anzeigen* XXXV (24 August 1733): 553–56.

Review of *Dissertatio chorographica*, by A. G. Baumgarten. *Wöchentliche Hallesche Anzeigen* XI (14 March 1735): 166–71; and XII (21 March 1735): 181–85.

Molesworth, Robert. *An Account of Denmark, as it was in the Year 1692*. London, 1694. Reprint, Copenhagen: Rosenkilde and Bagger, 1976.

Morren, Nathaniel. *Annals of the General Assembly of the Church of Scotland, from the Final Secession in 1739, to the Origin of the Relief in 1752*. Vol. 1 of 2. Edinburgh: John Johnstone, 1838.

Niemeier, Johann Barthold, praes. *Disputatio ethica ... de stoicorum ἀπαθεία*. Helmstadt, 1679.

Pasor, Georg. *Lexicon Graeco-Latinum In Novum Domini Nostri Jesu Christi Testamentum*. Leipzig, 1686.

Pollio, Lucas. *Pathologia sive de affectibus*. Leipzig, 1678.

Pritius, Johann Georg. *De renatorum experientia spirituali*. 2nd ed. Jena, 1723.

Profe, Gottfried, praes. *De affectibus demonstratio philosophica*. Halle, 1739.

Mathesis philosophiae filia, non mater. Halle, 1738.

Obituary of William Cleghorn. *Scots Magazine* XVI (August 1754): 404.

Quistorp, Theodor Johann. "Erweiß, daß die Poesie schon für sich selbst ihre Liebhaber leichtlich unglückselig machen könne." In *Frühe Schriften zur ästhetischen Erziehung der Deutschen*. Vol. 2 of 3. Edited by Hans-Joachim Kertscher and Günter Schenk. Halle (Saale): Hallescher, 1999.

Rambach, Johann Jakob. *Gedächtniß-Rede von dem Geheimniß der Evangelischen Weisheit*. 2nd ed. Halle, 1732.

Institutiones hermeneuticae sacrae. Jena, 1723.

Erläuterung über seine eigene Institutiones hermeneuticae sacrae. Edited by Ernst Friedrich Neubauer. Giessen, 1738.

Poetische Fest-Gedancken von den höchsten Wohlthaten Gottes. Jena, 1727.

Ramsay, Andrew Michael. *The Travels of Cyrus, In two volumes, to which is annex'd, A discourse on the theology and mythology of the ancients*. 2 vols. London, 1727.

Reichius, Joannes, praes. *Disputatio moralis de nature et indole adfectuum*. Halle, 1700.

Review of *A Treatise of Human Nature*, Book III, by David Hume. *Bibliothèque Raisonnée* 26.2 (April–June 1741): 411–27.

Review of *A Treatise of Human Nature*, Book III, by David Hume. *Bibliothèque Raisonnée* 26.2 (April–June 1741): 411–27. Translated by James Fieser. In *Early Responses to Hume's Moral, Literary and Political Writings, I. Hume's Moral Philosophy*. Edited by J. Fieser. Bristol: Thoemmes, 1999.

Robe, John. *An Appendix to Mr. Robe's Historical and Remarking Paper; Vindicating the Late Act of Assembly, concerning Mr. Leechman's Affair*. Edinburgh, 1744.

Schmidt, Johann Andreas, praes. *Dissertatio historico-theologica de modo propagandi religionem per carmina*. Def. Ludovicus Guntherus Gelhud. Helmstadt, 1710.

[Schneider, Johann Friedemann.] *Salebrae in via ad veritatem*. N.p., n.d.

Shaftesbury, Anthony Ashley Cooper, third Earl of. *Characteristicks of Men, Manners, Opinions, Times.* Edited by Philip Ayres. 2 vols. Oxford: Oxford University Press, 1999.

Characteristics of Men, Manners, Opinions, Times. Edited by Lawrence E. Klein. Cambridge: Cambridge University Press, 1999.

Letters. In *The Life, Unpublished Letters, and Philosophical Regimen of Anthony, Earl of Shaftesbury.* Edited by Benjamin Rand. London: Swan Sonnenschein, 1900.

Second Characters. Edited by Benjamin Rand. Cambridge: Cambridge University Press, 1914.

"A Short Account of the University of Edinburgh." *Scots Magazine* III (August 1741): 371–74.

Stolle, Gottlieb. *Anleitung zur Historie der Gelahrheit, denen zum besten, so den freyen Künsten und der Philosophie obliegen.* 3 vols. Jena, 1727.

Supplement to the Fourth, Fifth, and Sixth Editions of the Encyclopaedia Britannica. Edited by Dugald Stewart et al. Vol. 4 of 6. Edinburgh, 1824. S.v. "Ferguson (Adam, LL.D.)."

Thomasius, Christian. *Grundlehren des Natur- und Völkerrechts.* Translated by Johann Gottfried Zeidler. Halle, 1709. Reprint, Hildesheim: Olms, 2003.

A Vindication of Mr. Hutcheson from the Calumnious Aspersions of a Late Pamphlet, by Several of His Scholars. Glasgow, 1738.

Walch, Johann Georg. *Bescheidene Antwort auf Herrn Christian Wolffs Anmerkungen.* Jena, 1724.

Philosophisches Lexikon. Leipzig, 1726.

Weger, Laurentius. *Pathologia generalis sive de affectibus in genere dissertatio.* Königsberg, 1627.

Wishart, William. "Copy [of] Letter, or Speech, intended: and Letter to John Forrest. June 5, 1745." Transcribed and expanded by M. A. Stewart as "The Wishart Speedhand." In M. A. Stewart, *The Kirk and the Infidel: An Inaugural Lecture delivered at Lancaster University on 9 November 1994.* Corrected ed. Lancaster: Lancaster University, 2001.

The certain and unchangeable Difference betwixt Moral Good and Evil, a Sermon Preach'd before the Societies for Reformation of Manners, at Salters-Hall; on Monday the 3d of July, 1732. London, 1732.

[Wishart, William]. *A Vindication of the Reverend D—— B———y, from The scandalous Imputation of being Author of a late Book, intitled, Alciphron, or, the minute Philosopher.* London, 1734.

Wodrow, James. "The Life of Dr. Leechman, with some Account of his Lectures." In *Sermons,* by William Leechman. Vol. 1 of 2. London, 1789.

Wodrow, Robert. *Analecta, or Materials for a history of remarkable providences mostly relating to Scotch ministers and Christians.* Edited by Matthew Leisman. 4 vols. Edinburgh: printed for the Maitland Club, 1842–43.

Wolff, Christian. *Discursus preliminaris de philosophia in genere.* Frankfurt (Main), 1732.

Philosophia moralis sive ethica. Halle, 1753.

Psychologia empirica. Leipzig, 1738. Reprint, Hildesheim: Olms, 1968.

Vernünfftige Gedancken von der Menschen Thun und Lassen, zu Beförderung ihrer Glückseeligkeit [= *Deutsche Ethik*]. 4th ed. Frankfurt (Main) and Leipzig, 1733. Reprint, Hildesheim: Olms, 1996.

Vernünfftige Gedancken von Gott, der Welt und der Seele des Menschen, auch allen Dingen überhaupt [= *Deutsche Metaphysik*]. 11th ed. Halle, 1751. Reprint, Hildesheim: Olms, 2003.

Zedler, Johann Heinrich. *Grosses vollständiges Universal-Lexicon aller Wissenschaften und Künste.* Halle, 1732.

Zimmermann, Johann Liborius. *De actionum humanarum moralitate, legibusque stricte dictis.* Jena, 1728.

Das evangelische Predigt-Amt, wie es denen Menschen zur Seligkeit gereichen soll. Wernigerode, 1728.

"Gründliche Anweisung zum eigenen Nachsinnen." In *Kurzer Abriß einer Vollständigen Vernunft-Lehre.* Jena, 1730.

Natürliche Erkenntnis Gottes, der Welt und des Menschen. Jena, 1730.

Die Überschwengliche Erkenntnis Jesu Christi. Halle, 1731.

The Excellency of the Knowledge of Jesus Christ. London, 1772.

SECONDARY SOURCES

Adler, Hans. *Die Prägnanz des Dunklen: Gnoseologie, Ästhetik, Geschichtsphilosophie bei Johann Gottfried Herder.* Hamburg: Meiner, 1990.

Aesthetics. Produced by Camila O'Donnell. Directed by Pablo Garcia. 51 min. Films for the Humanities and Sciences, 2004. Digital video disc.

Ahnert, Thomas. *The Moral Culture of the Scottish Enlightenment, 1690–1805.* New Haven, CT: Yale University Press, 2014.

"The Moral Education of Mankind: Character and Religious Moderatism in the Sermons of Hugh Blair." In *Character, Self, and Sociability in the Scottish Enlightenment.* Edited by Thomas Ahnert and Susan Manning. New York: Palgrave, 2011.

Religion and the Origins of the German Enlightenment. Rochester, NY: University of Rochester Press, 2006.

Aichele, Alexander. Introduction to *Gedancken vom Vernünfftigen Beyfall auf Academien*, by A. G. Baumgarten. *Aufklärung* 20 (2008): 271–82.

Aldridge, A. O. "Shaftesbury and the Deist Manifesto." *Transactions of the American Philosophical Society* 41 (1951): 297–382.

Amoh, Yasuo. Introduction to *Collection of Essays*, by Adam Ferguson. Kyoto: Rinsen, 1996.

Aner, Karl. *Die Theologie der Lessingzeit.* Halle: Niemeyer, 1929.

Aronson, Jason. "Critical Note: Shaftesbury on Locke." *American Political Science Review* 53.4 (1959): 1101–4.

Aschenbrenner, Karl, and William B. Holther. Introduction to *Reflections on Poetry*, by A. G. Baumgarten. Berkeley: University of California Press, 1954.

Dictionary of Eighteenth-Century British Philosophers. Edited by John W. Yolton, John Valdimir Price, and John Stephens. 2 vols. Bristol: Thoemmes, 1999.

Dictionary of National Biography. Edited by L. Stephen and S. Lee. 22 vols. London: Oxford University Press, 1922.

Dictionary of National Biography. Edited by H. C. G. Matthew and Brian Harrison. 61 vols. Oxford: Oxford University Press, 2004.

Dussinger, John A. "'The Lovely System of Lord Shaftesbury': An Answer to Locke in the Aftermath of 1688?" *Journal of the History of Ideas* 42.1 (1981): 151–58.

Dwyer, Philip G. *The Rise of Prussia, 1700–1830*. Harlow: Pearson, 2000.

Dyck, Joachim. *Die Tradition der argumentativen Verknüpfung von Bibel und Poesie im 17. und 18. Jahrhundert*. Munich: Beck, 1977.

Eagleton, Terry. *Ideology of the Aesthetic*. Princeton, NJ: Princeton University Press, 1990.

Eco, Umberto. *Art and Beauty in the Middle Ages*. Translated by Hugh Bredin. New Haven, CT: Yale University Press, 1986.

Emerson, Roger L. "The 'Affair' at Edinburgh and the 'Project' at Glasgow: The Politics of Hume's Attempts to Become a Professor." In *Hume and Hume's Connexions*. Edited by M. A. Stewart and John P. Wright. Edinburgh: Edinburgh University Press, 1994.

"The Philosophical Society of Edinburgh, 1737–1747." *British Journal for the History of Science* 12.2 (1979): 154–91.

Encyclopedia of Aesthetics. 2nd ed. Edited by Michael Kelly. Oxford: Oxford University Press, 2014.

Fabian, Bernard. "English Books and Their Eighteenth-Century German Readers." In *Selecta Anglicana: Buchgeschichtliche Studien zur Aufnahme der englischen Literatur in Deutschland im achtzehnten Jahrhundert*, by B. Fabian. Wiesbaden: Harrassowitz, 1994.

Federlin, Wilhelm-Ludwig. *Kirchliche Volksbildung und bürgerliche Gesellschaft: Studien zu Thomas Abbt, Alexander Gottlieb Baumgarten, Johann David Heilmann, Johann Gottfried Herder, Johann Georg Müller und Johannes von Müller*. New York: Peter Lang, 1993.

Fehr, James Jakob. *"Ein wunderlicher nexus rerum": Aufklärung und Pietismus in Königsberg unter Franz Albert Schultz*. Hildesheim: Olms, 2005.

Fowler, Thomas. *Shaftesbury and Hutcheson*. London, 1882.

Franke, Ursula. *Kunst als Erkenntnis: Die Rolle der Sinnlichkeit in der Aesthetik des Alexander Gottlieb Baumgarten*. Studia Leibnitiana. Suppl. vol. 9. Wiesbaden, 1972.

Frängsmyr, Tore. "Christian Wolff's Mathematical Method and Its Impact on the Eighteenth Century." *Journal of the History of Ideas* 36.4 (1975): 653–68.

Friday, Jonathan, ed. Introduction to *Art and Enlightenment: Scottish Aesthetics in the Eighteenth Century*. Charlottesville, VA: Imprint Academic, 2004.

Fritz, Martin. *Vom Erhabenen*. Tübingen: Mohr Siebeck, 2011.

Frontius, Martin. "Baumgarten und die *Literaturbriefe*: Ein Brief aus Frankfurt/Oder an Louis de Beausobre in Berlin." *Deutsche Vierteljahrsschrift für Literaturwissenschaft und Geistesgeschichte* 80.4 (2006): 553–94.

Gawlick, Günter, and Lothar Kreimandahl, eds. Introduction to *Metaphysica*, by Alexander Baumgarten. Stuttgart-Bad Cannstatt: Frommann-Holzboog, 2011.

Geschichte der Universität Jena. 2 vols. Jena: Gustav Fischer, 1958.

Glauser, Richard. "Aesthetic Experience in Shaftesbury. Pt. I." *The Aristotelian Society*, suppl. vol. 76 (2002): 25–54.

Golden, Samuel L. *Jean LeClerc*. New York: Twayne, 1972.

Goldenbaum, Ursula. "Mendelssohn's Spinozistic Alternative to Baumgarten's Pietist Project of Aesthetics." In *Moses Mendelssohn's Metaphysics and Aesthetics*. Edited by Rainier Munk. New York: Springer, 2011.

Grant, Alexander. *Story of the University of Edinburgh during its first three hundred years*. 2 vols. London, 1884.

Greene, Robert A. "Instinct of Nature: Natural Law, Synderesis, and the Moral Sense." *Journal of the History of Ideas* 58.2 (1997): 173–98.

Greschat, Martin. *Zwischen Tradition und neuem Anfang: Valentin Löscher und der Ausgang der lutherischen Orthodoxie*. Wittenberg: Luther, 1971.

Gross, Steffen. *Cognitio Sensitiva*. Würzburg: Königshausen und Neumann, 2011.

Felix Aestheticus. Die Aesthetik als Lehre vom Menschen. Würzburg: Königshausen und Neumann, 2001.

"The Neglected Programme of Aesthetics." *British Journal of Aesthetics* 42.4 (2002): 403–13.

Grote, Simon. "Hutcheson's Divergence from Shaftesbury." *Journal of Scottish Philosophy* 4.2 (2006): 159–72.

The Moral Philosophy of William Cleghorn. MPhil dissertation. Cambridge University, 2005.

"Pietistische *Aisthesis* und moralische Erziehung bei Alexander Gottlieb Baumgarten." *Aufklärung* 20 (2008): 175–98.

"Religion and Enlightenment Revisited: Lucas Geiger (1682–1750) and the Allure of Wolffian Philosophy in a Pietist Orphanage." *Pietismus und Neuzeit* 41 (2015): 32–56.

"Shaftesbury's Egoistic Hedonism." *Aufklärung* 22 (2010): 135–49.

"Vom geistlichen zum guten Geschmack? Reflexionen zur Suche nach den pietistischen Wurzeln der Ästhetik." Translated by Claudia Drese. In *Schönes Denken: A. G. Baumgarten im Spannungsfeld zwischen Ästhetik, Logik und Ethik*. Edited by Andrea Allerkamp and Dagmar Mirbach. Hamburg: Meiner, 2016.

Grunert, Frank. Introduction to *Grundlehren des Natur- und Völkerrechts*, by Christian Thomasius. Hildesheim: Olms, 2003.

Guyer, Paul. "18th Century German Aesthetics." In *Stanford Encyclopedia of Philosophy*. Fall 2008 ed. Edited by Edward N. Zalta. http://plato.stanford.edu/archives/fall2008/entries/aesthetics-18th-german/.

A History of Modern Aesthetics. 3 vols. New York: Cambridge University Press, 2014.

Values of Beauty: Historical Essays in Aesthetics. Cambridge: Cambridge University Press, 2005.

Haakonssen, Knud. "German Natural Law Theory." In *The Cambridge History of Eighteenth-Century Political Thought.* Edited by Mark Goldie and Robert Wokler. Cambridge: Cambridge University Press, 2006.

"Natural Jurisprudence and the Identity of the Scottish Enlightenment." In *Philosophy and Religion in Enlightenment Britain: New Case Studies.* Edited by Ruth Savage. Oxford: Oxford University Press, 2012.

Natural Law and Moral Philosophy from Grotius to the Scottish Enlightenment. Cambridge: Cambridge University Press, 1996.

"Protestant Natural Law Theory: A General Interpretation." In *New Essays on the History of Autonomy: A Collection Honoring J. B. Schneewind.* Edited by Natalie Brender and Larry Krasnoff. Cambridge: Cambridge University Press, 2004.

Hammermeister, Kai. *The German Aesthetic Tradition.* Cambridge: Cambridge University Press, 2002.

Harris, James A. "The Early Reception of Hume's Theory of Justice." In *Philosophy and Religion in Enlightenment Britain: New Case Studies.* Edited by Ruth Savage. Oxford: Oxford University Press, 2012.

Hartung, Gerald. *Die Naturrechtsdebatte: Geschichte der Obligatio von 17. bis 20. Jahrhundert.* Freiburg: K. Alber, 1998.

Haubrich, Joachim. *Die Begriffe "Schönheit" und "Vollkommenheit" in der Ästhetik des 18. Jahrhunderts.* PhD dissertation. University of Mainz, 1998.

Hazard, Paul. *European Thought in the Eighteenth Century.* Translated by J. Lewis May. Cleveland, OH: Meridian Books, 1963.

Heimann, Mary. "Christianity in Western Europe from the Enlightenment." In *A World History of Christianity.* Edited by Adrian Hastings. Grand Rapids, MI: Eerdmans, 1999.

Henrich, Dieter. *Aesthetic Judgment and the Moral Image of the World: Studies in Kant.* Stanford, CA: Stanford University Press, 1992.

Hess, Jonathan. *Reconstructing the Body Politic.* Detroit, MI: Wayne State University Press, 1999.

Heussi, Karl. *Geschichte der theologischen Fakultät zu Jena.* Weimar: Böhlau, 1954.

Hinrichs, Carl. *Preussentum und Pietismus.* Göttingen: Vandenhoeck und Ruprecht, 1971.

Hochstrasser, T. J. *Natural Law Theories in the Early Enlightenment.* Cambridge: Cambridge University Press, 2000.

Holloran, Jonathan. *Professors of Enlightenment at the University of Halle, 1690–1730.* PhD dissertation. University of Virginia, 2000.

Holzhey, Helmut. "Christian Thomasius und der Beginn der deutschen Aufklärung." In *Grundriß der Geschichte der Philosophie: die Philosophie des 17. Jahrhunderts.* Vol. 4. *Das heilige Römische Reich.* Edited by H. Holzhey and W. Schmidt-Biggemann. Basel: Schwabe, 2001.

Horlacher, Rebekka. *Bildungstheorie vor der Bildungstheorie: Die Shaftesbury-Rezeption in Deutschland und der Schweiz im 18. Jahrhundert.* Würzburg: Königshausen und Neumann, 2004.

Hüning, Dieter. "Christian Wolffs Begriff der natürlichen Verbindlichkeit als Bindeglied zwischen Psychologie und Moralphilosophie." In *Die Psychologie Christian Wolffs*. Edited by Oliver-Pierre Rudolph and Jean-François Goubet. Hallesche Beiträge zur Europäischen Aufklärung 22. Tübingen: Niemeyer, 2004.

Hunter, Ian. "Multiple Enlightenments: Rival Aufklärer at the University of Halle, 1690–1730." In *The Enlightenment World*. Edited by Martin Fitzpatrick, Peter Jones, Christa Knellwolf, and Iain McCalman. London: Routledge, 2004.

———. *Rival Enlightenments: Civil and Metaphysical Philosophy in Early Modern Germany*. Cambridge: Cambridge University Press, 2001.

Israel, Jonathan. *Radical Enlightenment*. Oxford: Oxford University Press, 2001.

Jacob, Joachim. *Heilige Poesie*. Tübingen: Niemeyer, 1997.

Jacobs, Ed. "Johann Liborius Zimmermann und die pietistische Bewegung in Wernigerode." *Zeitschrift des Harz-Vereins für Geschichte und Altertumskunde* 31 (1898): 121–226.

Jones, Peter. "The Scottish Professoriate and the Polite Academy, 1720–46." In *Wealth and Virtue: The Shaping of Political Economy in the Scottish Enlightenment*. Edited by Istvan Hont and Michael Ignatieff. New York: Cambridge University Press, 1983.

Kang, Chi-Won. *Frömmigkeit und Gelehrsamkeit: die Reform des Theologiestudiums im lutherischen Pietismus des 17. und des frühen 18. Jahrhunderts*. Gießen: Brunnen, 2001.

Kennedy, Thomas D. "William Leechman, Pulpit Eloquence and the Glasgow Enlightenment." In *The Glasgow Enlightenment*. Edited by A. Hook and R. B. Sher. Phantassie: Tuckwell, 1995.

Kinnaman, Ted. "Aesthetics before Kant." In *A Companion to Early Modern Philosophy*. Edited by Steven Nadler. Malden, MA: Blackwell, 2002.

Kittsteiner, Heinz D. *Die Entstehung des modernen Gewissens*. Frankfurt (Main): Suhrkamp, 1995.

Kivy, Peter. "The 'Sense' of Beauty and the Sense of 'Art': Hutcheson's Place in the History and Practice of Aesthetics." *Journal of Aesthetics and Art Criticism* 53 (1995): 349–57.

Klein, Lawrence E. *Shaftesbury and the Culture of Politeness: Moral Discourse and Cultural Politics in Early Eighteenth-Century England*. Cambridge: Cambridge University Press, 1994.

Kliche, Dieter. "Die Institutionalisierung der Ästhetik." In *Ästhetische Grundbegriffe*. Edited by Karlheinz Barck et al. Stuttgart: Metzler, 2000. S.v. "Ästhetik/ästhetisch."

Kristeller, Paul Oskar. "The Modern System of the Arts." *Journal of the History of Ideas* 12 (1951): 496–527 and 13 (1952): 17–46.

Koch, Ernst. "De Theologia experimentali. Akademische Diskurse um 1700 in Leipzig, Halle und Wittenberg." In *"Aus Gottes Wort und eigener Erfahrung gezeigt": Erfahrung – Glauben, Erkennen und Handeln im Pietismus. Beiträge zum III. Internationalen Kongress für Pietismusforschung*. Edited by Christian Soboth and Udo Sträter. Halle: Franckesche Stiftungen, 2012.

Linn, Marie-Luise. "A. G. Baumgartens 'Aesthetica' und die antike Rhetorik." *Deutsche Vierteljahrsschrift für Literaturwissenschaft und Geistesgeschichte* 41.3 (1967): 424–43.

Lodewigs, Siegfried. *Der Pietismus im Spiegel seiner theologischen Kritiker.* PhD dissertation. University of Göttingen, 1972.

Lütteken, Anett, and Barbara Mahlmann-Bauer, eds. *Johann Jakob Bodmer und Johann Jakob Breitinger im Netzwerk der europäischen Aufklärung.* Göttingen: Wallstein, 2009.

Mackenzie, Henry. "Account of the Life and Writings of John Home." In *Works.* By John Home. Vol. 1 of 3. Edinburgh, 1822.

Mackintosh, James. "Preface to a Reprint of the *Edinburgh Review.*" In *Miscellaneous Works of the Right Honourable Sir James Mackintosh.* Vol. 2 of 3. London, 1854.

Martens, Wolfgang. *Literatur und Frömmigkeit in der Zeit der frühen Aufklärung.* Tübingen: Niemeyer, 1989.

Martineau, James. *Types of Ethical Theory.* 2 vols. 3rd rev. ed. Oxford: Oxford University Press, 1901.

McElroy, Davis D. *Scotland's Age of Improvement: A Survey of Eighteenth-Century Literary Clubs and Societies.* Pullman: Washington State University Press, 1969.

McManners, John. "Enlightenment: Secular and Christian (1600–1800)." In *The Oxford Illustrated History of Christianity.* Edited by J. McManners. Oxford: Oxford University Press, 1990.

Menck, Peter. *Die Erziehung der Jugend zur Ehre Gottes und zum Nutzen des Nächsten: Die Pädagogik August Hermann Franckes.* Tübingen: Niemeyer, 2001.

Menke, Christoph. *The Sovereignty of Art.* Translated by Neil Solomon. Cambridge, MA: MIT Press, 1998.

Miersemann, Wolfgang. "Ein 'Liebes-Poet' als geistlicher Dichter: Zu dem Menantes- Gedicht 'Bey Betrachtung der Liebe Gottes'." In *Menantes: Ein Dichterleben zwischen Barock und Aufklärung.* Edited by Cornelia Hobohn. Jena: Quartus, 2006.

Mirbach, Dagmar. "*Ingenium venustum* und *magnitudo pectoris*: Ethische Aspekte von Alexander Gottlieb Baumgartens *Aesthetica.*" *Aufklärung* 20 (2008): 199–218.

Moore, James. "Evangelical Calvinists versus the Hutcheson Circle: Debating the Faith in Scotland, 1738–1739." In *Debating the Faith: Religion and Letter Writing in Great Britain, 1550–1800.* Edited by A. Dunan-Page and C. Prunier. Dordrecht, Netherlands: Springer, 2013.

"Hume and Hutcheson." In *Hume and Hume's Connexions.* Edited by M. A. Stewart and John P. Wright. Edinburgh: Edinburgh University Press, 1994.

"Hutcheson's Theodicy: The Argument and the Contexts of a System of Moral Philosophy." In *The Scottish Enlightenment: Essays in Reinterpretation.* Edited by Paul Wood. Rochester: University of Rochester Press, 2000.

"Natural Rights in the Scottish Enlightenment." In *The Cambridge History of Eighteenth-Century Political Thought.* Edited by Mark Goldie and Robert Wokler. Cambridge: Cambridge University Press, 2006.

Preface to *Logicae Compendium*, by Francis Hutcheson. In *Logic, Metaphysics, and the Natural Sociability of Mankind*. Edited by James Moore and Michael Silverthorne. Indianapolis, IN: Liberty Fund, 2006.

"Presbyterianism and the Right of Private Judgment: Church Government in Ireland and Scotland in the Age of Francis Hutcheson." In *Philosophy and Religion in Enlightenment Britain: New Case Studies*. Edited by Ruth Savage. Oxford: Oxford University Press, 2012.

"A Scots-Irish Bookseller in Holland: William Smith of Amsterdam (1698–1741)." *Eighteenth-Century Scotland: The Newsletter of the Eighteenth-Century Scottish Studies Society* 7 (Spring 1993): 8–11.

"The Two Systems of Francis Hutcheson: On the Origins of the Scottish Enlightenment." In *Studies in the Philosophy of the Scottish Enlightenment*. Edited by M. A. Stewart. Oxford: Oxford University Press, 1990.

Moore, James, and M. A. Stewart. "William Smith and the Dissenters' Book Trade." *Bulletin of the Presbyterian Historical Society of Ireland* 22 (April 1993): 26–27.

Mossner, Ernest Campbell. *The Life of David Hume*. 2nd ed. Oxford: Oxford University Press, 1980.

Müller, Ernst. *Ästhetische Religiosität und Kunstreligion*. Berlin: Akademie, 2004.

Müller-Bahlke, Thomas. "Der Hallesche Pietismus und die Kunst: Bemerkungen zu einem alten Vorurteil." In *Das Echo Halles: Kulturelle Wirkungen des Pietismus*. Edited by Rainer Lächele. Tübingen: Niemeyer, 2001.

Mulsow, Martin. "Gundling vs. Buddeus." In *History and the Disciplines*. Edited by Donald Kelley. Rochester, NY: University of Rochester Press, 1997.

Moderne aus dem Untergrund. Hamburg: Meiner, 2002.

Munzel, G. Felicitas. *Kant's Conception of Moral Character*. Chicago: Chicago University Press, 1999.

Neugebauer, Wolfgang. "Brandenburg-Preusßen in der Frühen Neuzeit. Politik und Staatsbildung im 17. und 18. Jahrhundert." In *Handbuch der Preussischen Geschichte*. Edited by Wolfgang Neugebauer. Vol. 1. Berlin: Walter de Gruyter, 2009.

Nobbs, Douglas. "The Political Ideas of William Cleghorn, Hume's Academic Rival." *Journal of the History of Ideas* 26.4 (1965): 575–86.

Norton, David Fate. "Hume and Hutcheson: The Question of Influence." *Oxford Studies in Early Modern Philosophy* 2 (2005): 211–56.

Norton, David Fate, and Manfred Kuehn. "The Foundations of Morality." In *The Cambridge History of Eighteenth-Century Philosophy*. Edited by Knud Haakonssen. Vol. 2 of 2. Cambridge: Cambridge University Press, 2006.

Norton, Robert. *The Beautiful Soul: Aesthetic Morality in the Eighteenth Century*. Ithaca, NY: Cornell University Press, 1995.

Nüssel, Fredericke. Introduction to *Institutiones theologiae dogmaticae*, by J. F. Buddeus. Hildesheim: Olms, 1999.

Nuzzo, Angelica. *Ideal Embodiment: Kant's Theory of Sensibility*. Bloomington: Indiana University Press, 2008.

O'Connor, Thomas. *Irish Jansenists: Religion and Politics in Flanders, France, Ireland and Rome.* Dublin: Four Courts Press, 2008.

——. *An Irish Theologian in Enlightenment France: Luke Joseph Hooke 1714–96.* Dublin: Four Courts Press, 1995.

Osterwalder, Fritz. "Theologische Konzepte von Erziehung. Das Verhältnis von Fénelon und Francke." In *Das Kind im Pietismus und Aufklärung.* Edited by J. N. Neumann and U. Sträter. Tübingen: Niemeyer, 2000.

Oxford Classical Dictionary. 2nd ed. Edited by N. G. L. Hammond and H. H. Scullard. Oxford: Oxford University Press, 1970. Reprint, 1992.

Paton, Henry. *Scottish Record Society, Register of Marriages for the Parish of Edinburgh 1701–1750.* Edinburgh, 1908.

Peach, Bernard. "The Correspondence between Francis Hutcheson and Gilbert Burnet: The Problem of the Date." *Journal of the History of Philosophy* VIII.1 (January 1970): 87–91.

Pembroke, S. G. "Oikeiōsis." In *Problems in Stoicism.* Edited by Anthony A. Long. London: Athlone Press, 1971.

Peschke, Erhard. Introduction to *Manuductio ad lectionem scripturae sacrae.* In *Schriften zur biblischen Hermeneutik*, by A. H. Francke. Vol. 1. Berlin: Walter de Gruyter, 2003.

——. *Studien zur Theologie August Hermann Franckes.* 2 vols. Berlin: Evangelische Verlagsanstalt, 1966.

Peters, Hans Georg. *Die Ästhetik Alexander Gottlieb Baumgartens und ihre Beziehungen zum Ethischen.* Berlin: Junker, 1934.

Phillipson, Nicholas. "The Scottish Enlightenment." In *Enlightenment in National Context.* Edited by Roy Porter and Mikuláš Teich. Cambridge: Cambridge University Press, 1981.

Piselli, Francesco. "Ästhetik und Metaphysik bei Alexander Gottlieb Baumgarten." *Aufklärung* 20 (2008): 101–16.

Pocock, J. G. A. *Barbarism and Religion: The Enlightenments of Edward Gibbon, 1737–1764.* 4 vols. Cambridge: Cambridge University Press, 1999–2005.

Poppe, Bernhard. *Alexander Gottlieb Baumgarten: seine Bedeutung und Stellung in der Leibniz-Wolffischen Philosophie und seine Beziehungen zu Kant.* Münster, 1907.

Porter, James. "Is Art Modern? Kristeller's 'Modern System of the Arts' Reconsidered." *British Journal of Aesthetics* 49.1 (2009): 1–24.

——. "Reply to Shiner." *British Journal of Aesthetics* 49 (2009): 171–78.

——. "Why Art Has Never Been Autonomous." *Arethusa* 43 (2010): 165–80.

Poser, Hans. "Pietismus und Aufklärung – Glaubensgewißheit und Vernunfterkenntnis im Widerstreit." In *Aufklärung und Erneuerung.* Edited by Günter Jerouschek et al. Halle: Werner Dausien, 1994.

Probyn, Clive T. *The Sociable Humanist: The Life and Works of James Harris, 1709–1780.* Oxford: Oxford University Press, 1991.

Raabe, Karl. *A. G. Baumgarten aestheticae in disciplinae formam redactae parens et auctor.* PhD dissertation. University of Rostock, 1873.

Rae, John. *Life of Adam Smith.* London, 1895. Reprint, with an introduction by Jacob Viner, New York: Augustus M. Kelley, 1965.

Raphael, D. D. *The Moral Sense.* London: Oxford University Press, 1947.

Ratschow, Carl. *Lutherische Dogmatik zwischen Reformation und Aufklärung.* 2 vols. Gütersloh: Mohn, 1966.

Raynor, David R. "Hutcheson's Defence against the Charge of Plagiarism." *Eighteenth-Century Ireland* 2 (1987): 177–81.

Riemann, Albert. *Die Ästhetik Alexander Gottlieb Baumgartens unter besonderer Berücksichtigung der Meditationes philosophicae de nonnullis ad poema pertinentibus nebst einer Übersetzung dieser Schrift.* Halle: Max Niemeyer, 1928. Reprint, Tübingen: Max Niemeyer, 1973.

Rind, Miles. "The Concept of Disinterestedness in Eighteenth-Century British Aesthetics." *Journal of the History of Philosophy* 40.1 (2002): 67–87.

Rivers, Isabel. *Reason, Grace, and Sentiment.* 2 vols. Cambridge: Cambridge University Press, 1991–2000.

Rogers, Christine R. *The Role of Reason and Emotion in the Thought of Johann Jacob Bodmer and Johann Jacob Breitinger.* BLitt dissertation. Oxford University, 1965.

Romanell, Patrick. Introduction to *Guide to Aesthetics,* by Benedetto Croce. Indianapolis, IN: Hackett, 1965. Reprint, 1995.

Routledge Encyclopedia of Philosophy. Edited by Edward Craig. 10 vols. London: Routledge, 1998.

Rüping, Hinrich. "Budde und die Naturrechtslehre der Thomasius-Schule." In *Grundriß der Geschichte der Philosophie: die Philosophie des 17. Jahrhunderts.* Vol. 4. *Das heilige Römische Reich.* Edited by H. Holzhey and W. Schmidt-Biggemann. Basel: Schwabe, 2001.

"Christian Thomasius und seine Schule im Geistesleben des 18. Jahrhunderts." In *Recht und Rechtswissenschaft im mitteldeutschen Raum.* Edited by Heiner Lück. Köln: Böhlau, 1998.

Schloemann, Martin. *Siegmund Jacob Baumgarten: System und Geschichte in der Theologie des Überganges zum Neuprotestantismus.* Göttingen: Vandenhoeck und Ruprecht, 1974.

Schmitt, Wolfgang. *Die pietistische Kritik der "Künste."* PhD dissertation. Universität Köln, 1958.

Schneewind, J. B., ed. *Moral Philosophy from Montaigne to Kant.* Vol. 2. Cambridge: Cambridge University Press, 2003.

Schneider, Ferdinand Josef. "Das geistige Leben von Halle im Zeichen des Endkampfes zwischen Pietismus und Rationalismus." *Sachsen und Anhalt* 14 (1938): 137–66.

Schneiders, Werner. *Naturrecht und Liebesethik.* Hildesheim: Olms, 1971.

Schrader, Wilhelm. *Geschichte der Friedrichs-Universität zu Halle.* 2 vols. Berlin: Ferd. Dümmlers Verlagsbuchhandlung, 1894.

Schubert, Anselm. *Das Ende der Sünde: Anthropologie und Erbsünde zwischen Reformation und Aufklärung.* Göttingen: Vandenhoeck und Ruprecht, 2002.

Schwaiger, Clemens. *Alexander Gottlieb Baumgarten: ein Intellektuelles Porträt: Studien zur Metaphysik und Ethik von Kants Leitautor.* Stuttgart-Bad Cannstatt: Frommann-Holzboog, 2011.

"Baumgartens Ansatz einer philosophischen Ethikbegründung." *Aufklärung* 20 (2008): 219–38.

Das Problem des Glücks im Denken Christian Wolffs: Eine quellen-, begriffs-, und entwicklungs-geschichtliche Studie zu Schlüsselbegriffen seiner Ethik. Stuttgart-Bad Cannstatt: Frommann-Holzboog, 1995.

"Ein 'missing link' auf dem Weg der Ethik von Wolff zu Kant." *Jahrbuch für Recht und Ethik* 8 (2000): 247–61.

Schweizer, Hans Rudolf. *Ästhetik als Philosophie der sinnlichen Erkenntnis.* Basel: Schwabe, 1973.

The Scots Peerage; founded on Wood's edition of Sir Robert Douglas's Peerage of Scotland; containing an historical and genealogical account of the nobility of that kingdom. Edited by James Balfour Paul. Edinburgh: D. Douglas, 1904–14.

Scott, Hew. *Fasti Ecclesiae Scoticanae: The Succession of Ministers in the Church of Scotland from the Reformation.* Vol. 1 of 11. Edinburgh: Oliver and Boyd, 1915.

Scott, William Robert. *Francis Hutcheson: His Life, Teaching and Position in the History of Philosophy.* Cambridge: Cambridge University Press, 1900.

Sedgwick, Romney. *The House of Commons 1715–1754.* Vol. 1. *The History of Parliament.* London: Her Majesty's Stationery Office, 1970.

Sefton, Henry. "'Neu-lights and Preachers Legall': Some Observations on the Beginnings of Moderatism in the Church of Scotland." In *Church Politics and Society: Scotland 1408–1929.* Edited by Norman MacDougall. Edinburgh: John Donald, 1983.

Selby-Bigge, L. A., ed. *British Moralists.* Oxford: Oxford University Press, 1897. Reprint, New York: Bobbs-Merrill, 1964.

Shaw, John Stuart. *The Management of Scottish Society, 1707–1764.* Edinburgh: John Donald, 1983.

Sheehan, Jonathan. *The Enlightenment Bible.* Princeton, NJ: Princeton University Press, 2005.

Shepherd, Christine. *Philosophy and Science in the Arts Curriculum of the Scottish Universities in the Seventeenth Century.* PhD dissertation. University of Edinburgh, 1974.

Sher, Richard B. "Blair, Hugh." In *Dictionary of National Biography.* Edited by H. C. G. Matthew and Brian Harrison. Oxford: Oxford University Press, 2004.

Church and University in the Scottish Enlightenment: The Moderate Literati of Edinburgh. Princeton, NJ: Princeton University Press, 1985.

"Professors of Virtue: The Social History of the Edinburgh Moral Philosophy Chair in the Eighteenth Century." In *Studies in the Philosophy of the Scottish Enlightenment.* Edited by M. A. Stewart. Oxford: Oxford University Press, 1990.

Shiner, Larry. *The Invention of Art.* Chicago: University of Chicago Press, 2001.

Sidgwick, Henry. *The Methods of Ethics.* Indianapolis, IN: Hackett, 1981.

Outlines of the History of Ethics for English Readers. 6th ed. London: Macmillan, 1931. Reprint, Bristol: Thoemmes, 1996.

Smith, Norman Kemp. *The Philosophy of David Hume: A Critical Study of Its Origins and Central Doctrines.* London: Macmillan, 1941.

Solms, Friedrich. *Disciplina aesthetica: Zur Frühgeschichte der ästhetischen Theorie bei Baumgarten und Herder.* Stuttgart: Klett, 1990.

Sparn, Walter. Introduction to *Elementa philosophiae practicae*, by J. F. Buddeus. Hildesheim: Olms, 2004.

Stephen, Leslie. "Blair, Hugh." In *Dictionary of National Biography*. Edited by Leslie Stephen and Sidney Lee. Oxford: Oxford University Press, 1921–22.

Stewart, M. A. "Academic Freedom: Origins of an Idea." *Bulletin of the Australian Society of Legal Philosophy* 16.57 (1991/1992): 1–31.

"Berkeley and the Rankenian Club." In *George Berkeley: Essays and Replies*. Edited by D. Berman. Dublin: Irish Academic Press, 1986.

"George Turnbull and Educational Reform." In *Aberdeen and Enlightenment*. Edited by J. Carter and J. Pittock-Wesson. Aberdeen: Aberdeen University Press, 1987.

"John Smith and the Molesworth Circle." *Eighteenth-Century Ireland* 2 (1987): 89–102.

The Kirk and the Infidel: An Inaugural Lecture Delivered at Lancaster University on 9 November 1994. Corrected ed. Lancaster: Lancaster University, 2001.

Letter to Richard Sher and Mark Box. 30 April 2005. Electronic mail in the possession of M. A. Stewart.

"Principal Wishart (1692–1753) and the Controversies of His Day." *Records of the Scottish Church History Society* 30 (2000): 60–102.

"Rational Dissent in Early Eighteenth-Century Ireland." In *Enlightenment and Religion*. Edited by Knud Haakonssen. Cambridge: Cambridge University Press, 1996.

"The Stoic Legacy in the Early Scottish Enlightenment." In *Atoms, Pneuma, and Tranquility: Epicurean and Stoic Themes in European Thought*. Edited with an introduction by Margaret J. Osler. Cambridge: Cambridge University Press, 1991.

"William Wishart, Early Critic of *Alciphron*." *Berkeley Newsletter* 6 (1982/83): 5–9.

Stewart-Robertson, J. C. "Cicero among the Shadows: Scottish Prelections of Virtue and Duty." *Rivista Critica di Storia della Philosophia* 38.1 (1983): 25–49.

Stöckmann, Ernst. *Anthropologische Ästhetik: Philosophie, Psychologie und ästhetische Theorie der Emotionen im Diskurs der Aufklärung*. Tübingen: Niemeyer, 2009.

Stolnitz, Jerome. "On the Origins of 'Aesthetic Disinterestedness.'" *Journal of Aesthetics and Art Criticism* 20.2 (1961): 131–43.

Stolzenburg, A. F. *Die Theologie des Jo. Franc. Buddeus und des Chr. Matth. Pfaff*. Berlin: Trowitzsch, 1927. Reprint, Aalen: Scientia, 1979.

Straßberger, Andres. *Johann Christoph Gottsched und die "philosophische" Predigt*. Tübingen: Mohr Siebeck, 2010.

Strube, Werner. "Alexander Gottlieb Baumgartens Theorie des Gedichts." In *Dichtungstheorien der Frühaufklärung*. Edited by Theodor Verweyen. Tübingen: Niemeyer, 1995.

——. "Die Entstehung der Ästhetik als einer wissenschaftlichen Disziplin." *Scientia Poetica* 8 (2004): 1–25.

Tatarkiewicz, Wladyslaw. *A History of Six Ideas: An Essay in Aesthetics*. London: Nijhoff, 1980.

——. *History of Aesthetics*. Edited by C. Barrett. 3 vols. Paris: Mouton, 1970–74.

Tholuck, F. August. *Geschichte des Rationalismus*. 2 vols. Berlin, 1865. Reprint, Aalen: Scientia, 1990.

Thorpe, C. D. "Addison and Hutcheson on the Imagination." *English Literary History* 2 (1935): 215–34.

Trevor-Roper, Hugh. "The Religious Origins of the Enlightenment." In *Religion, the Reformation and Social Change*. 3rd ed. London: Secker and Warburg, 1984.

Trianosky, Gregory W. "On the Obligation to Be Virtuous: Shaftesbury and the Question, Why Be Moral?" *Journal of the History of Philosophy* 14.3 (1978): 289–300.

Trop, Gabriel. "Aesthetic Askesis: Aesthetics as a Technology of the Self in the Philosophy of Alexander Baumgarten." *Das achtzehnte Jahrhundert* 37.1 (2013): 56–73.

Turco, Luigi. "Moral Sense and the Foundations of Morals." In *The Cambridge Companion to the Scottish Enlightenment*. Edited by A. Broadie. Cambridge: Cambridge University Press, 2003.

——. "Sympathy and Moral Sense: 1725–1740." *British Journal for the History of Philosophy* 7.1 (1999): 79–101.

Tuveson, Ernest. "The Importance of Shaftesbury." *English Literary History* 20.4 (1953): 267–99.

Voitle, Robert. "Shaftesbury's Moral Sense." *Studies in Philology* 52 (1955): 17–38.

——. *The Third Earl of Shaftesbury*. Baton Rouge: Louisiana State University Press, 1984.

Walford, David. Introduction to *An Inquiry Concerning Virtue, or Merit*, by Shaftesbury. Manchester: Manchester University Press, 1977.

Wallmann, Johannes. "Pietismus und Orthodoxie. Überlegungen und Fragen zur Pietismusforschung." In *Pietismus-Studien: Gesammelte Aufsätze*, vol. 2, by J. Wallmann. Tübingen: Mohr Siebeck, 2008.

Walton, K. L. "Aesthetics: Introduction." *Grove Art Online*. Oxford: Oxford University Press. Cited 2 July 2015.

Waniek, Gustav. *Gottsched und die deutsche Litteratur seiner Zeit*. Leipzig, 1897.

Whitmer, Kelly. *The Halle Orphanage as Scientific Community: Observation, Eclecticism and Pietism in the Early Enlightenment*. Chicago: University of Chicago Press, 2015.

Witte, Egbert. *Logik ohne Dornen*. Hildesheim: Olms, 2000.

Wood, Paul. "Introduction: Dugald Stewart and the Invention of 'the Scottish Enlightenment.'" In *The Scottish Enlightenment: Essays in Reinterpretation.* Edited by P. Wood. Rochester: University of Rochester Press, 2000.

Woodmansee, Martha. *The Author, Art, and the Market: Rereading the History of Aesthetics.* New York: Columbia University Press, 1994.

Wundt, Max. *Die deutsche Schulphilosophie im Zeitalter der Aufklärung.* Tübingen: Mohr, 1945. Reprint, Hildesheim: Olms, 1992.

 Die Philosophie an der Universität Jena in ihrem geschichtlichen Verlaufe dargestellt. Jena: Fischer, 1932.

Young, James O. "The Ancient and Modern System of the Arts." *British Journal of Aesthetics* 55.1 (2015): 1–17.

Zelle, Carsten. "Pietismus und Erhabenheit – Immanuel Jacob Pyras Beitrag zur Literaturkritik der Aufklärung." In *Aufklärung und Erneuerung: Beiträge zur Geschichte der Universität Halle im ersten Jahrhundert ihres Bestehens (1694–1806).* Edited by G. Jerouschek and A. Sames. Hanau: Dausien, 1994.

Zelle, Carsten, and Gregor Schwering, eds. *Ästhetische Positionen nach Adorno.* Munich: Fink, 2002.

Zuckert, Rachel. *Kant on Beauty and Biology.* Cambridge: Cambridge University Press, 2007.

Zurbuchen, Simone. "Aufklärung in der Schweiz." In *Grundriß der Geschichte der Philosophie: die Philosophie des 18. Jahrhunderts,* vol. 5, *Das heilige Römische Reich.* Edited by Helmut Holzhey and Vilem Mudroch. Basel: Schwabe, 2014.

Index

IDEAS IN CONTEXT

Edited by David Armitage, Richard Bourke, Jennifer Pitts and John Robertson